Introduction to U.S. Law, Policy, and Research

Introduction to U.S. Law, Policy, and Research: An Environmental Perspective

Peter M. Bower

Dana Neacşu

Published by:

Vandeplas Publishing, LLC – July 2019

801 International Parkway, 5th Floor
Lake Mary, FL. 32746
USA

www.vandeplaspublishing.com

ISBN 978-1-60042-502-8

Cover Photo: The ceiling tondo - IUSTITIA/JUSTICE by Raffaelo Sanzio, in the Stanza della Segnatura in the Vatican Palace. IUSTITIA, the Roman goddess of justice, is seated with her symbols of the law, the scales of justice that weigh the evidence pro and con, and the sword of righteous enforcement. She wears no blindfold in this depiction. *The Stanza della Segnatura* (or room of the tribunal) takes its name from the highest court of the Holy See that met in this room in the mid-16th century after the frescoes were painted in 1508-1511. (photo P. Bower)

INTRODUCTION TO U.S. LAW, POLICY, AND RESEARCH: AN ENVIRONMENTAL PERSPECTIVE

Peter M. Bower
Dana Neacşu

TABLE OF CONTENTS:

Acknowledgments

Dana Neacsu: This book is for Izzie, ZouZou, and Absy, my beloved daughters, who inspire me every day. Without my international education in Romania, France and the United States, I would not have been able to learn and practice dialectical, interdisciplinary, and experiential teaching. Without access to the fabulous resources of Columbia Law School, and the Arthur W. Diamond Law Library, this book would not have been conceived. I would also like to thank my co-author, our students, and all my co-workers who, since 2003, made my teaching at Barnard College possible. Special thanks to Anton Vandeplas for trusting our vision of teaching environmental law, policy, and legal research.

Peter Bower: I dedicate this book to my wife, Michele, my friend and the love of my life, as well as to the hope of the future, my four grandsons, Owen, Zachary, Eli, and Gavin, as well my granddaughter to be, Madison. I extend a special thank you to Dana, all our students, and especially to Daisy de Wolf, now a student at Fordham Law.

"It may be true that the law cannot make a man love me, but it can stop him from lynching me, and I think that's pretty important."

-Martin Luther King Jr.

Introduction

Introduction to U.S. Law, Policy, and Research – An Environmental Perspective is not the typical *environmental law* text that is often a compendium of the basic environmental case law, statutes and rules. Instead, it is process-oriented introduction to law and legal research, within the context of environmental law, policy and decision-making. In an experiential, interdisciplinary, and dialectical manner, this text book focuses on legal literacy, research skills, and writing; while introducing the common law origins and structure of the U.S. legal system, in general, and of environmental law. This book also guides in the reader in deciphering how to read and brief cases and how to analyze environmental statutes and regulations. As you read, be ready to find specific *terminology* in italics and underlined if the use of legal dictionaries is appropriate, and read titles in small caps as indicative of a source we deemed seminal for your learning, whether it is the United States Constitution, the Endangered Species Act, or an explanatory text.

LEARNING GOALS

Introduction to U.S. Law, Policy, and Research – An Environmental Perspective provides hands-on use of online legal resources, especially through our *Environmental Law and Policy companion website, http://www.environmentallaw-teach.org/,* so students achieve the following goals:

1. Develop legal literacy and learn how to read opinions of important cases that elucidate how courts create common law and especially environmental law through the interpretation and application of environmental statutes and regulations;

2. Use legal research tools to find "*good law*" by analyzing *precedent*; understand *citations*; locate statutes and their associated rules and regulations, and find cases that determine the meaning of statutes;

3. *Brief* cases; learn how to write internal (*office*) *memoranda of law* and how to incorporate relevant research about specific federal environmental statutes, their regulations, and their associated case law, and prepare a memorandum to explain how *case law* determines the meaning of a statute;

4. To understand the origins, history, and structure of the U.S. legal system; to understand the ecological and ethical bases of environmental law, its use in environmental policy and decision-making, and its role in cost-benefit analysis and risk management.

All of the above require learning the legal language. Legal literacy is a central focus of this book. The legal language, especially its vocabulary, is not only relevant, it is the sea in which we all swim. Important terms for the reader to look up in a legal dictionary are *italicized* and underlined throughout this book. Both general and specialized legal dictionaries are available in print and online.

BLACK'S LAW DICTIONARY is the classic tome for the desk and is considered to be the best legal dictionary of American Law. It contains definitions of legal terminology used in all fields of law, including definitions of Latin phrases, such as *stare decisis* and *pro se*. Specialized legal dictionaries for various fields of law, including Lee's DICTIONARY OF ENVIRONMENTAL LEGAL TERMS, provide specialized references. Lee's Dictionary contains environmental statutory and regulatory definitions, such as, "acid rain program." Another dictionary, BARRON'S LEGAL DICTIONARY is available in handy paperback editions. Online free dictionaries are abundant, but not all are easy to use or give a meaningful definition. Useful websites include:

Law.com Dictionary (http://dictionary.law.com/);
Legal Information Institute, Cornell (https://www.law.cornell.edu/wex); and,
The Free Dictionary (http://legal-dictionary.thefreedictionary.com/).

In addition to these sources, you can use the "Glossary" contained in this book. It is available also on the companion website at http:// www.environmentallaw-teach.org/.

Studying law is a fundamental imperative because of the pervasive role of the law in our country. Because ours is perhaps the most *litigious* society on the planet, *lawsuits* are commonplace. *Legal actions* are taken, and persons are sued. The law affects everybody, every day, from birth to death: both require legally mandated certificates. As individuals or other entities, we are all legal subjects.

The laws of a local municipality, county, state and federal government affect all of us: whether we enter into the contract of marriage, obtain a divorce or a driver's license, buy a book or real estate, change the oil in a car, discard trash, invest in the stock market, or engage in interstate commerce. More importantly, anyone born in the U.S.A. and any naturalized citizen automatically become entitled to specific rights and freedoms. Because of the above, INTRODUCTION TO U.S. LAW, POLICY, AND RESEARCH – AN ENVIRONMENTAL PERSPECTIVE is deeply rooted in basic civics, an understanding of the rights and duties of citizens and of how our country and government work. It is also deeply rooted in basic civics to encourage civic-mindedness and to address the fact that most citizens of the USA are woefully unprepared and ignorant of basic civics. This is why the UNITED STATES CONSTITUTION, its Amendments, and the DECLARATION OF INDEPENDENCE, as well as key FEDERALIST PAPERS and decisions of the Supreme Court, is required reading.

In spite of gross deficiencies in civic education, citizens of the USA have an enormous respect for the law and believe in the "rule of law". This fact was brought to the forefront dramatically in the events leading up to the case of *Bush v. Gore* (see our Companion Website, at http://www.environmentallaw-teach.org/, and Introduction Sidebar 1, http://www.environmentallaw-teach.org/sidebar-1.html). *Bush v. Gore* was decided in connection with the 2000 presidential election. Most citizens feel strongly about having their "rights" respected, including the right to free speech and to due process. Phrases such as "you are breaking the law," "I will take you to court," and "I have my rights" are part of the popular vocabulary. These feelings are deeply embedded in our culture.

American law is everywhere today because of its double nature as both a product of popular culture and a creator of popular culture. Talk about individual rights and due process of law thrive in school, at home, on TV, and in the digital media. Legal concepts generate perhaps more popular culture (including songs and movies) than they do academic writings. American general culture and especially the media often cover legal knowledge (e.g., A Civil Action by Jonathan Harr, John Grisham's series of novels, the TV series *Law & Order, Boston Legal, Suits, or Billions*). For this reason, we are never too far from law or legal discourse. We learn from the media but while we learn, we may not be learning the truth. We need to be able to think critically and debunk media myths and errors. The idea of "legal rights" has become an intrinsic value that is widespread in the American culture. The only way to understand the value of such belief is by being able to identify the specific right itself, whether it is mentioned by the CONSTITUTION, a statute, or issued by a court, and then by searching its historical interpretation and application by courts. This is the way to avoid legal information that comes from a source that lacks proper authority, instead of developing a critical approach to legal information.

Americans tend to believe that the *U.S. Supreme Court* acts as the guarantor of our individual freedoms and makes important decisions that affect the nation. Appreciation of the role and history of the Supreme Court and of the lower federal appeals and trial courts is limited. Indeed, who knows that in 1967, in a case called *Loving v. Virginia*, the U.S. Supreme Court invalidated laws prohibiting interracial marriage (see our Companion Website, Introduction, Sidebar 2, http://www.environmentallaw-teach.org/sidebar-2.html)? This is a riveting example of how the study of law combines theory and practice; that is, real cases and stories of real people. It demonstrates how theory is applied in a historical context and how the content they are learning has a real-life application.

Americans also are aware that *endangered species* are protected by statute but have little understanding of how regulations to carry out the law are created, of the role of the *Federal Register*, of the *Administrative Procedures Act*, and of the *Code of Federal Regulations*. How does a species become listed as endangered or threatened? What agencies protect endangered species? Are endangered species that live on private property protected? Or, how might violations of the law involve the FBI? And, most significantly, how does case law ultimately determine the meaning of statutes and regulations?

Study of the law has special meaning for environmental scientists and activists. Anyone who is seriously involved in protecting and improving the environment, or making a positive change in society, realizes that the effort is made within the law and nothing is done without the law. The law is a powerful tool for the environmental movement but this realization did not come until the citizens' movement and legal actions of the Storm King controversy (described in this book) paved the way for the new environmental movement. This movement included the rapid growth of environmental legislation in the late 1960s and early 1970s that created the *EPA*; the *Endangered Species Act*; the *Comprehensive Environmental Response, Compensation and Liability (Superfund) Act (C.E.R.C.L.A.); the Clean Air Act; the Clean Water Act; the Toxic Substances Control Act*; and a host of other major statutes. These statutes in turn created rapidly increasing opportunities for legal employment and environmental consulting.

Even if you do not become a lawyer, study of the law provides important opportunities for self-improvement. In INTRODUCTION TO U.S. LAW, POLICY, AND RESEARCH – AN ENVIRONMENTAL PERSPECTIVE, we call this self-renewing, intellectual resourcefulness. This means that whatever is learned by the use of this book and its companion website is only the beginning. We pay conscious attention to those tools and skills that will allow you to continue the study and learn about the law throughout a lifetime. These include the ability to research cases, statutes, regulations, and precedent. After reading this book, you may now be able to add new powerful dimension to that history or English paper. The deeper significance or truth of a newspaper article that covers a legal story can now be understood. The study of law provides the ability to move freely within a whole new language. It reinforces the ability to synthesize complex ideas, to read *primary sources* and think critically. The study of law also allows insight into a wide-range of disciplines because the law applies to everything under the sun. The emphasis on writing skills offered by this book and our companion website, at http://www.environmentallaw-teach.org/, for instance, the writing of briefs and memoranda, reinforces the ability to synthesize complex ideas and to think critically. And, most significantly, all of the skills mentioned above are transferable. Hopefully, this book and its companion website will be the starting points of what could become a lifetime interest in American law, starting with the way in which it works, and ending with the ability to critically think about how the law can be an instrument of social justice.

PERSONAL NOTES FROM THE AUTHORS

Peter Bower

Having co-founded the Department of Environmental Science at Barnard College, I continued teaching geology and environmental science at Barnard College and Columbia University for over forty years. During part of that time, 1988 -1996, I also served on the City Council and was Mayor of the Township of Teaneck (pop. ~ 40,000). It was there, in various environmental struggles such as creating parkland and Teaneck's first recycling program, fighting illegal dumping of refuse on township property and prosecuting wrongdoers, reversing zoning by ordinance and over-development, or protecting the Greenbelt along a major highway through town, that I understood the value of legally-informed citizens. As a mayor I learned that everything I did or wanted to do on the Town Council involved the law and was surrounded by and defined by the law.

As an elected member of the municipal government, I needed to become law-literate and learn what the law was, how it was created, and how it all worked. The first and most important decision I made upon becoming Mayor was to choose a Town Attorney. Of course, the most important factor of the City Council of seven was to be able to count to four. Without four votes nothing happened. My selection depended on two main factors: Did the attorney know the law (especially NJ state law)? And, could this attorney be creative enough to move us from A to B? I selected Martin Cramer, attorney for Jimi Hendrix and for Woodstock, who instilled in me a thirst to learn about the law and the ability to be able to ask the right questions.

For several years, I was at his side learning by doing. I spent days and weeks in the Columbia Law Library learning to read cases and do legal research. It was at this point that I was convinced that my undergraduates at Barnard and Columbia needed an environmental law class rooted in basic civics, reading cases, researching precedent, writing briefs, and researching statutes, and regulations. Given that the environmental law class has been taught for over twenty years, these roots have been well developed but, given the concern for environmental protection, deep roots of civic-mindedness and the role the law and lawyers may play have also been developed.

Dana Neacşu

This book has evolved from the teaching of Environmental Law at Barnard College, on a foundation of two decades of teaching Law, either as an abstraction hard to grasp, as concrete pieces of legislation, or as specific cases or regulations which affect everybody from birth to death. Having worked with Dr. Bower since 2003, I have reached the conclusion that Law ought to be taught organically and conceptually, and through its myriad of specific consequences, in its concrete aspect.

This book reflects what is taught in our class. We co-teach substantive environmental law and policy, with the necessary constitutional and torts components, as well as legal research and writing, with the added civil procedure elements for understanding the constraints of legal writing and reasoning. Law dictates behavior when it establishes social boundaries, the limits of socially tolerable. Certainly, legal tolerance is different than moral or religious tolerance, because if immoral behavior meets a raised eyebrow, illegality meets with various civil and penal liabilities. Just from this pragmatic approach to consequences, the logic behind our way of teaching law seems irrefutable. A society governed by the rule of law promotes a peaceful future, or better yet, the only future civilization should strive for.

We teach law dialectically, not like a compartmentalized abstraction, but as an organic societal component. Environmental law intertwines politics, science, and active citizenship, having been born from civic engagement, not long ago. Given our current climate crisis, and the need for immediate action, environmental law and politics have certainly moved to the forefront of all civics, politics, economics and jurisprudential teaching.

We teach law digitally, because technology is such an inseparable element of the law: one of the prerequisites of a norm to be binding is its publicity, which can be achieved using the technology of the day. Technology influences how law realizes itself as individual statutes, court and agency decisions, or agency rules, and how it produces its specific, fact-based consequences. Most of my professional life has involved legal teaching, and as such I have long been preoccupied with the way students are introduced to law.

In Bucharest, Romania, after a brief period as a trial court judge and a researcher in the Legal Institute of the Romanian National Academy, I taught introduction to civil law to 1L students. At Columbia University in New York City, I have taught legal research to 1L and LLM students since 2005, when I published my first book on law and legal research – INTRODUCTION TO U.S. LAW AND LEGAL RESEARCH (Transnational, 2005). My own research has a large pedagogical component. For instance, fifteen years ago I wrote about the elite law schools' curriculum, and argued that law was not taught within the confines of a free-market of ideas: important schools of ideas were missing from the elite law schools' curriculum, while variations of one school of thought were presented as a sign of intellectual diversity. Almost ten years later, in another law journal article, THE MANY TEXTS OF LAW (2014), that lack of intellectual diversity persisted, and the ignorance it produced continued to be compounded by the Socratic Method which makes students learn as they espouse their ignorance. Perhaps in 1870, the year when Christopher Columbus Langdell became Harvard's Dane Professor, and this method became associated with that illustrious institution of education, this carefully crafted elitist approach to law was exactly what was needed. Today, it is not satisfactory, because casebooks of edited snippets seem so paper limited. Today's age of technology is digital, and it is hailed as the new equalizer. Everyone has the chance to expand their horizon, except in legal education. Unlike exposure to all schools of ideas to nurture imagination, technology seems to encourage the reverse; narrowing things down and giving students the ability to be even more precise while avoiding the essential broader subject-matter connections.

And this is what we are set to avoid. Within the law school environment, technology and database-driven research, seem to accelerate what legal educators have been fighting against for 75 years, the closed universe. In our class, due to our legal, cultural, philosophical, policy, and scientific immersion into the world of environmental law, we are exposing the students to the essence of the rule of law, while enabling them to understand the dialectical nature of legal normativity. Because there is no rule of law outside a working legal regime whose specific rules ought to be constitutional while also mirroring our social mores, we engage in the most concrete form of interdisciplinary studies. Our mixed approach of scientific, political, and legal pragmatism has been well received by the thousands of students who took our Environmental Law and Policy class we teach at Barnard College. The enthusiasm with which our Barnard and Columbia students have received our endeavor has given us high hopes that we can inspire other programs around the country.

For I think it an undeniable position, that a competent knowledge of the laws of that society, in which we live, is the proper accomplishment of every gentleman and scholar; and highly useful, I had almost said essential, part of liberal and polite education.

- Blackstone's The Study, Nature,
and Extent of the Law

Chapter 1 – Historical Origins and Nature of the U.S. Legal System

THE LAW, LEGAL AND MORAL NORMS, POSITIVE LAW, AND THE *RULE OF LAW*

The word "*law*" has multiple meanings. *Law* is a means that society uses to attain its conception of legitimate order and stability. It is the entire system of rules that, when enforced, by consequence materializes a society's ideal of legitimate order.

Law has both abstract and concrete forms. Abstractly, it refers to the field of study of a society's rules regulating how individuals must behave toward one another. As a branch of knowledge, it studies the rules governing people's behavior in relation to each other. Law is both a discourse about power and power in action. As a discourse, legal studies embrace legal philosophy, in its wider sense as a general reflection on the nature of legal institutions. In the United States, at the federal level, abstract principles are actualized concretely in the CONSTITUTION, in statutes passed by Congress, in executive orders issued by the President, in regulations issued by agencies, and in decisions handed down by courts. Such a concrete form of law is the system of actual, written rules which materialize a society's ideal of legitimate order and is also known as positive law. Legal research teaches the most tangible and concrete aspects of the law. It explains law by explaining how government institutions (the legislative, executive, and administrative branches) work and how their products (statutes, cases, and administrative rules, regulations, or decisions) can be researched.

Law is not the only means a society uses to attain order and stability. Both legal and moral norms are rules of conduct. However, moral norms are rules that people, through customary behavior, have expected each other to follow. Laws, on the other hand, are binding rules of conduct which come from state legislative bodies and are enforced by other state institutions. Legal norms define what types of conduct are lawful, what types of conduct are unlawful, and how unlawful conduct should be punished. Religion is another means of attaining order and stability, where religious bodies enact and enforce those rules. There still are theocracies, where the state and religious institutions merge, and where both the state and religious institutions may enforce the dual character norms. For example, the five foundational tenets, or maqasid, of Islam are enforced by a caliphate, or the Vatican enforces laws governing Catholic priests. Sometimes, legal norms have a moral origin, and other times a religious origin. For instance, some may be derived from local, social norms, and some could be derived from the Mosaic Decalogue (the Ten Commandments).

How abstract legal rights and principles are actualized in a given place and at a given point in time depend upon prevailing legal norms. This concept is known as the *Rule of Law* and it is the intermediary between the concrete legal norm and the ideal of order that norm is supposed to achieve. While legal norms change as societal values evolve, the Rule of Law is one principle whose *hegemonic* value has remained the same.

American colonists inherited their reverence for the Rule of Law from the British. By the beginning of the thirteenth century, English commoners felt that they had *rights* that inherently belonged to them. They developed a strong respect for the Rule of Law. This history includes the struggle for the rights established in the MAGNA CARTA LIBERTATUM in 1215 (The Great Charter of the Liberties of England). Through this struggle the English nobility (the barons) limited the absolute and often arbitrary power of the king, subjecting the king to the law. Article 39 in the original 1215 Charter states:

> NO Freeman shall be taken or imprisoned, or be disseised of his Freehold, Liberties, or free Customs, or be outlawed, or exiled, or any other wise destroyed; nor will
> We not pass upon him, nor condemn him, but by lawful judgment of his Peers, or by the Law of the land.
> We will sell to no man, we will not deny or defer to any man either Justice or Right.

Of course, being disseised (i.e., dispossessed) of one's freehold was important to any Freeman (non-serf) in feudal times. "We will sell to no man" meant that the king could no longer demand payment to receive *justice* and to not be able to *deny or defer* meant the King could no longer stop lawsuits. These are all *due process rights* that have come down to us today as a historical gift and are part of the Rule of Law. Among its many important provisions, the MAGNA CARTA codifies the right of *habeas corpus*. The ENGLISH HABEAS CORPUS ACT of 1679 defines and strengthens the ancient prerogative *writ of habeas corpus*, which required a court to examine the lawfulness of a prisoner's detention and thus prevent unlawful or arbitrary imprisonment.

The first copy of the MAGNA CARTA to be published in the colonies was included in William Penn's THE EXCELLENT PRIVILEGE OF LIBERTY AND PROPERTY: BEING THE BIRTH-RIGHT OF THE FREE-BORN SUBJECTS OF ENGLAND_(1687). Almost a century later in 1780, John Adams prominently placed the idea of "a government of laws, not of men" in the Commonwealth of Massachusetts' initial state constitution. The idea that laws would govern the new nation rather than the arbitrary dictates of the king was held widely throughout the colonies and the CONSTITUTION's Fifth Amendment states that "no person shall be deprived of life, liberty, or property without due process of law." Indeed, the MAGNA CARTA lives with us today.

THE DECLARATION OF INDEPENDENCE: NATURAL LAW AND MORAL NORMS

The introduction to the Declaration of Independence consists of a single sentence stating that this document will "declare the causes" that impel "the thirteen United States of America" to dissolve their "political bands" with the British Empire.

> IN CONGRESS, JULY 4, 1776
>
> The unanimous Declaration of the thirteen United States of America:
>
> When in the Course of human events it becomes necessary for one people to dissolve the political bands which have connected them with another and to assume among the powers of the earth, the separate and equal station to which the Laws of Nature and of Nature's God entitle them, a decent respect to the opinions of mankind requires that they should declare the causes which impel them to the separation.

The preamble to the DECLARATION OF INDEPENDENCE sets out "certain unalienable Rights" and states that "governments are instituted" in order "to secure these rights" but that "the People" have the right to "institute new government" when existing government becomes "destructive" of these "unalienable rights."

> We hold these truths to be self-evident, that all men are created equal, that they are endowed by their Creator with certain unalienable Rights, that among these are Life, Liberty and the pursuit of Happiness. — That to secure these rights, Governments are instituted among Men, deriving their just powers from the consent of the governed, — That whenever any Form of Government becomes destructive of these ends, it is the Right of the People to alter or to abolish it, and to institute new Government, laying its foundation on such principles and organizing its powers in such form, as to them shall seem most likely to affect their Safety and Happiness.

What gives the people the right to rebel and "institute [a] new Government?" It is the "Laws of Nature and of Nature's God" that gives "one people" the right to a "separate and equal station," and it is "their Creator" who endows them with the "Rights" to "Life, Liberty, and the Pursuit of Happiness" that governments "instituted among Men" are to protect. This is an example of natural law, that is, certain inherent values or rights that are understood to exist via human reason. Humankind uses reason to analyze the laws of nature and determine just law and "rights." It must be recognized that the Founders were predominantly Christians who believed that the law of nature was infused into human beings, "endowed" in them by God at the time of Creation. While there were the "Laws of Nature," Nature also had a "God," a higher incarnation, but they both provided the authority for rebellion and for the founding of the United States of America. These laws were premier moral norms. They provided the foundation of a political philosophy that repudiated the theory of absolute monarchy whereby the king or queen was considered divine or selected by God, and the rights of subjects were only those afforded by the monarch.

Natural law has been an important philosophical issue through the ages, especially the relationship between positive law and natural law. There have been many theories and variants of natural law, such as Aristotle's theory of justice or the writings of Thomas Aquinas. John Locke and Thomas Hobbes' theories and ideas were especially important for the development of English law—the antecedent of American law.

Natural law is often thought of as virtuous and righteous, representing the best of human understanding. As recently as the last century, natural law was referenced in our jurisprudence, only for achieving unnatural results. In June 1958, two residents of Virginia, Mildred Jeter, an African-American woman, and Richard Loving, a white man, were married in the District of Columbia pursuant to its laws, and then chose to live in Virginia, which banned interracial marriages. Indicted for violating that law, the Lovings were then sentenced to 25 years in prison for the crime of *miscegenation*. The trial court judge suspended that sentence on condition that they leave the state. He reasoned his opinion stating:

> Almighty God created the races white, black, yellow, malay and red, and he placed them on separate continents. And but for the interference with his arrangement there would be no cause for such marriages. The fact that he separated the races shows that he did not intend for the races to mix *(Loving v. Virginia,* 388 U.S. 1, 3).

Ironically, racists relied upon natural law arguments to justify their insidious practices of segregation; in particular, slavery. However, this should not shock the student of history, because forty-one of the signers of the Declaration of Independence were slave owners and the institution of slavery had been an important influence on the framing of our Constitution of 1789.

It is important to read the rest of the Declaration of Independence, the body of which lists the specific grievances that compelled Americans to rebellion. Twenty-five of the fifty-six men who signed the Declaration of Independence were lawyers, including John Hancock, Thomas Jefferson, George Wythe, Roger Sherman, Samuel Huntington, John Adams, and Francis

Hopkinson. They had a deep knowledge and respect for English law and many of the grievances were concerned with legal rights that they presumed were theirs as colonists of the Crown. For instance, in reference to King George III:

> He has refused his Assent to Laws, the most wholesome and necessary for the public good.
> He has forbidden his Governors to pass Laws of immediate and pressing importance, unless suspended in their operation till his Assent should be obtained; and when so suspended, he has utterly neglected to attend to them.
> He has refused to pass other Laws for the accommodation of large districts of people, unless those people would relinquish the right of Representation in the Legislature, a right inestimable to them and formidable to tyrants only.
> He has dissolved Representative Houses repeatedly, for opposing with manly firmness his invasions on the rights of the people;
> He has obstructed the Administration of Justice by refusing his Assent to Laws for establishing Judiciary Powers.
> For depriving us in many cases of the benefits of Trial by Jury.
> For taking away our Charters, abolishing our most valuable laws, and altering fundamentally the Forms of our Governments.

All of these laws and grievances were in the realm of positive law, specifically the common law system of England.

HISTORICAL ORIGINS OF THE U.S. LEGAL SYSTEM: ENGLISH COMMON LAW, LAW IN THE THIRTEEN COLONIES, AND A UNIQUE FORM OF FEDERALISM

American law cannot be understood without an appreciation of both its English *common law* heritage and a unique form of *federalism* that is its foundation. Both are intimately intertwined with the origin and development of thirteen separate and diverse colonies of the British Empire.

Federalism is a system of government that unites separate subsidiary governing units (states in the U.S.) under the authority of a central or "federal" government. Of course, the United States did not start out with a central authority. It began with thirteen politically distinct colonies, created at different times, but all under the English Crown. Virginia, Massachusetts (including land that later became the state of Maine), New Jersey, New York, and New Hampshire were owned by the King and governed by Royal Charter in which the Crown appointed governors. North and South Carolina were owned by Lord Proprietors selected by King Charles II but eventually became Royal colonies. Delaware, Pennsylvania, Georgia, and Maryland were proprietary colonies owned by an individual or a group who appointed governors who reported to the King.

Rhode Island and Connecticut were charter colonies that were owned by the colonists via a joint-stock company. Charter colonies were self-governed and had greater independence than the other colonies. Massachusetts was a royal province but eventually was governed by a charter. All thirteen colonies had an appointed governor and governor's council (or upper house), a court system, and an elected legislature (or lower house) but the character of these was different in each colony. The right to vote was limited to men who owned land, paid taxes, and were members of a Christian church. Town meetings played an important role in the New England colonies. The southern colonies had county-level administration, and the middle colonies had a mixture of both.

Further seeds of rebellion were inherent in the political organization of the colonies wherein colonial legislatures could do nothing contrary to the laws of England, their actions and bills could be vetoed by the governors, and all laws passed and approved by a governor could be vetoed by the King (except for the charter colonies).

Each colony evolved in its own way. While slavery was widespread (e.g., in the late 1600s and early 1700s 40% of households in New York City had slaves), it was a more critical to the economic viability of the southern colonies.

Although English colonists were the majority, Germans, French, Dutch, Scots, Irish, and Swedes had important demographic impact. Each colony was also religiously diverse with Roman Catholics, Anglicans, Presbyterians, Puritans, Baptists, Huguenots, and Quakers all playing important economic, political, and social roles in specific colonies.

Given the ideological, cultural, and religious diversity of the American colonies, it is truly amazing that the Framers would be able to create a Constitution and federal republic out of thirteen separate legal systems, each with its own political and economic history. Of course, this diversity also sowed the seeds of trouble: those of states' rights and slavery in the South. There was the advantage that the English colonists were dominant and the English language was the common tongue. More importantly, by the beginning of the 18th century, the colonies had well-established court systems with trained, experienced lawyers and judges who had the English common law system as a model. This was necessitated in part by the need for business transactions in commerce. American jurists studied Sir William Blackstone's Commentaries on the Laws of England, a comprehensive treatise on English common law, and referenced it in developing the common law legal system of the United States. The specific grievances stated in the Declaration of Independence demonstrate that the colonists felt entitled to the rights that the English had under their common law system.

Common law is law that is established by judges through court decisions. These decisions, or case law, become "precedent" for future decisions following the logic that controversies involving similar situations or sets of facts should be decided similarly. The accumulated weight of these precedents became the common law that is relevant, if not binding, on future decisions of the courts. In addition, laws passed by legislatures often obtain their meaning when adjudications of a statute by agency action are tested and interpreted by courts.

It was under the reign of Henry II of England that judges were sent from his court at Westminster to ride "circuits" through the kingdom. With judges from the King's Court charged with administering justice nationwide, local customs of unwritten law were rationalized and centralized, creating a powerful and unified court system, as well as a law "common" to the country as a whole. The decisions of judges during this time were recorded and filed and Ranulf de Glanvill wrote and organized the writing of the fourteen books of THE TREATISE ON THE LAWS AND CUSTOMS OF THE KINGDOM OF ENGLAND (originally written in Latin in 1187-89 and first published in 1554). This book is a truly important historical document for the development of the common law in England because it codified the legal processes in place at that time and introduced the system of *writs*.

While writs will be discussed in more detail shortly, they produced the principle called *stare decisis* ("to stand by that which has been decided"). This principle came into being whereby decisions and reasoning used by previous judges were used by later judges if the cases had similar facts. Trial by jury has been practiced in various forms during medieval times but was reintroduced by Henry II and eventually became standard for both civil and criminal actions. Along with this came another important legal practice that has been passed down to us in American law, that of trials being adversarial, contentious proceedings, in which plaintiffs bring lawsuits or prosecutors bring criminal charges against defendants, each side presents their case, and judges and/or juries serve as neutral arbiters and determine liability or guilt (see our Companion Website, Chapter 1, Sidebar #5, "Juries and the Adversarial System," http://www.environmentallaw-teach.org/sidebar-5.html).

After the DECLARATION OF INDEPENDENCE, each of the thirteen independent states passed *reception statutes*, or Constitutions. The state constitutions incorporated existing English common law as their own. For instance, the NEW YORK CONSTITUTION, adopted in 1777, provided that:

> XXXV. And this convention doth further, in the name and by the authority of the good people of this State, ordain, determine, and declare that such parts of the common law of England, and of the statute law of England and Great Britain, and of the acts of the legislature of the colony of New York, as together did form the law of the said colony on the 19th day of April, in the year of our Lord one thousand seven hundred and seventy-five, shall be and continue the law of this State, subject to such alterations and provisions as the legislature of this State shall, from time to time, make concerning the same. That such of the said acts, as are temporary, shall expire at the times limited for their duration, respectively. That all such parts of the said common law, and all such of the said statutes and acts aforesaid, or parts thereof, as may be construed to establish or maintain any particular denomination of Christians or their ministers, or concern the allegiance heretofore yielded to, and the supremacy, sovereignty, government, or prerogatives claimed

> or exercised by, the King of Great Britain and his predecessors, over the colony of New York and its inhabitants, or are repugnant to this constitution, be, and they hereby are, abrogated and rejected. And this convention doth further ordain, that the resolves or resolutions of the congresses of the colony of New York, and of the convention of the State of New York, now in force, and not repugnant to the government established by this constitution, shall be considered as making part of the laws of this State; subject, nevertheless, to such alterations and provisions as the legislature of this State may, from time to time, make concerning the same.

WRITS AND THE LAW

Many have heard of the writ of habeas corpus. Fewer know that this Latin phrase meaning "produce the body" is found in Article 1 of the UNITED STATES CONSTITUTION. Section 9 of Article 1 states in part that

> The Privilege of the Writ of Habeas Corpus shall not be suspended, unless when in Cases of Rebellion or Invasion the public Safety may require it.

A *writ* is an order from a court, and a *writ of habeas corpus* is an order to "produce the body," that is, an order to the government authority holding a person prisoner to produce such person and demonstrate a valid reason for his or her incarceration. In order to obtain a writ of habeas corpus, the attorney for the imprisoned individual must file an application with the appropriate court. Habeas corpus rights have been and are currently and actively being litigated concerning detentions prior to deportation and Guantanamo detainees (see *Boumediene v. Bush*, 553 U.S. 723 (2008)). Presidents Lincoln and Roosevelt suspended this writ during the Civil War and WWII respectively. The Framers of the Constitution sought to prevent government authorities from imprisoning citizens without charging them with a crime and then keeping them from challenging their imprisonment. The Framers of the Constitution were acutely aware of this right because it had been abused by the British during the war for American independence.

Writs in current use in the U.S. include subpoenas and warrants, as well as the *writ of certiorari* ("to be informed"). In the U.S., plaintiffs or defendants who are unhappy with a decision of a lower court may petition for a writ of certiorari to a higher court. If granted, the higher court orders (through the writ) that the lower court send all of its records of the case in question to be reviewed by the higher court. The U.S. Supreme Court issues a writ of certiorari ("grants cert") in about 85 cases each year (roughly 1% of the total petitions for certiorari).

Of course, writs and the writ of habeas corpus came to us via English common law and have a long history going back to medieval times. The *Magna Carta* guaranteed the right to have a court determine the lawful-ness of a prisoner's detention. The right itself goes back to the Assize of Clarendon during the reign of Henry II, the formation of the royal court system, and the consolidation of the common law. The courts of assize or assizes were local courts. To use an assize, a plaintiff had to obtain a writ from the King to proceed (i.e., permission to use his royal courts). This process was administered by a royal judge. Obtaining a writ was costly, so writs and the legal system were only available to those with financial resources. Because court documents were written in formal Latin or French, aggrieved civil litigants and criminal defendants generally needed to hire trained advocates (lawyers or barristers) with the expertise necessary to prepare writs, translate them for their clients, and convey the facts of their clients' cases to the courts. Originally, permission from the king was required to use his courts and writs constituted a formal grant of the king's permission. However, it was possible to obtain a writ and, thereby, permission to use the royal court, only if a potential litigant's claim fit within the parameters of an existing writ. If the complaint did not fit the restrictive, predefined set of circumstances of a writ, then redress in the royal courts was not possible. These particular sets of circumstances to which writs applied were known as the "forms of action" and entailed a pre-established set of procedures and remedies. Today, the word "action" means a lawsuit, such as a civil or criminal action, and wrongdoings that may be redressed by a court are said to be "actionable." In medieval England, however, many complaints about wrongdoings did not match the "form of action" provided by any of the existing writs and, so, the types of writs increased in variety over time but still many complaints had no avenue for redress. PALGRAVE'S PARLIAMENTARY WRITS (1827) describes the nearly fifty types of writs developed by then, including such writs (or complaints) as the *Writ of Right*, the various forms of the *Writ of Assumpsit*, or the *Action of Detinue*.

With respect to the writ of habeas corpus, the HABEAS CORPUS ACTS OF 1640 and 1649 removed the authority of the king to arbitrarily detain people and made habeas corpus, a safeguard of individual liberty, into a general right of all citizens. Writs were no longer needed in Great Britain after the Forms of Action were abolished in 1832-33. Eventually, writs were transformed into an order (or summons) for the parties to appear in court. The thirteen colonies inherited from England the common law writ system, with its rigid set of forms of action and types of relief. While the American system evolved and lingered longer than it did in Great Britain, it also suffered from the same limitations. These limitations were in part resolved by the legal concept of equity.

EQUITY AND LAW

The UNITED STATES CONSTITUTION and its amendments repeatedly distinguish between cases at law and in equity. Article 3, Section 2 of the CONSTITUTION reads in part:

> The judicial Power shall extend to all Cases, in Law and Equity, arising under this Constitution..."
> The Seventh Amendment provides: "In Suits at common law, the right of trial by jury shall be

preserved..." And the Eleventh Amendment reads "The Judicial power of the United States shall not be construed to extend to any suit in law or equity, commenced or prosecuted against one of the United States by Citizens of another State, or by Citizens or Subjects of any Foreign State.

To understand *equity*, we must return to the English court system as it evolved from medieval times when complainants applied to the King's Court for the writ that matched their set of grievances. When no writ could be found to match their circumstances, legal redress was not possible. To provide judicial remedies in the absence of applicable writs, a court of equity was created where the Lord Chancellor sat as judge and jury. Only those of high social status were initially able to avail themselves of this court of equity. Nevertheless, this court was committed to fairness, that is, finding equitable solutions to legal issues that could not be redressed under the writ system. A lord whose land had been illegally seized while he was away on the Crusades could, if a jury rules in his favor, only receive monetary compensation in a court of law (i.e., the writ system) but a court of equity could order the property be returned to him because this was fair and just relief.

Initially, Lord Chancellors were churchmen. Without legal training, their decisions, while providing a measure of fairness and relief from the strictures of the writ system, could also seem arbitrary. When Sir Thomas More (for Catholics, Saint Thomas More, the patron saint of lawyers) was appointed Chancellor by Henry VIII, he became the first lawyer to hold the position. All subsequent Chancellors were lawyers. Lower courts of equity eventually came into being, and a system of precedents evolved making decisions of the courts of equity less arbitrary.

So, courts of law, with their prescribed writs and forms of action, and courts of equity evolved separately. These separate systems of justice were inherited by the thirteen colonies and developed and survived in the United States until 1938 when the Federal Rules of Civil Procedure abolished the forms of action and established one "civil action." Thus, remedies formerly available only by writ became possible via a civil action. As a result, in a single proceeding, plaintiffs could seek remedies at law in the form of monetary compensation, known as "damages," and equitable remedies, such as injunctions, that order the defendant to cease and desist or to perform a specific act. State courts have also unified law and equity in courts of general jurisdiction, but Delaware still maintains separate courts of law and equity. Other states, Illinois and New Jersey, have separate divisions for law and equity in a single court. Even where there has been a fusion of law and equity, equitable requests, such as a request for a temporary restraining order or a motion to dismiss, are heard and decided as before, by a judge alone. In most circumstances, a jury renders the verdict in cases where monetary damages are sought. Plaintiffs in many cases request both a "remedy at law" (damages) as well as injunctive relief. This is the essential motivating force behind the eventual fusion of law and equity. In the U.S., a jury, unless waived by the defendant, is the arbiter of fact and applies applicable law to determine liability and amount of damages; however, equitable relief is still left to the determination of a judge.

The common law may now seem a bit confusing because the term has been used both to distinguish common law from equity and to describe the legal system of England (including equity) that was inherited by the thirteen colonies and eventually the United States. In both cases, however, common law refers to law that is developed and determined by a system of courts, that is, judge-made law.

Another singularly important aspect of English law that was inherited in both federal and state court systems is that once a court has made a decision concerning a particular set of facts, another court reviewing similar facts is bound to reach the same decision. This is the principle of precedent that is also known as the doctrine of *stare decisis* ("to stand by that which has been decided"). While the doctrine of *stare decisis* provides a degree of predictability and might seem restrictive, it is also what gives U.S. law its dynamic nature.

Binding precedent is a court decision that requires (except in unusual circumstances) a lower court in the same jurisdiction to apply the "rule" in cases with similar facts. Both federal and state appellate decisions are binding on lower courts in their jurisdiction. State supreme courts bind all lower courts in that state. The Supreme Court of the United States binds all courts. Precedents established in one jurisdiction are not binding on other jurisdictions. These precedents are considered persuasive authority. When binding precedent does not exist, attorneys research and use persuasive authority to bolster their arguments in their briefs and in oral arguments before the court. Tensions are created when courts in different jurisdictions decide cases with similar facts differently. Often, when such a tension occurs between federal appellate jurisdictions, the Supreme Court will hear the case, make a decision, and establish the precedent. When the facts and issues in a case are considered to be slightly different as compared to a pertinent binding precedent, courts may reach a different result. The new precedent is said to be distinguished from the previous ruling. When a court decision is used to support a successful argument in another case, that decision becomes a precedent that has been affirmed. If this precedent is not overruled by a higher-level court and is affirmed again and again in other cases, then this precedent becomes *good law*.

In *Marbury v. Madison,* 5 U.S. 137 (1803), the Supreme Court announced for the first time the principle that a court may declare an act of Congress void if it is inconsistent with the Constitution. This principle of judicial review has been affirmed consistently for over 200 years and is thus well-established, "good law" (see our Companion Website, Chapter 1, Sidebar #3, "Marbury v. Madison," http://www.environmentallaw-teach.org/sidebar-3.html).

Many precedents, some established over many years and used in many cases, are overturned or reversed by a higher court. Social, economic, and political changes in society, and shifting standards of behavior and morality, are often reflected by changes in case law. Reversal of the anti-miscegenation statutes and case law by the Supreme Court in *Loving v. Virginia,* 388 U.S. 1

(1967) invalidated *Virginia's Racial Integrity Act* and similar laws in sixteen states. *Stare decisis* many times means to stand by what is right and to respond to changes in society. Indeed, *stare decisis* is, in reality, very dynamic.

The sources of U.S. law will be discussed in detail later in this book but it is important to state here that the meaning and significance of all the statutes passed by federal and state legislatures and of all the regulations promulgated by federal and state administrative agencies are determined in the courts. The meaning of the CONSTITUTION itself is determined through case law. The passage of the *Endangered Species Act in 1973* was momentous, but it was in *Tennessee Valley Authority vs. Hill,* 437 U.S. 153 (1978) that the Supreme Court gave endangered species incalculable value that takes priority over all other considerations. Case law determined the significance and impact of this statute. *Tennessee Valley Authority vs. Hill* and the *Endangered Species Act* will be discussed in detail later in this book.

Lawyers (and their law clerks) must be thorough, efficient, and skillful as they research the cases (and precedents) related to the case and set of facts before them. Does the new case have a set of facts that distinguishes it from prior binding precedents? Are there relevant persuasive precedents in other jurisdictions? Attorneys are aided today by large legal libraries and especially by advanced online information technology. In medieval times in England, most court decisions went unrecorded but were based on established customs and traditions and word of mouth. Eventually, written records were kept and with the introduction of the printing press, much more elaborate record keeping was possible and with it, a solid foundation for *stare decisis* and the legal profession.

Today, the enormous amount and complexity of litigation in the U.S. make legal researching abilities critical for success. The most advanced legal databases such as *LexisAdvance* and *Westlaw* are very costly. While their services may be licensed to a law firm, a business, a library system, or a university, their availability to the general public is limited to the package public libraries license. This book emphasizes the development of legal research capabilities utilizing the best of the free online legal databases.

AN ADVERSARIAL LEGAL SYSTEM

Trials in the U.S. are contentious, *adversarial proceedings* with lawyers for the plaintiffs or prosecutors and lawyers for the defense following rules of procedure while vying to win their case. These contests are often before a jury. As we further explain in our Companion Website, Chapter 1, Sidebar #5 "*Juries and the Adversarial System,*" http://www.environmentallaw-teach.org/sidebar-5.html, the Sixth and Seventh Amendments of the UNITED STATES CONSTITUTION guarantee the right to trial by jury in criminal and civil cases respectively. The Sixth Amendment has been incorporated into the Fourteenth Amendment; and therefore applies to all of the states.

Although the Seventh Amendment has not been formally incorporated into the Fourteenth Amendment, nearly all of the states assure jury trials in civil as well as criminal actions.

Judges are neutral and play a role similar to that of a referee. Along with *stare decisis* the adversarial nature of the U.S. legal system is a defining and dynamic core value. This distinguishes the U.S. common law system from civil law systems where, for instance, trials are not adversarial and a judge typically serves the role of both the plaintiff's attorney or prosecutor and defense attorney. Judges or magistrates play an active role; they develop evidence and arguments for both sides and may interview witnesses before rendering a decision. Precedent plays little if any, role in civil legal systems, as we further explain in our Companion Website, Chapter 1, Sidebar #4 "*Common Law and Civil Law Legal Systems*," http://www.environmentallaw-teach.org/sidebar-4.html.

Chapter 2 – The Structure and Function of the U.S. Legal System and Its Lawmaking Institutions

The United States legal system has a solid English common law foundation. Since its colonial days, that foundation has evolved into the complex system we experience today, whether we understand how it works or not. Because we believe that law works organically as a complex system, the next pages are devoted to explaining its lawmaking institutions.

HAVE YOU READ THE CONSTITUTION OF THE UNITED STATES?

This may sound like a basic question, but studies have shown that very few U.S. citizens have read the CONSTITUTION OF THE UNITED STATES OF AMERICA. Fewer yet have studied it and understood it as a living document. In order to understand why the CONSTITUTION was drafted in 1787, open our companion website, read the CONSTITUTION'S PREAMBLE, and consider both its specific and aspirational goals. From there, move on to Article VI of the CONSTITUTION and its accompanying commentary on our website. Paragraph two is known as the *supremacy clause*. The supremacy clause is of paramount importance because it declares the Constitution, which now includes twenty-seven amendments, as well as all federal laws and treaties which do not violate the CONSTITUTION to be the highest law in the United States.

While every state in the union has its own (usually much longer) constitution, the provisions of state constitutions may differ from, but may never contradict, the Constitution. Whenever there is a conflict between a state constitution or a state law and either the UNITED STATES CONSTITUTION or a constitutional federal law or treaty, state as well as federal judges must reject the state constitution or state law in favor of the CONSTITUTION and constitutional federal law. Paragraph three of Article VI requires all federal and state elected and appointed officials to take an oath or make an affirmation to support the CONSTITUTION.

It is important to note that the CONSTITUTION replaced a previous document, the ARTICLES OF CONFEDERATION. All of the Framers of the Constitution were elected by their respective state legislatures. Many Founders of the United States, such as Thomas Jefferson, were not Framers of the Constitution and vice versa. Many issues divided the Framers and these were hotly debated. These debates are most clearly understood by reading the Federalist Papers written by Alexander Hamilton, James Madison, and John Jay. Madison's essays have been the most often read and quoted because of their focus on the larger issues of government, especially federal governance, where one central authority shares power with subsidiary units (now fifty states). In *Federalist No. 78*, Madison argues:

> The interpretation of the laws is the proper and peculiar province of the courts. A constitution is in fact, and must be, regarded by the judges as the fundamental law. It therefore belongs to them to ascertain its meaning as well as the meaning of any particular act proceeding from the legislative body.

Here Madison, often considered the "Father of the Constitution," argues for a strong third, judicial branch of government with powers of judicial review. A strong judiciary becomes a reality after *Marbury v. Madison, 5 U.S. 137 (1803),* (see Sidebar #3 of the Companion Website).

WHO DETERMINES THE MEANING OF THE CONSTITUTION?

The first sentence of Article III, Section 1 reads: "The judicial power of the United States shall be vested in one supreme Court." The first sentence of Section 2 reads: "The judicial power shall extend to all Cases in Law and Equity, arising under this Constitution, the Law of the United States, and treaties made, or which shall be made, under their Authority..." This and the Supreme Court decision and precedent set in *Marbury v. Madison,* 5 U.S. 137 (1803), (see Sidebar #3 of the Companion Website) have established the Supreme Court of the United States (SCOTUS) as the final arbiter of the U.S. CONSTITUTION and federal laws and treaties. By virtue of its power of judicial review, the Supreme Court determines whether federal statutes, administrative regulations, and executive orders comply with constitutional requirements. The federal courts may also resolve contradictions between state constitutions or state laws and the U.S. CONSTITUTION and federal laws.

WHAT IS THE BILL OF RIGHTS?

At present, there are twenty-seven amendments to the CONSTITUTION. The first ten of these amendments comprise the BILL OF RIGHTS. Read the first ten Amendments (on the companion website) and then compare them to the ENGLISH BILL OF RIGHTS ("An Act Declaring the Rights and Liberties of the Subject and Settling the Succession of the Crown") enacted by the English Parliament in 1689. The English Bill of Rights established the sovereignty of parliament over all government institutions including the Monarchy. The enumeration of grievances against the CROWN IN THE ENGLISH BILL OF RIGHTS is reminiscent of the grievances listed in the DECLARATION OF INDEPENDENCE. The provisions of the ENGLISH BILL OF RIGHTS provide the motivation and template for the U.S. BILL OF RIGHTS as it declares "ancient rights and liberties" to include:

> That the pretended power of suspending the laws or the execution of laws by regal authority with-out consent of Parliament is illegal;
> That the pretended power of dispensing with laws or the execution of laws by regal authority, as it hath been assumed and exercised of late, is illegal;
> That the commission for erecting the late Court of Commissioners for Ecclesiastical Causes, and all other commissions and courts of like nature, are illegal and pernicious;
> That levying money for or to the use of the Crown by pretence of prerogative, without grant of Parliament, for longer time, or in other manner than the same is or shall be granted, is illegal;
> That it is the right of the subjects to petition the king, and all commitments and prosecutions for such petitioning are illegal;
> That the raising or keeping a standing army within the kingdom in time of peace, unless it be with consent of Parliament, is against law;
> That the subjects which are Protestants may have arms for their defence suitable to their conditions and as allowed by law;
> That election of members of Parliament ought to be free;
> That the freedom of speech and debates or proceedings in Parliament ought not to be impeached or questioned in any court or place out of Parliament;
> That excessive bail ought not to be required, nor excessive fines imposed, nor cruel and unusual punishments inflicted;
> That jurors ought to be duly impanelled and returned, and jurors which pass upon men in trials for high treason ought to be freeholders;
> That all grants and promises of fines and forfeitures of particular persons before conviction are illegal and void...

George Mason, a Virginia delegate, lost a motion at the Constitutional Convention to add a BILL OF RIGHTS TO THE CONSTITUTION and then unsuccessfully fought Virginia's *ratification*. James Madison, considered to be the "Father of the Constitution," pledged to amend the Constitution by adding a Bill of Rights at the First Congress to assuage anti-federalists fears that the U.S. CONSTITUTION did not sufficiently protect individuals from government incursions. After ratification (see Article VII) Congress followed through on Madison's promise.

The Ninth Amendment (1791) states that "[t]he enumeration in the CONSTITUTION, of certain rights, shall not be construed to deny or disparage others retained by the people." The Ninth Amendment indicates that there may be other rights "retained by the people" that were not included in the Bill of Rights. Other rights "retained by the people" that have been recognized by the courts include the right to vote, the right to freedom of movement, and the right to privacy. The right to privacy "enumerated" through application of the due process clause of the Fourteenth Amendment was central to the decision in *Roe v. Wade*, 410 U.S. 113 (1973), that protected a woman's reproductive decision-making and abortion rights. You can read more about the history behind that case on our Companion Website, Chapter 2, Sidebar #6, http://www.environmentallaw-teach.org/sidebar-6.html.

It should be emphasized again that the real meaning of the CONSTITUTION and its Amendments is determined by judicial interpretation. Consider, for example, the First Amendment. The words "*the freedom of speech*" have been given practical meaning through decisions in cases decided by numerous courts, especially SCOTUS (the Supreme Court of the United States). First Amendment litigation, like all litigation in the United States, always involves a case or controversy arising from specific events, for example, an arrest for flag burning. Does the First Amendment guarantee the right to yell "fire" in a crowded theater? Does it permit a speaker to advocate the commission of violent acts against other persons?

THE LAWMAKING BRANCHES OF GOVERNMENT

The U.S. government is one of separated powers. The first three articles of the U.S. CONSTITUTION delineate the structure of the federal government and distribute political powers among its three branches. The structure and powers of the legislative, executive, and judicial branches are described in Articles I, II, and III respectively. The following will briefly describe how the legislative branch passes statutes; how the executive branch and administrative agencies issue executive orders, create regulations, and adjudicate disputes; and how the judicial branch adjudicates cases and controversies.

ARTICLE I OF THE CONSTITUTION: THE LEGISLATIVE BRANCH AND STATUTORY LAW

Article I of the CONSTITUTION defines our form of government: a republic. Article I also states that the republican form of government was created so all citizens vote for individuals to represent them in the federal legislative bodies. Article I defines the federal legislature. At the federal level, there is a *bi-cameral* legislature known as Congress. Its chambers are called the Senate and the House of Representatives (Section 1).

From a structural point of view, the composition of the two chambers is different. First, the apportionment of representatives in the House changes for each state after each census and states with growing populations gain representation. However, each state, regardless of its population, has two senators to represent its interests in the Senate. Thus, unlike Members of the House of Representatives, who represent a specific part of their state's constituency, each Senator represents his or her entire state. Second, while all seats in the House of Representatives are filled simultaneously by elections held every two years (Section 2), Senators are elected to hold office for six-year terms, but only one-third of Senate seats are up for election in each biannual, congressional election (Section 3). Section 2 declares that Members of the House of Representatives were to be "chosen every second year by the People." The CONSTITUTION did not delineate who actually had the right to vote for federal officials and left that decision to the individual states. Most states initially gave the franchise only to free, white men over the age of twenty-one who owned property (in New Jersey, women who owned property could vote until women were disenfranchised in 1807). By the mid-1850s all white males over twenty-one could vote. The Fifteenth Amendment (1870) prohibited the denial of *suffrage*...on the basis of "race, color, or previous condition of servitude." The Nineteenth Amendment (1920) forbade states from denying the right to vote "on account of sex." The Twenty-fourth Amendment stipulated that the right to vote could not be denied "by reason of failure to pay any poll tax or other tax." The Twenty-sixth Amendment (1971) extended the right to vote to anyone "eighteen years of age or older."

For 125 years after the CONSTITUTION's ratification in 1788, Senators were not elected by popular vote. Instead, Senators were elected by state legislatures as stipulated by Article I, Section 3. The Seventeenth Amendment (1913) democratized Article I, Section 3 and provided for the direct election of U.S. Senators.

The Voting Rights Act of 1965 strengthened the Fifteenth Amendment protections by further prohibiting practices that contributed to racial discrimination in voting. The Voting Rights Act of 1965 banned discriminatory laws and practices that were designed to circumvent the Fifteenth Amendment. *The Voting Rights Act of 1965* prohibited voter qualification requirements, such as literacy tests and poll taxes, which were designed to disenfranchise African Americans. This statute has been the basis of active litigation, most notably in the Supreme Court decision in *Shelby County v. Holder*, 570 U.S. 2 (2013). You can read more about the history behind this case at our Companion Website, Chapter 2, Sidebar #7, http://www.environmentallaw-teach.org/sidebar-7.html.

The actual number of Members of the House of Representatives allotted to each state was initially set using a formula that counted the number of "free men" in each state and the infamous "three fifths of all other Persons" (referring to slaves) that provided extra representation for the slave states in the House of Representatives (Section 2). The other oblique allusion to slavery (the word "slavery" was not used until the CONSTITUTION'S THIRTEENTH AMENDMENT) can be found in the shockingly evil third paragraph of Article IV, Section 2, which required "free states" to return fugitive enslaved individuals to their owners. This paragraph was rendered null and void after the passage of the Thirteenth Amendment which abolished slavery.

Article I, Section 2 provides that: "The Number of Representatives shall not exceed one for every thirty Thousand, but each State shall have at Least one Representative." To account for population growth, the size of the House was regularly increased by Congress until it fixed the number at 435 in 1911. Section 2 indicates that

> Representatives...shall be apportioned among the several States...." and that this "enumeration shall be made" .... within every subsequent Term of ten Years, in such manner as they shall by Law direct.

So, while the total number of seats in the House is fixed at 435, they are apportioned among the population of each state as determined by the constitutionally mandated census conducted every ten years. As for not exceeding "one for every thirty Thousand," the population of the United States was about 326 million in 2017 and dividing by 435 yields about 75,000 people for each seat in the House.

From a lawmaking point of view, there are few differences between the House and the Senate. These distinctions are described in detail in Article I, Section 7. Members of each chamber can introduce a bill proposing a new law. A committee of that chamber will study the bill and reject it or recommend, with or without changes. If the bill passes out of committee, it is then brought to the floor of the entire chamber for debate. Amendments may be offered. If the bill receives an affirmative vote after debate, it is then sent to the other chamber where similar debates and vote take place. If there are proposed amendments, both chambers of Congress must agree on them. When Congress cannot agree on the content of a bill, the bill is referred to a special committee whose role is to resolve differences between the two legislative houses on the wording of a bill. Unless a bill passes both houses in the same form, it cannot be sent to the President for signing. At this point in the lawmaking process, the President has a few options. The President can sign the bill into law or the President can do nothing. If the President does not sign the bill, then, if Congress is in session, the bill becomes law automatically after ten days. If Congress is not in session when the ten-day period expires, the bill does not become law. This is known as a *pocket veto*.

The President can also actively veto the bill. Then, unless Congress overrides the veto by a two-thirds vote of both Houses, the bill does not become law. However, once the bill is signed into law, it becomes binding federal statutory law. But this is just the beginning. Who will execute the provisions of this law? Here the executive branch through its administrative agencies creates regulations to carry out the specifics of the law and then adjudicate disputes that arise. Later in this book, we will see that the true meaning of a statute and its regulations will be determined by the decisional law of the courts. But, amendments to and debates over bills become parts of a law's legislative history, and this legislative history is often used by courts in determining the meaning of statutory language.

Article I, Section 7 begins by stating that "All bills for raising Revenue shall originate in the House of Representatives; but the Senate may propose or concur with Amendments as on other bills." The issue of "no taxation without representation" was one of the key motivating forces in the decision of the American Colonies to declare their independence from King George III. It is therefore not difficult to understand the sensitivity of the Framers to the issue of who had the power of the purse. Because the House of Representatives was more closely connected to the people and was elected every two years, the sole power to initiate bills to raise revenue is vested in the House of Representatives.

The word *republican* also appears in Article IV, Section 4 in the form of a guarantee by the federal authority that each state shall have a representative government. Each state's *constitution* establishes the structure of that state's government, including the legislative body or bodies that can enact statutes. With one notable exception, Nebraska, both the federal and the state legislative bodies are bi-cameral. For example, the New York legislative body is composed of the New York State Senate and New York State Assembly. State lawmaking procedures are also nearly identical to the federal system. A legislator introduces a bill, and then the bill is referred to the appropriate standing committee of the chamber where it was introduced. When the bill passes both chambers of the state legislature, it is sent to the governor's office. Like the President, a governor can sign bills into law, veto them, or take no action on them. Once a bill is signed into law, it becomes binding, state statutory law.

Congressional Powers – Article I, Section 8

The Bill of Rights was added to the Constitution in the First Congress to protect individual rights and delineate what the federal government was not allowed to do. Article I, Section 8 enumerates the many important powers granted to the Congress and is often considered the core of the Constitution. The laws passed to carry out these powers have necessitated the establishment of a huge administrative bureaucracy. This federal administrative bureaucracy has become so massive that it is often referred to as our fourth branch of government. A fourth administrative, governmental branch is something that the Framers of the U.S. Constitution never envisioned. Read Article I, Section 8 and the accompanying commentary in the companion website.

The following are some overarching, critical congressional powers:

1. the power to collect taxes with federal tax collection now the responsibility of the Internal Revenue Service, a huge, federal bureau within the Department of the Treasury that is aided by the enforcement power of the Department of Justice;

2. the power to regulate commerce "among the several states," which has allowed the federal government to regulate many activities (including environmental protection) because of the very broad definition accorded "commerce" by the courts;

3. the power to create "[t]ribunals inferior to the supreme Court," which has permitted the creation of the present federal court system with trial and appellate courts, known as circuit courts; and,

4. the power to declare war and raise and support armies and the navy.

The "necessary and proper" clause found in the last paragraph of Section 8 is worth repeating:

> "To make all Laws which shall be necessary and proper for carrying into Execution the foregoing Powers, and all other Powers vested by the Constitution in the government of the Unites States, or any Department or Officer thereof."

The "necessary and proper" clause has been used to justify the creation of laws well beyond the types of legislation envisioned by the Framers, along with departments and agencies to carry out such laws. This over time has resulted in the growth of a vast and powerful federal bureaucracy within the executive branch.

ARTICLE II OF THE CONSTITUTION: THE EXECUTIVE BRANCH, EXECUTIVE ORDERS, AGENCIES AND ADMINISTRATIVE LAW

Article II, Section 1 vests the "executive Power" in the President of the United States. Go to the companion website and read the four sections of Article II along with the commentary. The chief executive is responsible for carrying out and enforcing the *law of the land*. The President may create law through executive orders or decrees. Executive orders have the full force of the law but are directed internally to the executive departments and agencies of the federal government. Executive orders, while not specifically mentioned in the CONSTITUTION, derive their authority from Article II, Section 3's exhortation to "take Care that the Laws be faithfully executed." Executive orders are, of course, subject to judicial review.

The President is elected for a term of four years. No term limit was included in the original text of the CONSTITUTION. By deciding not to seek election for a third four-year term in 1796, George Washington established the precedent that a president should only serve two terms. The precedent was the unwritten rule until Franklin D. Roosevelt was elected to four terms. In 1951, shortly after Roosevelt's death in office, the Twenty-second Amendment, which limited a presidency to a maximum of two full, elected terms, was ratified.

The election of Presidents has produced debate and consternation about the electoral college, which was mandated by the CONSTITUTION. Each state has a specific number of electors that is equal to the combined number of seats held in the House of Representatives and the Senate. In

2017, New Jersey, for instance, has twelve representatives and two senators for a total of fourteen electors. In a presidential election the winner of the popular vote in almost every state wins all the electoral votes in that state. Maine and Nebraska allocate their electors among the candidates in proportion to the popular vote. The electors subsequently meet and vote for the President.

The Electoral College was originally created by the Framers as a device to protect the election of the President from what the Framers viewed as the unsophisticated, uneducated votes of the masses. This truly elitist principle required that the most knowledgeable and accomplished men would be chosen as electors by their respective legislatures and that these electors would use their own judgment in voting for the best candidate for President. The CONSTITUTION says nothing about political parties. However, by 1792 the Federalist Party led by Alexander Hamilton opposed the anti-federalist Democratic-Republican Party of Thomas Jefferson. This was the beginning of what has largely been a two-party system in the United States. The advent of political parties made it necessary to create separate groups of electors who pledged to vote for their party. This was constitutionally allowed since the creation of the Electoral College was left to the states "in such Manner as the Legislature thereof may direct." Winning a majority of electoral votes is, therefore, the goal of any Presidential candidate. If no candidate secures a majority of votes in the electoral college, then the election is decided by the House of Representatives with each state having one vote. Because there is a total of 538 electors, corresponding to 435 representatives, 100 senators, and the three electors for the District of Columbia (as provided by the Twenty-third Amendment), the magic number is 270. Losers of the popular vote who won the presidency by winning the electoral college vote include John Quincy Adams (1824), Rutherford B. Hayes (1876), Benjamin Harrison (1888), George W. Bush (2000) and Donald Trump (2016). In the presidential election of 1824, John Quincy Adams was elected President but not until February 9, 1825. This election was the only one in history to be decided by the House of Representatives under the provisions of the Twelfth Amendment (1804) after no candidate secured a majority of the electoral vote.

The President exercises considerable lawmaking powers. As previously discussed, the President exercises his or her lawmaking powers by signing federal bills into law or vetoing them, or by issuing executive orders. Though Congress usually creates departments and agencies through "enabling acts," Congress (in Chapter 9, Title 5 of the *United States Code*) gave the President the power to issue an executive order to establish an administrative agency if the purpose is to consolidate responsibilities and make administration more efficient. Using this power, President Nixon established the *Environmental Protection Agency* (E.P.A.) in 1970 through a reorganization plan that consolidated in one agency a variety of environmental monitoring, standard-setting, enforcement, and research activities that at that time were dispersed among several existing agencies. See the Companion Website at http://www.environmentallaw-teach.org and search for *Reorganization Plan No. 3 of 1970,* which outlines the rationale for the consolidation of these activities within the new EPA.

Article II, Section 2 states that "The President shall be the Commander in Chief of the Army and Navy of the United States, and of the Militia of the several States, when called into the service of the United States...." Like the vaguely defined "executive Power" granted in Article II, Section 1, the President's commander-in-chief power has also expanded over the course of the past 200 years. Presidents have relied on Article II, Section 2 to commence military actions. Arguably, reliance by a President on Article II, Section 2 to enter military actions conflicts directly with the power to declare war given to the House of Representatives in Article I, Section 8.

The President's lawmaking powers may be also exercised indirectly through appointments. Article II, Section 2 states that the President "shall nominate, and by and with the Advice and Consent of the Senate, shall appoint ambassadors, other public Ministers and Consuls, Judges of the supreme Court, and all other Officers of the United States, whose Appointments are not herein otherwise provided for, and which shall be established by Law." The Foreword to the December 1, 2016 edition of the POLICY AND SUPPORTING POSITIONS (PLUM BOOK), states:

> Every four years, just after the Presidential election, the "United States Government Policy and Supporting Positions," commonly known as the Plum Book, is published, alternately, by the Senate Committee on Homeland Security and Governmental Affairs and the House Committee on Oversight and Government Reform. This publication contains data (as of June 30, 2016) on over 9,000 Federal civil service leadership and support positions in the legislative and executive branches of the Federal Government that may be subject to noncompetitive appointment (e.g., positions such as agency heads and their immediate subordinates, policy executives and advisors, and aides who report to these officials). (https:// www.govinfo.gov/content/pkg/GPO-PLUMBOOK-2016/pdf/GPO-PLUMBOOK-2016.pdf).

The PLUM BOOK gives you a clear sense of the magnitude of the unelected federal bureaucracy within the executive branch. Page 26 of the PLUM BOOK contains information regarding the number of positions filled by appointments within the Department of Defense.

Article II, Section 2 also provides that the President "may require the Opinion, in writing, of the Principal Officer in each of the executive Departments, upon any subject relating to the Duties of their respective Offices." Without using the word, this language created the justification for a *Cabinet* (discussed in more detail below). Advice and consent of the Senate formerly required only consultation with the Senate. Now, presidential appointees are required to attend hearings before Senate committees. If the Senate committee approves the appointment, then the appointment is brought before the full Senate for a vote. An affirmative vote by a simple majority confirms the appointment.

Section 2 of Article II provides that the President "shall have the Power, by and with the advice and consent of the Senate, to make Treaties, provided two-thirds of the Senators present concur." The Obama Administration negotiated on behalf of the United States in helping to draft the Paris Climate Accord in 2017. This agreement has been signed by 195 countries of the United Nations Framework Convention on Climate Change and ratified by 145 countries. The United States Senate never ratified the *Paris Climate Accord;* therefore, it does not have the force of law in the United States.

Article II, Section 3 provides that the President "shall from time to time give to Congress Information of the State of the Union, and recommend to their Consideration such Measures as he shall judge necessary and expedient; he may on extraordinary Occasions convene both Houses, or either of them...." The CONSTITUTION does not specifically require the President to deliver a speech to Congress for such purpose; however, every President since Woodrow Wilson in 1913 has addressed a joint session of Congress. Presidents Washington and Adams also gave their annual, constitutionally mandated reports in the form of addresses to joint sessions of Congress. President Jefferson discontinued this practice and, instead, transmitted his annual report in writing. Presidents continued to furnish annual, written reports until 1913. President Roosevelt established two traditions by calling in 1934 what was known as the "President's Annual Message to Congress" the "State of the Union Address" and by making the first address at night in 1936. This address has evolved from radio (President Coolidge in 1923) to television (President Truman in 1947) and now into a major media event. By tradition, the address is made in January or February. Since the development of nuclear weapons, a designated survivor is chosen to be absent from the State of the Union Address and to be secured in a safe location. This person is usually a cabinet member that, according to the Presidential Succession Act of 1947, is in the direct line of succession. The actual line of succession provided for in this statute is: Vice President, Speaker of the House of Representatives, President pro tempore of the Senate, the Secretary of State, and then the rest of the members of the U.S. Cabinet.

Article II, Section 1 dictates that the Vice President shall be "chosen for the same Term" as the President. Article I, Section 3 states that the "Vice President of the United States shall be President of the Senate, but shall have no Vote, unless they be equally divided". The most important responsibility of the Vice President is stated in Article II, Section 1 that makes the Vice President first in the line of succession if the president dies, is disabled, or is *impeached* and convicted. The Twenty-fifth Amendment (1967) restated and clarified Article II and also provided for Vice Presidential succession, by requiring Vice Presidential vacancies to be filled by the President and confirmed by both houses of the Congress. Previously, whenever a Vice President had succeeded to the Presidency or had otherwise left the office empty (through death, resignation, or removal from office), the Vice Presidency remained vacant until the next Presidential and Vice-Presidential terms began.

Article II, Section 4 states that "The President, Vice President and all civil Officers of the United States, shall be removed from Office on Impeachment for, and Conviction of, Treason, Bribery, or other high Crimes and Misdemeanors." Impeachment is the equivalent to an indictment. The understanding of the Framers was that "High Crimes" were those committed by those who have taken an oath of office and have special responsibilities because of their position of authority and public trust. These "Crimes and Misdemeanors" cover a wide range of abuses and illegal behavior. Article I, Section 2 provides that the House of Representatives "shall have the sole power of impeachment." Only officers of the U.S. federal government may be impeached. As previously mentioned, Article II, Section 2 gives the power (subject to the "advice and consent" of the U. S. Senate) to appoint "Officers of the United States" to the President. "Officers of the United States" are, therefore, appointed members of the executive or judicial branch of government. They are numerous (see the PLUM BOOK above) and include, for instance, all the heads of executive departments and agencies, all federal judges, and all officers of the U.S. military.

Members of Congress are not and cannot be "Officers of the United States." The "ineligibility clause" of Article 1, Section 6 states that "No Senator or representative shall, during the time for which he was elected, be appointed to any civil Office under the Authority of the United States" and "no Person holding any Office under the United States, shall be a member of either House during his continuance in office." While members of Congress cannot be impeached, the CONSTITUTION explicitly states in Article I, Section 5 that "each House may determine the Rules of its Proceedings, punish its members for disorderly Behaviour, and, with the Concurrence of two-thirds, expel a Member."

The procedure for impeachment of an "Officer of the United States" requires that the House Judiciary Committee by majority vote send the "Articles of Impeachment" to the floor of the House, where there is a hearing. By a majority vote, the House can confirm the impeachment. An impeachment is not a conviction but is a formal allegation and is analogous to an indictment in a criminal trial. Article I, Section 3 states that "The Senate shall have the sole Power to try all Impeachments. When sitting for that Purpose, they shall be on Oath or Affirmation. When the President of the United States is tried, the Chief Justice shall preside: And no Person shall be convicted without the Concurrence of two-thirds of the Members present." Presidents Andrew Johnson and William Jefferson Clinton are the only two Presidents to have been impeached. Neither was convicted by the Senate. One Cabinet member, William Belknap, the Secretary of War, was impeached in 1876 for taking kickbacks. He was not impeached until after he resigned from office. The Senate could not muster the two-thirds supermajority needed to convict Belknap because many Senators felt that they could not convict someone who had resigned. Fifteen federal judges have been impeached, and eight were convicted by the Senate since 1803 when Judge John Pickering of New Hampshire was impeached for excessive intoxication. More recently, Judge Thomas Porteous of Louisiana was convicted of bribery and perjury in 2010. The penalty for impeachment is stated in Article 1, Section 3 where "Judgment in Cases of Impeachment shall not extend further than to removal from Office, and disqualification to hold and enjoy any Office of honor, Trust or Profit under the United States: but the Party convicted shall nevertheless be liable and subject to Indictment, Trial, Judgment and Punishment, according to Law."

THE CABINET AND ADMINISTRATIVE AGENCIES. THE RISE OF A FOURTH BRANCH OF GOVERNMENT

The primary function of administrative agencies are: (1) making rules and regulations (used interchangeably here); and (2) adjudicating disputes between the agency and the persons or entities that they regulate. The U.S. CONSTITUTION does not explicitly mention administrative agencies. The authority to create administrative agencies has been inferred from the powers attributed to the other branches. For instance, Article II, Section 2 of the U.S. CONSTITUTION states that the President "may require the Opinion, in writing, of the principal Officer in each of his executive Departments, upon any subject relating to the Duties of their respective Offices." Most administrative agencies are part of the executive branch; however, they are formed by the legislative branch (e.g. Congress or a state legislature) through enabling statutes. Enabling statutes broadly delegate power to administrative agencies.

DEPARTMENTS AND INDEPENDENT AGENCIES

Federal administrative agencies are either executive or independent. The head of each administrative agency is appointed by the President, whose appointment must be confirmed by the Senate. The President may remove the head of an executive agency at any time for any reason. Executive agencies are usually located within the executive branch in a Cabinet-level department. The Bureau of Ocean Energy Management, for example, is a bureau within the Department of the Interior, a Cabinet-level department.

Congress must designate a department as having cabinet-level rank. The creation of a Cabinet-level department, which confers prestige, is made when the mission of the department is considered to be broad and significant to the nation. The President appoints the "principal Officer in each of his executive Departments" subject to the "advice and consent of the senate." The Cabinet includes the Vice President and the heads of the executive departments, who are called Secretaries, with the exception of the head of the Department of Justice, who bears the title Attorney General. The idea for a Presidential Cabinet comes from England where the Secretaries are called Ministers and the Cabinet is called the Privy Council. The Privy Council is assembled as a formal body of advisors. During George Washington's Presidency, there were only five Cabinet members: The Vice President, the Secretary of State, the Secretary of Treasury, the Secretary of War, and the Attorney General. At one time there was a Department of War and separate departments for the Army, Navy, and Air Force but these have been merged into the Department of Defense. There was also a separate Post Office Department, but the Post Office Department is now a separate, non-Cabinet level agency.

Today, in 2019, there are sixteen Cabinet members. Members of the Cabinet departments are listed below (with their dates of creation by Congress) in the order in which they would succeed to the Presidency in the event of a vacancy. Remember that the Speaker of the House and President pro tempore of the Senate follow the Vice President in order of succession, then the Secretary of State.

Vice-President
Secretary of State (1789)
Secretary of Treasury (1789)
Secretary of Defense (1947)
Attorney General (1870)
Secretary of Interior (1849)
Secretary of Agriculture (1889)
Secretary of Commerce (1903)
Secretary of Labor (1913)
Secretary of Health and Human Services (1953)
Secretary of Housing and Urban Development (1965)
Secretary of Transportation (1966)
Secretary of Energy (1977)
Secretary of Education (979)
Secretary of Veterans Affairs (1989)
Secretary of Homeland Security (2003)

Once a department is created, Congress must provide funding for employees to support the Department's mission. The four departments in Washington's Cabinet had approximately 1000 non-military employees. Today, the fifteen departments of the Cabinet have over 4.2 million employees, with 3 million of these in the Department of Defense. While the budget for the Department of Defense is over $600 billion per year, the Department of Health and Human Services with approximately 70,000 employees had an authorized budget of $1.020 trillion in 2015.

In addition to the Vice President and heads of executive departments, there are a number of Cabinet-level officials, who, though they are not officially members of the Cabinet, do attend Cabinet meetings. These presently include:

White House Chief of Staff
U.S. Trade Representative
Director of National Intelligence
Representative of the United States to the United Nations

Director of the Office of Management and Budget
Director of the Central Intelligence Agency
Administrator of the Environmental Protection Agency
Administrator of the Small Business Administration

The Cabinet meets when the President calls a meeting. In the past, these meetings were often weekly; however, meetings of the entire Cabinet have become more of a rarity recently. Now, Cabinet meetings are typically conducted with only a few Cabinet members, advisers, and other officials concerned with a particular issue.

The Cabinet has nearly doubled in size since the end of WWII. This has been the Congressional response to the growing demand for government action on a growing list of national social, political, and economic needs. The return of members of the armed forces, many of whom were injured, from the Vietnam War, following WWI, WWII, the Korean War, and other military actions, created the pressing need for the elevation of the *Veterans Administration* (created in 1930) into a *Department of Veteran Affairs* (established in 1989).

In addition to the fifteen executive departments with 1.2 million nonmilitary employees, you will find over 450 independent administrative agencies and sub-agencies with over 1.6 million non-military employees. You will discover among many, many others the *Environmental Protection Agency*, the Nuclear Regulatory Commission, the Central Intelligence Agency, the Federal Communications Commission, and the National Aeronautics and Space Administration. The President appoints the chairmen of independent agencies. Unlike executive agencies, which have a single head, there are usually several heads, or chairmen, of independent agencies. For example, the Federal Energy Regulatory Commission, an independent agency, has five chairmen. No more than a simple majority of independent agency chairmen may be from the President's political party. The President's appointments for independent agency chairmen must also be confirmed by the Senate.

All of the Cabinet-level departments and almost all of the independent administrative agencies are part of the executive branch. A few, such as the Congressional Budget Office, the Government Accounting Office, and the Library of Congress, are located within the legislative branch of government. The U.S. Sentencing Commission and the Judicial Conference of the U.S. are two of a handful of agencies of the judicial branch.

ADMINISTRATIVE LAW JUDGES

The Office of Personnel Management, itself an independent agency, administers the selection of Administrative Law Judges (ALJ)s, but the ALJs are hired by the specific agencies that require their service. Thus, all ALJs are employees of the executive branch. The *Administrative Procedures Act*

(A.P.A., 5 U.S.C. §§500 et seq.), discussed below, has protections in place to safeguard the independence of these ALJs. A.P.A. safeguards help to ensure that ALJs conduct trial-like hearings free from agency coercion or influence and that they objectively weigh the evidence. It is important to note the ALJs are considered Article I judges because they were created by the legislative branch through an act of Congress. These judges were at first called *hearing officers*. They do not have lifetime appointments. Article I courts are often called legislative courts or tribunals to distinguish them from the Article III courts (the Supreme Court and the federal inferior courts) to be discussed in the next section.

AGENCY RULEMAKING

An agency's enabling statute grants it the power to promulgate rules or regulations. Agencies may engage in formal, informal, or hybrid rulemaking. Agencies are often granted the power to create scientific or technical rules because, unlike Congress, agencies are staffed by individuals with expertise in the area being regulated. For example, an agency like the *Environmental Protection Agency* (E.P.A.) is staffed by individuals who have specific knowledge about the environment and environmental concerns and who are capable of passing regulations intended to protect the environment.

a. Formal Rulemaking

The A.P.A. governs the process of making rules and regulations and adjudicating claims and disputes. The A.P.A. was enacted in 1946 to ensure fairness in rulemaking and due process in adjudication, and to establish a means to oversee government agency action.

The A.P.A. established uniform administrative law procedures for a federal agency's promulgation of rules and adjudication of claims. The A.P.A. also sets forth the process for judicial review of agency action. Section 553 of the A.P.A. sets forth the general procedural requirements for federal agencies engaging in both formal and informal rulemaking. Section 553(c) of the A.P.A. specifically sets forth the procedures for a federal agency engaging in formal rulemaking. Section 553 (c) states that "when rules are required to be made on the record after opportunity for agency hearing, §§ 556 and 557 of the title apply instead of this subsection." Sections 556 and 557 set forth the procedural requirements for all administrative hearings, including the trial-like formal rulemaking process. When an agency's enabling statute requires rules and regulations to be promulgated after a formal hearing recorded and transcribed on the record, an agency must engage in "*Formal Rulemaking*." A notice of proposed rulemaking (NPRM) must be published in the *Federal Register (F.R.)*, which is published daily except on holidays. It is the official record of the proceedings of the federal executive branch of government. As required by the A.P.A., the *Federal Register* publishes all executive orders and Presidential proclamations, all proposed new rules and final rules, all changes to existing rules, and all notices of hearings, adjudicatory proceedings, and grant applications. The final rules are then published in the *Code of Federal Regulations (C.F.R.)*. Changes to the C.F.R. are published online daily, and all regulations old and new are published in an annual edition of approximately 200 print volumes, available digitally.

After the publication of an NPRM in the *Federal Register*, the agency conducts a public hearing at which witnesses may present testimony on the proposed rule. These witnesses may be subject to cross-examination. An official transcript of the hearing is kept. Following the hearing, the agency must publish its formal findings and determine whether to promulgate the regulation. If the agency proceeds to promulgate the regulation, the final rule is published in the *Federal Register*.

Most enabling statutes do not require agencies to engage in formal rulemaking. If an enabling statute is at all ambiguous about whether an agency must engage in formal or informal rulemaking, a court will always interpret the statute as requiring the agency to engage in informal rulemaking, because informal rulemaking is less expensive and less time-consuming than formal rulemaking.

b. Informal Rulemaking

Administrative agencies promulgate most of their rules through the process of informal rulemaking. The procedures set forth in Section 553 of the A.P.A. also govern informal rulemaking. Unlike formal rulemaking, informal rulemaking does not require rules be made on the record after opportunity for agency hearing, so informal rulemaking is not subject to the procedural requirements for agency hearings set forth in A.P.A. Sections 556 and 557. Like formal rulemaking, informal rulemaking begins with the publication of an NPRM in the *Federal Register* and an explanation of the legal authority for issuing the rule and a description of how interested members of the public can participate in the rulemaking process. Interested parties are encouraged to submit written comments which contain information that interested members of the public believe will influence the agency's decision to promulgate the regulation.

Departments and agencies are required to consider the concerns expressed in this period for comment. Participation in the process is important because it provides a unique opportunity for citizens to influence and shape their laws directly. Agencies engaging in informal rulemaking are not required to hold hearings but may receive oral testimony if they wish to do so. After considering the comments received by the public, the agency publishes the final rule and a concise general statement of the regulation's purpose and the date on which the regulation becomes effective, which must be at least 30 days after publication of the final draft of the rule in the *Federal Register*.

c. Hybrid Rulemaking

Hybrid rulemaking combines the most efficient features of formal and informal rulemaking. Hybrid rulemaking requires publishing an NPRM. in the *Federal Register* followed by an opportunity for interested members of the public to submit comments. The agency then holds an informal hearing with a limited opportunity for cross-examination of witnesses. The final proposed regulation is published in the federal register.

JUDICIAL REVIEW OF AGENCY RULES

After an agency has promulgated a rule, a regulated party may challenge the rule in federal district court or may ignore the rule. If fined for violating the rule, the party may challenge the fine it receives in front of an ALJ. And, if it is not satisfied with the ALJ's ruling, it may challenge the ALJ's ruling in a federal district court.

Courts are reluctant to strike down agency rules. Therefore, agency rules will only be struck down if the party challenging the rule can prove that:

1) the enabling statute was unconstitutionally vague;
2) the agency violated the Constitution;
3) the agency exceeded the power granted it by its enabling statute; and
4) the agency did not follow proper rulemaking procedures.

Courts tend to be deferential to agencies' findings of fact and it is therefore very unlikely that a reviewing court will strike down an administrative rule. Nonetheless, regulated individuals frequently challenge agency rules. For example, in *United States v. Nova Scotia Food Products Corp.*, 568 F.2d 240 (2^{d} Cir. 1977), Nova Scotia Food Products challenged an F.D.A. regulation requiring whitefish to be salted and heated to 180° Fahrenheit for at least 30 minutes to prevent botulism contamination. Nova Scotia Food Products argued that this requirement "completely destroy[ed]" the whitefish and rendered it unsalable, and that there were equally effective and less destructive alternative preparation methods. The Second Circuit agreed and struck down the regulation as applied to whitefish.

ADJUDICATION

Administrative agencies may also adjudicate individual cases. The A.P.A. sets forth the procedures an agency must follow in adjudication in 5 U.S.C. §§ 554, 556, and 557. Adjudication begins when a complaint is filed with an ALJ by the agency's staff. The party the agency is investigating is given notice of the time and place of the hearing, the remedy being sought, and the subject of the adjudication. The ALJ issues a preliminary decision which may be appealed to the head of the agency. If the ALJ's ruling is appealed to the head of an agency, the agency's head will issue a final order which may be appealed to a circuit court of appeals. Many agencies rely primarily on adjudications, which tend to be quicker, less costly, and less resource-intensive than non-administrative trials.

Many federal administrative agencies are headquartered in or near Washington D.C. The D.C. Circuit Court has original jurisdiction to review the rulemaking and other administrative activities of administrative agencies without a prior hearing by a district court. As you will see below, the United States Court of Appeals for the District of Columbia Circuit is considered the most important inferior appellate court. In 42 U.S.C. § 4915 (a), for example, the D.C. Circuit is given exclusive jurisdiction over petitions for review of E.P.A. standards and regulations and of Federal Aviation Administration (F.A.A.) standards and regulations.

OTHER ADMINISTRATIVE ACTIVITIES

Agencies also engage in *administrative activities*, including granting permits, managing properties, and conducting research relevant to proposed rules and regulations. Agency actions such as these, are subject to judicial review pursuant to the A.P.A., 5 U.S.C. § 704. An agency may also issue interpretive rules (statements issued by an agency to advise the public of the agency's construction of the rules and orders it administers) and policy statements (preliminary announcements by an agency stating how the agency intends to exercise its discretion in future cases). Interpretive rules and policy statements must be published in the *Federal Register* so that they are accessible to the general public.

OVERSIGHT BY THE THREE BRANCHES OF GOVERNMENT

All three branches of government oversee agency actions. Congress may hold oversight hearings and investigations, set agencies' budgets, and confirm appointments (the Senate must approve the President's nominees for the heads of Executive Agencies and each of the President's nominees for chairmen of Independent Agencies). The President may issue executive orders, which bind executive agencies and appoint the heads of executive agencies and the chairmen of independent agencies. Agencies are required to submit major rules to the Office of Information and Regulatory Affairs (O.I.R.A.), which was set up by President Reagan in 1981. O.I.R.A. requires agencies to show that the benefits of any major rule justifies the costs. A major rule is a rule that is likely to have an annual effect on the economy of $100 million or more. Courts may review agency statutory interpretation to determine if the agency's decision is sufficiently attentive to Congress's intent in enacting a given statute.

ENVIRONMENTAL ADMINISTRATIVE LAW

Congress delegates various powers to administrative agencies. Statutorily, their delegated power enables agencies to:

- issue and promulgate rules and regulations;
- apply executive power to investigate violations of agencies' rules and regulations; and
- enjoy judicial power to adjudicate disputes between agencies and other parties.

Consider these three powers in relation to the *Clean Water Act (C.W.A),* enacted by Congress in 1972. The C.W.A. is one of the most important pieces of environmental legislation in the United States. From this very complex statute, let's glance at one section, Section 404 of C.W.A, 33 U.S.C. § 1344, and see how it helps regulate the three powers mentioned above.

Upon reading Section 404, it becomes obvious that this section helps to protect wetlands by regulating the discharge of dredged or fill material into *wetlands* adjacent to "*waters of the United States*." Congress decided that the *Environmental Protection Agency* (E.P.A.) and the U.S. Army Corps of Engineers would share authority to enforce Section 404 of the C.W.A., 33 U.S.C. § 1344. While Section 404 is a small part of the C.W.A. it is illustrative of the regulatory process. In order to carry out the provisions of Section 404, the E.P.A. and Corps of Engineers needed to promulgate regulations that would provide definitions and procedures for doing so.

In order to regulate the discharge of dredge and fill material in wetlands, it is important to define what a *wetland* is and to be able to physically delineate where they are. To define what a *wetland* is, the E.P.A and Corps of Engineers must follow the procedures described in the A.P.A. The E.P.A. and the Corps of Engineers exercise their legislative power by promulgating regulations pursuant to the C.W.A, which define wetlands. They exercise their executive powers by sending agency employees to investigate individuals and inspect facilities suspected of violating the Clean Water Act by polluting regulated bodies of water, including wetlands. If the E.P.A. or the Corps of Engineers finds a violation, it will exercise its judicial power by imposing a fine. If the fine is challenged by the recipient, the applicable agency will hold a hearing before an administrative law judge (ALJ).

After following all procedures required by the A.P.A., the E.P.A. issued regulations to enforce Section 404 of the *Clean Water Act,* including the definition of a "wetland." See, e.g., *40 C.F.R. Ch. 1, PART 230-§ 404(b)(1)*-Guidelines for Specification of Disposal of Sites for Dredged or Fill Material on our Companion Website, at https://www.law.cornell.edu/cfr/text/40/part-230/subpart-A, and read 40 C.F.R. § 230.3(t). The 1987 CORPS OF ENGINEERS WETLANDS DELINEATION MANUAL AND REGIONAL SUPPLEMENTS, posted on our Companion Website, at https://www.cpe.rutgers.edu/Wetlands/1987-Army-Corps-Wetlands-Delineation-Manual.pdf, is used to define what a "wetland" is. But, Section 404 of the Clean Water Act only protects those wetlands "adjacent to waters of the United States." To learn what "waters of the United States" means, you must seek another C.F.R. definition. For that, go to our Companion Website again, at http://www.environmentallaw-teach.org/, and read 40 C.F.R. § 230.3. Now, when dredged or fill material is deposited in a wetland adjacent to waters of the United States, the E.P.A./Corps of Engineers will have a basis for taking the appropriate enforcement action.

IMPORTANCE OF THE ADMINISTRATIVE BRANCH OF GOVERNMENT

It is clear that the Framers who envisioned three branches of government and their checks and balances did not anticipate the exponential growth of a federal administrative bureaucracy. This administrative branch, frequently referred to as the *fourth branch* of the U.S. government, now has more authority and power over nearly every detail of the lives of the people than the three other branches combined.

ARTICLE III OF THE CONSTITUTION AND THE JUDICIAL BRANCH

The United States Judicial System

In the hierarchy of authorities, statutory law outranks case or decisional law created by the judicial system. The application of a statute or its regulations to specific circumstances is often the subject of litigation, and the courts interpret and give meaning to the statute and its regulations in these cases. However, case law can always be overturned by statutory law as long as the statute is constitutional. Yet, because of its common law foundation, the judiciary is still the preeminent source of law in the U.S. and, because of its unique form of federalism, the judicial system has evolved into a parallel system of federal and state courts. For a simple way to visualize the United States Judiciary, look at *Basic Structure of the United States Judiciary,* provided at the end of this chapter.

Federal Courts

Article III, Section 1 stipulates that the "judicial Power of the United States shall be vested in one supreme Court, and in such inferior courts as the Congress may from time to time ordain and establish." With the Judiciary Act of 1789, Congress established a six-member Supreme Court composed of one Chief Justice and five Associate Justices. This statute also created our tri-level federal court system by adding trial courts and intermediate appellate courts to the national judiciary. Each of the thirteen states became a federal judicial district. Each of the thirteen federal judicial districts was given its own trial court. The thirteen federal district trial courts were then grouped into three geographically-based judicial circuits. The federal judicial circuit courts were granted *appellate* jurisdiction over the decisions of the federal district trial courts within their geographic circuits. Judges on the circuit courts initially consisted of one district judge and two Supreme Court Justices who literally "rode the circuit" on horseback.

Eighty years later, the Judiciary Act of 1869 set the number of Supreme Court Justices at nine, which is the number of Justices on the Court today (though at various times during the intervening years the number fluctuated with seven, eight, nine, and even ten Justices). As states were admitted to the union, new district and Circuit Courts were added to the federal judiciary so that today there are twelve circuits covering the fifty states and the District of Columbia and ninety-four district courts within these eleven circuits. The courts for these circuits are officially referred to as United States Courts of Appeals. For example, the federal appellate court for the Second Circuit, which includes New York, bears the title "United States Court of Appeals for the Second Circuit." The District of Columbia also has a Circuit Court. It is sometimes referred to as the "Little Supreme Court" because it is the second most powerful court in the United States due in large measure to the influence it yields in overseeing the federal bureaucracy. In addition to hearing appeals of federal district court rulings on administrative agency regulations and actions, either under a specific congressional enabling act or pursuant to the A.P.A, many cases involving the review of federal administrative agency rulemaking or decisions are sent directly to the D.C. Circuit Court because the agency in question is headquartered in Washington D.C.

Go to the map of United States Circuit and District Courts that you can find on our Companion Website at http://www.environmentallaw-teach.org. The United States Court of Appeals for the Fourth Circuit is located in Richmond, Virginia. The Fourth Circuit consists of nine federal district courts. Locate the following: The Eastern, Middle, and Western Districts of North Carolina; the District of South Carolina; the Eastern and Western Districts of Virginia; the Northern and Southern Districts of West Virginia; and the District of Maryland. There are five judges authorized by Congress for the Northern District of West Virginia; but the thirty-two counties that it serves are divided into four divisions with courts located in Clarksburg, Elkins, Martinsburg, and Wheeling. In the District or trial courts, a single judge usually presides over both jury and non-jury trials. The Court of Appeals for the Fourth Circuit is authorized by Congress to have fifteen active judges. The number of judges in each Circuit is different, but appeals are usually heard by a group of three judges. For the ultimate federal court system resource, see www.uscourts.gov.

The Circuit Courts hear appeals from the district courts and from decisions of federal administrative agencies located within their circuits. For example, appeals of matters relating to the federal administrative agency called The National Labor Review Board (N.L.R.B.), will be heard either by the Court of Appeals of the place of the violation or by the United States Court of Appeals for the District of Columbia, where the N.L.R.B. is headquartered. The federal judiciary now also includes specialized courts charged with hearing appeals in specific types of cases. For example, the thirteenth federal circuit court, the Court of Appeals for the Federal Circuit, handles appeals that involve patents as well as appeals from the Court of Federal Claims and the Court of International Trade.

Federal district courts are courts of *general jurisdiction* that can hear both civil and criminal cases under the federal CONSTITUTION or a federal statute and controversies between citizens of different states. They are not restricted by law to hearing only disputes limited to a specific subject matter. District courts are the tribunal where a lawsuit is brought and tried. In 2016, just under 370,000 cases were filed in federal district courts. In civil actions, aggrieved parties, who may be persons, corporations, or other legal entities, rather than government prosecutors commence the case by filing a complaint. It is the responsibility of the party filing the civil action, referred to as the plaintiff, to assert both the factual and legal bases that would entitle them to the legal or equitable relief they are seeking. The party against the lawsuit, the defendant, attempts to contradict the plaintiff's narrative. The defendant joins the plaintiff in court and presents evidence to persuade the fact finder, either the jury or the judge, of the factual issues at hand in the lawsuit. Upon hearing the evidence and the arguments made by each party's lawyer, the jury or judge as finder-of-fact renders a verdict in favor of one of the parties. When a jury serves as the finder-of-fact, the jurors must reach their factual verdict according to the instructions about the applicable law given them by the judge.

District court decisions are open to changes on appeal. The appeal stage may involve two levels of scrutiny: one from an intermediary court and another from the court of last resort. At the federal level, the court of last resort is the Supreme Court. However, unlike in civil law countries, the appeal in the American legal system involves only a review of the application of the law by the lower court or courts and not of the facts of the case itself. Thus, except in cases of *reversible error*, the district court has the last word in factual matters. Additionally, in light of the very small number of appellate courts and the finite number of cases each can take on at any given time, it is obvious that only a small percentage of the district court decisions are appealed. In 2016, approximately 60,000 district court decisions were taken on appeal by the Circuit Courts. This may seem like a large number, but it represents just over 15% of the number of cases initiated in federal district courts in that year.

A party who wants to appeal a decision of a Federal Court of Appeals or of a state court files a *petition for writ of certiorari* with the Supreme Court. A minimum of four of the nine Justices must agree to grant a writ of certiorari. This is referred to as the "rule of four." If the Supreme Court grants the petition, a writ of certiorari is issued to the lower court. *Certiorari*, as mentioned earlier, comes from Latin, where it means "to be informed." The writ received by the lower court acts as an order to provide a record of the legal proceedings in the case and to send them to the Supreme Court for their review. When the Court *grants cert*, the case is then scheduled for the filing of *briefs* and for oral argument. Approximately 7,000 petitions for a writ of certiorari are received by the Supreme Court each year, but the Supreme Court grants certiorari in only an average of 100-150 cases.

> Parties who are not satisfied with the decision of a lower court must petition the U.S. Supreme Court to hear their case. The primary means to petition the court for review is to ask it to grant a writ of certiorari. This is a request that the Supreme Court order a lower court to send up the record of the case for review. The Court usually is not under any obligation to hear these cases, and it usually only does so if the case could have national significance, might harmonize conflicting decisions in the federal Circuit courts, and/or could have precedential value. In fact, the Court accepts 100-150 of the more than 7,000 cases that it is asked to review each year. Typically, the Court hears cases that have been decided in either an appropriate U.S. Court of Appeals or the highest Court in a given state (if the state court decided a Constitutional issue).
>
> (http://www.uscourts.gov/about-federal-courts/educational-resources/about-educational-outreach/activity-resources/supreme-1).

The fact that Supreme Court reviews so few cases each year means that in terms of important precedents most federal law is appellate law. The significance of the denial of certiorari by the U.S. Supreme Court has been debated, but the Supreme Court has explained that there are many reasons for the denial of certiorari and that a denial contains no implicit approval or disapproval of the rationale for the lower court decision. When the Federal Court of Appeals for two or more circuits disagree on a similar set of facts or issue, then the Supreme Court has discretion to intervene in order to resolve their conflicting holdings. It often takes several years for the Supreme Court to grant certiorari to cases involving an issue on which the circuit courts are split.

State Courts

Each of the fifty states of the United States has its own system of courts, the structure of which now mirrors the federal court system. While the court nomenclatures differ from state to state, they follow the same common law principles as the federal court system. "Lower" trial courts have to follow precedents established by decisions of higher appellate courts, both intermediate level appellate courts and courts of last resort, in cases involving similar facts. Likewise, intermediate appellate courts must adhere to precedents set in similar cases by the court of last resort.

In New York, most disputes that involve state law—either statutory or case law—will be tried in trial courts, which, in New York, are known as the *Supreme Court*. These decisions can be appealed to the Appellate Divisions of the Supreme Court. The court of last resort in New York, unlike in most other states, is known as the Court of Appeals. Information about the court system in each state can be found on the National Center for State Courts' website at www.ncsu.org.

The highest court in the state of New York is called (with some confusion) the *Court of Appeals*. According to the 2017 ANNUAL REPORT OF THE CLERK OF THE COURT TO THE JUDGES OF THE COURT OF APPEALS OF THE STATE OF NEW YORK,

> In 2017, the Court and its Judges disposed of 3,582 matters, including 142 appeals, 1,196 motions and 2,244 criminal leave applications. A detailed analysis of the Court's work follows.
> (https://www.nycourts.gov/ctapps/news/annrpt/AnnRpt2017.pdf)

Add to this caseload the caseload of the highest courts of the forty-nine other states and remember that the Supreme Court of the United States disposes of about 70 cases a year. It is abundantly clear that the overwhelming majority of lawmaking occurs in the states. In addition to the system of state courts that parallels the federal system, the trial appellate courts, and court of last resort, each state's judicial system contains a host of its own special courts, courts of limited jurisdiction. These include criminal courts, family/divorce courts, juvenile courts, and probate courts. There are also county and municipal courts as well as small claims, traffic, and police courts. These latter courts get little attention but this is where the majority of the U.S. population has contact with judges and the law.

Jurisdiction

Jurisdiction refers to the power or right of a court to hear and decide a lawsuit. The Tenth Amendment to the CONSTITUTION states:

> The powers not delegated to the United States by the Constitution, nor prohibited by it to the States, are reserved to the States, or to the people.

Thus, the judicial jurisdiction of the federal courts consists only of the power given to it by the CONSTITUTION or by federal legislation. Jurisdiction for any other type of litigation remains in the state courts.

Article 3, Section 2, Clause 1, of the CONSTITUTION states:

> The judicial Power shall extend to all Cases, in Law and Equity, arising under this Constitution, the Laws of the United States, and Treaties made, or which shall be made, under their Authority; --to all Cases affecting Ambassadors, other public Ministers and Consuls;--to all Cases of admiralty and maritime Jurisdiction;--to Controversies to which the United States shall be a Party;--to Controversies between two or more States;-- between a State and Citizens of another State;-- between Citizens of different States;--between Citizens of the same State claiming Lands under Grants of different States, and between a State, or the Citizens thereof, and foreign States, Citizens or Subjects.

Section 2 of Article III establishes the jurisdiction of the federal courts. Federal courts can decide all cases involving the CONSTITUTION, the laws of the United States, or its treaties. Federal courts also decide all cases concerning U.S. ambassadors, public officials and consuls, all cases involving national waters and international seas (admiralty and maritime), all cases in which the United States is a party, all cases between citizens of the same state who are claiming land under grants from other states, and all cases that involve one or more states, or the citizens of different states. The parts of Article 3, Section 2, Clause 1 in bold letters were rendered null and void by the 11th Amendment that states:

> The Judicial power of the United States shall not be construed to extend to any suit in law or equity, commenced or prosecuted against one of the United States by Citizens of another State, or by Citizens or Subjects of any Foreign State.

This simply means that no state can be sued in federal court by a citizen of another state or by anyone from another country. It is an example of sovereign immunity for states. In another example of how case law defines the CONSTITUTION, this sovereign immunity was extended in *Hans v. Louisiana*, 134 U.S. 1 (1890) to suits by residents of the same state. This decision left open the question of whether a state can be sued in state court by a citizen of that state. In *Alden v. Maine*, 527 U.S. 706 (1999), the Supreme Court ruled that a state's sovereign immunity did not allow suits against a state in state court. Thus, case law has fully defined the meaning of the 11th Amendment.

Article 3, Section 2, Clause 2 states:

> In all Cases affecting Ambassadors, other public Ministers and Consuls, and those in which a State shall be Party, the supreme Court shall have original Jurisdiction. In all other Cases before

mentioned, the supreme Court shall have appellate Jurisdiction, both as to Law and Fact, with such Exceptions, and under such Regulations as the Congress shall make.

Original jurisdiction means that the Supreme Court serves as the trial court and hears the case first before any lower court. This original jurisdiction has been limited to cases between states and cases involving ambassadors and the Supreme Court has consistently ruled that the CONSTITUTION prevents Congress from expanding the Supreme Court's original jurisdiction. Since President Washington appointed the first two justices of the Supreme Court two days after Congress passed the Judiciary Act of 1789, there have been nearly two hundred state-versus-state original jurisdiction cases and only two cases involving ambassadors. Thus, the overwhelming majority of cases heard by the Supreme Court arrive on appeal from lower federal courts or state courts.

Article 1, Section 8, Clause 4 of the CONSTITUTION places bankruptcy under federal jurisdiction and gives Congress the authority to pass laws that establish "uniform Laws on the subject of Bankruptcies throughout the United States." The first federal bankruptcy laws were passed by Congress in 1800. These laws have been repealed or amended several times. Modern bankruptcy law began in 1898 with the Nelson Act that was amended by the Bankruptcy Reform Act of 1978 now found in Title 11 of the *United States Code* (U.S.C.). Bankruptcy cases are always filed in United States Bankruptcy Courts. There is a federal bankruptcy court in each of the ninety-four federal judicial districts. These courts can only hear cases relating to bankruptcy, i.e., situations in which a debtor becomes insolvent and is unable to pay creditors. This is an example of subject matter jurisdiction. An appeal of a District Court bankruptcy case is handled like any other civil appeal.

Article 1, Section 8, Clause 8 gives Congress the authority to enact laws that "promote the progress of science and useful arts, by securing for limited times to authors and inventors the exclusive right to their respective writings and discoveries." While this clause is known as the "copyright clause," it is also the source for U.S. patent law found in Title 35 of the *United States Code.*

The first federal copyright law was passed in 1790 and was succeeded most recently by the Copyright Act of 1976, which together with its subsequent amendments, is found in Title 17 of the *United States Code.*

Article 1, Section 8 states that "Congress shall have the Power" to "provide for the Punishment of counterfeiting the Securities and current Coin of the United States" (Clause 6) and to "define and punish Piracies and Felonies committed on the high Seas, and Offenses against the Law of Nations" (Clause 10). Federal laws covering these types of financial crimes are found in Title 18, Chapter 25: Counterfeiting and Forgery and Chapter 81: *Piracy and Privateering.*

For the crimes listed above the CONSTITUTION granted the power and conferred a duty upon Congress to pass appropriate legislation. In addition, the last clause of Article 1, Section

8 states that Congress shall have the power to "make all Laws which shall be necessary and proper for carrying into Execution the foregoing Powers, and all other Powers vested by this CONSTITUTION in the Government of the United States, or in any Department of Officer thereof." This *necessary and proper* clause gave Congress one of the most powerful (and controversial) tools to pass legislation for many other federal crimes. Again, the jurisdiction of the federal courts is exclusive when Congress has passed legislation authorizing it.

Title 18 of the *United States Code* is dedicated to statutory provisions about crimes and criminal procedure. Section 3231 of that title defines the original jurisdiction of the federal trial courts, called district courts. It states:

> The district courts of the United States shall have original jurisdiction, exclusive of the courts of the States, of all offenses against the laws of the United States.

The district courts are therefore the first line of defense against crimes against the United States.

A multitude of crimes are codified in Title 18 of the *United States Code* but many other crimes are codified under other titles. For instance, wildlife trafficking crimes are listed in Title 16. They include crimes listed in Chapter 35, as they appear in the *Endangered Species Act*, against endangered species and crimes listed in Chapter 53 as they appear in the *Lacey Act*, against wildlife, fish, and plants. Many federal agencies have been granted powers to investigate federal crimes. Wildlife trafficking crimes mentioned above are investigated by special agents of the *U.S. Fish and Wildlife Service and the National Oceanic and Atmospheric Administration* and are prosecuted by attorneys of the *Department of Justice's Environment and Natural Resources Division (E.N.R.D.).*

Criminal violations of the Clean Water Act (Chapter 23 of Title 33- Navigation and Navigable Waters) are investigated by special agents of the *Environmental Protection Agency's Office of Criminal Enforcement* and prosecuted by the Environmental Crimes Section of the Department of Justice's E.N.R.D. and/or through one of the ninety-four U.S. Attorney's Offices across the country. Other federal crimes include tax evasion, child pornography, kidnapping, immigration violations, hate crimes, and many others.

The Sixth Amendment calls for trial "by an impartial jury of the State and district wherein the crime shall have been committed." Within the federal court system, Rule 18 of the Federal Rules of Criminal Procedure specifies which federal court may hear a particular criminal case:

> Unless a statute or these rules permit otherwise, the government must prosecute an offense in a district where the offense was committed. The court must set the place of trial within the district with due regard for the convenience of the defendant and the witnesses, and the prompt administration of justice.

For civil actions in which the United States is a plaintiff, Title 28 of the *U.S. Code* (Judiciary and Judicial Procedure), Section 1345 states:

> Except as otherwise provided by Act of Congress, the district courts shall have original jurisdiction of all civil actions, suits or proceedings commenced by the United States, or by any agency or officer thereof expressly authorized to sue by Act of Congress.

Per U.S. District Courts - Judicial Business 2016, 2016, 369, 208 civil and criminal actions were filed in U.S. District Courts. 291,851 of them were civil filings and 77,357were criminal prosecutions. Of these, the U.S. government was the plaintiff in only 4,793. This means that over 98% of the civil filings did not involve the U.S. government as a plaintiff and thus did not involve exclusive federal jurisdiction, but relied on other types of jurisdiction not governed by federal statute. Civil offenses against the United States are contained in many statutes. For more information, access https://www.uscourts.gov/statistics-reports/us-district-courts-judicial-business-2016.

The Endangered Species Act, for instance, contains provisions regarding both criminal and civil crimes. As codified as 16 U.S. Code §1540 (see the companion website), it provides penalties and enforcement for both civil and criminal violations. Cases and controversies arising out of this provision would be litigated in federal courts.

According to title 28 of the *U.S. Code*, Section 1331, "district courts shall have original jurisdiction of all civil actions arising under the Constitution, laws, or treaties of the United States." Thus, federal courts have original jurisdiction to hear cases involving a *federal question*. That is a controversy between private litigants in a civil action over the Constitution, federal laws or treaties. All crimes prohibited by the *Endangered Species Act* involve a federal question and thus would be first tried in federal district courts.

Federal jurisdiction may also include *diversity jurisdiction* where the litigants are from different states. If a couple in Illinois sues a company in Wisconsin for breach of contract, the plaintiffs have the choice of filing the suit in Illinois state court or in federal district court. In this situation, the jurisdiction is also said to be "concurrent," and the plaintiff may bring suit in either federal or state court. However, if they file the suit in state court, the defendant has the right to remove the case to a federal district court. In contrast, a dispute arising between two citizens of the same state with regard to a matter arising entirely within that state would have to be brought in a court of that state absent a claim of infringement of a federal statutory or constitutional right. Adding to the complexity of litigation within the United States, state courts frequently apply federal law or the laws of other states, and federal courts make rulings based upon applicable state laws. Federal law is amplified by state law in some places where federal law fails to speak or expressly defers to state law. It should come as no surprise that in the United States, litigation arises over the issue of which court or courts (federal or state) are empowered to decide specific cases. Likewise, litigants argue in court about what law (federal or state) a court must apply or about which court or courts have jurisdiction to settle a jurisdictional dispute. The outcome of either of these determinations can have a significant impact on the ultimate judicial ruling.

Sovereign Immunity

Can a person sue the United States? The answer to this question depends on many issues, including the definition of a _person_. *The Endangered Species Act* at 16 U.S.C. §1532(13) states that:

> The term "person" means an individual, corporation, partnership, trust, association, or any other private entity; or any officer, employee, agent, department, or instrumentality of the Federal Government, of any State, municipality, or political subdivision of a State, or of any foreign government; any State, municipality, or political subdivision of a State; or any other entity subject to the jurisdiction of the United States.

While we know the definition of a _person_—a public or private legal entity, as well as a human being,—we still need to answer whether within that confine, the United States can nevertheless be sued.

As mentioned above, the *Eleventh* Amendment, and cases interpreting it, deny that right. The United States possess _sovereign immunity_ and are therefore immune from being sued in federal court without their consent. The principle of _sovereign immunity_ in U.S. law is a legal doctrine inherited from the English common law (also known as crown immunity) by which the king or a national government or state cannot commit a legal wrong and is immune from civil suit or criminal prosecution unless they consent to be sued. The principle of _sovereign immunity_ is not mentioned in the U.S. CONSTITUTION. The courts, however, have strongly supported this doctrine. As stated in the Supreme Court decision of *Alden v. Maine*, 527 U.S. 706 (1999), "the State's immunity from suit is a fundamental aspect of sovereignty which the States enjoyed before the ratification of the CONSTITUTION, and which they retain today . . ." and further, "sovereign immunity derives not from the Eleventh Amendment but from the structure of the original Constitution itself. ... Nor can we conclude that the specific Article I powers delegated to Congress necessarily include, by virtue of the Necessary and Proper Clause or otherwise, the incidental authority to subject the States to private suits as a means of achieving objectives otherwise within the scope of the enumerated powers." Also, the U.S. Court of Appeals for the Fifth Circuit in *Price v. United States,* 81 F. 3d 520 (5th Cir. 1996) stated: "It is an axiom of our jurisprudence. The government is not liable to suit unless it consents thereto, and its liability in suit cannot be extended beyond the plain language of the statute authorizing it."

Statutes that authorize lawsuits against the *United States* include:

- *the Federal Tort Claims Act of 1946 (28 U.S. Code § 1346* - United States as defendant) that allows a person to sue the U.S. for the harmful acts of a federal employee, and

- the *Tucker Act of 1881 (28 U.S. Code § 1491 - Claims against United States generally; actions involving Tennessee Valley Authority),* that allows lawsuits over breaches of federal contracts or improperly assessed internal revenue taxes.

Jurisdiction for lawsuits for monetary damages under the *Tucker Act* devolves on the United States Court of Federal Claims in Washington, D.C. When the claims are less than $10,000, the Court of Federal Claims has concurrent jurisdiction with the appropriate U.S. District Court. Other claims against the U.S. are filed in the appropriate U.S. District Court. Both the *Tucker Act* and the *Federal Tort Claims Act* are not broad waivers of sovereign immunity. These two statutes contain many limitations, and the courts have further defined the meaning of these two statutes. For example, in *Feres v. United States*, 340 U.S. 135 (1950), the Supreme Court ruled that the *Federal Tort Claims Act* did not apply to injuries or death to members of the military sustained while on active duty that resulted from the negligence of other members of the military. Here sovereign immunity has been extended to the military. This issue will be thoroughly revisited later in this book when Howard Ball's JUSTICE DOWNWIND is discussed.

Solicitor General

The Solicitor General is (after the Attorney General and Assistant Attorney General) the third highest-ranking member of the Department of Justice. The Solicitor General is in charge of and represents the United States in all litigation at the Supreme Court. Because the United States is involved in nearly 70% of all the cases that the U.S. Supreme Court decides, this position is extremely important, especially in the development of landmark cases discussed below. The Solicitor General and Deputy Solicitor-General are appointed by the President with the advice and consent of the Senate. The Office of Solicitor General also consists of staff attorneys and Assistants to the Solicitor General, who help prepare briefs, petitions and other legal documents. The Solicitor General determines the cases in which the United States will seek review before the Supreme Court as well as the legal position the government will take. The Solicitor General usually personally participates in oral arguments before the Supreme Court, though a number of cases are argued by the Deputy Solicitor General or Assistants. The Office of the Solicitor General often files *amicus curiae* briefs in cases where the United States is not a party but has a significant interest in the outcome of the case. The Office of the Solicitor General reviews cases decided against the United States in the federal courts of appeal and will determine if the government will appeal to the Supreme Court. The Office of the Solicitor General also reviews cases decided adversely to the government in the federal district courts and will determine whether the government will file an appeal.

Landmark Cases

Landmark cases establish a significant new precedent or substantially change an existing precedent. The importance of these landmark decisions results from the significant social, political, and economic changes they cause. Such decisions may establish a completely new principle. For example, *Marbury v. Madison*, 5 U.S. 137 (1803) (which you can find on our Companion Website http://www.environmentallaw-teach.org/sidebar-3.html) introduced the principle of *judicial review*. They may reverse an established principle. For instance, the *separate but equal* established by *Plessy v. Ferguson*, 163 U.S. 537 (1896) was overturned by *Brown v. Board of Education*, 347 U.S.483 (1954). The opinion is also available on our Companion Website, Chapter 2, Sidebar #8, http://www.environmentallaw-teach.org/sidebar-8.html). They may define the real practical meaning of a statute. *TVA v. Hill*, 437 U.S. 153 (1978). It *could* be said *TVA v. Hill* gave the *Endangered Species Act* real teeth. *TVA v. Hill* will be examined in detail in the chapter on the *Endangered Species Act*. See the Companion Website for the Landmark Cases link to find resources for further reading.

It is natural that most landmark cases are decided in the Supreme Court but remember that of the roughly 7000 appeals each year from lower courts the Supreme Court hears only about seventy cases. This means that the U.S. courts of appeals make landmark decisions that are not reviewed by the Supreme Court. While the CONSTITUTION is the bedrock of the U.S. legal system, its practical meaning, as well as the meaning of federal statutes, has always been determined by decisions of the courts, especially the Supreme Court. These cases involve the application of the CONSTITUTION or of federal statutes to specific facts that are in controversy between the parties. The true meaning of the CONSTITUTION and federal statutes is determined by the decisional law.

As we end the brief introduction to our legal system, it becomes obvious that the American and English legal institutions have remained similar with two notable exceptions: America lacks the lawmaking institution of the monarchy, and, unlike England, our legal system has a judicial institution at its pinnacle, the United States Supreme Court. The role of the judiciary can be thus viewed as a most foundational feature of our common law system, even in our present times when statutory provisions have become much more prevalent than ever in our legal history. That makes case law research a must-have skill. Case law research involves finding binding and persuasive cases, as well as learning how to read opinions. Many cases regard statutory and administrative law controversies, which require statutory and administrative legal research skills to find those provisions. With the next three chapters, we continue building your legal literacy generally, and environmental law and policy proficiency, especially, by adding legal research skills.

BASIC STRUCTURE OF UNITED STATES COURT SYSTEM

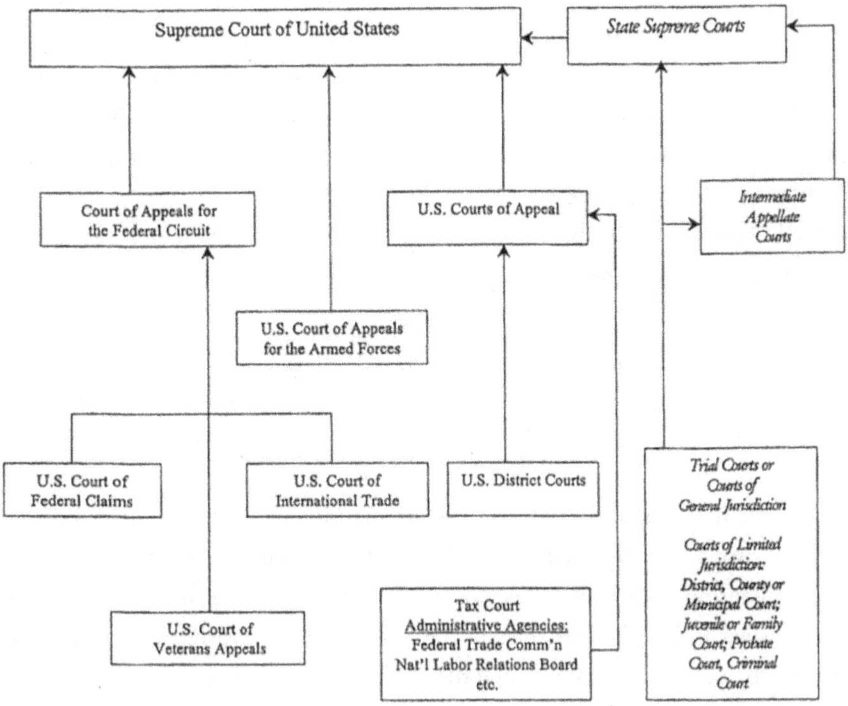

Chapter 3 – Thinking about Law as an Object of Research – Basic Principles of Legal Research

As you have noticed from the previous chapters, it is very hard to talk about the law in any concrete way without mentioning specific names and specific repositories where the various statutes, cases, or rules and regulations are published. Learning about the law is a long process. It requires familiarity with its specific language and the formal organization or hierarchy of the legal system. It requires knowledge about what constitutes the law, generally, abstractly, and specifically. Where a specific norm is published often establishes its binding value, its normativity, within the United States legal system. Through legal research, you will become more at ease with the entire legal learning process.

In this book, legal research is presented as an intrinsic component of any class on law and policy. Here are its basic principles:

1. FIRST PRINCIPLE OF LEGAL RESEARCH: KNOW (A) THE AREA OF THE LAW TO RESEARCH AND (B) HOW LEGAL INFORMATION IS PUBLISHED

The first basic rule has two prongs: a) your research is as good as your understanding of the substantive legal issue at hand, and b) your research depends on your knowledge of how legal information is published. This book focuses on environmental law and policy, and the research necessary to answer legal questions related to these topics. As a result, you need to become familiar with both environmental issues and the information gathering process.

Environmental law represents the normal growth of the administrative state where people engage in more and more complex activities which need to be regulated by state agencies. Environmental issues are of such magnitude, that only government agencies might be able to safeguard the interests of the society at large when they come into conflict with powerful economic interests of the few.

Originally, there was no environmental jurisprudence *per se.* Environmental law started in courts, and it developed through torts cases, such as *Boomer v. Atlantic Cement Co,* 26 N.Y.2d 219 (N.Y. 1970). Today, we say that cases such as *Boomer* mark the beginning of the modern environmental era. Our journey in environmental law and policy is a step-by-step process, which differentiates between public nuisance as an unreasonable interference with the right to common enjoyment of public spaced by the general public, and private nuisance as unreasonable interference with individuals enjoying the same sets of rights. In fact, President Nixon signed the

Clean Air Act Amendments of 1970, only a few months before the *Boomer* decision. Soon afterward, in December 1970, the *Environmental Protection Agency* (E.P.A.) was created.

Since then, environmental law has flourished at the federal, state, and municipal level, with all three branches of the government participating in creating what could be called the Environmental Rule of Law. There are federal statutes delegating powers to agencies to explain and apply statutory provisions which are further interpreted by courts in instances of conflict and controversies. There are also state statutes which establish higher standards of environmental protection, and sometimes even more stringent municipal ordinances. In this very complex environment, it makes sense to understand the issues, and have a plan for how to find your research answer, as stated in 1.a). You also need to understand the limits of authoritative free online publications, so your answer contains the relevant binding law, as addressed in 1.b).

2. SECOND PRINCIPLE: STRATEGIZE YOUR RESEARCH

All research implies a macro and a micro level. At the macro level, you use a plan of research. At the micro level, you implement that plan.

Part of your research plan is to find ways to understand both the question, as well as the names of the places (repositories) containing the answer. Vocabulary helps us focus our thoughts. Similarly, legal research language enables you to strategize your options. So, let's see how it works.

Primary vs. Secondary Sources of Legal Research

We will devote separate chapters to the ways to research primary and *secondary sources*. But before we do that, here are a few general research tips. As a legal researcher, think about yourself as a house builder. You need to use bricks and mortar. In this analogy, *primary sources* are the bricks, and secondary sources are the mortar.

Primary Sources

The law itself represents these bricks, and they are, listed hierarchically:

- the Constitution;
- statutes, state and federal (where federal statutes can sometimes ratify international treaties);
- court decisions, often called opinions; and

- administrative rules, as well as administrative hearings, and Executive Orders.

Secondary Sources

The mortar of legal research, the secondary sources, is the glue which makes your answer coherent. It may contain:

- dictionary definitions,
- legal analysis provided by
  - academic writings, which have been published in
    - treatises for the benefit of law students and sometimes legal practitioners; or
    - law review articles;
  - commentaries which come from various restatements of the law; or even
  - brief notes one found by searching the Internet and clicking on research guides written by librarians.

It is always hard to say whether one should start with the primary sources or begin with the relevant available secondary sources because it always depends on what the researcher knows and has available. Students at large universities have more resources than students at smaller universities. Students at universities with law schools on the same campus will have an easier time strategizing their research. Another distinction is created by the general civic knowledge the students have as well as their previous exposure to legal research.

Assuming that you have no previous experience with legal research, you may find it reassuring to learn that legal research is quite rigorous and thus manageable. But let's continue the discussion of basic principles before we learn the steps that may produce the most efficient way to find the answer to our question: Who pays for cleaning up a dump site?

3. THIRD PRINCIPLE OF LEGAL RESEARCH: ARE YOU ABLE TO REFORMULATE YOUR RESEARCH QUESTION?

Once you have thought about your research question, reformulate it. Use the simplest legal terminology as possible without losing meaning. Keep in mind that sometimes, the best terminology is the one already used.

For instance, contract is the best legal research term you can use to describe a deal, a treaty, or an agreement. But most of the time, the fact pattern requires you to clarify it. The process can be tedious, but it is extremely useful. That is how you can generate searchable keywords.

Environmental law is a relatively new area of law. Moreover, like intellectual property, it is a federal legislative product, rather than the result of the common law. But, although many environmental law questions would inevitably direct you towards federal statutes, the answer often has a heavy administrative component. As a result, many environmental law questions can be difficult to research because the answer is rarely only one-dimensional.

Consider a scenario where a battery manufacturer dumps rejected batteries on a piece of private land and years later, when it restructures its business it donates it as the ground for a future public playground. If the municipality accepts private land to be used as the location for a public playground, without proper cleanup, a myriad of negative health consequences may happen. Under this set of circumstances, you can imagine a follow-up research question about who should pay for the health care bills for the eventual necessary medical treatment. When it becomes apparent that the land was used as a dump site and litigation occurs the cleanup cost will be shared among all the owners who either polluted or who took advantage of a reduced price of the property, knowing it had been used as a dumping site.

In another hypothetical, the original business sells the piece of land to other businesses which use it as a dump site. Eventually, someone has to pay for its cleanup. Who should it be? Would a statutory provision contain the correct answer? Would there be cases interpreting such statutory provisions?

Because environmental law research is primarily statutory research, we need to start with the specific statutes. Thus, your research strategy should be to simplify the question and use your basic knowledge. The main research terms would be: "federal statute," "environmental" and "liability."

Through your research, you will find out that indeed, Congress passed the law deciding how the cost of cleanup is shared as a provision of the statute entitled *The Comprehensive Environmental Response, Compensation, and Liability Act* (C.E.R.C.L.A). This provision explains how the cost of environmental cleanup may be shared among parties deemed to have legal responsibility for mitigating the contamination.

C.E.R.C.L.A., a federal statute, states that any person may seek contribution from any other person who is liable or potentially liable for having polluted the area. In this instance, the primary source, C.E.R.C.L.A., contains the legally binding norm, the official pronouncement of the government.

Before we start thinking about ways to find the statute and then the provision about liability under C.E.R.C.L.A., let's make sure that we understand what we are looking for.

i. Use an explanatory research guide

- The best way to be sure that you do not stumble over confusing, outdated, or unreliable secondary sources is to use a subject-based guide or a library catalog.

- Conduct a quick search using the search engine of your choice by typing the relevant keywords, "C.E.R.C.L.A." and "liability," will bring up a long list of research guides.
- Some research guides are produced by government agencies, such as the EPA's Superfund Liability, available at https://www.epa.gov/enforcement/superfund-liability.
- Because legal research is performed mostly digitally, you should be aware of its transient quality. For instance, the address of digital information, its URL, often changes over time. To combat this problem, you should know how to use various mirror sites. In this instance, I made a copy of this page using perma.cc, https://perma.cc/FGG6-5KBB.
- Other guides have a different URL. The first way to distinguish which research guide you are going to use is the date of publication associated with the URL which identifies the educational institution that authored it.
- The next step is to separate the guides based on their content. It is a good idea to choose the ones which identify necessary secondary sources, such as reference materials, as well as treatises and hornbooks on this issue. Then, decide which treatise to consult based on its title mirroring your research.
  For instance, a treatise with the name of the statute in the title would presumably have more useful information for your research than a treatise which only references environmental law.

ii. When you have identified a research guide by a title that looks like it will be useful, use a university library catalog.

- Using a library catalog, you can find out what research material is available to you.
- For instance, try to locate *Escaping Superfund Liability* in your library collection. If you locate it, note its location and call number if it is a print or microform book, or its URL if it is a digital source.

iii. If at any point during the research you need explanations for the terms encountered, including names of the sources, such as "treatises" or "hornbooks," try looking them up in a legal dictionary.

- Can you find a legal dictionary in your library collection?
- If you locate it, note its location and call number if it is a print or microform book, or its URL if it is a digital source.

iv. Once you find what you need, you will soon discover that legal writing is filled with footnotes. If at any point you feel the need for further explanation, explore the sources mentioned in the footnotes.

v. Some of the footnoted material may be available to you from the law school library's collection of law reviews and journals. Some of those articles may be available from various universities' digital common spaces, usually called Academic Commons. Unfortunately, you need to identify those Academic Commons and then search their content, because the indexing is not picked up by a mere search. Of course, remember Google Scholar and its content of secondary legal sources.

- Use a library catalog, or Google Scholar and locate the law review article entitled: *The end of joint and several liability in Superfund litigation.*
- If you locate it, note down the title of the journal where it is published (in this instance, Duquesne Law Review), its location and call number if it is a print or microform journal, or the database containing it, such as HeinOnline, if it is a digital source.

4. FOURTH PRINCIPLE OF LEGAL RESEARCH: REMAIN FLEXIBLE AND ALTERNATE USING SECONDARY AND PRIMARY SOURCES THROUGH THE ENTIRE RESEARCH PROCESS.

In legal research, you will use secondary sources when you strategize, but there is no rule which prohibits you from using other secondary sources to explain the primary source that represents your answer. Secondary sources are your best friends. Use them to make sure you know whether your issue is governed by a statute, what type of statute, federal or not, or whether it is a common law issue. Stay with the secondary source until you know what primary source you are searching for and then keep going back to that or other secondary sources to make sure that you are finding the correct answer.

Let's use our C.E.R.C.L.A. example. In this instance, we need to find the Superfund statute. How do you find out that C.E.R.C.L.A. is a synonym of "the Superfund statute"? You might have used a secondary source without even thinking about it as such. Any print or digital indexes or the Popular Name Table, which is a find-aid tool accompanying the United State Code, for instance, are secondary sources.

Many times, it is hard to separate planning from executing your research plan. Research flexibility has many facets, as you will see briefly sketched below.

1) Finding the Superfund statute, C.E.R.C.L.A.

A. We will talk more about this aspect of legal research. But for now, it is important to understand that the benefit of starting with a secondary source is that locating the primary source becomes so much easier. For example, in a secondary source that mentions C.E.R.C.L.A., there is usually a footnote providing readers with C.E.R.C.L.A.'s full, legal citation (codified at 42 U.S.C. 9613(f)(1)). Once you click on the citation you will find the text of the statute.

B. Even when there is no such link, the secondary source identifies the primary source, the statute, by its citation so you can easily locate it.

C. Citations identify the type of document, the collection where it is located, and a specific document itself within the collection.

2) Understanding how statutes are published.

A. Before you can take advantage of the information provided by citation you need to understand how the legal information is published.

B. Statutes are published in chronological and in subject matter collections.

C. Federal statutes are published in the *United States Statutes at Large*, commonly known as *Statutes at Large* (Stat.), and in the *United States Code* (U.S.C.).

   (i) The first Superfund public law (P.L.) started as a bill introduced in the House as "Hazardous Waste Containment Act of 1980" (H.R. 7020) by James Florio (D-NJ) on April 2, 1980. It passed the House on September 23, 1980, and then it passed the Senate on November 24, 1980. President Jimmy Carter signed it into law on December 11, 1980, under its current title, abbreviated C.E.R.C.L.A. and nicknamed "Superfund legislation." Because it was enacted by the 96th United States Congress, C.E.R.C.L.A. received the following citation: P.L. 96-510. It became published in 94 Stat. 2767.

volume	repository	page where it starts
94	Statutes at Large	267

(ii) Go to United States Statutes at Large, https://www.govinfo.gov/app/collection/statute and locate the 2002 C.E.R.C.L.A. amendments, PL 107-108.

(iii) Each statute is identified by the number of the Congress and by a sequential number, as well as by its title, "Brownfield Amendments."

D. C.E.R.C.L.A. is also published in the United States Statutes at Large, and that version contains section 113(f)(1), and in the *United States Code* (U.S.C), where that section doesn't exist. Instead, you'll be referred to 42 U.S.C. § 9613, where that provision was codified, as we will explain later.

Title	repository	Section
42	United States Code	9613

(i) Go to the United States Code, https://www.govinfo.gov/app/collection/uscode and find Title 42

(ii) All the statutes published within Title 42 regard the same subject matter.

(iii) Some questions to consider:

- What subject matter does Title 42 cover?
- How many titles are currently in the U.S.C.?
- Can you find 42 U.S.C. § 9613?
- Why do you think it is easier to find 42 U.S.C. § 9613 than the original C.E.R.C.L.A. statute?

E. The difference between the chronological publication and the subject matter publication is crucial. The chronological publication contains a static version of the statutory language while the codified version available from the *United States Code* is a dynamic version of the statute incorporating all of the subsequent amendments which followed the original chronological publication.

3) The answer represents the binding authority, the law, that is in force at the time of your research.

A. To find the liability rule under C.E.R.C.L.A. is to find what the law in force is. For that, you need to know how legal information is published. For instance, all federal statutes compiled in the *United States Code* (which is the subject matter compilation) are published every year on the government's Publishing Office website, as well as in print. That annual publication of the United States Code contains the law in force as of the time of its publication.

B. Any academic library will be able to help you locate the official subject matter compilation of federal statutes and most academic libraries will be able to give you access to various commercial databases containing that information. Public libraries may have only the print version of the U.S.C.

4) Finding the relevant statutory provision governing your issue is not the end of the legal research process. Let's find cases interpreting the relevant statutory provision.

A. Courts accept complaints involving specific statutory violations, which come out of specific facts. Naturally, facts occur within a specific geographical area, which defines the jurisdiction of the potential litigation of the issue. Each jurisdiction has its own legal precedent, which will govern subsequent litigation of that issue within similar factual circumstances.

B. Finding the cases that represent the *stare decisis* (use a legal dictionary to find its meaning) is the hardest part of the research.
   (i) Unlike statutory and administrative law research which you can perform knowing the date or the subject matter of the law or rule, case law research cannot be performed without using commercial databases.
   (ii) Some commercial databases are more expensive than others.
   (iii) Let's use *Casetext*, https://casetext.com/, which is relatively new in the legal research market, to find a case on C.E.R.C.L.A. liability.
   (iv) If we were to type "C.E.R.C.L.A." and "liability," we would notice a large number of returns which would be impossible to skim through.
   (v) To avoid missing relevant results because of a large number of hits, you should use "filters" to focus your search as much as possible.

   - One primary filter is the jurisdiction of your case, which is determined by the place where the facts occurred.
     - When the applicable statute is a federal statute, the jurisdiction is federal. For instance, if the dumpsite was located within the geographical boundaries of New York State, then the appellate jurisdiction is the Second Circuit, where the state of New York is located.

- Another way to reduce the number of results is by using all of the relevant keywords you can think of:
    - Synonyms: "Superfund" in addition to "C.E.R.C.L.A." and "The Comprehensive Environmental Response, Compensation, and Liability Act."
    - Other relevant terms include "joint liability;" which defines a type of liability among wrongdoers. (If you do not know the meaning of these terms, you can look them up in a legal dictionary).

- Finally, remember to use connectors, the symbols which ensure that your research results contain all of the keywords in a specific order:
    - within the same paragraph (/p) or sentence (/s) ((/p) will allow you to search for two words in the same paragraph and (/s) will allow you to search for two words within the same sentence).
    - C.E.R.C.L.A. /p liability /s joint.

- The cases you will locate are identified in multiple ways.
    - All cases have a "name," which generally is given by the name of the plaintiff (the party which started the lawsuit, the party which suffered the wrong) and the name of the defendant (the wrongdoer). For instance, *United States v. Alcan Aluminum Corp.,* identifies a case where the *United States* government, sued *Alcan Aluminum Corporation* for the cleanup of two waste sites.
    - All cases have a citation. For *United States v. Alcan Aluminum Corp.,* the citation is 990 F.2d 711 (2[d] Cir. 1993).

Volume	Repository (Federal Reporter, 2d series)	Page opinion starts	Court + year of decision
990	F.2d	711	(2d Cir. 1993)

When you settled on a number of relevant cases from the relevant jurisdiction, remember that you need to make sure they are still good law. "Good law" means that those cases have not been overturned, or otherwise negatively affected, by a higher court within the same jurisdiction, or by the respective legislative body.

- Cases can be upheld, reversed, or amended by a superior court from the same jurisdiction;
- A Superfund case decided by the trial court located in Manhattan, the Northern District Court of New York (N.D.N.Y.) is reviewed by the Court of Appeals for the Second Circuit (2nd Cir), and the appellate judges may

decide to affirm the lower court's decision, reverse and remand to the lower court for another trial, or as in our example, do both.

- For instance, this is the history of the case used earlier: *United States v. Alcan Aluminum Corp.*, 755 F.Supp. 531 (N.D.N.Y. 1991), *aff'd in part, rev'd in part and remanded*, 990 F.2d 711 (2^{d} Cir. 1993).

C. In our example, with the less expensive databases, the only way to make sure that the cases are still good law is to rely on your research skills. With more expensive databases, such as *Lexis* and *Westlaw*, or even *Bloomberg Law*, this step is performed easily by using their citing services, *Shepards, KeyCite* or *BCite.*

Let's research the applicable administrative rules. Because environmental law is a relatively recent creation of the administrative state, it is paramount that you cover administrative rules and regulations and, in some cases, administrative decisions.

A. Since the early 20th century, all agencies are required to publish their rules.

B. The *Environmental Protection Agency* (E.P.A.) protects human health and safeguards the natural environment. It was established in the executive branch as an independent agency pursuant to REORGANIZATION PLAN NO. 3 OF 1970 (5 U.S.C. app.), effective December 2, 1970. It was created to permit coordinated and effective governmental action on behalf of the environment. The Agency is designed to serve as the public's advocate for a livable environment. You can read it from our Companion Website, https://archive.epa.gov/epa/aboutepa/reorganization-plan-no-3-1970.html.

C. Like all agency rules, the E.P.A. rules are published chronologically in the *Federal Register* (F.R.), which is available at https://www.govinfo.gov/app/collection/fr.
   - The *Federal Register*, (F.R.) is published by the Office of the Federal Register, National Archives and Records Administration (NARA), https://www.govinfo.gov/app/collection/fr,. The *Federal Register* is the official daily publication for rules, proposed rules, and notices of Federal agencies and organizations, as well as executive orders and other presidential documents.
   - A recent E.P.A. rule regarding "Approval and Revision of Air Quality Implementation Plans" was published in 83 F.R. 33.

Annual volume	repository	Page where the rule starts
83	Federal Register	33

- and then, republished topically, in the *Code of Federal Regulations*, at https://www.govinfo.gov/app/collection/cfr.
    - The *Code of Federal Regulations* (C.F.R.) is published in annual editions. The *Code of Federal Regulations* is the codification of the general and permanent rules published in the *Federal Register* by the departments and agencies of the Federal Government. It is divided into 50 titles that represent broad areas subject to Federal regulation. The 50 subject matter titles contain one or more individual volumes, which are updated once each calendar year, on a staggered basis. The annual update cycle is as follows: titles 1-16 are revised as of January 1; titles 17-27 are revised as of April 1; titles 28-41 are revised as of July 1; and titles 42-50 are revised as of October 1. Each title is divided into chapters, which usually bear the name of the issuing agency. Each chapter is further subdivided into parts that cover specific regulatory areas. Large parts may be subdivided into subparts. All parts are organized in sections, and most citations to the C.F.R. refer to material at the section level.
    - For instance, under 40 C.F.R. 3.2(a)(2), electronic reporting of documents required under Title 40 of the *Code of Federal Regulations* may occur after the E.P.A. has first published a document in the Federal Register announcing that the E.P.A. is prepared to receive, in electronic form, documents required or permitted by the identified part or subpart of Title 40. All rules published in Title 40 regard the protection of the environment.

Title	repository	Section
40	Code of Federal Regulations	3.2(a)(2)

D. Because there is no precedential value in older administrative decisions, there is no mandate for any agency to publish their decisions. However, most agencies publish their decisions on their website.

- To find the rules of filing complaints with the E.P.A., the hearing procedures, and to locate orders and decisions of E.P.A.'s Administrative Law Judges, go to https://www.epa.gov/alj.

5. FIFTH PRINCIPLE OF LEGAL RESEARCH: AT EVERY SINGLE STEP IN THE LEGAL PROCESS, USE COMMON SENSE

Legal research is as much science as it is art. It requires you to review the question and the answer and determine if it makes sense. Remember that legal research is a process, and until it all makes sense there is no one way of progression towards the end. You can start with a text, then move to a statute, then go back and read more about the issue at hand and find a case that seems relevant.

For instance, you need to find out if only licensed farmers can sell milk at greenmarkets in New York State. You come up with a plan. You start with a Google search and realize that this is a New York state law issue and that the answer will combine statutory and administrative law provisions, and perhaps even cases. But while executing your plan you keep a log, and you may even want to see if there is an encyclopedia entry which might make sense of all the primary sources you find. You may read an explanation and click on the primary source it cites. Then, you may go back for more explanatory analysis. Because, remember, everything eventually has to make sense.

If your plan does not make sense, then your answer has a good chance to be mistaken too. When this occurs, you need to go back and search again with an eye for the missing piece of the puzzle. The only way to do a correct and comprehensive research job is to read the question and the answer you found and see if indeed, within the set of factual circumstances, it makes sense. If it does not make sense, then return to the secondary source, the explanatory analysis, and read it again. If necessary, start planning again. Eventually, you will be able to complete the entire research puzzle.

6. SIXTH PRINCIPLE OF LEGAL RESEARCH: ONLY *GOOD LAW* IS BINDING

Your research needs to be current, so your answer contains the binding authority, the law. You may resist this rule thinking that you are not a practicing attorney so why should you care what the law is as of the moment of your handing in your assignment? But, in the same way that you cannot serve apples as oranges, you cannot represent unconstitutional or "expired" laws as the relevant, binding law.

For instance, while there is statutory law, 18 U.S.C. § 700, making it illegal to burn the U.S. flag, there is also subsequent Supreme Court jurisprudence holding such activity is expressive conduct protected by the First Amendment. So, merely finding the statute, though responsive and relevant, is not the correct answer. The correct answer is mentioning that burning the flag, while a crime under 18 U.S.C. § 700, it is expressive conduct and therefore protected under the law according to *U.S. v. Eichman*, 496 U.S. 310 (1990).

When it comes to federal statutory research, the official government website contains annual updates of the codified statutory provisions. The administrative rules detailing those provisions are updated daily through the Federal Register. The only problem remains with the case law interpreting the statutory provisions as detailed by federal administrative rules. At the state level, this problem only persists. The good news is that all academic libraries subscribe to a legal database which will allow you to update your results with the click of a button. The bad news is that due to their prohibitive costs, the access to those databases changes quite unpredictably and once you graduate, you will not have access to them. Of course, this may all change with the open access movement and continuing to spread the news that law needs to be publicly available in a true democracy.

7. SEVENTH PRINCIPLE OF LEGAL RESEARCH: DO YOUR FINDINGS MAKE SENSE IN LIGHT OF YOUR SUBSTANTIVE KNOWLEDGE OF THE LAW?

Now that you think you are done with your research, assemble all your findings and read through them. Does your statutory provision, as interpreted by the cases you found make sense in light of your substantive knowledge of the law? For instance, only a few years ago, when the algorithm of the two major databases, Westlaw and LexisNexis was not as sophisticated as it is today, if you searched for "nuclear family" using a *natural language technique*, and relying only on their algorithm, you would have received results about nuclear arms. Also, if you search for cases about divorce in Washington State, you would have been surprised to find none. Given that the divorce rate is far bigger than null, you would have realized that your results are erroneous, and your research was not done yet. Eventually, probably by consulting a *secondary source*, such as a *treatise* or an *encyclopedia*, you would have learned that the legal terminology used by the Washington State legislature for divorce was *dissolution of marriage*. These particular mistakes have been corrected because the algorithm used does more than relying on crowd sourcing results and promoting hits that users have clicked on the most. But reading through the final list of results before incorporating it in your research memo, or any other document, is sound advice which you have probably heard before.

Chapter 4 – Applying the Second Principles of Legal Research. Using Secondary Sources

Learning about the law is more than just memorizing the organization of our system of government or its law-making functions. Law is something that requires a lot of thought and deliberation, whether it is at the legislative level, in the judicial chambers, or in various agencies. Our democracy works by requiring expertise in order to perform many of these functions. To achieve that expertise, students of law often start by reading legal analysis, and only then, the text of the law itself. The reason behind this approach to legal studies is multifaceted. This chapter will present it from the legal researcher's perspective.

Earlier we talked about the principles of legal research. The first rule stated that there is no legal research without jurisprudential understanding of the issues at hand. We translated that axiom by saying:

> The first basic rule has two prongs: a) your research is as good as your understanding of the substantive legal issue at hand, and b) your research depends on your knowledge of how legal information is published.

APPLYING THE SECOND PRINCIPLE OF LEGAL RESEARCH TO MAP OUT YOUR RESEARCH

Use the second principle enunciated here. Map out your expectations and start strategizing. If you are a novice in this area, you may still be confused by this suggestion, and rightfully so. When you are faced with a legal research question you need to be able to read it. Depending on how versed you are in American law before you even start thinking about research, you may need help understanding English legal jargon, which, at times, may sound like a foreign language.

DEFINING SECONDARY SOURCES

That is why when conducting legal research, you want to start with specific points of information, called <u>*secondary sources*</u>. Conceptually, secondary sources have multiple meanings, but their main role is well-settled. Secondary sources help the researcher find the answer, the *primary sources*. How that role is performed depends on many factors, and most importantly perhaps, their meaning.

Secondary sources direct the research to legal analysis, to jurisprudence, "la doctrine" or "la dottrina," and to primary sources, the law itself. Thus, secondary sources might only be explanatory and persuasive.

Secondary sources in American law do not share the unique pervasive role "la doctrine" or "la dottrina" has in both international and civil law systems. While "la doctrine" should never be confused with legislation of judicial decisions, it nevertheless influences the law differently in the two legal systems mentioned above. One reason may be that in other legal systems, experts and professional publishing houses are the gatekeepers of jurisprudential wisdom, while in the United States, law students decide what is published in law journals, and thus what becomes the bulk of legal scholarship.

Certainly, legal scholarship exerts some influence over legislators and judges in the United States legal system too, but its influence is further removed and less predictable. Secondary sources may persuade judges to accept a certain interpretation of the statute versus another interpretation. They may persuade legislators during hearings to accept a certain version of a bill versus another one.

Nevertheless, secondary sources are the first place to go for legal researchers. Typically, their role is that of a tool used to understand the scope of the research. Secondary sources thus offer analysis and background information.

1. Typically, secondary sources are useful because they function as a fundamental finding-aid tool. For instance, indexes help locate relevant legal scholarship. Legal scholarship both helps to explain issues and to locate relevant primary sources.

REMEMBER

- Sources are *binding* when they influence a court directly.
- All secondary sources and primary sources from another jurisdiction are only *persuasive*.

For example, if you write a paper about the New York law regarding non-criminal "unconscious aiding and abetting," reading a piece of legal scholarship may be all you need to do. There are many strategies to find what you need in the most effective way. If you deem that the issue is esoteric enough, then rather than consulting a book, an article, such as a law review article, may be the fastest way to find what you need. Once you identify the best index to locate relevant law review articles, you can use it to perform a search for articles. In this instance, you may find that a law article, entitled *Concert of Action by Substantial Assistance,* identified by the following *citation* as 16 Touro L. Rev. 25 (1999), offers you the information you need. In addition to that explanation, it would direct you to the binding law in that area, as of the date of its writing.

Legal practitioners look at a secondary source in a different way than a non-practitioner. Secondary sources help them start the legal research process, and may help them frame a legal argument when they present their client's case in front of a judge. When practitioners cannot find a binding primary source, then they look for sources of persuasive authority. Thus, for practitioners, whether attorneys or law librarians, secondary sources rarely represent the end of the legal research process. By their very essence, they are a commentary on specific legal rules, and not the law itself.

2. For a student of law, because they summarize, restate, review, analyze, and interpret the law, secondary sources, especially legal scholarship, often represent only the beginning of the legal research process.

Secondary sources, by their very own nature, incorporate various time gaps between the moment they are authored and the moment they are published. From the moment an author produced a commentary and a publication published it, many primary sources could have changed their status; statutory amendments or court appeals could have taken place. Certainly, with the new movement toward open publishing, the time from finalizing a secondary source and its public accessibility is substantially minimized. But even if secondary sources might become explanations written as soon as the law is passed, and the fee-based databases, such as *Westlaw, LexisAdvance,* and *Bloomberg Law,* aim to present the researcher with an integrated approach to legal research where primary and secondary sources are amassed in one relevant-looking answer, secondary sources are only persuasive. Of course, they remain the pivotal starting point in legal research, because the law due to its highly abstract content is hard to decipher. Below are some of the reasons for mastering secondary sources. I will start with what a Berkeley Librarian, Bob Berring, called "research-aid tools," then move to finding-aid tools, and end with legal scholarship, jurisprudence, and practitioners' tools.

YOUR FIRST TIME READING THE QUESTION

Legal research, like any research process, benefits the researcher if the researcher has some familiarity with the topic and the legal publishing. But there is always a first time, and secondary sources are here to help anybody who just is just starting this process.

Legal Dictionaries

Legal dictionaries are indispensable for reasons explained earlier – legal jargon often sounds like a foreign language – and also because American law contains Latin phrases for which translation requires a legal dictionary.

For instance, when the United States Supreme Court is asked to review a lower court's decision, that procedural demand takes the form of a *writ of certiorari*. The *writ of certiorari*, as you might already know, comes from the Latin *certiorari*, a verbal derivative of *certior*, which means to inform. Through a *writ of certiorari*, the Court decides whether it will hear a case or not. For a brief, but illuminating definition, in this and any other similar instance, legal dictionaries are a must. For more than a century BLACK'S LAW DICTIONARY has been the golden standard of the language of law.

Originally authored by Henry Campbell Black, and first published in 1891, BLACK'S LAW DICTIONARY, now in its 10th edition, contains "definitions of the terms and phrases of American and English jurisprudence, ancient and modern." The up-to-date BLACK'S LAW DICTIONARY is available online for a fee, through the legal database *Westlaw*. The 2nd edition, however, is freely available at https://thelawdictionary.org/.

BLACK'S LAW DICTIONARY is not the only legal dictionary practitioners and students of U.S. law use. For instance, WEX is a free legal dictionary and encyclopedia sponsored and hosted by the Legal Information Institute at the Cornell Law School. WEX entries are collaboratively created and edited by legal experts. It is available at https://www.law.cornell.edu/wex. BALLENTINE LAW DICTIONARY, 3rd ed., is available for a fee from *LexisAdvance*, and freely from http://citizenlaw.com/pdf/a.pdf.

The Bluebook and Free-of-Charge Digital Decoders

Continuing with our example, most of the time, the United States Supreme Court will deny the writ. That outcome is further abbreviated as *cert. den.* What do you do to decipher its meaning, *cert. den.= certiorari denied*? Google may help, but in law, Google searches are insufficient because their relevance comes from source crowding rather than expertise. Furthermore, legal information is identifiable by legal citations, which also need to be deciphered.

Legal Citations

- identify the type of the document, whether it is a primary or secondary source

—and—

- within that typology, what hierarchical place it occupies (whether it is a case, its precedential value, or if it is a federal or state statute, or a federal or state administrative regulation)

Legal jargon is filled with abbreviations and rules governing these abbreviations. There are many secondary sources to help decipher legal abbreviations. For instance, BIEBER'S DICTIONARY OF LEGAL ABBREVIATIONS, edited by Mary M. Price, assistant director of the Law Library at Vanderbilt Law School, and available on *LexisAdvance*, provides extensive coverage of all legal abbreviations within the U.S. legal system. It is a useful tool to understand the abbreviations for titles, terms, and names used in American legal literature.

The Bluebook and Other Systems of Citation

Law students, who decide what is published in law journals and thus, what constitutes American doctrine, also decide those rules of citations. The rules of citations are published in THE BLUEBOOK: A UNIFORM SYSTEM OF CITATION, uniformly known as THE BLUEBOOK. THE BLUEBOOK is compiled by the editors of the COLUMBIA LAW REVIEW, THE HARVARD LAW REVIEW, the UNIVERSITY OF PENNSYLVANIA LAW REVIEW, and THE YALE LAW JOURNAL, or the main repositories of American jurisprudence.

THE BLUEBOOK was first published in the early 1920s. Its origin is murky because both Harvard and Yale claim it. According to Harvard, the origin of THE BLUEBOOK was a pamphlet for proper citation forms for articles in the Harvard Law Review written by its editor in 1920s[1]. According to two Yale librarians, Harvard's claim is incorrect. They trace the origin of THE BLUEBOOK to a 1920 publication by Karl N. Llewellyn at Yale on how to write law journal materials for the Yale Law Journal[2]. Today, in its 20th edition, THE BLUEBOOK remains published and distributed by the Harvard Law Review Association. The purchase of the print edition enables the user to access it digitally as well.

THE BLUEBOOK is the golden standard for journal publications. However, there are other ways to decipher abbreviations, and the following page is memorized by all U.S. law students. In addition to citation rules, THE BLUEBOOK is also useful because it lists all federal and state primary sources, and identifies them both by their full title and their legal abbreviations. For example, if you are interested in learning the name of the repositories that cover the Supreme Court decisions, all you need to do is go to the section of THE BLUEBOOK called the "Table on United States Jurisdiction" (T.1) and search for the names of the Supreme Court reporters. In addition to their names, you will also learn the time frame covered. For example, just by using THE BLUEBOOK, you find out that the name of one of the reporters is the UNITED STATES REPORTS that it covers all opinions starting with those decided in 1790 and that its abbreviation is "U.S."

Quick Reference: Law Review Footnotes

This table gives examples of commonly used citation forms printed in the typefaces used in law review footnotes (as explained in **rule 2**). The last page and inside back cover present examples in the typefaces used in court documents and legal memoranda (as explained in the **Bluepages**).

CASES rule 10	
reporter **rule 10.3**	Jackson v. Metro. Edison Co., 348 F. Supp. 954, 956–58 (M.D. Pa. 1972), *aff'd*, 483 F.2d 754 (3d Cir. 1973), *aff'd*, 419 U.S. 345 (1974).
service **rule 19**	*In re* Looney, [1987–1989 Transfer Binder] Bankr. L. Rep. (CCH) ¶ 72,447 (Bankr. W.D. Va. Sept. 9, 1988).
pending and unreported cases **rule 10.8.1**	Albrecht v. Stanczek, No. 87-C9535, 1991 U.S. Dist. LEXIS 5088, at *1 n.1 (N.D. Ill. Apr. 18, 1991).
	Jackson v. Virginia, No. 77-1205, slip op. at 3 (4th Cir. Aug. 3, 1978) (per curiam), *aff'd*, 443 U.S. 307 (1979).
	Ross v. Weissman, No. 90-345 (D. Mass. filed Sept. 18, 1990).
	Cleary v. Rizkalla, 925 F.2d 314 (1st Cir. 1991), *petition for cert. filed*, 60 U.S.L.W. 3422 (U.S. Jan. 14, 1992) (No. 92-212).
CONSTITUTIONS rule 11	N.M. CONST. art. IV, § 7.
STATUTES rule 12	
code **rule 12.3**	Administrative Procedure Act § 6, 5 U.S.C. § 555 (2006).
	22 U.S.C. § 2567 (Supp. I 1983).
session laws **rule 12.4**	Department of Transportation Act, Pub. L. No. 89-670, § 9, 80 Stat. 931, 944–47 (1966).
LEGISLATIVE MATERIALS rule 13	
unenacted bill **rule 13.2(a)**	S. 516, 105th Cong. § 2 (1997).
hearing **rule 13.3**	*Transforming the Federal Government To Protect America from Terrorism: Hearing Before the H. Select Comm. on Homeland Sec.*, 107th Cong. 23–25 (2002) (statement of John Ashcroft, Att'y Gen. of the United States).
report **rule 13.4**	S. REP. No. 95-797, at 4 (1978), *as reprinted in* 1978 U.S.C.C.A.N. 9260, 9263.
UNPUBLISHED MANUSCRIPTS rule 17.2.1	Victoria E. Anderson, Company Outing: How Consensual Relationship Agreements Adversely Affect Homosexual Employees 12 (Mar. 15, 2004) (unpublished comment) (on file with the University of Pennsylvania Journal of Labor and Employment Law).
LETTERS rule 17.2.3	Letter from Pierre Arsenault, Exec. Editor, Harvard Law Review, to Bryan M. Killian, Supreme Court Chair, Harvard Law Review (Apr. 2, 2004) (on file with the Harvard Law School Library).

Peter Martin, a former Harvard Law librarian, publishes another guide to legal citation, INTRODUCTION TO BASIC LEGAL CITATION, which is available at https://www.law.cornell.edu/citation/. It comes with a companion blog, CITING LEGALLY, at http://citeblog.access-to-law.com, for those with an interest in current issues of citation practice, policy, and instruction.

Another database which allows the search for the meaning of abbreviations for English language legal publications, from the "British Isles, the Commonwealth and the United States, including those covering international and comparative law" is CARDIFF INDEX TO LEGAL ABBREVIATIONS, available at http://www.legalabbrevs.cardiff.ac.uk/. It covers a wide selection of major foreign language law publications. The database mainly covers law reports and law periodicals, but some other legal publications are also included. THE INDEX is under continuous development with new abbreviations and titles being added on a regular basis.

THE PROCESS OF UNDERSTANDING THE QUESTION

Once you can read the research question, you are ready to start your research journey. As mentioned earlier, the first basic rule of legal research has two prongs: a) your research is as good as your understanding of the substantive legal issue at hand, and b) your research depends on your knowledge of how legal information is published. In this book we focus on environmental law and policy, so it becomes necessary to understand environmental issues and then the legal information gathering process.

Fundamental Secondary Sources:

- decipher legal meaning (dictionaries)
- decipher citations (citators)

Meta-Research - Mapping out Your Research

One of the daunting pre-research tasks is to know where to start your legal research. You want a reliable starting point which will also give you an idea of what information is out there. You would like a Google Map of your research if possible.

Your first instinct may be to Google the answer to your research question. Not a bad first step if your digital literacy is strong enough to bypass the ads and figure out what is reliable and what is junk. Frequently, even what seems reliable may not be useful. Pay attention to legal research guides. Often, they are authored by a law librarian. If maintained up to date, then go ahead and use them. For example, law reference librarians at Georgetown Law Library have preempted your effort by posting such a library guide. http:// guides.ll.georgetown.edu/home.

There is no fixed point for using secondary sources in the process of legal research. When we talked about the basic principles of legal research it became clear that you need to understand the issue at hand, but understanding C.E.R.C.L.A. liability may require more than a one-time reading of any relevant explanation.

For another example, if you want to learn about the legal status of nuclear reactors you may want to use a research guide even after you have started your research. Linda Tashbook's NUCLEAR LAW RESEARCH GUIDE, available from the NYU Law Library's website, at http://www.nyulawglobal.org/globalex/Nuclear_Research1.html offers a quick and rather slim overview of the international and comparative aspects of nuclear law, easing the finding of sources or confirming earlier suggestions. Even when a guide lacks clarity, or its scope is too limited, it may still be a useful starting point because it identifies relevant research terms in addition to potentially relevant statutes, which in itself is daunting for a beginner.

Similar finding tools are guides created by specialized institutes or consortium of higher education, or the legislative (administrative) body itself. For instance, ORAU, a non-profit consortium of major Ph.D.–granting academic institutions, cultivates collaborative partnerships that enhance the scientific research and education enterprise of our nation. *ORAU's* CITIZEN'S GUIDE TO U.S. NUCLEAR REGULATORY COMMISSION INFORMATION, https://www.orau.org/ptp/PTP%20 Library/library/NRC/NUREG/0010.pdf, is a detailed, though limited in scope, guide to the work of the agency.

This first step is the beginning of the process. As soon as the language of the question is clear, then you need a *research plan.* A research plan encourages you to organize the information you know and focus on how you can use what you know to find what you do not know. The steps of an easy research plan are mentioned below.

Meta-Research and the Role of Secondary Sources

Preliminary Research Plan

- identify what you know;
- identify what you do not know;
- make a list of what secondary sources you think might be useful to clear your confusion.

If we define legal research narrowly as finding the answer to a particular question, usually that answer consists of primary sources, the law.

- "What are the rules for dumping nuclear waste?" or
- "Where can nuclear waste be dumped on the territory of the United States?"

The questions identify the final answer "the rules." But they do not tell you where you should start. Perhaps you already know that statutory provisions are further detailed by administrative rules. Perhaps you already know that the correct and comprehensive answer also needs to contain additional case law research to confirm that the rules you found are still "good law."

But depending on where you are in your research, you may find it useful to avoid going directly to the law itself. You may find it useful to first have an understanding of the issues.

You can achieve an understanding of the related issues through secondary sources. If primary sources represent the official pronouncement of the governmental lawmakers or the opinions of the judiciary, and I call that the tangible aspect of American law, then secondary sources are texts that explain the law.

Legal scholarship is authored by members of the academe, whether faculty members, or students, members of the academe auxiliary, law librarians, or even practitioners to explain what the law is in a particular area. They have an academic audience in mind (the pool that produced the authors), but these materials can be used by practitioners as tools of persuasion.

If you know that you have a good grasp of the issues in question and that you understand them sufficiently that searching for secondary sources will be meaningful and bring you a responsive source that covers your topic, then the next step is to learn how you can locate those commentaries about the law.

Finding-Aids, Google, and Google Scholar

By now, everybody is familiar with various search engines. The most popular search engine in the United States is Google, https://www.google.com, and for scholarship, its companion, Google Scholar, https://scholar.google.com/.

Thus, searching for the rules for nuclear waste disposal on Google Scholar will prompt two types of results: citations and full-text sources. With Google Scholar, it is imperative to enable library catalog searches, especially if you are affiliated with a specific university. The larger the library holdings collection, the more relevant the Google Scholar results will be.

Library Catalogs and More

It is hard to explain legal research without being involved in a practical exercise. That is why at the end of this book you can follow along with this explanatory part by undertaking to answer Question 1 in *Introduction to the U.S. Law and Legal System: An Environmental Perspective – Legal Research Exercise.*

Legal scholarship, as well as many sources of legal analysis published in book-format can and should be located through online library catalogs. Library catalogs are a better first stop than a mere Google search, because like Google, they are free-of charge. Unlike Google, their access is available even from China. Library catalogs limit the results to their holdings and library-produced research guides. Additionally, unlike Google Books, a catalog search has the benefits of an index search conceived by a legal expert. For example, through "title" or "keyword" field restrictions and a geographical location restriction, an index can quickly give the researcher an idea of the best starting point because of the substantive expertise of the legal academia and the information management expertise of the librarian.

For instance, using Columbia University's Catalog, CLIO, https://clio.columbia.edu/, the results cover multiple sources, from book-format to articles and from print to digital sources. Also, all sources available using a library catalog have been vetted by experts rather than users, which impacts scholarly pursuits differently.

Law library catalogs are even more limited in their results because they index their law collection and offer the researcher quick access to their highly specialized holdings. For example, Pegasus, www.pegasus.law.columbia.edu, the online 2nd generation catalog of the law school library at Columbia Law School, offers the researcher the advantage of quickly locating the most popular treatises on any general subjects such as "contracts" or "torts," through a title and limited-collection search. By typing "contracts" in the title field and limiting the search to "Third Floor," the researcher obtains a limited number of hits. They represent those treatises and other legal monographs that the Columbia Law School faculty found to be the most relevant as of the date of the search, which, librarians located in the most selective part of the library, the third-floor reserves.

In a catalog-search the user should avoid the search option in the "subject headings" because those subjects are designated by the Library of Congress and they often are far removed from the ordinary meaning of a concept. You will be well-advised to start with the well-established authors in the field, and the most recent edition, because it contains the most relevant explanation. In legal research, we always want the law applicable the day of the inquiry, and thus the most recent explanation.

Google, as well as *Lexis Advance, Westlaw, Bloomberg Law* or new legal services, such as *Casetext*, have search features similar to the field search offered by any library catalog. For example, if you know the title of the treatise you want to locate you may do so through "Find a Source" on Lexis or "Find a Database" on *Westlaw. Bloomberg Law* offers a "secondary sources" option which can be further limited by expanding it to more specific secondary sources, including their version of AMERICAN LAW REPORTS, BLOOMBERG LAW REPORTS.

Repositories of Jurisprudence and Legal News

Going back to our nuclear waste questions, imagine that you need to explain the results of your search to someone with no background. To be able to do that, you will need to make sure you have a good grasp of those issues. Thus, perhaps finding out more about nuclear energy and its corollary, nuclear waste, is the way to go. But what secondary source is best suited to give you that background analysis?

Before we tackle that question, let's review the rules of citation for secondary sources. Citing monographs, book-like sources, requires only a three-part identifier: The Name of the Author, The Title of the Book, and (the year of its publication).

- Carlton Stoiber, HANDBOOK ON NUCLEAR LAW (2003).

Journal articles have a similar structure: Author name, Title of the Article, volume number, Title of the Periodical, first page number, and (year of publication). For instance, let's look at the following article:

- Emily M. Farah, *Reviving Spent Nuclear Fuel Reprocessing in the U.S.*, 16 *U.* Pittsburgh J. Tech. L. Policy 183, (2016).

In law, as in any other academic area, encyclopedias continue to remain the first place to search for a brief, meaningful explanation. There are two major legal encyclopedias, CORPUS JURIS SECUNDUM, and AMERICAN JURISPRUDENCE, available in print and digitally from the major legal databases, *Lexis Advance* and *Westlaw*.

Treatises

Unlike any other academic area, legal scholarship consists predominantly of journal articles, because academic tenure requires academic journal publications. Treatises are works of comprehensive analysis written by experts, often members of the legal academe, offering a general overview of the specific subject matter. Journal articles often advocate the author's perspective, but in doing so cover a more limited subject matter in more depth than a treatise.

There are many treatises that students of the law use. Some are called *Hornbooks*, while others are called *Nutshells*.

Treatises are used when (1) the research fits within a traditional area of legal doctrine, and (2) the researcher is not comfortable with a specific legal area. Treatises have the advantage of explaining issues in a larger context. For example, if you are interested in nuisance start with a treatise. You should start with a treatise on torts, such as PROSSER AND KEETON ON THE LAW OF TORTS, because this treatise will briefly but comprehensively explain the different types of nuisance. If you are interested in nuisance in the context of environmental law, you will find it easier by starting with an environmental law treatise, such as Grad's TREATISE ON ENVIRONMENTAL LAW, which will cover public nuisance as an environmental tort, as well.

Treatises are useful because they summarize court decisions, and give you an insightful view of the development of our common law system based on a complex interplay of court decisions, statutes, and administrative regulations. While all treatises are useful, those usually identified as "hornbooks" are of special value because they are written for students, albeit law students, and not legal practitioners. Like PROSSER'S LAW OF TORTS, they are more likely to give an overview of the area in a more comprehensive way. Similarly, useful for those who need to learn fast about a legal subject, are those treatises published by West in its nutshell treatises. For example, if you are interested in a quick and reliable overview of the U.S. patent system, MILLER AND

Davis's Intellectual Property: Patents, Trademarks, and Copyright in a Nutshell will be the right place to start your search.

Law Review Articles

If you find yourself doing research in a more esoteric area of law, a law review article that expounds on the primary source of your interest may be a better starting point. You can try to answer Question 2 in *Introduction to the U.S. Law and Legal System: An Environmental Perspective – Legal Research Exercise,* to find the explanation below easier to understand.

Law review articles are authored by members of the academe, practitioners, and law students. They follow a well- established practice of analyzing and discussing the chosen topic so that the reader can get an accurate view of what the law is in the very specific and often quite narrow area that constitutes the topic of that article. Law review articles, or law journal articles, have the advantage of covering obscure areas in more detail than a treatise. For example, while Prosser's Law of Torts explains the different standards for concert of action by substantial assistance, including as it relates to toxic torts (such as illegal dumping where more than one individual or company may be involved in the wrongdoing) it does not explain state law subtleties. To the contrary, a law review article, such as Neacşu's *Concert of Action by Substantial Assistance: What Ever Happened to Unconscious Aiding and Abetting?* will devote its entire content to explaining that issue according to New York law. In other words, if treatises have the advantage of explaining the law that covers a larger body of legal norms—torts, environmental law, criminal procedure, etc.—then law review articles have the advantage of advocating a point of view that may be similar to that of the reader, and thus offer ready-made support for an argument. Treatises mostly refrain from challenging any given status quo.

Going back to our questions about the rules governing nuclear waste disposal, the most relevant answer came from a student note. Its Bluebook citation is:

> Emily M. Farah, Reviving Spent Nuclear Fuel Reprocessing in the U.S., 16 *U. Pittsburgh J. Tech. L. Policy* 183, (2016).

From Farah's note, one can learn that Congress enacted the Nuclear Waste Policy Act (NWPA) in 1982 and that the NWPA mandated the Department of Energy (D.O.E.) to implement a blueprint for the nuclear waste repositories and established a goal for the federal government to take over wastes by 1998.

> In 1987, Congress designated Yucca Mountain in Nevada as the national repository, but the Obama Administration has since terminated the Yucca Mountain repository's license. However, the D.O.E. authority to withdraw the Yucca Mountain license from the NRC has been challenged and is currently being litigated. Even if courts decide that the NWPA does not allow the D.O.E. to prohibit the licensing

of Yucca Mountain, there will still be challenges. For example, Congress, which has previously refused to appropriate monies for the Yucca Mountain project, would have to find a way to fund it. This leaves the country without any long-term plan or back-up plan for radioactive waste. Even if Yucca Mountain ultimately receives a license from the NRC and becomes operational, it is not big enough to store all of the nation's nuclear waste. According to the Nevada Attorney General, seventy-seven reactor sites across the country are holding 70,000 metric tons of high-level nuclear waste and spent nuclear fuel, and it is estimated that each site accumulates 2,000 tons each year. Yucca's design capacity is only 77,000 metric tons. Thus, by the time Yucca Mountain would be filled to capacity in 2036, "there will still be at least the same amount of spent fuel still stored at the reaction sites, even if no new plants are built" (Farah, 196–97).

Other Repositories of Jurisprudence - Academic Commons & SSRN

Jurisprudence is available in print and online. Online, it is available in all legal mega databases, as well as through free-of-charge specialized portals, such as *Academic Commons, SSRN,* and *Bepress,* that may provide you access to legal information authored by legal practitioners, or even law professors. Here are a few words on when you would use some of these sources of legal information.

For instance, *Columbia University's Academic Commons* are described as the digital repository where faculty, students, staff of Columbia, and its affiliate institutions can deposit the results of their scholarly work and research. *Academic Commons* stand for free access to scholarship. The name and the platform vary. For instance, the Harvard law faculty use the *NELLCO* platform, a law library consortium platform, at https://lsr.nellco.org/harvard_faculty/. The Columbia University law faculty used the B*epress* platform until recently when they migrated to a platform which is still under construction.

The *Social Science Research Network, SSRN,* available at ssrn.com, is another way to locate texts on current and obscure issues of law. SSRN is composed of a number of specialized research networks in social sciences, including law. The SSRN eLibrary consists of a Full Text and an Abstract Database. SSRN has recently been purchased by a digital publisher, Elsevier.

Blogs as Repositories of Legal News

A few years ago, using blogs as a source of legal information might have looked sketchy. Today, members of the legal academia have their own blogs where they explain changes in their area of law. For example, the *TaxProfBlog,* http://taxprof.typepad.com/, is maintained by Paul C. Caron from Pepperdine University School of Law. Another useful blog is SCOTUS Blog, http://www.scotusblog.com/, maintained by Aaron Nielson, who is an associate law professor at Brigham Young University and the weekly author of D.C. Circuit Review–Reviewed at the Notice & Comment Blog.

FindLaw Professionals: News and Commentaries

"FindLaw Professionals" present themselves as a "group of well-respected authorities in their legal practice areas." Their legal summaries are advertised to help any "individual legal consumer" learn more about the legal system. Since this book was first published, the database has improved both its search capabilities and its content. Now, you can search for both legal analysis, called a law firm article, or a legal news article, and legal commentary.

HAVING MAPPED OUT YOUR RESEARCH EXPECTATIONS, THE RESEARCH PROCESS CONTINUES

In conclusion, when you believe that you are done with secondary sources, make sure you read the summary you settled upon to convey the analysis needed to present your research memo. If it doesn't make sense, remember the fourth principle of legal research. *Do not move on to primary sources until you know what you need*, and more importantly, make sure that it all makes sense when you read your research plan.

The Role of Scholarship in Legal Research To:

- explain the research question
- explain research options
- focus the researcher's attention to a specific legal area
- identify potentially relevant primary sources

In our most recent example about nuclear waste and where it can be dumped, a brief research plan would contain the information obtained from research guides and various texts of legal scholarship. It would be more specific, but along these lines, because it would mention:

- the area of law, and
- the research terms
    - for identifying the applicable federal statute, and
    - the relevant binding case law interpreting that statute, within the specific jurisdiction, according to the particular set of facts.

Now, you may want to try your research skills and answer the first two questions of *Applying the Second Principle of Legal Research.* This research exercise is printed at the end of this chapter.

APPLYING THE SECOND PRINCIPLE OF LEGAL RESEARCH. PRACTICE EXERCISE.

The following exercise will introduce you to some secondary sources: library catalogs, monographs, and law review articles.

Questions highlighted in *Italicized **Bold** can* be completed by anyone with internet access. Questions highlighted in underlined <u>**Bold**</u> may only be completed by students with access to *Nexis Uni* or *Westlaw Campus.*

Question 1 - Using a library catalog, such as Pegasus, http://pegasus.law.columbia.edu, locate the catalog record for any treatise or other secondary source on endangered species. For instance, locate the record for *The Endangered Species Act: history, implementation, successes, and controversies.*

a) What is the name of the author? What is its call number and location?
b) Is it currently checked out? (In Pegasus, if the space under Status is empty, the source is on the shelf)
c) Now, go to http://clio.columbia.edu/. Can you can locate that title as an ebook?

****

Question 2 –Use http://clio.columbia.edu/ and find an article considering a species-loss domino-effect before the implementation of endangered species legislation. (While only Columbia University students have access to the entire Columbia library catalogue, even non-Columbia University students should be able to answer the following questions).

a) What is the title of the article?
b) What is its citation? Can you use the Bluebook citation format as explained below?

The Bluebook citation of a law review article contains:

- the name of the author;
- the title of the article;
- the volume number of the journal;

- the abbreviation of the journal;
- the page where the article starts; and
- the year of its publication.

Here is an example, E.D. *Neacşu, Concert of Action by Substantial Assistance*, 16 Touro L. Rev. 25 (1999).

Chapter 5 – Applying the Principles of Legal Research. Finding the Relevant, Binding, "Good Law"

In this chapter, we will focus on the mechanics behind the sixth principle of legal research, finding the relevant good law, while also applying the third, fourth, and fifth principles. Our goal becomes finding the most efficient way to perform legal research. To find primary sources, which are the main object of legal research, you engage in both macro (meta-research) and micro-level legal research. At the end of this chapter you will find a legal research exercise which introduces you to the main repositories of U.S. law, *Introduction to the U.S. Law and Legal System: An Environmental Perspective – Legal Research Exercise: Federal and State Law Repositories.*

DEFINING PRIMARY SOURCES

In legal research, primary sources and are the product of the three branches of the federal, state, and local government. Primary sources cover statutes, cases, and administrative law.

(a) Statutes:

Statutes are the primary sources of law that come from the federal, state, or municipal legislature. Generically, it is called statutory law. Statutes are compiled in various statutory collections, which can be accessed in different ways, according to the information needed.

(b) Case law:

Case law can be found in the compilations of court opinions. They represent the way the judiciary body ensures social order.

(c) Administrative law:

Administrative law comes from the executive branch and administrative agencies. Administrative law covers rules and regulations, as well as administrative decisions. The rules and regulations can be found in the compilations of presidential executive orders, those of administrative rules and regulations, and the compilations of administrative decisions.

Locating primary sources:

Primary sources are relatively easy to locate, because they represent the tangible aspect of American law. Compilations of primary sources are publicly available whether in print or digitally. Generally, they have various limitations. Some are available for a fee while others are available free-of-charge.

1. THE MACRO-LEVEL APPROACH TO LOCATING PRIMARY SOURCES

Before you start choosing a specific repository, think about the larger picture, about a "plan of action." Once you have a macro understanding of research, you can move to the micro level and engage in research.

- What primary sources do I need to access?
  (i.e., statutes, cases, administrative regulations)

- What do I need from those sources?
  (e.g., a statute as passed by Congress on a specific date, or the statute and its amendments, as of the date of your research)

- Why do I need that specific primary source? (reformulating your research question to make sure you are on the right research path)

You should aim for your research to be linear and progress toward a clear answer. First, start with a plan which maps out your understanding of the question, and how you think you should answer it. Next, identify the secondary sources which you believe are most relevant to your research. Finally, once you understand the contextual background information, you may move from secondary sources to primary sources, to the law itself: the statute, case law, or administrative rule.

But legal research is not a mere mechanical process. It involves a continuously revolving door from secondary to primary sources, and then from one repository of primary sources to another. Often you start with a treatise, then you read a case, then a law review article, and from there, locate another case. The question I will tackle in this section is how to find the most reliable collections of primary sources in the most efficient way.

2. REPOSITORIES OF PRIMARY SOURCES

In this book, collections of primary sources are called repositories. In this way you get a better understanding of their tangibility, and with that the finality of the legal research process.

Legal information is largely hierarchical, so we will start by identifying legal repositories according to their authoritative role in the American legal system:

(a) the Federal (and state) Constitution and municipal charters;

(b) federal and state statutes, and municipal ordinances;

(c) federal, state, and municipal court decisions; and

(d) administrative rule, regulations, and decisions.

Some repositories contain only one type of legal norms. Others are an amalgamation of primary sources and even secondary sources. More noteworthy, only some repositories have the built-in features to allow the researcher to update the results, and check whether they are still good law. Because updating is the last necessary step of any reliable legal research process, choosing a repository is often the result of its research features.

Repositories of Federal and State Constitutions and Municipal Charters

The federal CONSTITUTION is our fundamental law. In its current embodiment, it is available both in print as well as online. Historical versions of the CONSTITUTION are part of the official federal statutory collections, the United States Statutes at Large commonly known as "Statutes at Large." The *Statutes at Large* compilation contains all statutes in chronological order. For instance, the 1789 CONSTITUTION is available in vol. 1, on page 10 of that print collection.

The federal CONSTITUTION is available from digital, free-of-charge repositories, as well. For example, the site of the U.S. Government Publishing Office, https:// www.govinfo.gov contains and disseminates official information from all three branches of the Federal Government[3]. It naturally contains past and current versions of the CONSTITUTION, including the Centennial Edition of our federal CONSTITUTION, which is available at https:// www.gpo.gov/fdsys/pkg/GPO-CONAN-2017/pdf/GPO-CONAN-2017.pdf. Congress.gov also contains a portal to the text of the CONSTITUTION of the United States well as a legal analysis of the CONSTITUTION based on U.S. Supreme Court Cases, https://www.congress.gov/constitution- annotated/.

The federal CONSTITUTION is also available from the fee-based, mega amalgamations of legal information: *LexisAdvance, Westlaw,* and *Bloomberg Law,* as well as smaller competitors, such as *HeinOnline.*

All state constitutions are available in print and digitally from their state statutory compilations. They are also available from each state's official website, as well as from the mega databases mentioned above. For instance, the NEW YORK STATE CONSTITUTION is available from the state statutory compilations, from the official website of the State of New York, at https://www.dos.ny.gov/info/pdfs/Constitution%20January%202015%20amd.pdf, and also from a myriad of commercial sources, whether they are fee-based or not.

Municipal charters are compiled digitally by various publishers and are available free-of-charge, or from the mega databases. For instance, the laws and rules of the City of New York, including the NEW YORK CITY CHARTER, are now available on the Web, published by the American Legal Publishing Corporation, http://www.amlegal.com/codes/client/new-york-city_ny/.

Repositories of Federal and State Statutory Law and of Municipal Ordinances

Federal statutes are available both in print and online. Statutes are officially collected chronologically, in the order they are passed by each Congress, and by subject matter. The official chronological collection is called the *United States Statutes at Large,* abbreviated Stat. The official codified version, which contains federal statutes published by subject matter, is called the *United States Code,* and it is abbreviated U.*S.C.*

The *Statutes at Large* contains every law, public and private, enacted by Congress in order of the date of its passage from 1789. Each *Statutes at Large* volume is numbered sequentially. To access the entire collection of *Statutes at Large* free-of-charge, you need to have access to both a library that carries the print collection and to the Internet in order to access the electronic collection, because it is not available in its entirety in a single format. The print collection of the *Statutes at Large* does not contain the most recent statutes.

The *United States Statutes at Large* is evidence of all the laws enacted during a session of Congress. Additionally, it also contains resolutions, reorganization plans, proposed and ratified amendments to the CONSTITUTION, as well as proclamations by the President. It is published under the direction of the Office of the Federal Register through the Congressional Printing Management Division, U.S. Government Publishing Office. The *United States Statutes at Large* can be obtained digitally and in print.

The *Stat.* collection of electronic, free-of-charge, documents resides on the GPO's Federal Digital System (https://www.govinfo.gov/app/collection/statute) and is maintained by the U.S. Government Publishing Office. This collection is incomplete. It starts with Volume 65, which covers the federal statutes passed by the 82nd Congress, in 1951. In paper format, *Statutes at*

Large are available either by purchase from the Superintendent of Documents or at any Federal Depository Library.

The *Stat.* collection is also available electronically from *LexisAdvance, Westlaw, Bloomberg Law,* and *HeinOnline.* They offer complete electronic coverage of the *Statutes at Large.* Unlike the *Statutes at Large,* the *United States Code* (*U.S. Code* or *U.S.C.*) contains only the general and permanent public laws of the United States. The *United States Code* is divided by broad subjects into 53 titles and is published by the Office of the Law Revision Counsel of the U.S. House of Representatives.

The *U.S. Code* was first published in 1926. The next main edition was published in 1934, and subsequent main editions have been published every six years since 1934. In between editions, annual cumulative supplements are published in order to present the most current information. Thus, unlike the *Statutes at Large,* the *United States Code's* function is more than recording federal statutes: it is to ensure easy access to the applicable law. In addition to its topical organization, the second most important aspect of this codification is that it is periodically updated to include all subsequent amendments, as explained above.

In print, a title may be made up of a few bound volumes. For example, federal statutes on education are located in Title 20 of the *United States Code.* Currently, there are six volumes of statutes that make up Title 20.

There are a few free-of-charge e-legal repositories which contain federal statutes in their codified version. For example, the 1994, 2000, and the 2006 editions are also available online from the full-text database offered by GPO, at https://www.govinfo.gov/app/ collection/uscode. The *United States Code* is also available electronically from https://www.loc.gov/law/help/us-code.php, which connects you with the version published by the Office of the Law Revision Counsel of the U.S. House of Representatives, at http://uscode.house.gov/. This version is also available from The Public Library of Law, the free arm of Fastcase, FindLaw (another free-of-charge portal) and Cornell University Law School – Legal Information Institute (LII), a free-of-charge legal information database, and soon from https://www.govinfo.gov/help/uscode. Another free-of-charge statutory portal is *The Public Library of Law* (PLol), created by Fastcase.

State statutes are available for free from each state official site, and from FindLaw, The Public Library of Law, and LII. Topical access to state statutes is also available from various organizations. For example, the Children's Bureau and the U.S. Department of Health and Human Services have put together an information gateway site, which is a portal to all state statutes focused on child welfare.

State statutes, like their federal counterparts, are published chronologically and republished in topical compilations, which are also called "codes." State statutes are published both in print and digitally, on the official website of each state government. Current New York State statutes, for instance, are available at http://public.leginfo.state.ny.us/lawssrch.cgi?NVLWO. The major three fee-based databases, *LexisAdvance, Westlaw,* and *Bloomberg Law* contain the current version of all state statutes, as well as some historical versions.

At the municipal level, ordinances are most often digitally published. Some municipalities, such as New York City, publishes them chronologically and in a topical codification, named "Administrative Code." Municipal ordinances are digitally available from various publishers, often free-of-charge. Library guides to municipal ordinances, such as NEACȘU'S MUNICIPAL LAW – RESEARCH TIPS, http://library.law.columbia.edu/guides/Municipal_Law, are the best starting point to identify those repositories. Some municipal ordinances are also available from *LexisAdvance, Westlaw,* and *Bloomberg Law.* However, as with every piece of legal information, look at when it was last updated, so you can evaluate its content.

Locating Repositories of Federal, State, and Municipal Case Law

Case law is law created by courts through their court decisions. A decision, or holding, is usually included in the written opinion that marks the end of most legal disputes. Opinions have been collected in "court reporters"—usually in a West publication— for hundreds of years. These collections are available both in print and online.

In print, in order to locate a specific reporter, first, you need to know its name. *The Bluebook*—as mentioned before—is a useful tool in identifying the correct name of each reporter. Once you know the title, and especially the abbreviation of the reporter, you can easily locate its print version by using any library catalog in the same way you would search for any book or monograph.

Those reporters are also available electronically. They are available from both free-of-charge and fee-based databases. The free-of-charge legal repositories and portals are *Google Scholar,* which has incorporated *AltLaw.org, The Public Library of Law,* and *Casetext,*

(a) *Google Scholar* has incorporated *AltLaw.org*, and perhaps formed a better product, especially in light of the fact that it contains the print reporter's pagination (even if it is West reporter). *AltLaw.org* brought to the mega search engine its database of United States Supreme Court case law (1803 to the present); and United States Circuit Courts of Appeal case law (published cases from 1950 to the present and unpublished cases from 1996 to the present).

(e) T*he Public Library of Law (PLol),* created by *Fastcase,* is a free public resource with searchable federal case law from 2004 to present, state case law from 1997 to present, and Supreme Court cases from 1754.

(f) C*asetext* provides access to federal and state case law both free-of-charge and for a fee, with various research tools only available to the fee-based clients.

(g) Recent court opinions are also available from each court's website, which can be accessed from https://www.govinfo.gov/app/collection/uscourts. Federal courts tend to be better equipped to deal with electronic archiving of their opinions than state courts. The United States Supreme Court website is accessible directly from the web, from the Court's website http://www.supremecourtus.gov/, from *govinfo.gov,* or from *Oyez,* available at http://www.oyez.org/. *The Oyez Project* is a multimedia archive which aims to be a complete and authoritative source for all audio recorded in the Court since the installation of such a recording system. Another e-resource for the Supreme Court cases is Justitia, http://supreme.justia. com/, which is powered by Google.

Of course, the fee-based databases *LexisAdvance, Westlaw,* and *Bloomberg Law* cover federal and state case law. With the advent of *Bloomberg Law,* the competition has only accelerated, with everyone trying to incorporate the menu-driven features of *Bloomberg Law.* A somewhat recent alternative to case law research is *Fastcase,* which charges only a fraction of what the other proprietary databases charge for downloading or printing a case ($5), and *Casetext.* The future will tell how many fee-based databases American lawyers can support financially. Municipal court cases are often only available through each municipal court website, or through each state's e-courts system. In New York State, municipal courts are covered by the e-courts system. For civil courts, the repository is called *WebCivilLocal,* and its access points are:

(a) Index search;
(b) Party Search;
(c) Attorney/Firm Search;
(d) Judge Search;
(e) Court calendars; and
(f) Attorney/Firm Calendars.

A list of the specific courts covered by this centralized portal is available at https://iapps.courts.state.ny.us/webcivilLocal/LCAvailableCourts.

Locating Repositories of Administrative Rules, Regulations, and Decisions

For more than half a century, federal administrative rules and regulations have been published in two official publications: The *Federal Register (F.R.),* and the *Code of Federal Regulations (C.F.R.).* Since 1936, the *Federal Register* has been the official daily publication of rules, proposed rules, and notices of federal agencies and organizations. Additionally, the *Federal Register* publishes executive orders and other presidential documents.

Each year, a new volume of the *Federal Register* is published. The current volume for the year 2018 is 83. All volumes since 1994 are available at https://www.federalregister.gov/. Unlike the *Federal Register*, the *Code of Federal Regulations*, like the *United States Code*, is divided into topics. However, the topics of the two codified compilations do not necessarily correspond. For example, the 17th topic in both compilations is called "Title 17." However, in the *United States Code*, Title 17 covers statutes on copyrights, while in the *Code of Federal Regulations*, Title 17 covers rules and regulations on commodity and securities exchanges. Thus, if you are interested in learning how statutory provisions regarding copyright arbitration have been further detailed by administrative agencies, going to the C.F.R. volumes that cover Title 17 would be a mistake. The rules and regulations regarding copyright arbitration are available in Title 37 of the *Code of Federal Regulations*, which is entitled "Patents, Trademarks, and Copyrights."

From 1996 onward, the *Code of Federal Regulations* is available from govinfo.gov, at https://www.govinfo.gov/app/collection/cfr, while the *Federal Register* is available from 1994 onward from govinfo.gov, at https://www.govinfo.gov/app/collection/fr, and NARA, at https:// www.federalregister.gov/.

State and federal rules are available for free from The Public Library of Law at http://www.plol.org/Pages/Search.aspx. Federal and state administrative law is also available from each agency's official website, much like municipal agency which is available from each municipal agency website. For instance, federal motor vehicle emission standards, such as 40 C.F.R. Part 59, are available from the United States *Environmental Protection Agency*, https://www.epa.gov/, while the New York state rules are available from the Department of Environmental Conservation, at https://www.dec. ny.gov/regulations/regulations.html. New York City rules about emission standards are available from the New York City Department of Environmental Protection, at http://rules.cityofnewyork.us.

Administrative law contains both administrative rules and administrative decisions. When delegated by the appropriate legislative body, administrative agencies have the authority to solve disputes and issue administrative decisions. Federal administrative decisions are available both in print and online, though not necessarily in both formats. While older decisions may be available in print, more recent ones are available electronically free-of-charge from their official website. For example, since 1942, the U.S. Department of Agriculture publishes the decisions issued by its administrative judges in *Agriculture Decisions*. Its post-2000 decisions are also available on its website. However, the administrative decisions issued by both the Office of Hearings and Appeals of the Department of Education and the Secretary of Education are more difficult to find. As another example, the decisions issued by the U.S. Securities and Exchange Commission are available both in commercial as well as in official publications, in print and electronically. The Commission's Opinions and orders issued from 1996 onward are available electronically free-of-charge from its official website, https://www.sec.gov/.

In addition to the free-of-charge databases, all three fee-based databases, *LexisAdvance*, *Westlaw*, and *Bloomberg Law*, contain both the current administrative rules published in the *Code of Federal Regulations* and the *Federal Register*, as well as some older versions and some federal administrative decisions. This type of coverage is similar for their coverage of state administrative law, while their coverage of municipal administrative law is very selective.

3. THE MICRO-LEVEL APPROACH TO LOCATING PRIMARY SOURCES

Once you have identified the correct repository of primary sources, you need to find the particular piece of legislation, case law, or administrative law that answers your question. This step depends on the information you have at hand.

If you found a citation, you need to translate it correctly within that repository, whether it is electronic or in print. If you know the name of the specific statute, or the name of one of the parties involved in the lawsuit, you need to use the appropriate finding-aid tool within that repository. When you start your search with a citation at hand, you need to interpret it.

As mentioned earlier, legal citations identify a document as part of a print multi-volume legal collection, whether you will use a print version of the document or its online counterpart. Thus, it is usually composed of three parts: a number that precedes the abbreviation and which identifies the number of the volume of the collection, the abbreviation of the collection, and a number that follows the abbreviation, and which identifies the page where the document starts. For example, if the citation you have is 78 STAT. 252 that means that what you are looking for is a public law that is published in the 78th volume of the *Statutes at Large* and it starts on page 252.

Abbreviating Federal Primary Sources. Citing Federal Sources:

1. Federal Statutes are published in

    (a) Session laws (Pub. L. 88-352);

    (b) Statutes at Large (78 STAT. 252); and

    (c) United States Code (42 U.S.C. § 2000d)

2. Court Opinions are published in *Reports* or *Reporters* which are tied to a specific court. For instance, U.S. Supreme Court Opinions are published in

    (a) United States Reports - 532 U.S. 275;

(*b*) *Supreme Court Reporter* - 121 S.Ct. 1511;

(*c*) *United States Supreme Court Reports, Lawyers' Edition,* 149 L.Ed.2d 517.

3. Administrative Rules and Regulations are published in

(a) Federal Register • F.R.
65 F.R. 39775

(b) Code of Federal Regulations • C.F.R.
34 C.F.R. § 100.1

Sometimes a citation will contain more than the three parts mentioned above. For example, the citation of a court's opinion contains the name of the parties, as well as the abbreviation of the reporter where it is published that is proceeded by the volume number and followed by the page where the opinion starts, and then by a parenthetical which contains the year when the case was decided. Those situations will be explained later when we will discuss in detail how to find each type of legal document.

When you start your legal research without a citation, you need to fully use the information you have. For example, if you know the name of the statute and the number of the Congress that passed it, then it becomes manageable to locate it in the *Statutes at Large.* Each volume contains a list of the statutes it houses, and it identifies them by their public law number and their name. For example, for the *Civil Rights Act of 1964,* you will go to the volumes of the 88th Congress and browse through the lists. Thus, you will find out that the statute was published in the 78th volume of the *Statutes at Large* and it starts on page 240.

If you want to read only a part of the *Civil Rights Act on 1964* in its current version, then you should use the *United States Code* and its *General Index.* For example, if you want to read its Title VI which focuses on the prevention of discrimination in federally assisted programs on racial grounds, then you go the General Index C-D, and search under the "civil rights" heading for "federal aid" and for "exclusion for participation...on grounds of race." You will find that that statutory provision is codified in the 42nd Title of the *United States Code* in section 2000d. Of course, you can find the codified section by going to the electronic version of the U.S.C, either directly to govinfo.gov, or any of the other ways mentioned above. You will follow the instructions from the *United States Code*'s page that explain what type of Boolean search will be more effective.

Sometimes, your task will be more than to locate legislation whose name or citation you know. You will try to locate the law in a particular area. For instance, when you want to locate the legislation implementing climate change policy, you will start mapping out a different research approach, which you will subsequently execute.

In this instance your research encompasses a larger scope than we have previously discussed. Your macro-level approach will start with a topical plan that will cover an international treaty never ratified by the United States, *The Kyoto Protocol.* Skip federal legislation, because there is none, and continue to state and municipal law. *The Kyoto Protocol* extended the 1992 *United Nations Framework Convention on Climate Change* (UNFCCC) in an attempt to have the signatories reduce greenhouse gas emissions and thus to attempt to reverse global warming. Because the Protocol was never ratified, it is not binding law, and it does not have a corresponding Public Law. Thus, there is neither macro nor micro research at the state level. Climate change legislation may still happen at the state and municipal level. For instance, currently, there is legislation being considered by the New York legislative body, Senate Bill S7253, whose purpose is to establish the New York state climate action council to report on greenhouse gases, establish a greenhouse gas reduction plan, and to set statewide greenhouse gas emission limits and targets. You will find this proposed legislation by using the official website of the New York State Senate, at https://www.nysenate.gov/ legislation/bills/2017/s7253. At the municipal level, for instance, New York City Local Law No. 32, adopted January 8, 2018, requires the Commissioner of the Department of Buildings (DOB) to amend the New York City Energy Conservation Code (Energy Code) and raise the energy efficiency requirements. Again, this research can be performed on the official website of the municipal government, at https://www1.nyc.gov/assets/buildings/local_laws/ll32of2018.pdf.

However, when you do case law research, rarely can you perform research that is free-of-charge. In the rare instance, when you do have the citation of a case or you know where the case was adjudicated and the names of the parties involved, then by finding a public library and using its print reporter system, or accessing the website of the appropriate court, you might be able to perform the needed research. Otherwise, it is pretty much impossible to perform case law research free of charge. Remember that the print reporters are multi-volume sets that do not have indexes that accompany each set. Without even a partial citation that will identify the reporter and the volume where the opinion is published, you cannot locate it. Each set of reporters published by West are accompanied by the *West Digest*, which indexed the entire realm of case law into almost 450 large topics and thousands of subtopics whose key numbers unified the rich conceptualization across federal and state jurisdictions. For instance, all federal and state cases covering any issue connected to environmental law are listed under topic 149. Then, they are distinguished according to a variety of subtopics and key numbers. As such, cases about particular pollutants and regulating gas emissions are further identified as

- 149EKey Number Symbol276 > Particular pollutants > In general.

A variety of indexing devices are available digitally. All three databases, *Westlaw, LexisAdvance* and *Bloomberg Law* use an indexing system for their case law collection. To date, the most comprehensive indexing is that provided by *Westlaw*, whose legal issues precede the cases identified as covering the area of law thus identified (149K276). Those editorialized summaries are called "keynotes" in *Westlaw* and "headnotes" in *LexisAdvance.* In the latter product, the editors pride themselves in using the dicta to summarize the issue, rather than the editors' work.

When it comes to administrative law, both the macro and micro aspects of research are similar at the federal, state, and municipal level. At the federal level, both the *Federal Register* and the *Code of Federal Regulations* have finding-aid tools. Therefore, whether you know the citation of the document—65 F.R. 38775, or 34 C.F.R. 100.1—or only its subject matter, you should be able to locate it easily. At the state and municipal level, the official agency website will contain the current version of the rules relevant to your research.

Nevertheless, you need to remember that legal research does not end with you finding what you believe is the binding relevant legislation, case law, or administrative rule. You need to find the proof, and that proof is always offered for a large fee by the same databases mentioned before, *LexisAdvance, Westlaw* and *Bloomberg Law,* and some new ones, such as *Fastcase* or *Casetext.*

Making Sure Your Research Is "Good Law"

When we discussed the principles of legal research, we mentioned that only "good law" is binding. But what constitutes "good law"? The last step of legal research requires you to make sure your findings are still good law.

The big problem with legal research is related to the porous nature of law. Often in law, there is no clear answer. There is no rock to be located as in geology or a new insect to be described as in entomology. When do you know that what you have is the answer to your query? What represents the law? Is it a statute, a case, an administrative rule, or all of the above? Is there a Supreme Court decision that has declared your findings unconstitutional? All these questions are pertinent, and because of their intrinsic value, this book has offered you a few research tips. Assuming that you have decided what the correct answer to your question is; the final question remains, is it still binding? Is it still the law of the land? Has the Supreme Court held it unconstitutional? Has it been amended or reversed?

What constitutes "good law?"

Good law is a statute that is still on the books and has not been declared unconstitutional by the court of last resort of the appropriate jurisdiction. In our example about the criminalization of flag burning, we discovered that while the statute is still on the books, the U.S. Supreme Court declared such punishment unconstitutional. While burning the flag is a crime under 18 U.S.C.A. § 700, it is expressive conduct and protected under the law according to *U.S. v. Eichman,* 496 U.S. 310 (1990). Thus, limiting your answer to the statutory provision would be incorrect; as it does not represent "good law."

Similarly, the good federal law governing the right to bear and beget a child is not *Roe v. Wade,* 410 U.S. 113 (1972). The good law is *Roe v. Wade,* 410 U.S. 113 (1972) as amended by *Planned*

Parenthood of S.E. Pennsylvania v. Casey, 505 U.S. 833 (1992), which circumscribed that private liberty to the first trimester of pregnancy.

The unifying pattern here is the case law treatment of legislation (administrative law) and cases. Without covering the relevant cases which interpret the legislation, earlier cases, or administrative law, your answer is incorrect because it is incomplete.

Unfortunately, to find the subsequent treatment of a statute, case, or administrative law, you will need to use one of the fee-based databases mentioned here because they offer intuitive, user-friendly updating services, such as Shepard's (*LexisAdvance*), KeyCite *(Westlaw)*, and *B-CITE (Bloomberg Law)*, as well as *Fastcase* and *CaseText*. By the virtue of being a digital database, they all offer such services implicitly. With every full-text search, you discover the "good law" if you can distinguish it. Similarly, within the limits of their coverage, both *Google Scholar* - https://scholar.google.com/ - and *The Public Library of Law (Plol)* - http://www.plol.org/Pages/Search.aspx - offer such updating service.

4. INTRODUCTION TO THE U.S. LAW AND LEGAL SYSTEM: AN ENVIRONMENTAL PERSPECTIVE – LEGAL RESEARCH PRACTICE EXERCISE: FEDERAL AND STATE LAW REPOSITORIES.

The following exercise will introduce you to some of the free repositories of primary law, as well as some fee-based repositories. Questions highlighted in *Italicized **Bold** can* be completed by anyone with internet access. Questions highlighted in underlined **Bold** may only be completed by students with access to *Nexis Uni* or *Westlaw Campus.*

Primary Sources: Case Law

Question 1- Supreme Court Reporters (part of the Federal Reporter system)

Cases are published in many print and digital places. For instance, *Citizens to Preserve Overton Park, Inc. v. Volpe*, 401 U.S. 402, 91 S.Ct. 814, 28 L.Ed.2d 136 (1971) is available in the three "reporters" identified by their abbreviations above: U.S., S.Ct, and L.Ed.

a) In the official citation, 401 U.S. 402, the official reporter is abbreviated **"U.S."** What is its full title?
b) Did you find it by searching for it online? If so, did you use a dictionary of legal abbreviation?
c) Google "*Citizens to Preserve Overton Park, Inc. v. Volpe*, 401 U.S. 402" and write down the URL identifying this U.S. Supreme Court decision in any digital repository Google lists on the first screen.

Question 2 - New York Reporters

State law cases are published in multiple ways, too. Let's locate the following case: *Boomer v. Atlantic Cement Co.*, 287 N.Y.S.2d 112 (N.Y. Sup. Ct. 1967). To locate the opinion, go to the New York courts website (nycourts.gov) and type "*Boomer v. Atlantic Cement Co.*" into the search bar to complete the following questions.

a) What is the name of the court which decided that case (read the information provided in the question)?
b) If this is the case citation: "287 N.Y.S.2d 112," what number designates the first page of that decision?

An essential part of case law research is to determine how courts have interpreted or treated an earlier case. By recording every mention of a case by every later court, *Shepards* allows the researcher to determine if a specific case is still good law, has been criticized, or has been overruled. An online version of *Shepards* is available from *LexisNexis Academic.* Court Listener, the "Free Law Project" is creating a free case citator to allow legal researchers to see a case's citing references.

Question 3 – Fee-Based and Free-of-Charge Case Citators

Shepard's Reports

Go to any version of *Lexis* (Columbia University students have access through http://www.columbia.edu/cu/lweb, go to Nexis Uni link and log in with your Columbia University UNI). When you have logged into Nexis Uni, type the following citation into the main search bar: **515 U.S. 687**.

a) Is there a symbol next to the name of the case?
b) If so, what is the symbol and what does it indicate?

Click on the link which says: *Shepardize* this document. The resulting screen contains the *Shepard's Report.* See the number next to "Citing Decisions," and answer the next question:

a) How many subsequent cases [**opinions or court decisions (NOT DOCUMENTS)**] have cited *Babbitt v. Sweet Home Chapter of Communities for a Greater Or.*"?

Free-of-Charge Case Citators:

CourtListener (https://www.courtlistener.com) has a free legal citator; however, it is much more limited than *Shepherds* on *LexisAdvance* or *Keycite* on *Westlaw*. CourtListener has a limited database of cases – *Boomer v. Atlantic Cement Co.* is not in the CourtListener database, but *Citizens to Preserve Overton Park v. Volpe* is.

Search for "**401 U.S. 402.**" A blue box will pop up saying "It looks like you're trying to search for *Citizens to Preserve Overton Park, Inc. v. Volpe*, from 1971." Click on that box to go to the case. CourtListener presents the text of the opinion but there is no information on that page to indicate whether the *Overton Park* has been overturned. (On NexisUni it is listed as "Questioned" by thirteen other cases).

b) How many citing references does CourtListener have listed for *Overton Park*?

Here is the main limitation – using CourtListener, a reader must in theory read each of *Overton Park*'s citing references to determine whether *Overton Park* remains good law. This is obviously not practical; therefore, it is clear that there is almost no good way to determine a case's citing references without using a fee-based database.

Question 4 – Case Headnotes

Court decisions are published in various repositories randomly. To help researchers, database editors identify issues and briefly note them in a section preceding the decision itself. On *LexisAdvance*, they are called "Headnotes" and on *Westlaw* they are called "Keynotes." Headnotes and Keynotes categorize topics that appear in court opinions. For example, the Headnote 1 in *Boomer v. Atlantic Cement Co.* is "Remedies and Injunctions." Clicking on Headnote 1 will lead to cases citing *Boomer*'s discussion of "Remedies and Injunctions."

Now, look up *U.S. v. Billie*, 667 F. Supp. 1485 (1987), on Nexis Uni by typing its citation (667 F. Supp. 1485) into the search box. Then, scroll down the case until you find "LexisHeadnotes."

a) What is the title of the Third Headnote?
b) How many other cases cite *U.S. v. Billie* for the information contained in Headnote 3?
   (**REMEMBER**. The verb used by Nexis Uni to denote subsequent cases citing a particular case is "shepardize," so, imagine you were to *Shepardize U.S. v. Billie* and search for cases that referenced just its Third Headnote).

Primary Sources: Federal Statutes

Statutes are published in more than one form. Laws printed in chronological order as passed by the legislature are called ***session laws.*** Federal session laws are called (for the most part) ***Public Laws.*** When Congress passes a new law, it is assigned a Public Law number. For instance, the fourth law passed by the 105th Congress is P.L. 105-4. The number before the hyphen refers to the number of the Congress that passed the law. The numbers after the hyphen are a chronological serial numbering of the laws passed by that Congress.

Question 5 – Statutes at Large

The Library of Congress's legislation web site is called *Thomas.* The archived version of the Endangered Species Act of 1973, Pub. L. 93-205, Dec. 28, 1973; 87 Stat. 884, can be retrieved by using Google and searching for "Pub. L. 93-205."

a) If the citation is 87 Stat. 884, which number indicates the volume containing the statute?

Though the Library of Congress's legislation website, *Thomas*, available at <http://thomas.loc.gov>, carries many PDFs of public laws, remember that it does not cover all of them.

Next, you will look at the other form in which statutes are published – ***codes.*** The government-published ***federal statutory code*** is the *United States Code* (U.S.C.). The two most popular commercial alternatives are Lexis' *United States Code Service* (or *U.S.C.S*), and Westlaw's *United States Code Annotated* (or *U.S.C.A.).*

The advantages of the *U.S.C.A.* and the *U.S.C.S.* over the official *United States Code* are that they are much more timely (the official set is always at least two years behind) and these commercially produced sets are also heavily annotated with historical notes, C.F.R. sections, citations to leading cases interpreting code sections, and a variety of useful tables, indexes, and other research aids.

Question 6- The Federal Code (U.S.C.).

The Endangered Species Act of 1973, Pub. L. 93-205, Dec. 28, 1973; 87 Stat. 884, is codified at Title 16 U.S.C. §§ 1531-1543. Go to Govinfo (https://www.govinfo.gov/) and locate one section of the Act.

a) Which section § did you locate?

b) How many titles does the U.S.C. contain? ______(include titles which are currently reserved)
c) What do you think the term "title" represents (what does it contain)?
d) Is there a title containing all environmental statutes?____What about the title labeled "Conservation," what statutes do you think it covers?

Primary Sources: Federal Rules and Regulations

Most statutes cannot regulate behavior without the details found in administrative regulations. Like federal statutes, federal administrative rules are published as they are issued in the *Federal Register*, and are also organized by topic, in the code federal regulations, which is the *Code of Federal Regulations* (commonly known as the *C.F.R.*). Unlike the *Federal Register*, the *C.F.R.* carries only the final rules and regulations that the executive branch agencies issue.

***Question** 7*- The *C.F.R.*

Go to Govinfo, https://www.govinfo.gov/, and find the C.F.R. (https://www.govinfo.gov/app/browse/category/regulatory-info). Then, locate the 2018 edition of the C.F.R.

a) How is this codification generally organized?
b) What is a title?
c) Can you find the title that covers environmental regulations?

Chapter 6 – Learning to Read a Case: Environmental Torts and the BOOMER *Case*

In the previous chapters, you read about the United States legal system, its history, and its present. You also read about finding specific legal norms, whether statutory, decisional, or administrative. For the next few chapters, you will read about environmental law in a manner that mirrors its progression: incrementally.

Environmental law started with a few cases, then a handful of statutes, and within a matter of decades it came to encompass a significant legal area. The beauty of environmental law is that citizens can still make a significant impact, whether they petition municipal ordinances to establish pollution limitations, or whether they sue polluters in citizen lawsuits. In New York, it seems that it all started with one case which became known as *Boomer v. Atlantic Cement Company.* The trial (**BOOMER I**), appellate division (**BOOMER II**), and Court of Appeals (**BOOMER III**) opinions are reprinted at the end of this chapter and on the Companion Website, at http://www.environmentallaw-teach.org/chapters.html. Before you continue, read **BOOMER I** and **BOOMER II**, so you have an understanding of the socio-economic reality of mid-20th century New York State, as well as the facts and the parties. In addition, by reading these opinions, you will be exposed to the area of law that is being litigated: *civil wrongs*, or *torts*. A tort is a wrong or harmful act for which the wronged party (*the plaintiff*) seeks a remedy in a civil court against the wrongdoer (*the defendant*). Litigating harm caused by polluting the environment was starting to become an important source for lawsuits and for the growth of environmental law. The **BOOMER** cases are the first in a series of environmental torts you will read about here.

In learning to read a case, there are several initial obstacles.

a) The most important of these is the legal language. It takes time to build a solid foundation of legal vocabulary, and the use of a legal dictionary is a must.
b) At a minimum, use the glossary in the back of this book may be of help. It is also available on the Companion Website at http://www.environmentallaw-teach.org/.
c) Do not assume that you know the meaning of a legal term. Often, the meaning is counterintuitive or very specific to the circumstances at hand. There are also terms that are specific to the case. Sometimes there are scientific or medical terms. These need to be defined as well.
d) Read all three opinions slowly, starting with **BOOMER I.** Go paragraph by paragraph and within each paragraph underline all legal terms and then look up the definitions.
e) Make notes where your understanding is not clear and try to formulate a question.

In this book, we will refer to reading a *case* interchangeably with the *decision*, or *opinion*. More accurately, each time, you will read the opinion that is written by the trial court judge or if the case is heard by a panel of judges at a higher, *appellate*, level, you will read the opinion written by the judge selected to write the majority opinion. The opinion contains the holding, the court's ruling on the issue or issues raised by the parties, and it provides the reasoning or an explanation for the court's decision. This usually includes a review of relevant cases and often provides background information as well as historical and social context. Some opinions are well-organized and concise, others are not. Often there are remarks or material, known as *dicta*, that are not directly relevant to the *holding* or final decision. The reader must approach each case with a critical mind. Judges write their opinions believing that their decision in a particular case was the only logical course of action. As such, opinions take the form of an argument in which the judge is an advocate. For this reason, the reader must not read and absorb, but rather, read and analyze. Were relevant precedents followed, distinguished, or reversed? Is the decision supported by the facts? Critical thinking skills are essential to reading and understanding opinions.

The flow chart below shows you what happened once the *plaintiff* decided to bring his *complaint* against the *defendant* to court. Read it as a *procedural* X-Ray of **Boomer I**.

Flow Chart for a Civil Trial

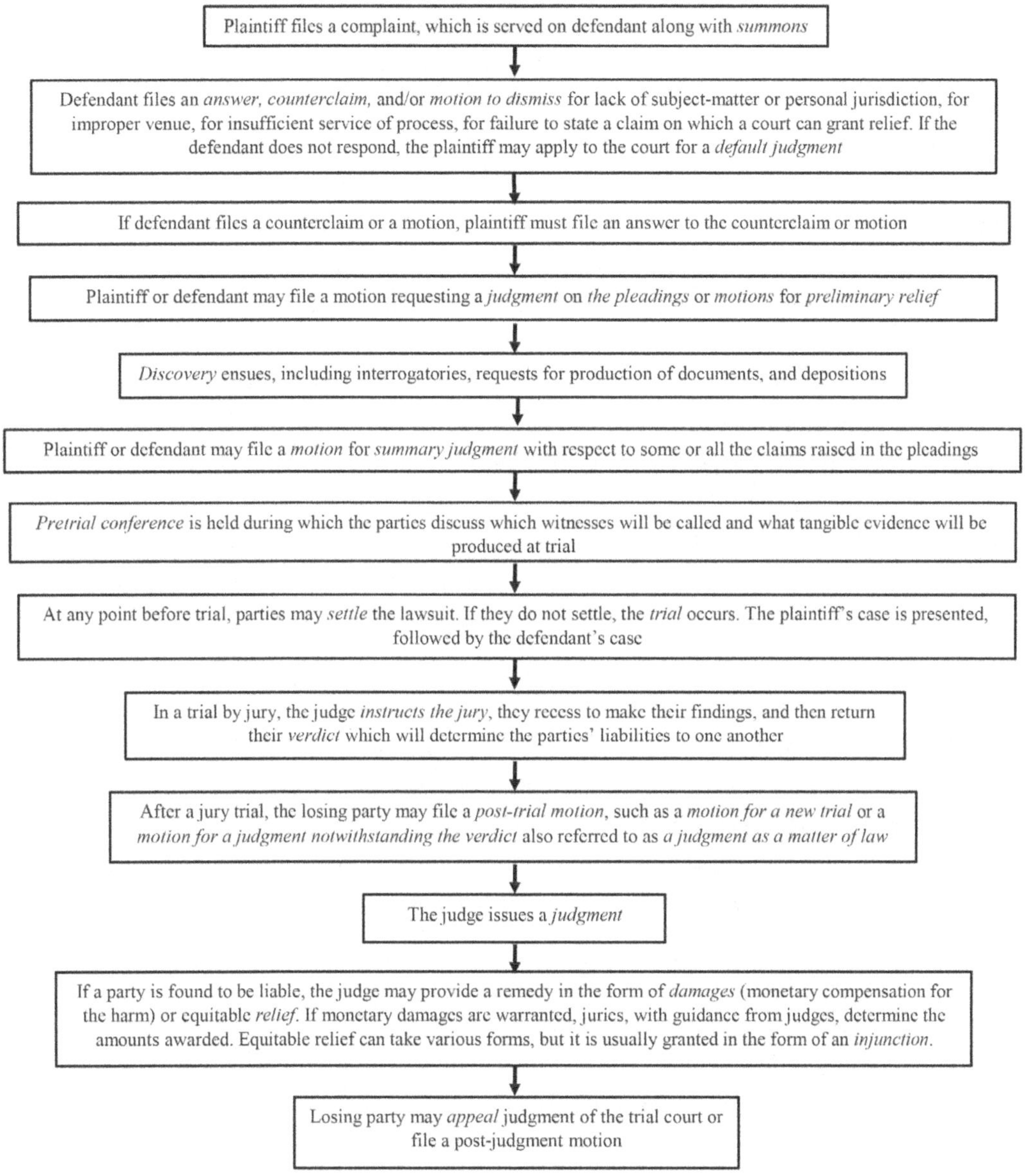

From this flowchart, it becomes clear that all *civil actions* start with the *plaintiff*'s *attorney* preparing a *complaint* that describes the harm that has occurred, the basis for the claim against the *defendant* (the *cause of action*), and how the *alleged injury* should be *remedied*.

Complaints are thus documents which a *plaintiff* (usually through their attorney) file with a *court of competency* (a court with *jurisdiction*) setting forth the claims against the defendant.

The defendant is officially *served* by the court with this complaint along with a *summons* that requires the defendant to file a *reply* or *answer* to the complaint by a certain date and then to *appear* in court to answer the charges. *Service of a summons and complaint* initiate the civil trial process, as you can see it illustrated in the flowchart. Civil trial procedure will be discussed in much more detail with the reading of Jonathan Harr's A CIVIL ACTION. Unless defendants specifically request *a bench trial* (in which the judge acts as the trier-of-fact in lieu of a *jury*), a jury will determine *liability*, that is, whether the defendant is substantially responsible for the harm experienced by the plaintiff. The trier-of-fact's determination is called a *verdict*. In federal courts, juries must be unanimous in both civil and criminal trials. For criminal trials, almost every state requires the jury to produce a unanimous verdict; however, for civil trials, almost one-third of states only require a *majority for a verdict*. The standard of proof is very different for juries in criminal versus civil trials. For criminal trials, the defendant is found guilty or not guilty using the *beyond a moral doubt* and to *a moral certainty* standard. For civil trials, liability is *found* based on the *preponderance of the evidence* or *the more likely than not* standard. After a verdict has been rendered, the judge issues a *judgment*. If liability has been found, then the judgment includes the *remedy* for the harm suffered by the plaintiffs. Remedies fall into two categories: *damages* (monetary compensation for the harm) and *equitable relief*. Equitable relief can take various forms, but it is usually granted in the form of an *injunction*. Juries with guidance from the judge determine the amount of damages. This can be a complicated process (as we shall see in *BOOMER*). Injunctions come in several forms. The most common types of *injunction* prevent a party from doing something or from continuing to do something. Injunctions which prohibit a certain act are sometimes referred to as a *cease and desist order*. Injunctions may also order the performance of specific remedial acts.

Civil trials can end in many ways. For instance, they can end in a *settlement* outside the court, a settlement sanctioned by the court, or with an *opinion*.

THE STRUCTURE OF ANY REPORTED COURT OPINION

To be binding, court opinions need to be *reported* or published. Whether they are reported in an *official* government reporter, or in a *commercial* reporter, all printed opinions will contain some basic elements. The first important piece of information is the title or *heading* that is at the top of the first page where the opinion is published in the case law repository designated for the court handling it. Because BOOMER III is a Court of Appeals opinion, and the Court of Appeals is the highest court in New York State, there are a few repositories of such opinions. For copyright reasons, the opinion included in this book is the one published by the Law Reporting Bureau, NEW YORK REPORTS, the official New York State Court of Appeals reporter. There are other places where the identical opinion can be found. Those additional or alternative *reporters* are commercial publications, available to you for a hefty fee. *Westlaw* and *LexisAdvance* have their own proprietary reporters. West Publishing Company (*Westlaw*) offers two case law repositories for New York State cases, a regional reporter, NORTH EASTERN REPORTER (Volume 257, Second Edition, the first page where the case starts in the reporter, 870), and WEST'S NEW YORK SUPPLEMENT (Volume 309, Second Edition, the first page where the case starts in the reporter, 312). These alternative reporters will be cited as parallel citations, such as 309 N.Y.S.2d 312.

a. BOOMER III - Heading

The official heading for BOOMER III is its official citation: *Boomer v. Atlantic Cement Co.*, 26 N.Y.2d 219 (1970). From it, you learn the name of the parties, where you can find it and read it, and the date of its argument and decision, although only the year makes it into the citation.

Next, there is a summary of the case, usually written by the judge's clerks, and information about the parties' representation, their attorneys. The case itself starts after the name of the judge. In BOOMER III, that is "Bergan, Judge". Read the case including the *dissent* of Judge Jansen.

BOOMER III represents the final judgment in this matter because it comes from the Court of Appeals, which in the state of New York is the highest court, or the *court of last resort*. This opinion is therefore mandatory, not persuasive, authority in the state of New York. There are multiple appellants. We know this because the case reads "Oscar H. Boomer et al." "Et al." is the abbreviation of a Latin phrase *et alia*, which means "and others". Because this is a case that has been appealed from lower courts, the parties are called *appellants* and *respondent*, rather than *plaintiffs* and *defendant*.

As you must have understood from reading BOOMER I and BOOMER II, Oscar Boomer, and the other appellants are appealing the lower court decisions won by the *defendant*, the Atlantic Cement Company. The date listed at the bottom, March 4, 1970, is the date on which the case was decided.

b. BOOMER III - Procedural History

From the Summary and the Points of Counsel, you have access to the information you already know from BOOMER I and BOOMER III, also known as the *procedural history*. Here we learn that the *Boomer et al. v. Atlantic Cement* Company case was litigated at the trial court level in the Supreme Court, Trial Term, of Albany County with Judge R. Waldron Herzberg presiding (BOOMER I). We also learn that the plaintiffs appealed the trial court decision, that this appeal was heard by the Supreme Court, Appellate Division, and that the trial court decision was *affirmed* (BOOMER II). There was also a second action (*Meilak et al. v Atlantic Cement Company*) that suffered the exact same fate as the Boomer action. All of the initial plaintiffs appealed to the highest court in the state of New York, The Court of Appeals. The Court of Appeals *granted certiorari* and, because the cases were nearly the same, they were combined for reasons of efficiency. It is necessary to mention here that the review of a case at the appellate level is not a trial. Unless there have been gross errors in the management of the trial, the verdict of the trial court is not disturbed. Absent gross errors, the appeal concerns itself with the basis for the judgment as applied to the given *verdict*.

Before we continue with the structure of all opinions, let's focus on BOOMER III. Because reading a case requires a different approach than pleasure reading or newspaper reading, we will go paragraph by paragraph and extract the elements that are common to all opinions.

c. BOOMER III – Opinion, paragraph #1, 26 N.Y.2d at 222

Briefly, Judge Bergan reminds the reader that every case involves real people in real places. Here, in the case at hand, it involves the geographic and historic importance of the cement industry along the Hudson River. We need to remember every moment we read any opinion because otherwise, we engage in an instructive but often sterile exercise.

From this paragraph, we learn the location of the defendant, a "large cement plant." Near what municipality is it located? We also learn quickly that neighboring landowners have sued the cement company "alleging injury to property from dirt, smoke, and vibration emanating from the plant." They have asked for "injunction and damages" as a remedy for this harm. The lower courts have found a nuisance, but instead of granting an injunction the only remedy was temporary damages.

And, if we really read carefully, we understand that we have come across the *main issue*, the *gist* of this case: why damages for a nuisance? Damages are monetary compensation for the harm, but temporary damages compensate for harms up to the time of the trial and allow the plaintiffs to maintain their cause of action after the trial is over; that is, they can sue again if the harm continues. A nuisance is a type of tort. The two main types are private and public nuisance. *Private nuisance* involves the actions, conduct, or use of property by one party so as to substantially or unreasonably interfere in the use and enjoyment of another's property or to injure life or health of another. *Public nuisance* involves the actions, conduct, or use of property by one party so as to offend the senses or violate public standards of decency or to obstruct the free passage or use of public rights, parks, beaches, roads, or navigable streams. Analytically, BOOMER is a private nuisance, intentional tort.

d. Boomer III – Opinion, paragraphs ##2-7, 26 N.Y.2d at 222-3

This paragraph continues to allude to the *issue at hand*, the appropriate remedy for the wrong in Boomer, by indicating the *reasoning* of the court. This paragraph contains statements which constitute *dicta*. The paragraph is also political as it reads like a call to action for other branches of the government. "Ever wider recognition" of pollution (air pollution in this case) and the "growing sense of responsibility in State and Federal Governments to control it" presages the creation of the Environmental Protection Agency in December of 1970. The E.P.A. provided standard setting, monitoring, and enforcement capabilities for the powerful 1970 amendments to the Clean Air Act of 1963 that among other things, regulated stationary, industrial sources of pollution.

The "specific relief" sought by the homeowners is, of course, an injunction that would force the Atlantic Cement Company to cease operation. The key, central, "threshold question raised by the division of view," (or difference of opinion) is also *dicta*. This question concerns so-called "activist" and "conservative" judges. Activist judges "channel private litigation into broad public objectives." Conservative judges "resolve the litigation between the parties" as fairly as possible without concern for "broad public objectives." This difference between activist and conservative judges is as old as our legal system and is part of today's litigious legal environment. However, it should not be confused with politics of the left and right. A particular judge may be considered an activist in one case but rule conservatively in another. Activist judges are found on both the right and left.

Interestingly, while the threshold question or *legal issue* has not been directly addressed, the reader has a clear sense of how the court will solve the issue. It will channel its decision, or holding, to fit a private wrong.

e. Boomer III – Opinion, paragraph #8, 26 N.Y.2d at 223

Finally, *the legal issue* and the *reason for appeal* is introduced clearly: the plaintiff was denied injection, notwithstanding having suffered the wrong alleged, the nuisance. Additionally, we read the reason for the denial of injunction. "The total damage to plaintiffs' properties is, however, relatively small in comparison with the value of defendant's operation and with the consequences of the injunction which plaintiffs seek."

f. Boomer III – Opinion, paragraphs ##9-12, 26 N.Y.2d at 223-4

Here the court continues its reasoning by introducing the existing precedent established by the Court of Appeals 50 years earlier, in *Whalen v. Union Bag & Paper Co.*, 208 N. Y. 1 (1913). As you have read in the earlier chapters, the genius of the common law system is that once there is a "rule" or precedent, the lower courts have to follow it. However, the Boomer court is not a lower court. It is the same Court of Appeals; therefore, the reader realizes that Boomer might be decided as if there were no precedent.

Judge Bergan reminds us the gist of *Whalen,* and we learn that the established precedent in nuisance cases allows no mediation, negotiation, conditions, or middle ground; that is, a *balancing of the equities* when substantive damages accrued from nuisance. Balancing of the equities never occurs during the deliberations of a jury or plays a role in the jury's verdict. If equitable relief has been requested, the judge must weigh all the hardships, benefits, and consequences of an injunction to both plaintiffs and defendants before arriving at a final judgment. We will carefully read and brief *Whalen* in the next chapter, but it is worth noting that in *Whalen* the defendant was a pulp mill, which polluted a stream along which the plaintiff owned a *riparian* farm (riparian = along the bank of a stream). While the economic loss to the plaintiff was small, it was considered substantial (> $100) and the trial court granted an injunction to close the mill in spite of the fact that "the slight advantage to plaintiff and the great loss that will be inflicted on defendant." Judge Werner's 1913 opinion stated that "such a balancing of the injuries cannot be justified..." Indeed, he overturned the Appellate Division that had overturned the trial court and reinstated the injunction.

After introducing the precedent, Judge Bergan cites three of the more significant, relevant cases that have affirmed the *Whalen* decision. There were many, many more between 1913-1970. For those who have an interest, all three of these opinions have been posted on the Companion Website, http://www.environmentallaw-teach.org/, Chapter 4.

Similarly, Judge Bergan cites cases where an injunction was denied. These cases, however, do not reject or overturn the precedent set in *Whalen* because they are *distinguished* from *Whalen* by the fact that the damage suffered was not substantial. *Supra* means "above" or earlier in this writing while *infra* means "below" or later in this writing.

g. Boomer III – Opinion, paragraphs ##13-14, 26 N.Y.2d at 224-5

After restating the procedural history concerning the injunction being denied by the Appellate Division, Judge Bergan tackles the issues with regard to the damages awarded. Damages were examined and awarded at the trial court level. The awards were, however, *temporary damages.* This means that the monetary awards compensated for all harms past and present, but left the plaintiffs with their cause of action, i.e., the right to sue for any future harms. In the opinion of the trial court, "in awarding damages to the time of trial I am bound by precedent to grant only the loss of rental value or loss of usable value sustained." The key words are "to the time of trial" which makes the damages temporary. This was affirmed at the Appellate Division.

However, the court at Special Term, the trial court, awarded $185,000 in permanent damages "in the event that both sides stipulated to the payment and acceptance of such permanent damage as a settlement of all the controversies between the parties." A stipulation is a signed agreement between the parties in court or by their attorneys. No such stipulation was ever agreed upon, so the damages assigned by the lower court remained temporary.

h. Boomer III – Opinion, paragraph #15, 26 N.Y.2d at 225

While the two-prong holding to the issue is not directly expressed, the court tells us how one prong of the issue, the type of remedy requested, is solved, indirectly. There will be no injunctions because the court majority has "fully agreed" not to "close-down the plant at once and, as a result, will make a "departure from a rule that has become settled."

i. Boomer III – Opinion, paragraph #16-23, 26 N.Y.2d at 225-6

These paragraphs explain in detail the reasoning of the court for denying an injunction. They contain a discussion of "how best to avoid" an injunction. Somewhat hidden by an asterisk is some important information that was much more fully discussed in the trial and appellate court opinions. These are important *facts*. Namely, that the *defendant*, Atlantic Cement Co., hires over 300 people and has an investment of over $45 million in the plant. Not mentioned but just as important are the *ratable sot* tax dollars that the company provides to the local municipality that help fund schools, police, and other town activities as well as all the local businesses that thrive because employees spend their paycheck locally. All this would be lost if an injunction was issued and the former precedent (not allowing balancing of the equities in the Bergan court opinion).

There are also two hypothetical alternatives discussed: One is to postpone the issuance of an injunction to some future date pending the implementation of pollution abatement technology. The other alternative, the one the court will choose, is explained in a confusing manner. To "grant the injunction conditioned on the payment of permanent damages" means that when the permanent damages are paid, the injunction that hangs over the head of the Atlantic Cement Co. will be lifted (denied). Finally, the court states its intentions about solving the dispute between the parties as equitably as possible and remaining within the "four corners of these actions" and not (as stated in paragraphs #3 and #4) using "a decision in private litigation as a purposeful mechanism to achieve direct public objectives."

What we would like you to think about reading its *dicta* is its political and economic implications for that area. Were there other homeowners in the Hudson Valley who at that time had their properties damaged by the pollution of this and many other cement plants? Could you imagine how, given this Court of Appeals decision, cement plant attorneys would simply settle the damages out of court once a complaint was filed? Would this induce cement companies to improve pollution control? Was there a spate of complaints on the same issues that followed BOOMER? What happened to the cement industry in the Hudson Valley? To the Atlantic Cement Co.?

j. BOOMER III – Opinion, paragraph #24, 26 N.Y.2d at 225-6

The court continues discussing its holding: denying an injunction. This paragraph is interesting merely because of its language. Here is the term *conditioned* again, but explained once the language is understood. A *continuance*, contrary to intuitive readers, means a postponement. The court restates that the court will issue an injunction but postpone it when permanent damages are paid and then providing two supporting precedents.

k. BOOMER III – Opinion, paragraphs ##25-31, 26 N.Y.2d at 226-8

These next paragraphs provide further justifications (*dicta, reasoning*) for the denial of an injunction and awarding of permanent damages through the use of supporting cases and other legal authorities. The court uses various *persuasive authority*.

It cites *66 C.J.S. Nuisances §140, p.947*. The symbol § means "section." C.J.S. stands for *Corpus Juris Secondum,* which is a hybrid secondary source, known for its concise legal analysis and abundance of primary source citations. Here is some legal trivia: *Corpus Juris* means "body of law" in Latin and is a reference to the codification of Roman and civil law in Corpus *Juris Civilis in* the 6th Century. It is worth noting that although *secondary authority*, the quote used here is persuasive because it is supportive of the permanent damage theory chosen by this court. Judge Bergan then uses a Kentucky case, this time a persuasive primary source, to bolster the permanent damage theory where the cost of removal of the nuisance is large compared to the cost of the damages.

These paragraphs introduce *persuasive primary sources* from other jurisdictions, such as an Indiana state case similar in many respects to BOOMER . There, balancing of the equities allows the "continuance of the gas plant" (here continuance means that it stays open) in the interest of the public and permanent damages give "full relief" (in the common sense of the term) in "one action" of all harm past, present, and future." The court also cites to a Texas case with a "continuing and recurrent nuisance" where permanent damages were awarded, along with numerous cases where permanent damages were awarded in lieu of an injunction. It is worth noting that these are all persuasive references, while *Whalen* is a mandatory, binding authority this is overturned by this court.

l. BOOMER III – Opinion, paragraphs ##32-36, 26 N.Y.2d at 226-8

Finally, the court states its two-prong holding: denying the permanent injunction and granting permanent damages, while reversing and remanding the case to the trial court so an injection would be granted conditioned upon defendant paying permanent damages.

The court provides the theory of the damage for which permanent damages are awarded to the plaintiffs in this case. The theory is that of a "servitude on the land," the recurrent nuisance that has been imposed on the plaintiffs' properties. Permanent damages "would preclude recovery," that is, future lawsuits for the continuing nuisance. So, the permanent damages awarded are to compensate for a "servitude on the land."

What we would like to you to retain is that the Court of Appeals has affirmed both the trial and appellate courts' decisions: there is no closure of the defendant's factory. What has been reversed here are the temporary damages that have now been replaced with permanent damages. The cases of all the plaintiffs are to be "remitted," or sent back, to the Supreme Court, Albany County (the trial court) where an injunction will be "granted" but "vacated" (or voided) "upon payment by defendant of such amounts of permanent damage" that are "determined by the court." The Supreme Court, Trial Term, where this litigation originated (see BOOMER I), can now "be entirely free to reexamine the subject" of how much the permanent damages should be. It will be recalled that the Trial Term did determine "permanent damages as a possible basis for settlement of the litigation" but, because the parties could not agree to this, temporary damages were awarded. The temporary damages were in turn reversed by the Court of Appeals and replaced with permanent damages based on a "servitude upon the land."

m. BOOMER III –The Dissenting Opinion, 26 N.Y.2d at 228-32

The dissenting opinion by Judge Jasen begins with the confusing statement that he agrees "with the majority that a reversal is required here," but the reversal he wants is the reversal of the Appellate Division's refusal to grant an injunction. He objects to the "newly enunciated doctrine of assessment of permanent damages, in lieu of an injunction where substantial property rights have been impaired by the creation of a nuisance." He reiterates the longstanding "rule" of *Whalen v. Union Paper Bag Co.* and cites several cases that supported this precedent. He objects to permitting the "cement company to continue polluting the air indefinitely upon the payment of permanent damages" and, while he discusses several aspects of air pollution, he finally states that he objects to the "licensing of a continuing wrong," that is, likening the use of the payment of permanent damages to the purchase of a permit to continue polluting the air. The argument that payment of permanent damages would eliminate "the incentive to alleviate the wrong" is weakened by the fact that the potential for other plaintiffs taking action remains.

Judge Jasen's argument that the promotion of the private interest of the cement company serves no public use or benefit is belied by the facts of the situation. However, Judge Herzberg writes in the trial court opinion (Boomer I) that "I have given careful consideration to the plea of plaintiffs that an injunction should issue in this action. Although the Supreme Court has the power to grant and enforce an injunction, equity forbids its employment in this instance. The defendant's immense investment in the Hudson River Valley, its contribution to the Capital District's economy, and its immediate help to the education of children in the Town of Coeymans through the payment of substantial sums in school and property taxes lead me to the conclusion that I should adhere to the often quoted words of Judge Collin in *McCann v. Chasm Power Co.*, 211 N. Y. 301, 305 (1914):

> It is not safe to attempt to lay down any hard and fast rule for the guidance of courts of equity in determining when an injunction should issue. The ownership of property will be protected unless there are other considerations which forbid, as inequitable, the remedy of the prohibitive or mandatory injunction. A court of equity can never be justified in making an inequitable decree. If the protection of a legal right even would do a plaintiff but comparatively little good and would produce great public or private hardship, equity will withhold its discreet and beneficent hand and remit the plaintiff to his legal rights and remedies."

After reviewing all the evidence in this action, Judge Jasen finds that an injunction "would produce great public ... hardship." Indeed, the public was deeply invested in the 300 jobs the company provided as well as the concomitant spur to local businesses and the significant tax ratables that supported education, the police, and other public services. The constitutional arguments about a "taking" of property for a private use were found largely irrelevant and overblown since no property had been taken.

Judge Jasen also states that he would impose an injunction in 18 months unless the cement company "abated" the pollution during this time, but no standard for what the scale of this abatement is was provided. In the next paragraph, he states that it is not his "intention to cause the removal of the cement plant from the Albany area," but, of course, an injunction would do precisely this. He also speaks not of "18 months" but now of a "specified period of time to develop a means to alleviate this nuisance." Again, the amount of time required and the standard for "alleviation" seem elusive.

Finally, the dissenting judge acknowledges that the cement company already has the "most modern control devices." During retrial, in April-May 1972, the cement company showed that "it had made three significant developments in the control of emissions: 1. It had converted the primary fuel of the plant from coal to oil. 2. It had put "an additional spray system in the conveying apparatus from the quarry to the stockpiles at the plant site." 3. It had replaced the multi-clone dust collectors on the clinker cooler with a fiberglass bag-type collector all at the cost of $1,600,000."

When you read the dissenting opinion remember that the "cement company, at the time the plant commenced production (1962), was well aware of the plaintiffs' presence in the area." Had Boomer bought his property and moved in after the cement plant was in operation, he would have "come to the nuisance." The result of the litigation would have been totally different. As you will enlarge the scope of your knowledge about civil wrongs, you will see that for a while, that fact would have constituted an affirmative defense for the cement factory.

THE ELEMENTS OF A TORTIOUS PRIMA-FACIA CASE – THE BOOMER CASE

The elements of a lawsuit are the constituent parts that the plaintiffs must prove in order for a jury or a judge sitting as finder-of-fact to find the defendant liable. There are three basic elements for a tortious *prima-facia* case:

a) proof of harm (in violation of plaintiff's right);
b) proof of causation; and,
c) proof of fault.

Because *Boomer* was a private nuisance tort, *proof of harm* involved a showing of *substantial, unreasonable* interference in the use and enjoyment of their property, which meant that the alleged damages was greater than $100 and was unreasonable. A common sense term, *unreasonable* means outside of normal limits. What available evidence would show the nature and extent of the harm? Litigators call this *probative evidence* because it proves the truthfulness of the claims of harm. For Boomer, this might include physical evidence, such as photos and exhibits of corroded gutters, damaged exteriors of cars and buildings, cement dust coated trees, plants, and clothes, grit and dust on rooftops and windows, and a recording of noise and vibrations. Testimonial evidence would also be probative and include testimony by the aggrieved plaintiff, by individuals hired to clean buildings and property, by a chemist who can testify about the exact nature of the dust and grit, and, especially, by real estate agents who can testify to the loss of property value.

Proof of causation requires plaintiffs to show a factual connection between the defendant's conduct, actions, and/or use of property and the plaintiff's injury. Defendant's conduct must be found to be a "substantial factor" in a plaintiff's injury even though the defendant's conduct may not be the only factor, as other concurrent forces may have contributed to the plaintiff's injury. What is considered a "substantial factor" has been largely determined by many precedents of case law and lines have been drawn between substantial factors and those that are not. For Boomer, showing that the cement dust and vibration come from the operations of the Atlantic Cement Co. was not difficult. Here, the particles are visible and the vibrations and noise tangible. We can imagine, however, the difficulties in proving causation where the chemicals and the pathways by which they travel are not visible. In our examination of the toxic tort litigation in *A Civil Action,* we will see the enormous difficulties faced in proving causation for diseases allegedly caused by chronic low-level exposure to toxins.

Proof of fault is determined by reliance on one of three theories: intent, negligence, and strict liability. We will examine environmental torts that use all three of these theories. Analytically, BOOMER is a private nuisance intentional tort. Negligence theories are also difficult to prove but represent most of the tort litigation, especially because of personal injury torts. In *complaints,* plaintiff attorneys have to make clear the theory they use so they do not run the risk that the judge and opposing attorneys assume the use of a different theory, which the facts do not support. Civil intent is often misunderstood and confused with criminal intent where a culprit acts purposely and means or intends to cause harm. Civil intent maintains a legal presumption that the defendant intends the natural consequences of an act. Plaintiffs only need to show that the consequences of a defendant's action were *substantially foreseeable.* There does not need to be a showing of purposeful intent to harm. The Atlantic Cement Co. cast prodigious quantities of dust into the air and wind and gravity will naturally carry this dust and deposit it on nearby properties. Noise and vibrations from explosions travel as waves through the air and ground; again, a natural consequence imposed upon nearby properties. In addition, the plaintiffs repeatedly made complaints to the defendant, and documentation of these complaints provided virtual proof that the defendant knew of the consequences of the production of dust, noise, and vibrations.

BOOMER is an example of a *prima facie* case (Latin for "at first look"). On their face, the allegations in BOOMER were found sufficient to satisfy all the requirements of the cause of action, or some of its elements. The jury's verdict of liability was not difficult to reach. Judge Herzberg states in his trial court opinion that "although the evidence in this case establishes that Atlantic took every available and possible precaution to protect the plaintiffs from dust...., nevertheless, I find that the plaintiffs have sustained the burden of proof that Atlantic in the operation of its cement plant between September 1, 1962 and June 1, 1967 (a period of 57 months) created a nuisance insofar as the lands of the plaintiffs are concerned. The discharge of large quantities of dust upon each of the properties and excessive vibration from blasting deprived each party of the reasonable use of his property and thereby prevented his enjoyment of life and liberty therein."

The remedy for the finding of private nuisance involved considerable wrangling over the nature and amount of damages, but this case is remembered as a landmark ruling in which a longstanding precedent was overturned, balancing of the equities was allowed, and an injunction to close down the plant was denied.

1. BOOMER I

55 MISC.2D 1023

OSCAR H. BOOMER ET AL., PLAINTIFFS,

V.

ATLANTIC CEMENT COMPANY, INC., DEFENDANT. (AND SEVEN OTHER ACTIONS.)

SUPREME COURT, ALBANY COUNTY

AUGUST 14, 1967

CITE TITLE AS: Boomer v Atlantic Cement Co.

Torts
Nuisance

Emission of dust from cement plant--cement plant created nuisance by emission of dust preventing plaintiffs from enjoying their properties*1024 --no injunction is granted--loss of monthly rental value and permanent damages are fixed.

() Although a cement manufacturing company took every available precaution, when erecting its $40,000,000 modern cement plant, to prevent the discharge of dust and polluted air into the atmosphere, the evidence establishes that in the operation of its plant between September 1, 1962 and June 1, 1967, the cement company created a nuisance insofar as plaintiffs' lands are concerned. The discharge of large quantities of dust upon each of the properties and excessive vibration from blasting deprived each party of the reasonable use of his property and thereby prevented his enjoyment of life and liberty therein.

() Considering defendant's immense investment, its contribution to the area's economy, its immediate help to the education of children in the township through payment of substantial sums in school and property taxes, injunctive relief would produce great public hardship and is not warranted.

() Plaintiffs are granted as damages only the loss of rental value or usable value per month which are fixed. The court also fixes the amount of loss in the reasonable market value of each property which is the permanent loss of each plaintiff.

APPEARANCES OF COUNSEL

E. David Duncan for Oscar H. Boomer and others, plaintiffs. John J. Biscone and Daniel H. Prior, Jr., for Charles J. Meilak and another, plaintiffs. Ainsworth, Sullivan, Tracy & Knauf (Thomas F. Tracy of counsel), for defendant.

OPINION OF THE COURT
R. Waldron Herzberg, J.

Plaintiffs in this action seek an injunction against defendant cement company (Atlantic) to restrain it from emitting dust and raw materials and conducting excessive blasting in operating its plant in such a manner as to constitute a nuisance upon plaintiffs' lands. In addition damages to the time of trial are sought.

Atlantic commenced the production of Portland Cement at its plant in the Town of Coeymans in the County of Albany on or about September 1, 1962. Prior to that date defendant expended more than $40,000,000 in the erection of one of the largest and most modern cement plants in the world. The company installed at great expense the most efficient devices available to prevent the discharge of dust and polluted air into the atmosphere.

Although the evidence in this case establishes that Atlantic took every available and possible precaution to protect the plaintiffs from dust (see Freidman v. Columbia Mach. Works, 99 App. Div. 504; De Muro v. Havranek, 153 Misc. 787, 790-791), nevertheless, I find that the plaintiffs have sustained the burden of proof that Atlantic in the operation of its cement plant between September 1, 1962 and June 1, 1967 (a period of 57 months) created a nuisance insofar as the lands of the plaintiffs are concerned. The discharge of large quantities of dust upon each of the properties and excessive vibration from blasting *1025 deprived each party of the reasonable use of his property and thereby prevented his enjoyment of life and liberty therein (see Campbell v. Seaman, 63 N. Y. 568, 577; Bohan v. Port Jervis Gas & Light Co., 122 N. Y. 18, 23; Booth v. Rome Watertown & Ogdensburg R.R. Co., 140 N. Y. 267; McCarty v. Natural Carbonic Gas Co., 189 N. Y. 40, 46; Waters v. McNearney, 8 A D 2d 13, 16, affd. 8 N Y 2d 808; Dixon v. New York Trap Rock Corp., 293 N. Y. 509, 513; Dillon v. Cortland Baking Co., 224 App. Div. 303, 305; Moore v. Newport Quarries, 285 App. Div. 640, 642; 42 N. Y. Jur., Nuisances, §§ 14, 39).

I have given careful consideration to the plea of plaintiffs that an injunction should issue in this action. Although the Supreme Court has the power to grant and enforce an injunction, equity forbids its employment in this instance. The defendant's immense investment in the Hudson River Valley, its contribution to the Capital District's economy and its immediate help to the education of children in the Town of Coeymans through the payment of substantial sums in school and property taxes lead me to the conclusion that I should adhere to the often quoted words of Judge Collin in McCann v. Chasm Power Co. (211 N. Y. 301, 305): "'It is not safe to attempt to lay down any hard and fast rule for the guidance of courts of equity in determining when an injunction should issue.' [Quoting from Judge Werner's opinion in Whalen v. Union Bag & Paper Co., 208 N. Y. 1, 4.] The ownership of property will be protected unless there are other considerations which forbid, as inequitable, the remedy of the prohibitive or mandatory injunction. A court of equity can never be justified in making an inequitable decree. If the protection of a legal right even would do a plaintiff but comparatively little good and would produce great public or private hardship, equity will withhold its discreet and beneficent hand and remit the plaintiff to his legal rights and remedies." (See Forstmann v. Joray Holding Co., 244 N. Y. 22, 29-30; Howland v. Union Bag & Paper Corp., 156 Misc. 507, 515-516.) After reviewing all the evidence in this action, I find that an injunction "would produce great public ... hardship".

In awarding damages to the time of trial I am bound by precedent to grant only the loss of rental value r loss of usable value sustained. (See Uline v. New York Cent. & Hudson Riv. R. R. Co., 101 N. Y. 98; Francis v. Schoellkopf, 53 N. Y. 152, 155; Hoffman v. Edison Elec. Illuminating Co., 87 App. Div. 371, 373.) After considering the testimony of the experts called by the parties and the other evidence in this case, I find that the loss of usable value per month of each party is as follows: *1026

Oscar H. Boomer and June C. Boomer	$50
Theodore J. Richard and Miriam W. Richard	125
Avie Kinley, Martha Kinley and Mary L. Kinley	150
Kenneth R. Livengood and Dolores M. Livengood	40
Floyd W. Millious and Barbara A. Millious	40
Joseph L. Ventura and Carrie Ventura	40
James W. McCall	40
Charles J. Meilak and Angelina Meilak	50
Total	$535

In addition the plaintiffs Oscar H. Boomer and June C. Boomer are entitled to judgment against Atlantic pursuant to a stipulation made during the trial in the amount of $14,370 for damages to automobiles stored on their premises.

Since the trial of this action extended for several weeks and in order to effect a final determination, I find that the reasonable market value of each property as of September 1, 1962 (the date of the commencement of operations by Atlantic), the reasonable market value as of June 1, 1967 (the time of trial) and the permanent loss to each plaintiff, are as follows:

	Reasonable Market Value 9/1/1962	Reasonable Market Value 9/1/1962	Permanent Damage
Oscar H. Boomer and June C. Boomer	25,000	12,500	12,500
Theodore J. Richard and Miriam W. Richard			
Real Property	30,000	12,000	18,000
Business	40,000	16,000	24,000
Avie Kinley, Martha Kinley and Mary L. Kinley	140,000	70,000	70,000
Kenneth R. Livengood and Delores M. Livengood	18,000	7,000	11,000
Floyd W. Millious and Barbara A. Millious	20,000	8,000	12,000
Joseph L. Ventura and Carrie Ventura	25,000	12,500	12,500
James W. McCall	22,000	11,000	11,000
Charles J. Meilak and Angelina Meilak	26,000	12,000	14,000
Total			$185,000

In the event any plaintiff or plaintiffs and the defendant agree in writing to accept the permanent damages found herein within 30 days after the rendering of this decision with the provision that no subsequent action shall be brought by either the plaintiff or plaintiffs or any successor in title against this defendant or any successor to it, judgment for said amount with costs may be entered in said action. *1027

This decision in no way makes any findings in respect to the conduct of Atlantic in the operation of its plant between September 1, 1962 and June 1, 1967, except insofar as the plaintiffs herein are concerned. Further, I make no findings in respect to the operation by Atlantic of its plant subsequent to June 1, 1967.

All motions reserved upon the trial are denied.

Judgments for the plaintiffs as hereinbefore set forth, with costs.

2. BOOMER II

BOOMER V ATLANTIC CEMENT CO., 30 A.D.2D 480 (1968)

OSCAR H. BOOMER ET AL., APPELLANTS,

V.

ATLANTIC CEMENT COMPANY, INC., RESPONDENT. (AND FIVE OTHER ACTIONS.)

SUPREME COURT, APPELLATE DIVISION, THIRD DEPARTMENT, NEW YORK

NOVEMBER 4, 1968

CITE TITLE AS: Boomer v Atlantic Cement Co.

HEADNOTES

Torts
Nuisance
Injunctions

Application to enjoin defendant from emitting dust and other raw materials and conducting excessive blasting operations properly denied--award of damages based on loss of usable value properly applied.

() After giving due consideration to all of the relevant factors, the trial court properly refused to grant an application to enjoin defendant from emitting dust and other raw materials and conducting excessive blasting operations in such a manner as to create a nuisance. *481

() There is no ground for interfering with the trial court's award of damages based upon the loss of usable value sustained.

Boomer v. Atlantic Cement Co., 55 Misc 2d 1023, affirmed.

SUMMARY

Appeals from judgments of the Supreme Court, entered September 26, 1967 in Albany County, upon a decision of the court at a Trial Term (R. Waldron Herzberg, J.).

APPEARANCES OF COUNSEL

E. David Duncan for appellants.

Ainsworth, Sullivan, Tracy & Knauf (Thomas F. Tracy of counsel), for respondent.

OPINION OF THE COURT

Aulisi, J.

These are appeals from judgments of the Supreme Court in favor of the plaintiffs, entered September 26, 1967 in Albany County, upon a decision of the court at a Trial Term.

Involved in this appeal are eight separate actions commenced by residents of the Town of Coeymans whose homes and businesses are in the immediate vicinity of defendant's main cement plant and quarry located in the Town of Coeymans, Albany County, adjacent to U. S. Route 9W. The relief sought in these actions was an injunction restraining defendant from emitting dust and other raw materials and conducting excessive blasting operations in such a manner as to create a nuisance and the recovery of damages sustained as a result of the nuisance so created.

Despite its conclusion that the defendant in the operation of its plant had, in fact, created a nuisance with respect to plaintiffs' properties, the trial court refused to issue an injunction. In reaching its decision on the propriety of granting the injunctive relief sought, the court carefully considered, weighed and evaluated the respective equities, relative hardship and interests of the parties to this dispute and the public at large. Re-examining the record, we note the zoning of the area, the large number of persons employed by the defendant, its extensive business operations and substantial investment in plant and equipment, its use of the most modern and efficient devices to prevent offensive emissions and discharges, and its payment of substantial sums of real property and school taxes. After giving due consideration to all of these relevant factors, the trial court struck the balance in defendant's favor and we find no reason to disturb that determination.

The trial court did award damages based upon the loss of usable value sustained. Plaintiffs' contention to the contrary notwithstanding, we find no ground for interfering with either the court's determination of the proper measure of damages (see *482 Uline v. New York Cent. & Hudson Riv. R. R. Co., 101 N. Y. 98; Francis v. Schoellkopf, 53 N. Y. 152) or its application of same to the facts of this case.

The judgments should be affirmed, without costs. Herlihy, J. P., Reynolds, Staley, Jr., and Gabrielli, JJ., concur. Judgments affirmed, without costs. Copr. (C) 2019, Secretary of State, State of New York.

3. BOOMER III

BOOMER V. ATLANTIC CEMENT CO., 26 N.Y.2D 219 (1970)

OSCAR H. BOOMER ET AL., APPELLANTS,

V.

ATLANTIC CEMENT COMPANY, INC., RESPONDENT. (AND FIVE OTHER ACTIONS.)

CHARLES J. MEILAK ET AL., APPELLANTS,

V.

ATLANTIC CEMENT COMPANY, INC., RESPONDENT.

COURT OF APPEALS OF NEW YORK

ARGUED OCTOBER 31, 1969;

DECIDED MARCH 4, 1970.

HEADNOTES

Torts
Nuisance

Grant of injunction conditioned upon payment of permanent damage

Plaintiffs are entitled to enjoin operation of cement plant found to be nuisance causing damage to plaintiffs' properties--since injunction would close plant at once, court conditions injunction on payment to plaintiffs of permanent damages, with provision in judgment that acceptance of permanent damages shall be compensation for servitude on land.

() The operation of defendant's cement plant having been found to be a nuisance and to cause substantial damage to plaintiffs' properties from dirt, smoke and vibration emanating from the plant, plaintiffs are entitled to an injunction.

() The granting of an injunction would result in the closing down of defendant's plant at once. Defendant's investment in the plant exceeds $45,000,000 and over 300 people are employed. To avoid such result, the injunction should be conditioned upon the payment to plaintiffs of permanent damages which would compensate them for the total economic loss to their property present and future caused by defendant's operations. There should be a provision in the judgment that the payment by defendant and the acceptance by plaintiffs of permanent damages shall be compensation for a servitude on the land.

Boomer v. Atlantic Cement Co., 30 A D 2d 480, reversed.

Meilak v. Atlantic Cement Co., 31 A D 2d 578, reversed. See, also, 30 A D 2d 254.

SUMMARY

Appeals, by permission of the Court of Appeals, from orders of the Appellate Division of the Supreme Court in the Third Judicial Department, entered November 8, 1968 in the first above-entitled actions, and November 25, 1968 in the second above-entitled action, which unanimously affirmed judgments of the Supreme Court, entered in Albany County upon a decision of the court at a Trial Term (R. Waldron Herzberg, J.; opinion 55 Misc 2d 1023) which, in actions for (1) an injunction restraining defendant Atlantic Cement Company from emitting dust and raw materials and conducting excessive blasting in operating its plant in the Town of Coeymans, in such a manner as to constitute a nuisance upon plaintiffs' lands, buildings and equipment, and (2) damages sustained as a result of the nuisance so created, awarded damages to plaintiffs for the loss of rental or *220 usable value sustained but refused to grant the injunctive relief sought by them.

POINTS OF COUNSEL

E. David Duncan for appellants in first above-entitled actions.

I. The trial court, as well as the Appellate Division, erred as a matter of law by depriving plaintiffs of their property rights when the courts failed to grant an injunction against the nuisances created by The Atlantic Cement Company, Inc. (Campbell v. Seaman, 63 N. Y. 568; Whalen v. Union Bag & Paper Co., 208 N. Y. 1; Strobel v. Kerr Salt Co., 164 N. Y. 303; Stowers v. Gilbert, 156 N. Y. 600; Pappenheim v. Metropolitan El. Ry. Co., 128 N. Y. 436; Hulbert v. California Portland Cement Co., 161 Cal. 239; McCann v. Chasm Power Co., 211 N. Y. 301; Forstmann v. Joray Holding Co., 244 N. Y. 22; Howland v. Union Bag & Paper Corp., 156 Misc. 507; Wormser v. Brown, 149 N. Y. 163.) II. The trial court and Appellate Division in our instant cases have devised a new "economic utility doctrine", which if left unchallenged will leave in jeopardy the rights of small property owners throughout the State of New York. III. The trial court and the Appellate Division erred in their decision by leaving plaintiffs with an inadequate remedy at law, which results in a multiplicity of suits. (Campbell v. Seaman, 63 N. Y. 568; Henderson v. New York Cent. R. R. Co., 78 N. Y. 423; Madison Ave. Baptist Church v. Baptist Church in Oliver St., 73 N. Y. 82.) IV. The lower courts erroneously based their limitation on the scope of damages that could be awarded. (Uline v. New York Cent. & Hudson Riv. R. R. Co., 101 N. Y. 98; Francis v. Schoellkopf, 53 N. Y. 152; Henderson v. New York Cent. R. R. Co., 78 N. Y. 423.) V. The temporary damages granted by the trial court to plaintiffs were inadequate. (Reisert v. City of New York, 174 N. Y. 196; Bates v. Holbrook, 89 App. Div. 548; Bohan v. Port Jervis Gaslight Co., 122 N. Y.

18.) VI. The reasonable market value of the real property of plaintiffs and of the business known as the Coach House Restaurant as well as the permanent damage found by the trial court were grossly inadequate as a matter of law.

Daniel H. Prior, Jr. and John J. Biscone for appellants in second above-entitled action.I. It was error of law for the trial court and the Appellate Division to deny a permanent injunction to plaintiffs. (*221 Forstmann v. Joray Holding Co., 244 N. Y. 22; Howland v. Union Bag & Paper Corp., 156 Misc. 507; McCann v. Chasm Power Co., 211 N. Y. 301; Squaw Is. Frgt. Term. Co. v. City of Buffalo, 246 App. Div. 472; Whalen v. Union Bag & Paper Co., 208 N. Y. 1; Spano v. Perini Corp., 25 N Y 2d 11; Hay v. Cohoes Co., 2 N Y 159.) II. The trial court and the Appellate Division, by its affirmance, erroneously held that plaintiffs' damages were limited to loss of rental value. (Uline v. New York Cent. & Hudson Riv. R. R. Co., 101 N. Y. 98; Francis v. Schoellkopf, 53 N. Y. 152; Hoffman v. Edison Elec. Illuminating Co., 87 App. Div. 371; Henderson v. New York Cent. R. R. Co., 78 N. Y. 423; Kilbourne v. Board of Supervisors of Sullivan County, 137 N. Y. 170; Campbell v. Seaman, 63 N. Y. 568; Baumann v. City of New York, 180 App. Div. 498.)

Thomas F. Tracy and Frank J. Warner, Jr. for respondent.

I. The appeals should be dismissed since they do not raise any questions which are reviewable by this court. (Matter of Seagram & Sons v. Tax Comm. of City of N. Y., 14 N Y 2d 314; Bethlehem Steel Co. v. Turner Constr. Co., 2 N Y 2d 456; St. Agnes Cemetery v. State of New York, 3 N Y 2d 37; Zipprich v. Smith Trucking Co., 2 N Y 2d 177; Serano v. New York Cent. & Hudson Riv. R. R. Co., 188 N. Y. 156; Dimon v. New York Cent. & Hudson Riv. R. R. Co., 173 N. Y. 356; Flagg v. Nichols, 307 N. Y. 96; Caponigri v. Altieri, 165 N. Y. 255.) II. The trial court properly found that a permanent injunction should not be granted. (Bentley v. Empire Portland Cement Co., 48 Misc. 457; Canfield v. Quayle, 170 Misc. 621; Andrews v. Perry, 127 Misc. 320; Strobel v. Kerr Salt Co., 164 N. Y. 303; Whalen v. Union Bag & Paper Co., 208 N. Y. 1.) III. The rule of damages applied by the trial court and the Appellate Division was correct. (Uline v. New York Cent. & Hudson Riv. R. R. Co., 101 N. Y. 98; Henderson v. New York Cent. R. R. Co., 78 N. Y. 423; Williams v. New York Cent. R. R. Co., 16 N. Y. 97; Pappenheim v. Metropolitan El. Ry. Co., 128 N. Y. 436; Lynch v. Metropolitan El. Ry. Co., 129 N. Y. 274; Westphal v. City of New York, 177 N. Y. 140; Ferguson v. Village of Hamburg, 272 N. Y. 234; Jamaica Sav. Bank v. M. S. Investing Co., 274 N. Y. 215.) IV. The questions of damages, including their adequacy, was properly determined in the court below. (Fitzgerald v. New York Cent. R. R. Co., 215 App. Div. 1; *222 Jamaica Sav. Bank v. M. S. Investing Co., 274 N. Y. 215; Uline v. New York Cent. & Hudson Riv. R. R. Co., 101 N. Y. 98; Francis v. Schoellkopf, 53 N. Y. 152; Hoffman v. Edison Elec. Illuminating Co., 87 App. Div. 371; Tubiola v. Baker, 225 App. Div. 420; Matter of Sebring, 238 App. Div. 281.)

OPINION OF THE COURT
Bergan, J.

P#1: Defendant operates a large cement plant near Albany. These are actions for injunction and damages by neighboring land owners alleging injury to property from dirt, smoke and vibration emanating from the plant. A nuisance has been found after trial, temporary damages have been allowed; but an injunction has been denied. The public concern with air pollution arising from many sources in industry and in transportation is currently accorded ever wider recognition accompanied by a growing sense of responsibility in State and Federal Governments to control it. Cement plants are obvious sources of air pollution in the neighborhoods where they operate.

P#2: But there is now before the court private litigation in which individual property owners have sought specific relief from a single plant operation. The threshold question raised by the division of view on this appeal is whether the court should resolve the litigation between the parties now before it as equitably as seems possible; or whether, seeking promotion of the general public welfare, it should channel private litigation into broad public objectives.

P#3: A court performs its essential function when it decides the rights of parties before it. Its decision of private controversies may sometimes greatly affect public issues. Large questions of law are often resolved by the manner in which private litigation is decided. But this is normally an incident to the court's main function to settle controversy. It is a rare exercise of judicial power to use a decision in private litigation as a purposeful mechanism to achieve direct public objectives greatly beyond the rights and interests before the court.

P#4: Effective control of air pollution is a problem presently far from solution even with the full public and financial powers of government. In large measure adequate technical procedures are yet to be developed and some that appear possible may be economically impracticable. *223

P#5: It seems apparent that the amelioration of air pollution will depend on technical research in great depth; on a carefully balanced consideration of the economic impact of close regulation; and of the actual effect on public health. It is likely to require massive public expenditure and to demand more than any local community can accomplish and to depend on regional and interstate controls.

P#6: A court should not try to do this on its own as a by-product of private litigation and it seems manifest that the judicial establishment is neither equipped in the limited nature of any judgment it can pronounce nor prepared to lay down and implement an effective policy for the elimination of air pollution. This is an area beyond the circumference of one private lawsuit. It is a direct responsibility for government and should not thus be undertaken as an incident to solving a dispute between property owners and a single cement plant -- one of many -- in the Hudson River valley.

P#7: The cement making operations of defendant have been found by the court at Special Term to have damaged the nearby properties of plaintiffs in these two actions. That court, as it has been noted, accordingly found defendant maintained a nuisance and this has been affirmed at the Appellate Division. The total damage to plaintiffs' properties is, however, relatively small in comparison with the value of defendant's operation and with the consequences of the injunction which plaintiffs seek.

P#8: The ground for the denial of injunction, notwithstanding the finding both that there is a nuisance and that plaintiffs have been damaged substantially, is the large disparity in economic consequences of the nuisance and of the injunction. This theory cannot, however, be sustained without overruling a doctrine which has been consistently reaffirmed in several leading cases in this court and which has never been disavowed here, namely that where a nuisance has been found and where there has been any substantial damage shown by the party complaining an injunction will be granted.

P#19: The rule in New York has been that such a nuisance will be enjoined although marked disparity be shown in economic consequence between the effect of the injunction and the effect of the nuisance. *224

P#10: The problem of disparity in economic consequence was sharply in focus in Whalen v. Union Bag & Paper Co. (208 N. Y. 1). A pulp mill entailing an investment of more than a million dollars polluted a stream in which plaintiff, who owned a farm, was "a lower riparian owner". The economic loss to plaintiff from this pollution was small. This court, reversing the Appellate Division, reinstated the injunction granted by the Special Term against the argument of the mill owner that in view of "the slight advantage to plaintiff and the great loss that will be inflicted on defendant" an injunction should not be granted (p. 2). "Such a balancing of injuries cannot be justified by the circumstances of this case", Judge Werner noted (p. 4). He continued: "Although the damage to the plaintiff may be slight as compared with the defendant's expense of abating the condition, that is not a good reason for refusing an injunction" (p. 5).

P#11: Thus the unconditional injunction granted at Special Term was reinstated. The rule laid down in that case, then, is that whenever the damage resulting from a nuisance is found not "unsubstantial", viz., $100 a year, injunction would follow. This states a rule that had been followed in this court with marked consistency (McCarty v. Natural Carbonic Gas Co., 189 N. Y. 40; Strobel v. Kerr Salt Co., 164 N. Y. 303; Campbell v. Seaman, 63 N. Y. 568).

P#12: There are cases where injunction has been denied. McCann v. Chasm Power Co. (211 N. Y. 301) is one of them. There, however, the damage shown by plaintiffs was not only unsubstantial, it was non-existent. Plaintiffs owned a rocky bank of the stream in which defendant had raised the level of the water. This had no economic or other adverse consequence to plaintiffs, and thus injunctive relief was denied. Similar is the basis for denial of injunction in Forstmann v. Joray Holding Co. (244 N. Y. 22) where no benefit to plaintiffs could be seen from the injunction sought (p. 32). Thus if, within Whalen v. Union Bag & Paper Co. (supra.;) which authoritatively states the rule in New York, the damage to plaintiffs in these present cases from defendant's cement plant is "not unsubstantial", an injunction should follow.

P#13: Although the court at Special Term and the Appellate Division held that injunction should be denied, it was found that plaintiffs *225 had been damaged in various specific amounts up to the time of the trial and damages to the respective plaintiffs were awarded for those amounts. The effect of this was, injunction having been denied, plaintiffs could maintain successive actions at law for damages thereafter as further damage was incurred.

P#14: The court at Special Term also found the amount of permanent damage attributable to each plaintiff, for the guidance of the parties in the event both sides stipulated to the payment and acceptance of such permanent damage as a settlement of all the controversies among the parties. The total of permanent damages to all plaintiffs thus found was $185,000. This basis of adjustment has not resulted in any stipulation by the parties.

P#15: This result at Special Term and at the Appellate Division is a departure from a rule that has become settled; but to follow the rule literally in these cases would be to close down the plant at once. This court is fully agreed to avoid that immediately drastic remedy; the difference in view is how best to avoid it.*

- Respondent's investment in the plant is in excess of $45,000,000. There are over 300 people employed there.

P#16: One alternative is to grant the injunction but postpone its effect to a specified future date to give opportunity for technical advances to permit defendant to eliminate the nuisance; another is to grant the injunction conditioned on the payment of permanent damages to plaintiffs which would compensate them for the total economic loss to their property present and future caused by defendant's operations. For reasons which will be developed the court chooses the latter alternative.

P#17: If the injunction were to be granted unless within a short period -- e.g., 18 months -- the nuisance be abated by improved methods, there would be no assurance that any significant technical improvement would occur.

P#18: The parties could settle this private litigation at any time if defendant paid enough money and the imminent threat of closing the plant would build up the pressure on defendant. If there were no improved techniques found, there would inevitably be applications to the court at Special Term for extensions of time to perform on showing of good faith efforts to find such techniques.

P#19: Moreover, techniques to eliminate dust and other annoying by-products of cement making are unlikely to be developed by *226 any research the defendant can undertake within any short period, but will depend on the total resources of the cement industry Nationwide and throughout the world. The problem is universal wherever cement is made.

P#20: For obvious reasons the rate of the research is beyond control of defendant. If at the end of 18 months the whole industry has not found a technical solution a court would be hard put to close down this one cement plant if due regard be given to equitable principles.

P#21: On the other hand, to grant the injunction unless defendant pays plaintiffs such permanent damages as may be fixed by the court seems to do justice between the contending parties. All of the attributions of economic loss to the properties on which plaintiffs' complaints are based will have been redressed.

P#22: The nuisance complained of by these plaintiffs may have other public or private consequences, but these particular parties are the only ones who have sought remedies and the judgment proposed will fully redress them. The limitation of relief granted is a limitation only within the four corners of these actions and does not foreclose public health or other public agencies from seeking proper relief in a proper court.

P#23: It seems reasonable to think that the risk of being required to pay permanent damages to injured property owners by cement plant owners would itself be a reasonable effective spur to research for improved techniques to minimize nuisance.

P#24: The power of the court to condition on equitable grounds the continuance of an injunction on the payment of permanent damages seems undoubted. (See, e.g., the alternatives considered in McCarty v. Natural Carbonic Gas Co., supra.;, as well as Strobel v. Kerr Salt Co., supra.;.)

P#25: The damage base here suggested is consistent with the general rule in those nuisance cases where damages are allowed. "Where a nuisance is of such a permanent and unabatable character that a single recovery can be had, including the whole damage past and future resulting therefrom, there can be but one recovery" (66 C. J. S., Nuisances, § 140, p. 947). It has been said that permanent damages are allowed where the loss recoverable would obviously be small as compared with the cost of removal of the nuisance (Kentucky-Ohio Gas Co. v. Bowling, 264 Ky. 470, 477). *227

P#26: The present cases and the remedy here proposed are in a number of other respects rather similar to Northern Indiana Public Serv. Co. v. Vesey (210 Ind. 338) decided by the Supreme Court of Indiana. The gases, odors, ammonia and smoke from the Northern Indiana company's gas plant damaged the nearby Vesey greenhouse operation. An injunction and damages were sought, but an injunction was denied and the relief granted was limited to permanent damages "present, past, and future" (p. 371).

P#27: Denial of injunction was grounded on a public interest in the operation of the gas plant and on the court's conclusion "that less injury would be occasioned by requiring the appellant [Public Service] to pay the appellee [Vesey] all damages suffered by it* * * than by enjoining the operation of the gas plant; and that the maintenance and operation of the gas plant should not be enjoined" (p. 349).

P#28: The Indiana Supreme Court opinion continued: "When the trial court refused injunctive relief to the appellee upon the ground of public interest in the continuance of the gas plant, it properly retained jurisdiction of the case and awarded full compensation to the appellee. This is upon the general equitable principle that equity will give full relief in one action and prevent a multiplicity of suits" (pp. 353-354).

P#29: It was held that in this type of continuing and recurrent nuisance permanent damages were appropriate. See, also, City of Amarillo v. Ware (120 Tex. 456) where recurring overflows from a system of storm sewers were treated as the kind of nuisance for which permanent depreciation of value of affected property would be recoverable.

P#30: There is some parallel to the conditioning of an injunction on the payment of permanent damages in the noted "elevated railway cases" (Pappenheim v. Metropolitan El. Ry. Co., 128 N. Y. 436, and others which followed). Decisions in these cases were based on the finding that the railways created a nuisance as to adjacent property owners, but in lieu of enjoining their operation, the court allowed permanent damages.

P#31: Judge Finch, reviewing these cases in Ferguson v. Village of Hamburg (272 N. Y. 234, 239-240), said: "The courts decided that the plaintiffs had a valuable right which was being *228 impaired, but did not grant an absolute injunction or require the railway companies to resort to separate condemnation proceedings. Instead they held that a court of equity could ascertain the damages and grant an injunction which was not to be effective unless the defendant failed to pay the amount fixed as damages for the past and permanent injury inflicted." (See, also, Lynch v. Metropolitan El. Ry. Co., 129 N. Y. 274; Van Allen v. New York El. R. R. Co., 144 N. Y. 174; Cox v. City of New York, 265 N. Y. 411, and similarly, Westphal v. City of New York, 177 N. Y. 140.)

P#32: Thus it seems fair to both sides to grant permanent damages to plaintiffs which will terminate this private litigation. The theory of damage is the "servitude on land" of plaintiffs imposed by defendant's nuisance. (See United States v. Causby, 328 U. S. 256, 261, 262, 267, where the term "servitude" addressed to the land was used by Justice Douglas relating to the effect of airplane noise on property near an airport.)

P#33: The judgment, by allowance of permanent damages imposing a servitude on land, which is the basis of the actions, would preclude future recovery by plaintiffs or their grantees (see Northern Indiana Public Serv. Co. v. Vesey, supra.;, p. 351).

P#34: This should be placed beyond debate by a provision of the judgment that the payment by defendant and the acceptance by plaintiffs of permanent damages found by the court shall be in compensation for a servitude on the land.

P#35: Although the Trial Term has found permanent damages as a possible basis of settlement of the litigation, on remission the court should be entirely free to re-examine this subject. It may again find the permanent damage already found; or make new findings.

P#36: The orders should be reversed, without costs, and the cases remitted to Supreme Court, Albany County to grant an injunction which shall be vacated upon payment by defendant of such amounts of permanent damage to the respective plaintiffs as shall for this purpose be determined by the court.

Jasen, J. (Dissenting).

I agree with the majority that a reversal is required here, but I do not subscribe to the newly enunciated doctrine of assessment of permanent damages, in *229 lieu of an injunction, where substantial property rights have been impaired by the creation of a nuisance.

It has long been the rule in this State, as the majority acknowledges, that a nuisance which results in substantial continuing damage to neighbors must be enjoined. (Whalen v. Union Bag & Paper Co., 208 N. Y. 1; Campbell v. Seaman, 63 N. Y. 568; see, also, Kennedy v. Moog Servocontrols, 21 N Y 2d 966.) To now change the rule to permit the cement company to continue polluting the air indefinitely upon the payment of permanent damages is, in my opinion, compounding the magnitude of a very serious problem in our State and Nation today.

In recognition of this problem, the Legislature of this State has enacted the Air Pollution Control Act (Public Health Law, §§1264--1299-m) declaring that it is the State policy to require the use of all available and reasonable methods to prevent and control air pollution (Public Health Law, §1265).[1]

The harmful nature and widespread occurrence of air pollution have been extensively documented. Congressional hearings have revealed that air pollution causes substantial property damage, as well as being a contributing factor to a rising incidence of lung cancer, emphysema, bronchitis and asthma.[2]

The specific problem faced here is known as particulate contamination because of the fine dust particles emanating from defendant's cement plant. The particular type of nuisance is not new, having appeared in many cases for at least the past 60 years. (See Hulbert v. California Portland Cement Co., 161 Cal. 239 [1911].) It is interesting to note that cement production has recently been identified as a significant source of particulate contamination in the Hudson Valley.[3] This type of pollution, wherein very small particles escape and stay in the atmosphere, has been denominated as the type of air pollution *230 which produces the greatest hazard to human health.[4] We have thus a nuisance which not only is damaging to the plaintiffs,[5] but also is decidedly harmful to the general public.

I see grave dangers in overruling our long-established rule of granting an injunction where a nuisance results in substantial continuing damage. In permitting the injunction to become inoperative upon the payment of permanent damages, the majority is, in effect, licensing a continuing wrong. It is the same as saying to the cement company, you may continue to do harm to

1 See, also, Air Quality Act of 1967, 81 U. S. Stat. 485 (1967).

2 See U. S. Cong., Senate Comm. on Public Works, Special Subcomm. on Air and Water Pollution, Air Pollution 1966, 89th Cong., 2d Sess., 1966, at pp. 22-24; U. S. Cong., Senate Comm. on Public Works, Special Subcomm. on Air and Water Pollution, Air Pollution 1968, 90th Cong., 2d Sess., 1968, at pp. 850, 1084.

3 New York State Bureau of Air Pollution Control Services, Air Pollution Capital District, 1968, at p. 8.

4 J. Ludwig, Air Pollution Control Technology: Research and Development on New and Improved Systems, 33 Law & Contemp. Prob., 217, 219 (1968).

5 There are seven plaintiffs here who have been substantially damaged by the maintenance of this nuisance. The trial court found their total permanent damages to equal $185,000.

your neighbors so long as you pay a fee for it. Furthermore, once such permanent damages are assessed and paid, the incentive to alleviate the wrong would be eliminated, thereby continuing air pollution of an area without abatement.

It is true that some courts have sanctioned the remedy here proposed by the majority in a number of cases,[6] but none of the authorities relied upon by the majority are analogous to the situation before us. In those cases, the courts, in denying an injunction and awarding money damages, grounded their decision on a showing that the use to which the property was intended to be put was primarily for the public benefit. Here, on the other hand, it is clearly established that the cement company is creating a continuing air pollution nuisance primarily for its own private interest with no public benefit.

This kind of inverse condemnation (Ferguson v. Village of Hamburg, 272 N. Y. 234 may not be invoked by a private person or corporation for private gain or advantage. Inverse condemnation should only be permitted when the public is primarily served in the taking or impairment of property. (Matter of New York City Housing Auth. v. Muller, 270 N. Y. 333, 343; Pocantico Water Works Co. v. Bird, 130 N. Y. 249, 258.) The *231 promotion of the interests of the polluting cement company has, in my opinion, no public use or benefit.

Nor is it constitutionally permissible to impose servitude on land, without consent of the owner, by payment of permanent damages where the continuing impairment of the land is for a private use. (See Fifth Ave. Coach Lines v. City of New York, 11 N Y 2d 342, 347; Walker v. City of Hutchinson, 352 U. S. 112.) This is made clear by the State Constitution (art. I, § 7, subd. [a]) which provides that "[p]rivate property shall not be taken for public use without just compensation" (emphasis added). It is, of course, significant that the section makes no mention of taking for a private use.

In sum, then, by constitutional mandate as well as by judicial pronouncement, the permanent impairment of private property for private purposes is not authorized in the absence of clearly demonstrated public benefit and use.

I would enjoin the defendant cement company from continuing the discharge of dust particles upon its neighbors' properties unless, within 18 months, the cement company abated this nuisance.[7]

It is not my intention to cause the removal of the cement plant from the Albany area, but to recognize the urgency of the problem stemming from this stationary source of air pollution, and to allow the company a specified period of time to develop a means to alleviate this nuisance.

---

6 See United States v. Causby (328 U. S. 256); Kentucky-Ohio Gas Co. v. Bowling (264 Ky. 470, 477); Northern Indiana Public Serv. Co. v. Vesey (210 Ind. 338); City of Amarillo v. Ware (120 Tex. 456); Pappenheim v. Metropolitan El. Ry. Co. (128 N. Y. 436); Ferguson v. Village of Hamburg (272 N. Y. 234).

7 The issuance of an injunction to become effective in the future is not an entirely new concept. For instance, in Schwarzenbach v. Oneonta Light & Power Co. (207 N. Y. 671), an injunction against the maintenance of a dam spilling water on plaintiff's property was issued to become effective one year hence.

I am aware that the trial court found that the most modern dust control devices available have been installed in defendant's plant, but, I submit, this does not mean that better and more effective dust control devices could not be developed within the time allowed to abate the pollution.

Moreover, I believe it is incumbent upon the defendant to develop such devices, since the cement company, at the time the plant commenced production (1962), was well aware of the plaintiffs' presence in the area, as well as the probable consequences of its contemplated operation. Yet, it still chose to build and operate the plant at this site. *232

In a day when there is a growing concern for clean air, highly developed industry should not expect acquiescence by the courts, but should, instead, plan its operations to eliminate contamination of our air and damage to its neighbors.

Accordingly, the orders of the Appellate Division, insofar as they denied the injunction, should be reversed, and the actions remitted to Supreme Court, Albany County to grant an injunction to take effect 18 months hence, unless the nuisance is abated by improved techniques prior to said date.

Chief Judge Fuld and Judges Burke and Scileppi concur with Judge Bergan; Judge Jasen dissents in part and votes to reverse in a separate opinion; Judges Breitel and Gibson taking no part.

In each action: Order reversed, without costs, and the case remitted to Supreme Court, Albany County, for further proceedings in accordance with the opinion herein.

Chapter 7 – Learning to Brief a Case: Whalen v. The Union Bag and Paper Co.

An important skill in legal research is learning how to read a case. You read a case to understand what the judge wanted to say. The best way to read a case is to learn its structure through a process that is called "case briefing."

Case briefs can be written in a variety of different formats, but their purpose is the same. Briefs allow you to outline the important aspects of a case. As we go through the format and procedure of briefing a case, follow along with the sample brief provided after this section. We will use the following format to brief *Whalen v. Union Bag Paper Co.*, 208 N.Y. 1 (1913), referred below as WHALEN:

1. Heading
2. Facts
3. Procedural History
4. Legal Issues
5. Holding or Decision
6. Reasoning
7. Dissenting Opinions

After reading the court's opinion, you can then go back and sort the information in it into these seven categories. As stated above, the heading identifies the parties involved in the case. For your brief, identify the plaintiff, defendant, and court in which the case is being heard. Also, include the full citation of the case and any parallel citations as well as the authoring judge.

In the *Facts* section, summarize the facts of the case as stated in the opinion. Only include facts relevant to the legal reasoning and decision of the case. Superfluous facts will not help you to understand the legal issues of the case. This section should include a statement of why the plaintiff has brought action against the defendant and what remedies they seek.

In the *Procedural History* section, note the disposition of any prior proceedings and how the case reached its present court. For example, if the case is before the U.S. Supreme Court, was the case appealed as of right or did the Supreme Court grant a writ of certiorari to review the lower courts' decisions? Include decisions from lower courts such as trial and appellate courts. This will be important to understand the present court's decision as it relates to previous lower court decisions.

In the *Legal Issues* section, *Legal Issues* should be phrased as a specific question that requires a "yes" or a "no" answer. The *Legal Issues* are the key questions which the court must answer in order to reach its decision on the case. Sometimes the court itself explicitly sets forth the legal issues it will address in its opinion. Other times the legal issues must be discerned from the main points that the court addresses in reaching its decision.

In the *Holding* or *Decision* section, give the factually specific answer to the *Legal Issues* question.

In the *Reasoning* section, provide the court's rationale for the decision reached. Did the court found its decision on older legal principles, i.e., previously established good law, or did it create new legal principles? How did this case transform existing law in this jurisdiction? Remember that dicta in a judicial opinion are statements that are irrelevant for the holding.

In the *Dissenting Opinions* section, discuss the alternative views on this case provided by other members of the court.

The first case that you will brief is *Whalen v. The Union Bag and Paper Co.* Find it on the Companion Website, or at the end of this chapter, and read it. Before you begin to brief, it is important to understand all of its components and where they came from. To begin, our case heading clearly identifies the Appellant, Whalen, and the Respondent, The Union Bag and Paper Company. The Appellant is the party who lost in the previous round and who is now bringing the case to the appellate court. This means that the appellant is not necessarily the original plaintiff and the respondent is not necessarily the original defendant. Many times, the words "Appellant" and "Respondent" will not appear in the heading of the case, but the Appellant is the party whose name is listed on the left side of the "v." and the Respondent's name is listed on the right. Sometimes there are multiple appellants and respondents.

On our Companion Website and at the end of this chapter we include the official version of WHALEN, structured by paragraph numbers. Start reading it. In reading the Opinion section of WHALEN, it is important to note that not all Opinion sections will follow the same format. Sometimes sections within the Opinion will be labeled, such as a "Facts" section, and many times the Opinion section will be much longer than in *Whalen.* Opinions can also contain errors—either by the court or the reporter. It is important to cite these followed by [*sic*] to indicate the mistake is within the text being cited.

There are no *concurring* nor *dissenting* opinions in WHALEN. A concurring opinion is one that agrees with the majority's decision in the case but does so for reasons that differ from those given by the majority. WHALEN was decided over one hundred years ago in 1913. Since that time, it has been cited in over 30 cases. By using *Lexis*' Shepardizing system or *Westlaw*'s citator, KeyCite, you can find all cases in which WHALEN has been mentioned. Additionally, both of these case citators will indicate whether citing references have followed, distinguished, or overturned a specific case.

Based upon the above, let's read the case again and brief it as shown below.

WHALEN V. UNION BAG & PAPER CO., 208 N.Y. 1. (N.Y, 1913): A CASE BRIEF

Heading

1. Heading. *Robert E. Whalen, v. The Union Bag and Paper Co.*, 208 N.Y. 1 (NY, 1913)

   b. Plaintiff: Robert E. Whalen

   c. Defendant: The Union Bag and Paper Company

   d. Court: Court of Appeals of New York

After the summary sections or syllabus, the attorneys and judges are listed. Sometimes these sections will also include an Issue Statement. In *Whalen*, an Issue Statement is given for each party. In some cases, an Issue Statement may appear after the judges are named. This statement summarizes what issues the court had to decide. Counsel is listed first for the Appellant and then for the Respondent. The judges are listed first as all of the judges that tried the case followed by the judge (or judges) that wrote the opinion.

The following section is the *Opinion*. In this section, the court briefly presents the case, discusses the applicability of precedents and persuasive authority, and arrives at a decision.

Facts

2. Facts. Riparian owner *Robert E. Whalen* started an action against the *Union Bag and Paper Company* to restrain the defendant from continuing to pollute the stream.

In WHALEN, the first and the third paragraph of the Opinion (P#1 & #3) summarize the facts of the case. These facts have been previously tried in court and are not now being debated. The facts are given only at a level of detail necessary for the reader to follow the legal reasoning of the court. The plaintiff is a lower riparian owner upon Kayaderosseras Creek in Saratoga County. He owns a farm of two hundred-and-fifty-five acres, while the defendant conducts a business in which it has invested a large sum of money and employs great numbers of the inhabitants of the locality.

> The plaintiff owns and operates on this stream a pulp mill a few miles above plaintiff's land. This mill represents an investment of more than a million dollars and gives employment to 400 or 500 operatives. It discharges into the waters of the creek large quantities of a liquid effluent containing sulphurous acid, lime, sulphur, and waste material consisting of pulp wood, sawdust, slivers, knots, gums, resins and fibre. The pollution thus created, together with the discharge from other industries located along the stream and its principal tributary, has greatly diminished the purity of the water. 208 N.Y. at 2.

Procedural History

3. Procedural History. This is an appeal by the plaintiff from the Appellate Division of the Supreme Court in the Third Judicial Department (New York). The Appellate Court had amended the trial court's decision and reversed the grant of an injunction.

The second paragraph in WHALEN (P#2) contains some of the procedural history of the case. This paragraph presents the previous findings from the trial court and Appellate Division. It also states the plaintiff's reasoning for appealing the lower courts' decisions.

Legal Issues

4. Legal Issues. One of the main issues in this case is:

Shall injunction granting depend on who suffers a greater injury once their injuries are balanced?

All paragraphs from three through eight (P#3-8) delve into the issue at hand and the court's reasoning in deciding this case. It becomes apparent that the court has a holistic or dialectical approach to this complex problem. In briefing the case, often you choose one issue which will be the practical reason for which you read that particular case. We chose this issue because for over 50 years, WHALEN represented the New York Law regarding the principle of granting an injunction when both parties are faced with injuries from the nuisance: the plaintiff continues to be injured if the nuisance continues and the defendant starts to be injured if the nuisance-causing industrial activity ceases.

Holding or Decision

5. Holding or Decision. The court decided:

Shall injunction granting depend on who suffers a greater injury once their injuries are balanced? **No, an injunction cannot be denied if nuisance is found just because when balancing the injuries, the defendant's would be larger than the plaintiff's.**

The decision is reached in paragraphs 9 and 10.

Reasoning or Dicta

6. Reasoning or Dicta

In its reasoning, the court relies on a precedent, *Weston Paper Co. v. Pope.* In *Weston,* the court reasoned that the large monetary value of the plant should not allow the defendant to escape the consequences of polluting a stream. The slight injury to the plaintiff in comparison to the large expense the injunction would impose on the defendant is not sufficient reason to deny injunction. The court reasons that the balancing of injuries could not be used as the ultimate standard to determine the granting of injunction, followed to its logical conclusion, "it would deprive the poor litigant of his little property by giving it to those already rich."

The court explores this issue in each paragraph. For instance, the third paragraph discusses balancing the equities and if the defendant's cost of complying with the injunction is greater than the cost of the harm to the plaintiff, the injunction is denied. An injunction is a legal order to stop a certain activity. In this case, the plaintiff, a farm owner, sought to stop the defendant, Union Bag and Paper Company, from polluting a stream running through his property with chemicals and debris from the operation of its paper mill. Here, the damage caused to the farmer's property was small compared to the cost to the paper mill of abating the pollution. The court cites two cases (*Strobel v. Kerr Salt Co.* and *Sammons v. City of Gloversville*) and distances itself from their holdings because "such a balancing of injuries cannot be justified by the circumstances of this case." The fourth paragraph covers *Weston Paper Co. v. Pope,* which the court uses by *analogy* to decide the case *at bar*, meaning the case presently before the court. The sixth paragraph briefly states the court's agreement with the case cited above in the fifth paragraph and its application in the present case.

Dissenting Opinion

7. Dissenting Opinions: None.

WHALEN, 208 N.Y. 1 (1913)

ROBERT E. WHALEN, APPELLANT,

V.

THE UNION BAG AND PAPER COMPANY, RESPONDENT.

COURT OF APPEALS OF NEW YORK.

ARGUED MARCH 5, 1913.

DECIDED MARCH 25, 1913.

CITE TITLE AS: Whalen v Union Bag & Paper Co.

***1 Nuisance**

Injunction -- Pollution of a stream -- When injunction cannot be denied because injury to plaintiff is small as compared with loss to defendant caused by injunction

1. Where the evidence in an action for an injunction clearly establishes an unlawful invasion of plaintiff's rights by the defendant an injunction cannot be denied because the actual damage to the plaintiff from the continuance of the alleged wrong will be slight as compared with the defendant's expense of abating the condition.

2. Where in an action by the owner of a farm against a large and important paper manufacturing company for an injunction to restrain the defendant from continuing to pollute the waters of a stream running through his farm, the facts proved and found establish a clear case of pollution of the stream by the discharge therein of large quantities of noxious and destructive chemicals, pulp wood, sawdust and other refuse, and that the use and value of plaintiff's farm have been and are injuriously affected thereby, it is error for the Appellate Division to reverse the injunction granted by the trial court, because of the great loss likely to be inflicted on the defendant by the injunction as compared with the small injury caused to the plaintiff's land by that portion of the pollution which was regarded as attributable to the defendant. Such a balancing of injuries cannot be justified by the circumstances of the case.

Whalen v. Union Bag & Paper Co., 145 App. Div. 1,modified.

*2 APPEAL from a judgment of the Appellate Division of the Supreme Court in the third judicial department, entered May 26, 1911, modifying and affirming as modified a judgment in favor of plaintiff entered upon a decision of the court on trial at Special Term.

The nature of the action and the facts, so far as material, are stated in the opinion.

Robert E. Whalen, appellant, in person. Upon the Special Term's findings of fact, modified only as to the quantum of money damages, plaintiff is entitled to a permanent injunction as matter of law. (Strobel v. Kerr Salt Co., 164 N. Y. 303; Gardner v. Village of Newburgh, 2 Johns. Ch. 162; Corning v. T. I. & N. Co., 40 N. Y. 191; Chapman v. City of Rochester, 110 N. Y. 273; Moody v. Village of Saratoga Springs, 17 App. Div. 207; 163 N. Y. 581; Butler v. Village of White Plains, 59 App. Div. 30; Sammons v. City of Gloversville, 34 Misc. Rep. 459; 175 N. Y. 346; Warren v. City of Gloversville, 81 App. Div. 291; Sammons v. City of Gloversville, 81 App. Div. 332; Pendorf v. City of Rome, 203 N. Y. 645.)

J. S. L'Amoreaux and *James Boyd Potter* for respondent. The granting of injunctive relief is discretionary. (Loukes v. Payne, 140 App. Div. 777; Gray v. M. R. Co., 120 N. Y. 499; Knoth v. Manhattan R. Co., 187 N. Y. 243; McClure v. Leaycroft, 183 N. Y. 41; Thomas v. M. M. P. Union, 121 N. Y. 45.) In view of the slight advantage to plaintiff and the great loss that will be inflicted on defendant, equity requires the denial of injunctive relief. (Genet v. D. & H. C. Co., 122 N. Y. 505; People v. Canal Board, 55 N. Y. 390; 2 Farnham on Waters & Water Rights, 1691, 1709, 1710; Claude v. Weir, 4 Mont. 197; People v. Transit Dev. Co., 115 N. Y. Supp. 304; McCarthy v. B. H. Mining Co., 164 Fed. Rep. 940; Bliss v. Anaconda Mining Co., 167 Fed. Rep. 371; Health Dept. v. Purdon, 99 N. Y. 237; Townsend v. Bell, 167 N. Y. 462; *3 Penrhyn v. Granville, 181 N. Y. 80; Knoth v. Manhattan R. Co., 187 N. Y. 243; McCarty v. Gas Co., 189 N. Y. 40; Riedman v. Light Co., 56 App. Div. 23; Bentley v. Cement Co., 48 Misc. Rep. 457.)

WERNER, J.

P#1: The plaintiff is a lower riparian owner upon Kayaderosseras creek in Saratoga county, and the defendant owns and operates on this stream a pulp mill a few miles above plaintiff's land. This mill represents an investment of more than a million dollars and gives employment to 400 or 500 operatives. It discharges into the waters of the creek large quantities of a liquid effluent containing sulphurous acid, lime, sulphur, and waste material consisting of pulp wood, sawdust, slivers, knots, gums, resins and fibre. The pollution thus created, together with the discharge from other industries located along the stream and its principal tributary, has greatly diminished the purity of the water.

P#2: The plaintiff brought this action to restrain the defendant from continuing to pollute the stream. The trial court granted an injunction to take effect one year after the final affirmance of its decision upon appeal, and awarded damages at the rate of $312 a year. The Appellate Division reversed the judgment of the Special Term upon the law and facts, unless the plaintiff should consent to a reduction of damages to the sum of $100 a year, in which event the judgment as modified should be affirmed, and eliminated that part of the trial court's decree granting an injunction. The plaintiff thereupon stipulated for a reduction of damages, and then appealed to this court from the modified judgment. The facts found by the trial court--which do not appear to have been disturbed by the Appellate Division--establish a clear case of wrongful pollution of the stream, and need not be set forth in detail.

P#3: The plaintiff is the owner of a farm of two hundred and fifty-five acres, and the trial court has found that its ***4** use and value have been injuriously affected by the pollution of the stream caused by the defendant. The defendant conducts a business in which it has invested a large sum of money and employs great numbers of the inhabitants of the locality. We have recently gone over the law applicable to cases of this character (Strobel v. Kerr Salt Co., 164 N. Y. 303; Sammons *v. City of Gloversville,* 175 id. 346), and it is unnecessary now to restate it. The majority of the learned court below reduced the damages suffered by the plaintiff to $100 a year, and reversed that portion of the decree of the trial court which awarded an injunction. The setting aside of the injunction was apparently induced by a consideration of the great loss likely to be inflicted on the defendant by the granting of the injunction as compared with the small injury done to the plaintiff's land by that portion of the pollution which was regarded as attributable to the defendant. Such a balancing of injuries cannot be justified by the circumstances of this case. It is not safe to attempt to lay down any hard and fast rule for the guidance of courts of equity in determining when an injunction shall issue. As Judge Story said: 'It is impossible to foresee all the exigencies of society which may require their aid and assistance to protect rights or redress wrongs.' (2 Story's Eq. Juris. [10th ed.] § 959b.)

P#4: One of the troublesome phases of this kind of litigation is the difficulty of deciding when an injunction shall issue in a case where the evidence clearly establishes an unlawful invasion of a plaintiff's rights, but his actual injury from the continuance of the alleged wrong will be small as compared with the great loss which will be caused by the issuance of the injunction.

P#5: This appeal has been presented as though that question were involved in the case at bar, but we take a different view. Even as reduced at the Appellate Division, the damages to the plaintiff's farm amount to $100 a year. It can hardly be said that this injury is unsubstantial, even if we should ***5** leave out of consideration the peculiarly noxious character of the pollution of which the plaintiff complains.

P#6: The waste from the defendant's mill is very destructive both to vegetable and animal life and tends to deprive the waters with which it is mixed of their purifying qualities. It should be borne in mind also that there is no claim on the part of the defendant that the nuisance may become less injurious in the future.

P#7: Although the damage to the plaintiff may be slight as compared with the defendant's expense of abating the condition, that is not a good reason for refusing an injunction. Neither courts of equity nor law can be guided by such a rule, for if followed to its logical conclusion it would deprive the poor litigant of his little property by giving it to those already rich. It is always to be remembered in such cases that 'denying the injunction puts the hardship on the party in whose favor the legal right exists instead of on the wrongdoer.' (Pomeroy's Eq. Juris. vol. 5, § 530.)

P#8: In speaking of the injustice which sometimes results from the balancing of injuries between parties, the learned author from whom we have just quoted, sums up the discussion by saying: 'The weight of authority is against allowing a balancing of injury as a means of determining the propriety of issuing an injunction.' To the same effect is the decision in Weston Paper Co. v. Pope (155 Ind. 394). 'The fact that the appellant has expended a large sum of money in the construction of its plant and that it conducts its business in a careful manner and without malice can make no difference in its rights to the stream. Before locating the plant the owners were bound to know that every riparian proprietor is entitled to have the waters of the stream that washes his land come to it without obstruction, diversion or corruption, subject only to the reasonable use of the water, by those similarly entitled, for such domestic purposes as are inseparable from and necessary for the free use of their land; and they were bound also to know the character of their proposed business, and to ***6** take notice of the size, course, and capacity of the stream, and to determine for themselves at their own peril whether they should be able to conduct their business upon a stream of the size and character of Brandywine creek without injury to their neighbors; and the magnitude of their investment and their freedom from malice furnish no reason why they should escape the consequences of their own folly.'

P#9: This language very aptly expresses the rule which we think should be applied to the case at bar.

P#10: The judgment of the Appellate Division, in so far as it denied the injunction, should be reversed and the judgment of the Special Term in that respect reinstated, with costs to the appellant.

CULLEN, Ch. J., GRAY, WILLARD BARTLETT, CHASE, COLLIN and HOGAN, JJ., concur.

Judgment accordingly.

Chapter 8 – Case Studies in Common Law Environmental Torts

This chapter continues the explanation of the creation of environmental law on a case by case basis. It begins with a discussion and analysis of *Village of Wilsonville v. SCA Services*, 86 Ill.2d 1 (Ill. 1981), then it continues with *Spur Industries, Inc. v. Del E. Webb*, 108 Ariz. 178 (Ariz., 1972). The next two case studies focus on *Borland v. Sanders Lead Co.*, 369 So.2d 523 (Ala., 1979), and *Branch v. Petroleum, Inc.* 657 P.2d 267 (Utah, 1982). Each case covers a civil wrong, whose elements are established by the governing state law, which made the results highly unpredictable. The cases were litigated in the 1970s and early 1980s, which corresponds to the statutory creation of environmental law as a federal area of law. This change from state common law to federal law has made the application of the law more uniform and has streamlined the procedural demands upon plaintiffs.

CASE STUDY I: VILLAGE OF WILSONVILLE V. SCA SERVICES, 86 ILL.2D 1 (ILL. 1981)

Public nuisance is the unreasonable or unlawful use of one's property that causes unreasonable interference in rights common to the public, such as health and safety, or in the free passage or use of public rights such as public parks, beaches, roads, and streams. Public nuisance may also include behavior that offends the senses and violates principles of decency. SCA Services legally constructed and operated a toxic waste dump in Wilsonville. The twist, in this case, is that the lawsuit claims that the toxic waste dump constitutes a prospective public nuisance; that is, a nuisance that has not yet occurred but, as the plaintiff, the Village of Wilsonville claims, a nuisance that is substantially certain to occur. Two factors are considered when calculating risk: a) the magnitude of the harm or damage caused by an event or act and b) the probability that this event or act will occur. What is the nature of this possible future nuisance? What is the risk? Indeed, what level of harm and what probability of that harm occurring must be shown in order to be granted equitable relief in the form of an injunction? It is important for environmentalists and lawyers alike to appreciate the power of environmental tort actions. Even today when many environmental harms are adjudicated and/or remedied by enforcement of relevant statutes and regulations, environmental torts allow plaintiffs injured by these environmental harms to maintain their cause of action and to sue, recover damages, and seek equitable relief.

Note the location of the Village of Wilsonville on the maps in Study Questions for *Wilsonville*, available at the end of this chapter and on the Companion Website. You will see that Wilsonville is situated in southern Illinois, northeast of St. Louis. Read the *Wilsonville* opinion, which is printed in this chapter after the *Study Questions*, and in the *Companion*. As you read, notice the paragraph numbering, color code the paragraphs, if that helps you organize the information, and focus on how the material in each paragraph fits into one of the rubrics for a brief as indicated below. The brief structure below is the same as in *Boomer*, and *Whalen*.

1. Heading
2. Facts
3. Procedural History
4. Legal Issues
5. Holding or Decision
6. Reasoning
7. Dissenting Opinions

Heading

The heading is based on the citation: *Village of Wilsonville v. SCA Services*, 86 Ill.2d 1 (Ill. 1981). The formatting is similar to the example we offered in *Whalen* and *Boomer*.

Facts

Paragraphs 1-21 are devoted to the facts of this case. The court notes that "the record in this matter is over 13,000 pages long." As we shall see, scientific evidence and expert testimony play a key role in this case. Indeed, there is an abundance of facts. Many of these facts are repeated and expanded upon later in the opinion. But which facts are central to the holding and reasoning?

The level of danger can be assessed from facts presented in paragraphs 32, 39, and 49-50. Here we learn that the chemical waste disposal site consists of seven trenches (each about 15 feet deep, 30 feet wide, and 250-350 feet long). 95% of the chemical waste deposited into these trenches is contained in 55-gallon steel drums with the remainder deposited in double-wall paper bags. We also learn that the waste deposited in these trenches consists of "polychlorinated biphenyls (PCBs), a neurotoxic, possibly carcinogenic chemical which has been illegal to produce in this country since 1979....." as well as "cyanide.... paint sludge, asbestos, pesticides, mercury, and arsenic." The plaintiffs' attorneys and expert witnesses convinced the jury that "considerable evidence was adduced to show that these and other substances deposited at the site are extremely toxic to human beings." Paragraph 60 states that: "[t] here was considerable testimony that trucks carrying the waste materials to the disposal site via Wilson Avenue, the main street of the Village, sometimes spilled toxic liquids onto the street. The evidence is undisputed, both from the defendant's receiving reports and testimony from IEPA (Illinois Environmental Protection Agency) inspectors, that many drums arrived on the site leaking waste materials." Furthermore, in paragraph 35, "defendant's own site manager testified that the 55-gallon drums and paper bags used to transport the materials to the site were not intended to and would not contain the materials forever. There was evidence in fact that several of the drums were rusting, leaking, and spilling when they arrived at the site and that others were rolled over the edge of the tranches." In addition to the fact that the wastes were presently leaking, the 55-gallon drums and paper bags were never meant to be a permanent barrier, and the wastes are toxic to humans. Paragraph 7 indicates another potential for future harm: the active use of the groundwater resource by local residents from springs and 73 nearby wells.

The probability of the danger occurring can be understood from paragraphs 52, 53, and 55. Here, we learn that the toxic waste dump sits 300 feet above an abandoned coal mine. The coal was mined using the room and pillar method (see the images and diagrams in the Study Questions for *Wilsonville* on the Companion Website, http://www.environmentallaw-teach.org/). Expert witness testimony indicated that the earth would eventually crack and collapse due to the empty space left behind by the "room and pillar" method of mining. Subsidence produces fractures or cracks in the overlying soil and sediment and underlying rock. Dr. Augenbaugh, one of the expert witnesses who testified at trial, provided evidence (photos and interviews with farmers) of actual subsidence on properties near the toxic waste trenches. These cracks provide a "pipeline" for fluids to migrate. In paragraph 15 of the opinion, Dr. Augenbaugh even describes an experiment demonstrating the rapid movement of liquids into and through these fractures. In paragraph 16 Mr. Glover, a mining engineer, testifies that "subsidence can be expected to appear, on the average, about 40 years after a mine closed down" and that "there is a possibility of subsidence wherever coal is mined and underground support is removed."

Procedural History

Paragraphs 1 and 2 provide a summary of Wilsonville's procedural history. The Village of Wilsonville filed a complaint in April of 1977 in the circuit court of Macoupin County, Illinois, a local trial court. The "gravamen" or main point of the complaint was that the "defendant's chemical-waste-disposal site presents a public nuisance and a hazard to the health of the citizens of the village, the county, and the State." The complaint seeks injunctive relief as a remedy;

that is, the closing and cleanup of the site, but the village does not seek damages. "Leave to intervene" means that, although the county and the County Farm Bureau were not part of the original complaint, they were granted the right to join the lawsuit (and file a complaint of their own) because the county and the County Farm Bureau's rights would be sufficiently affected by the prospective nuisance. Eventually and remarkably, they were joined by the State of Illinois. Ultimately, for efficiency's sake, all of these actions were consolidated. The opinion, therefore, considers the prospective harm to the "citizens of the village, the county, and the State." In August of 1978, the trial court concluded that the hazardous chemical waste landfill constituted a public nuisance and issued both a permanent injunction (to cease operation of the landfill) as well as a mandatory injunction (requiring the cleanup and restoration of the site). The defendant appealed, and the Appellate Court for the Fourth District affirmed. The Supreme Court of Illinois also accepted the defendant's appeal and also affirmed the lower court's decision. In paragraph 23, the court concludes that "the evidence in this case sufficiently establishes by a preponderance of the evidence that the chemical-waste-disposal site is a nuisance both presently and prospectively."

Legal Issues

What level of future danger or hazard and what level of probability of this hazard occurring must be present in order to enjoin a prospective nuisance? Have these been met here?

Holding

The court concluded that the evidence in this case sufficiently establishes by a preponderance of the evidence that the chemical-waste-disposal site is a nuisance both presently and prospectively.

Reasoning

While the opinion refers to a public nuisance which consists of spillage of leaking chemicals, odors from the same as well as dust from the trucks hauling the waste, the court does not wish to "belabor this point" since the plaintiffs have not asked for a remedy for this present nuisance. The issue at hand involves the prospective nuisance. Thus, it may seem to you somewhat odd that a prospective or a potential future nuisance (which is the main legal issue in this case) is explicitly mentioned here and in the previous paragraph for the first time.

Quite often courts would start their reasoning by stating the applicable law. In this instance, the court explains the standard, or the test that the Illinois Supreme Court applied in order to determine whether a person is liable for a prospective nuisance. Unfortunately, this is not discussed until much later in the opinion. Paragraphs 51-53 begin with the defendant arguing that the decisions of the lower courts were incorrect because "they failed to require a showing of a substantial risk of certain and extreme future harm before enjoining operation of the defendant's site." According to the defendant, the prospective harm must be "extreme" and the probability of it happening must be "certain." The court responds by stating that the defendants "argue that the trial court did not follow the proper standard for determining when a prospective nuisance may be enjoined. The defendant argues that the proper standard to be used is that an injunction is proper only if there is a 'dangerous probability' that the threatened or potential injury will occur." The court distinguished between the defendant's *extreme* and *certain* requirements by stating that "we agree with the defendant's statement of the law, but not with its urged application to the facts of this case." Using a treatise, a secondary legal authority (Prosser's Law of Torts, 4th ed.), the court quotes "[t]he defendant may be restrained from entering upon an activity where it is highly probable that it will lead to a nuisance, although if the possibility is merely uncertain or contingent he may be left to his remedy after the nuisance has occurred." The court then cites as authority in Illinois, an intermediate appellate court decision and one of its own prior decisions in support of using the *highly probable principle*. Paragraph 55 begins by applying this principle with the statement "[i]n this case there can be no doubt but that it is highly probable that the chemical waste disposal site will bring about a substantial injury." It needs to be emphasized that this application of the "dangerous probability" standard is used only in fashioning a verdict. The trial court judge presumably instructed the jury about the "dangerous probability" test in its determination of liability.

The legal question can now be posed, and with this, it will now be possible to review the facts presented and to weigh their relevance to the holding and reasoning.

What level of future danger or hazard and what level of probability of this hazard occurring must be present in order to enjoin a prospective nuisance?

In applying the *dangerous probability* test to determine if a prospective nuisance exists, we see that there is a substantial risk of movement of toxic waste through underground fractures that contaminates the groundwater resource. The probability of this harm occurring is nearly certain because the dump sits on top of an abandoned coal mine. Thus, the jury finds by the preponderance of the evidence that the standard is met, and SCA Services is found liable for a prospective nuisance. The remedy (after balancing the equities) is a permanent injunction—closing the facility—and a mandatory injunction—requiring the removal of all wastes and restoration of the site to its original condition.

No Dissenting Opinion, but There Is a Concurring Opinion

Justice Ryan's concurring opinion reinforces the significance of this case, that is, the standard for the dangerous probability test and its use in determining if a prospective nuisance exists. At the end he states "[a]lthough the "dangerous probability" test has certainly been met in this case, I would be willing to enjoin the activity on a showing of probability of occurrence substantially less than that which the facts presented to this court reveal, due to the extremely hazardous nature of the chemicals being dumped and the potentially catastrophic results." *Wilsonville* is a classic example of judicial line drawing. What risk is acceptable? How high must the probability of the occurrence of a prospective event be and how dangerous must the resulting harm be to pass the dangerous probability test? We have one example here in *Wilsonville.* One Illinois Supreme Court judge has indicated that the risk could be substantially lower and still, in his view, be enjoined.

Multiplicity of Legal Issues Raised in Wilsonville

It is quite often that parties raise a multiplicity of legal issues during litigation. In *Wilsonville,* almost all of the essential information summarized above can be gleaned from the first 21 paragraphs of the opinion; but there is much more that needs to be discussed. In paragraph 22, the court summarizes the issues that have been raised by the defendant on appeal. While this is largely a laundry list of complaints, the defense hopes that something will stick. Rather than simply dismiss these issues the court discusses each issue fully in order to buttress its final decision.

The defendant has raised several issues on appeal:

> (1) whether the finding of the circuit and appellate courts that the waste-disposal site is a prospective nuisance is contrary to the manifest weight of the evidence;
> (2) whether those courts applied the wrong legal standard in finding that the waste-disposal site constitutes a prospective nuisance;
> (3) whether the circuit and appellate courts erred in failing to balance the equities, either in finding a prospective nuisance or in fashioning relief;
> (4) whether the courts erred in failing to defer to, or to otherwise weigh, the role of the IEPA, the United States Environmental Protection Agency (USEPA), and the Illinois State Geological Survey (ISGS);
> (5) whether the courts erred in finding that plaintiffs have no adequate remedy at law;
> (6) whether the courts erred in ordering a mandatory injunction; and, finally,
> (7) whether the courts' decisions constituted a taking of property without due process of law. (Wilsonville, 86 Ill.2d at 14).

Each of these issues is discussed in the paragraphs that follow. The question is, in part, what paragraph deals with what issue.

In preparation for a full discussion of issue #1, paragraph 22 (previously quoted) emphasizes the sufficiency of the "evidence" for the finding of a prospective nuisance. But there is a digression, irrelevant to the holding in this case, about the fact that there is also a present nuisance, i.e., that the "spillage from improperly contained chemical waste, the odors, and the dust created by the site constitute a present interference with the right of the plaintiffs to enjoy and use their property." Clearly, the local residents have a cause of action in private nuisance much like the plaintiffs in *Boomer.* As we will see later, the residents do indeed sue SCA Services in private nuisance for damages.

Paragraph 23 of the opinion informs us that the defendant argued that "there are three areas where....the trial court made erroneous findings of fact." See #1 above. If this were the case, then the finding of liability would be "contrary to the manifest weight of the evidence" and would be overturned. The three areas in which the trial court made erroneous findings of fact are: 1a) the possibilities of "explosive interaction," 1b) soil permeability, and 1c) migration of chemical waste from the trenches via fractures due to subsidence.

Paragraph 24 of the opinion states that "while the defendant vigorously challenged the evidence," they have not "overcome the natural and logical conclusions which could be drawn from the evidence." And, "findings of fact made by the trial court will not be set aside unless they are contrary to the manifest weight of the evidence." So, with this quick summary that the defendant's claims are going nowhere, the court then debunks the claims that the trial court made erroneous findings of fact that now follows a long discussion debunking each of the three claims above.

Paragraphs 25-29 and 33-34 of the opinion address the issue of the "explosive interaction" (#1a above) and the qualifications of the expert witnesses who testified on this issue. In its "motion to strike," the defense wants the testimony of Dr. Zahalsky and Dr. Hall thrown out because the defendants claim that these witnesses weren't qualified. The court rejects this argument. Further, their testimony that interactions of the chemicals disposed of at the site could produce fires and explosions was considered by the court as entirely relevant.

The qualifications of Doctors Zahalsky and Hall are described in paragraphs 25 and 26 of the opinion. In paragraphs 29-30, the testimony of Dr. Harbison, the defendant's expert witness, was "discounted" by the court for being "erroneous" in part as well as not supported by the evidence. Thus, "the trial court's findings.... are amply supported by the manifest weight of the evidence."

The court discusses the issue of soil permeability (#1b) in paragraph 31 of the opinion. Both plaintiff's and defendant's expert witnesses testified about the significant permeability of the soil and, thus, "the trial court was correct in finding that the permeable nature of the soil.... poses a threat of migration of chemical waste away from the disposal site."

The issue of migration of chemical wastes via subsidence related fractures (issue #1c) is discussed in paragraphs 32 and 33 of the opinion. The trial court found that "subsidence warrants closing of the site." Subsidence is, as we have learned, unavoidable because the waste disposal site sits on top of a former coal mine. The Supreme Court of Illinois found Dr. Augenbaugh's testimony and photographs (discussed in paragraphs 14 and 4) compelling.

Again, the trial court was upheld.

Paragraphs 35 and 55 were already discussed concerning the possibility of "explosive interactions." Paragraphs 37 and 62 further discuss the spillage, dust, and odors which eventually led to a private nuisance tort as in *Boomer.* Paragraph 38 contains a discussion of private and public nuisance, already discussed at the beginning of this chapter. We also learn that the trial court found both a private and public nuisance.

Paragraphs 39-42 focus on issue #3 raised by the defendants on appeal, i.e., that the "courts erred in failing to balance the equities, either in finding a prospective nuisance or in fashioning relief." In the court's somewhat confused response, it is important to understand that balancing of the equities has no place in the verdict or liability phase of a trial. The existence of a private or public nuisance depends on whether the facts presented at trial prove the elements of a case. Balancing of the equities occurs only during the remedy phase of the trial. The argument that the "law of Illinois requires that the circuit court engage in a balancing process before reaching a conclusion that the waste disposal site presents a prospective nuisance" is therefore erroneous. There was no balancing in *Boomer* until the remedy phase; otherwise, one might expect that the private nuisance action would have been dismissed because of the critical economic importance of the cement factory to the community. Paragraph 46 of the opinion contains a long quote from the trial court opinion. The distinction between the liability phase and the remedy phase for equitable balancing is not clearly stated. The trial court opinion states "[w]hether or not a business is useful or necessary or whether it contributes to the welfare and/or prosperity of the community are elements to be considered in a serious manner but said elements are not determinative as to whether or not an operation is a nuisance." It is not clearly stated that the "elements to be considered in a serious manner" will only be considered in the remedy phase. If a nuisance is found, then permanent and mandatory injunctions are the remedy. Only at this point will the equities will be balanced.

The quote in paragraph 42 also contains a reference to a "coming-to-the nuisance" defense. This defense will become central for us in *Spur v. Del Webb*, which will be discussed later in this chapter. Assuming that both cases were tried under the same state law, then SCA Services could have raised the same affirmative defense, or the "estoppel" defense, and bar any subsequent to legal action. The opposite, of course, would have been imaginable.

In paragraph 42 of the opinion, the court dismisses issue #3 raised on appeal, stating that "the trial court did engage in a balancing process" and that the defendant's claim to the contrary is therefore "without merit."

Issue #2 raised on appeal, that "that the wrong legal standard was applied in determining that the "waste-disposal site constitutes a prospective nuisance," is discussed in paragraphs 41-43 of the opinion and goes to the heart of the reasoning behind the holding that a prospective nuisance exists. The defendant claims that the correct legal standard to be used in determining if a prospective nuisance exists would "require a showing of substantial risk of certain and extreme future harm." The court again confuses the liability phase (where the issue of whether a nuisance exists is determined) and the remedy phase (where equitable relief and balancing of the equities will take place in the determination of a remedy). Injunctive relief has nothing to do with the proper legal standard for finding a prospective nuisance. Whether "an injunction is proper" will be determined only after a prospective nuisance is found. This "showing of substantial risk of certain and extreme future harm" is also known as the "dangerous probability" test. The court agrees "with the defendant's statement of the law, but not with its urged application to the facts of this case." The court quotes *Prosser* (a persuasive, secondary authority), "[t]he defendant may be restrained from entering upon an activity where it is highly probable that it will lead to a nuisance." The standard for finding a prospective nuisance is not "certain and extreme future harm" but a high probability of the harm occurring. And yes, a "defendant may be restrained," but whether a defendant must be restrained would only be determined after a prospective nuisance is found during the remedy phase. The court then cites two Illinois cases in support of the highly probable standard. Finally, the court reiterates the findings of the trial court.

Paragraph 56 of the opinion deals with issue #4, i.e., that the "courts erred in failing to defer to the IEPA" and issue #5, i.e., that the "courts erred in finding that plaintiffs have no adequate remedy at law." Both of these claims involve the permits issued to SCA Services by the Illinois EPA. These include the permit to develop and operate the hazardous-waste landfill, as well as 185 permits for the delivery of waste. The defendant claims that the trial court "failed to defer to the IEPA" and "failed to give weight" to these permits. The court states that this "assertion has no merit" because the permits were issued using inaccurate information. In addition, the court is not required to "defer" to the IEPA. The court will determine whether there is a prospective nuisance regardless of the IEPA's decisions. The issue before the court is a prospective nuisance that the court will consider regardless of the decisions of this agency. Moreover, the defendant claims that the plaintiffs have not exhausted their remedies because the plaintiffs "have an adequate remedy at law" by seeking review of the IEPA's decision to grant these permits. The court simply states that the "plaintiffs are not seeking a review of the issuance of permits," but instead "seek to enjoin a nuisance, a matter which is properly brought in a court of equity."

Issue #6 raised on appeal, that the "courts erred in ordering a mandatory injunction" is a repeat of issues #2 and #3. In paragraph 58 of the opinion, the court says that it has already addressed the issue of the use of the dangerous probability test as well as the defendant's concern about balancing the equities and states that the court "will not unduly prolong this already lengthy opinion with duplicative discussion." The court then does precisely this by discussing the balancing of the equities further in paragraphs 52-60 of the opinion. The long discussion presents a number of alternatives to closing the site (permanent injunction) and removing all wastes and restoring the site (mandatory injunction) presumably to show that the court considered all these alternatives in its balancing of the equities.

Issue #7 raised on appeal, that the "courts' decisions constituted a taking of property without due process of law," is readily dismissed. The defendant argues that this "taking" has been caused by recent changes in state law. In paragraph #73, the court states that this "argument has no merit" because "the principles of law applied in this case are neither new, unreasonable, nor unpredictable. Manifestly, a party cannot expect to operate a site in this manner and in the location the defendant has chosen and expect to be immune from liability for creating a public nuisance."

In paragraph #75 of the opinion, the court affirms the lower court's decisions and remands the case back to the trial court to supervise the "enforcement of its order."

Explaining the Role of Expert Testimony

The verdict in *Wilsonville* demonstrates the importance of expert testimony in an adversarial proceeding. Finding the *truth* is often difficult when experts' testimony on the same set of facts is diametrically opposed. Sometimes the truth lies somewhere in between, with both sides presenting "truths" but only those truths that help their side. But in *Wilsonville*, why was the testimony presented by some experts believed while the testimony of other experts was rejected by the jury and by reviewing courts at the appellate level? The selection, vetting, and preparation of expert witnesses is, of course, key. Mistakes were made by SCA's expert witnesses; and this should never have happened. Also, since expert witnesses are paid, the appearance of purchased testimony can be a slippery slope if an expert witness is seen as a *hired gun*.

Jurisdiction

Jurisdiction is the legal right of a particular court to hear and decide a lawsuit. A court must have personal jurisdiction and subject matter jurisdiction to hear an issue. Whether a court has this legal right depends on both subject matter and personal jurisdiction. Cases that fall within the exclusive subject matter jurisdiction of the federal courts include federal criminal prosecutions, bankruptcy, admiralty, copyrights, trademarks, patents, claims against the U.S. government, and claims under statutes that explicitly provide for exclusive federal jurisdiction. State court systems have jurisdiction over all cases that do not fall within the exclusive subject matter jurisdiction of the federal courts. Many cases can be heard in either federal or state courts. These cases fall within what is called concurrent jurisdiction. Since most federal statutes do not provide for exclusive subject matter jurisdiction of federal courts, these cases involving a federal question can be heard in either federal or state courts. It is not uncommon for a state court to rule on an issue involving a federal statute or even the U.S. Constitution.

Concurrent jurisdiction also includes cases where there is a diversity of citizenship. This means that the plaintiff and defendant are from different states. If a case involving a federal question or diversity of citizenship is brought in state court, the defendant has the right to remove the case to federal court. If this case were brought to a federal court first, it must remain there.

Why do we mention all this? Because the attorneys for SCA Services did not choose to exercise their jurisdictional rights. The landfill was owned by SCA Services of Boston. The original complaint was filed in the trial court of Macoupin County in the State of Illinois. It is not clear why the attorneys for SCA Services chose to leave the case in this local court. The disadvantages of doing so include a jury selected from the local population (usually more sympathetic to local concerns of the type adjudicated in *Wilsonville*) rather than from the much larger pool used by a federal district court in Illinois, and the fact that the federal courts are generally less sympathetic to tort actions than the state court systems.

Organized Crime and SCA Services

While likely inadmissible in the *Wilsonville* trial, it is interesting to learn that SCA Services had substantial ties to organized crime, especially in the state of New Jersey. This is fully described in *Giants of Garbage* by Harold Crooks, *Space, Times, and Organized Crime* by Alan Block, and Maurice Hinchey's Report to the NY State Assembly entitled *Organized Crime's Involvement in the Waste Hauling Industry*. SCA Services owned a toxic waste dump in Niagara Falls, NY near the infamous Love Canal site that was noted for dangerous explosions and fires. Reflect on the testimony in the *Wilsonville* trial about the "explosive interaction" of toxic chemicals. Tony Viola, a mobster, became vice-president of SCA. The company's criminal connections would become known after the murder of several independent waste haulers in New Jersey that were replaced with SCA Services.

The actual trial itself, however, provided evidence that the officials in the Village of Wilsonville were not told by SCA Services that toxic wastes would be dumped and buried at the site. When the citizens of Wilsonville discovered that SCA services was, in fact, dumping toxic wastes, the resulting anger of the citizens of Wilsonville did play a role in the relentless efforts to stop the waste disposal site from operating and have it cleaned up and restored to its original condition. *Wilsonville* became a classic instance of NIMBY (not in my back yard).

In 1982 the residents of Wilsonville filed a private nuisance action alleging that the waste landfill had lowered property values and caused various health issues. The public nuisance lawsuit was filed in 1977, with the Supreme Court of Illinois issuing its ruling in 1981. Waste Management, Inc., the world's largest waste company, bought 60% of SCA Services in 1984 and then settled the lawsuit in 1987 by offering $2.5 million to 700 residents of Wilsonville. This amounted to about $2000 per resident with larger amounts going to property owners.

Thought Question

What if a municipality decided (after catastrophic incidents at Three Mile Island, Chernobyl, and the four reactors at Fukushima) that the local nuclear power plant is a prospective risk (nuisance) and went to court? What legal remedies may be available? This would be an interesting and important issue for the court. Where would the line be drawn? Look at the graph below where harm is plotted on the vertical axis, and the probability of that harm occurring is plotted on the horizontal axis. The harm in *Wilsonville* is indicated at point "X" with very high probability (actually 100%) because we learned after the trial that contamination indeed had migrated offsite in the groundwater. The harm is considered to be much lower than the other catastrophic harms plotted on the vertical axis, but like the harm caused by the contamination in Love Canal or Woburn, the harm caused by the contamination could be severe and have a local impact on human health. Where would *Fink v. Board of Trustees*, cited as persuasive precedent in *Wilsonville*, fit on this graph?

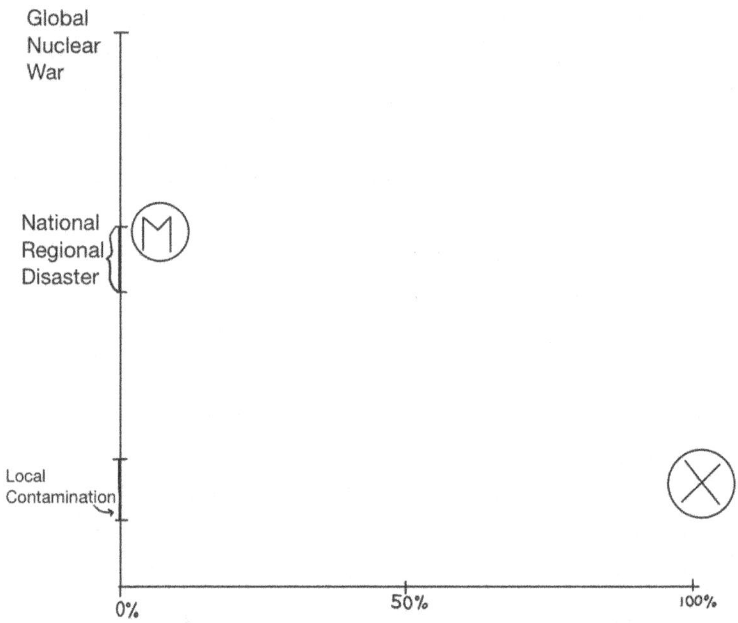

Probability of occurrence:
X = toxic chemicals released to the environment in Wilsonville
M = meltdown of nuclear reactor

The meltdown of a nuclear reactor is plotted as "M." Would the known risk involved with a nuclear reactor be sufficient to allow a court to enjoin its operation? Surely the probability of occurrence is low but nowhere near as low as the nuclear power industry and government proclaimed. The risk, however, would never be litigated in court because of the Price-Anderson Act, which limits the liability of nuclear power companies and shields them from common law tort actions. This statute, passed by Congress in 1957 and reauthorized and amended every 15 years or so, allows the civilian nuclear power industry to exist. Insurance companies refused to insure nuclear power companies given the fantastic liabilities involved. While the nuclear power companies are required to pay into a liability pool, the amounts involved, though in the hundreds of millions, would be woefully insufficient for a Chernobyl-type disaster. The taxpayer would pick up the cost as well as the harm inflicted on the environment and human health.

Boomer and Wilsonville Compared and Contrasted

Although these two civil wrong cases apply different state law (New York and Illinois), there are many similarities that sprang from reading them side by side.

1. <u>Plaintiffs and defendants</u>: The plaintiffs in *Boomer* are private property owners while the plaintiffs in *Wilsonville* are the Village of Wilsonville, Macoupin County, and the State of Illinois. The defendants in both cases are private companies.

2. <u>The elements</u>: Analytically, both are intentional torts. *Boomer* is a private nuisance tort, and *Wilsonville* is a public nuisance tort. The elements in both are proof of harm, proof of causation, and proof of intent. Proof of harm in *Wilsonville* is, of course, the main issue because the public nuisance is prospective and the "dangerous probability" standard of proof must be defined and met.

3. <u>Requested remedy</u>: The plaintiffs in *Boomer* request both damages and an injunction that would close down the cement plant. The plaintiffs in *Wilsonville* request an injunction that would close and clean up the chemical waste landfill.

4. <u>The verdict</u>: In both cases, a nuisance was found. In *Boomer,* this was a private nuisance while in *Wilsonville* it was a prospective public nuisance.

5. <u>The judgment and balancing the equities</u>: Considerable time is spent in the *Wilsonville* opinion discussing the balancing of the equities because the defendant had claimed that the trial court had "erred in failing to balance the equities." The Illinois Supreme Court determined and demonstrated that the trial court did, in fact, balance the equities. That is, the court weighed the benefits to the public from preventing environmental contamination from a toxic waste landfill against

the economic cost to SCA Services to close and clean up the site. The court also considered various proposed technological solutions to make the site safe but determined that these would not solve the problem. Hence, the prospective nuisance was enjoined and SCA Services ended up paying over five million dollars to close and clean up the site. The central issue in the *Boomer* decision was, in fact, the balancing of the equities. The court had to weigh the cost to the cement plant and community if its operation would be enjoined. Well over 300 million dollars had been invested in the plant, hundreds of local residents were employed there, and there was considerable tax revenue flowing into the coffers of the local municipality. The decision not to enjoin the operation of the plant weighed the foregoing economic consequences against the longstanding New York State precedent that required an injunction if a nuisance were found. In balancing the equities in favor of the cement plant and community, the highest court in the State of New York upheld the trial court and overturned a long-standing precedent. The court also reversed the lower court's award of temporary damages to the plaintiffs which allowed the plaintiffs to maintain their cause of action for future nuisance actions and replaced this with permanent damages, a one-time award for "servitude on the land."

Study Questions for *Wilsonville*

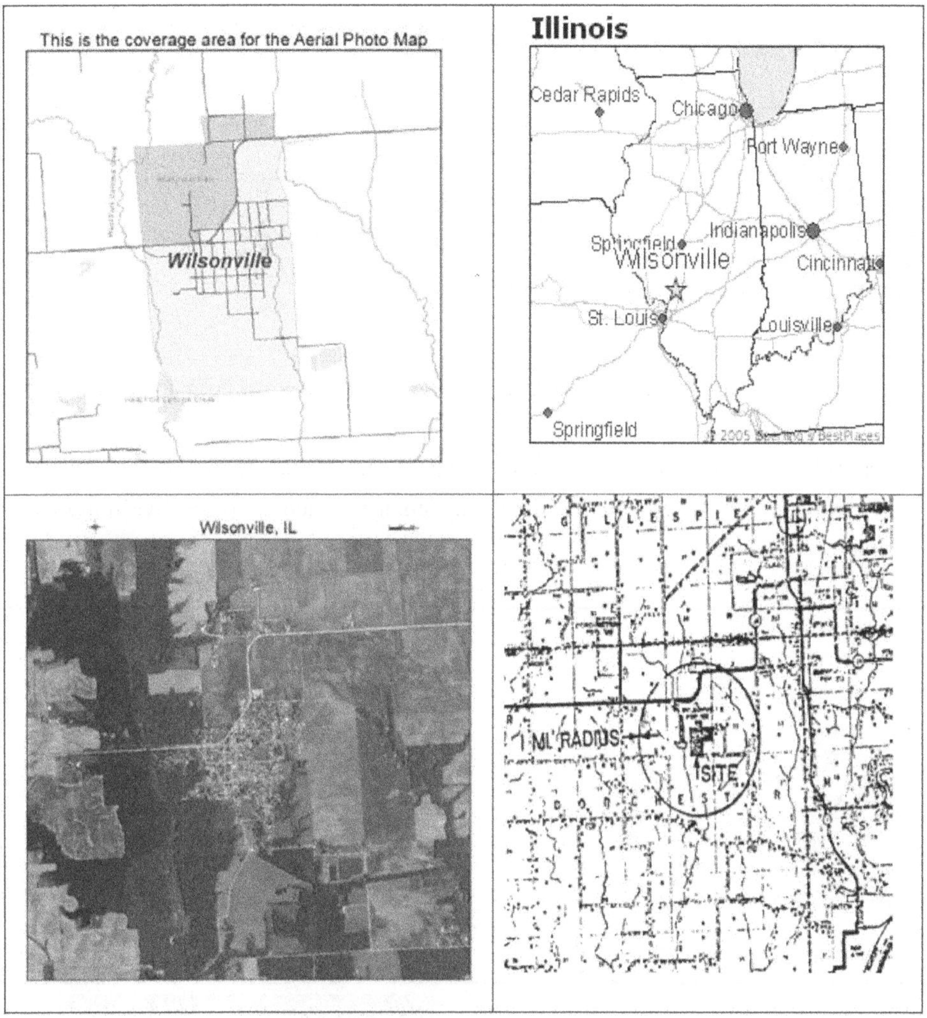

This diagram shows the location of the 130-acre toxic waste disposal site. For reference to the maps above, note the main road that runs east-west but turns sharply to the north in the Village of Wilsonville.

1. According to *Wilsonville*, what is a prospective public nuisance? (Be sure to define all terms).
2. Discuss the general criteria used here to decide whether or not a prospective public nuisance exists.
3. List and describe the elements of the prospective nuisance in *Wilsonville*.
4. What was the verdict in *Wilsonville*? Explain the basic reasoning for the finding of liability for this prospective nuisance.

5. What was the remedy in *Wilsonville*? Discuss this remedy in terms of both a mandatory and permanent injunction.
6. Did the court balance the equities in fashioning this remedy? If so, explain how.
7. What did the court in *Wilsonville* decide about damages when a prospective nuisance is found? Explain.

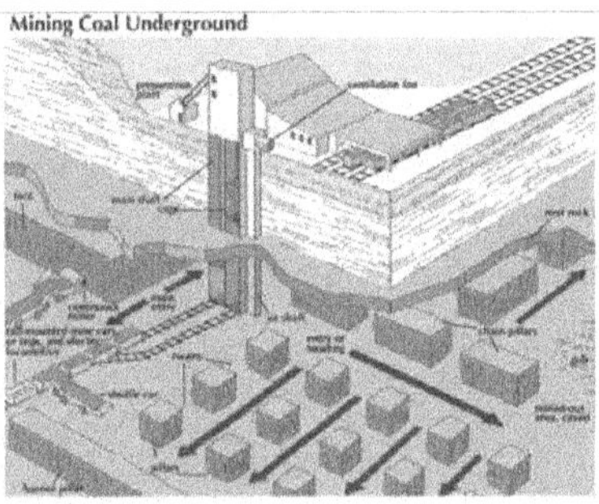

https://images.app.goo.gl/hC8SDvVw7FvdV2Bv5

cardcow.com

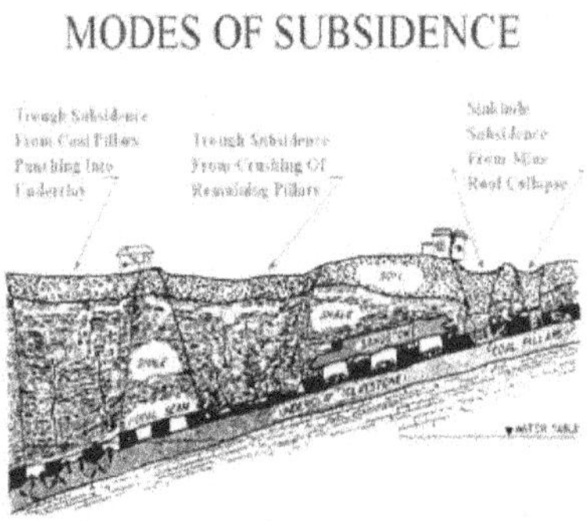

https://www.dep.pa.gov/Citizens/MSI/Pages/Mine-Subsidence-Loss-and-Coverage.aspx

https://www.mininghistoryassociation.org/ScrantonHistory.htm

Village of Wilsonville (Court opinion)

86 ILL.2D 1

SUPREME COURT OF ILLINOIS.

THE VILLAGE OF WILSONVILLE ET AL., APPELLEES,

V.

SCA SERVICES, INC., APPELLANT.

NO. 52885.

|MAY 22, 1981.

Rehearing Denied Oct. 19, 1981.

Synopsis

Operator of a chemical-waste-disposal site appealed from a judgment of the Circuit Court, Macoupin County, John W. Russell, J., enjoining it from continued operation of the site. The Appellate Court, Green, J., 77 Ill.App.3d 618, 33 Ill.Dec. 163, 396 N.E.2d 552, affirmed, and petition for leave to appeal was granted. The Supreme Court, Clark, J., held that: (1) a preponderance of the evidence sufficiently established that the site was a nuisance both currently and prospectively; (2) trial court had subject matter jurisdiction to enjoin operation of the site as a public nuisance, despite plaintiffs' failure to seek review from State Environmental Protection Agency's decision to grant permits for the operation of the site; (3) trial court balanced the relative hardship to be caused to the plaintiffs and the operator of the site and fashioned reasonable relief when it permanently enjoined operation of the site and ordered exhumation of all material from the site and reclamation of the surrounding area; and (4) the decision to enjoin operation of the site as public nuisance did not constitute a sudden change in state law and did not deprive the operator of its property without due process of law.

Affirmed and remanded.

Ryan, J., filed concurring opinion.

Attorneys and Law Firms

*5 Henry L. Mason, III, Thomas M. McMahon and Robert M. Olian of Sidley & Austin, Chicago, Fred C. Prillaman of Mohan, Alewelt & Prillaman, Springfield, and Stuart Dobbs of Denby, Dobbs, Meno & Bloomer, Carlinville (William C. Brashares and Melvin J. Duvall, Jr., of Cladouhos & Brashares, Washington, D. C., and Lawrence C. Hutchings, Boston, Mass., of counsel), for appellant.

Paul C. Verticchio, Gillespie, for appellees Village of Wilsonville and Macoupin County Farm Bureau.

Tyrone C. Fahner and William J. Scott, Attys. Gen., Springfield (Richard W. Cosby, Ann L. Carr, and A. L. Zimmer, Asst. Attys. Gen., of counsel), for the People.

Kenneth R. Boyle, State's Atty., Carlinville, for appellee the County of Macoupin.

Eugene H. Bernstein of Isham, Lincoln & Beale, Chicago, for amicus curiae Commonwealth Edison Co.

John M. Cannon and Susan W. Wanat, Chicago, for amici curiae Chicago Ass'n of Commerce and Industry, Illinois Mfrs.' Ass'n, and Mid-America Legal Foundation.

Mary C. Bryant, Chicago, and Dorothy A. Darrah and Richard S. Mallory, Washington, D. C., for amicus curiae United States Environmental Protection Agency.

David O. Ledbetter, Washington, D. C., for amicus curiae U. S. Dept. of Justice.

Kirkland & Ellis, Chicago (Daniel W. Vittum, Jr., *6 Frank L. Winter, and Donald W. Rupert, Chicago, of counsel), for amici curiae John Sexton Sand & Gravel Corp. and John Sexton Contractors.

Opinion

CLARK, Justice:

P#1. On April 18, 1977, the plaintiff village of Wilsonville (the village) filed a complaint seeking injunctive relief in the circuit court of Macoupin County. Plaintiffs Macoupin County and the Macoupin County Farm Bureau were granted leave to intervene on April 29, 1977, and May 9, 1977, respectively. They filed complaints substantially similar to the village's complaint. The gravamen of the complaints was that the operation of the defendant's chemical-waste-disposal site presents a public nuisance and a hazard to the health of the citizens of the village, the county, and the State. The Attorney General of Illinois filed a complaint on May 26, 1977, seeking an injunction pursuant to the Environmental Protection Act (Ill.Rev.Stat.1975, ch. 1111/2, pars. 1003(d), 1003(n), 1012(d), 1043). After several amendments to the complaints and several motions were made and decided, the Attorney General's action and the other action were consolidated and set for trial. Trial began on June 7, 1977, consumed 104 days, and resulted in judgment for the plaintiffs on August 28, 1978. The trial court's judgment order concluded that the site constitutes a nuisance and enjoined the defendant from operating its hazardous-chemical-waste landfill in Wilsonville. It ordered the defendant to remove all toxic waste buried there, along with all contaminated soil found at the disposal site as a result of the operation of the landfill. Further, the court ordered the defendant to restore and reclaim the site.

P#2. The defendant appealed. The Appellate Court for the Fourth District unanimously affirmed the trial court's judgment. (77 Ill.App.3d 618, 33 Ill.Dec. 163, 396 N.E.2d 552.) We allowed the defendant's *7 petition for leave to appeal. (73 Ill.2d R. 315.) We affirm.

P#3. The record in this matter is over 13,000 pages long. The appellate court opinion sets out many pertinent facts. It is only necessary to summarize them here.

P#4. The defendant has operated a chemical-waste landfill since 1977. The site comprises approximately 130 acres, 90 of which are within the village limits of the plaintiff village. The remaining 40 acres are adjacent to the village. The defendant enters into agreements with generators of toxic chemical waste to haul the waste away from the generators' locations. The defendant then delivers it to the Wilsonville site, tests random samples of chemical waste, and then deposits the waste in trenches. There are seven trenches at the site. Each one is approximately 15 feet deep, 50 feet wide, and 250 to 350 feet long. Approximately 95% of the waste materials were buried in 55-gallon steel drums, and the remainder is contained in double-wall paper bags. After the materials are deposited in the trenches, uncompacted clay is placed between groups of containers and a minimum of one foot of clay is placed between the top drum and the top clay level of the trench.

P#5. The site is bordered on the east, west, and south by farmland and on the north by the village. The entire site, the village, and much of the surrounding area is located above the abandoned Superior Coal Mine No. 4, which operated from 1917 to 1954. The No. 6 seam of the mine was exploited in this area at a depth of 312 feet. The mining method used to extract coal was the room-and-panel method, whereby about 50% of the coal is left in pillars which provide some support for the earth above the mine. There was testimony at trial by Dr. Nolan Augenbaugh, chairman of the Department of Mining, Petroleum and Geological Engineering at the University of Missouri at Rolla, that pillar failure can occur in any mine where there is a readjustment of stress. Also on the defendant's *8 site is a 30- to 40-feet-high pile of "gob," or mine spoil of coal, shale, and clay, which was accumulated over the time the mine was operated. Acid drainage from the mine has seeped into the ground and contaminated three surface drainage channels at the site. The defendant has attempted to remedy this situation by covering the surface of the "gob pile" with excess soil from the trenches.

P#6. There are 14 monitoring wells along the perimeter of the site. They are designed to detect liquids which seep through the soil and into the wells. They are not designed to contain liquids, however. In fact, monitoring wells Nos. 5 and 6 are 650 feet apart, which would allow many materials to pass between those two wells and not be discovered. The wells are sampled quarterly by a private laboratory, and test results are submitted to the Illinois Environmental Protection

Agency (IEPA). Additional water samples are taken from three surface channels and are tested and reported in the same manner as samples taken from the wells. The surface drainage and the groundwater drainage from the site are to the south, away from the village and toward farmland.

P#7. The village has no sewage-treatment plant and no municipally owned sewage system. Most homes are served by septic tanks, and some homes and businesses are connected to private sewers. The water-distribution system is centralized, and water is purchased from Gillespie, Illinois. The system was built in 1952 after the village tried unsuccessfully to find sufficient water by drilling municipal wells in the area. There are still 73 water wells in the village, some of which are used to water gardens or wash cars. At least one well is used to water pets, and another is used for drinking water. South of defendant's site, approximately one-half mile from the gob pile, is the Vassi Spring, the owner of which intends to use it as his water supply when he builds his home. Further south are four more springs used to water livestock.

P#8. *9 On February 11, 1976, the defendant applied to the IEPA for a permit to develop and operate the hazardous-waste landfill. A developmental permit was issued by the IEPA on May 19, 1976. After a preoperation inspection was conducted by the IEPA, an operational permit was issued to the defendant on September 28, 1976. Each delivery of waste material to the site must be accompanied by a supplemental permit issued by the IEPA. A supplemental permit specifies the chemical nature and quantity of the waste to be deposited at the sites. Between November 12, 1976, and June 7, 1977, the first day of trial, the defendant had obtained 185 such permits.

P#9. The materials deposited at the site include polychlorinated biphenyls (PCBs), a neurotoxic, possibly carcinogenic chemical which it has been illegal to produce in this country since 1979. Due to the extensive use of PCBs in electrical equipment such as transformers, capacitors, and heat-transfer systems, and in hydraulic systems, any PCBs that were produced legally now have to be disposed of when they are no longer in use. PCBs have been stored at the site in liquid, solid and semi-solid form. Additionally, there are a number of now-empty drums which had once contained PCBs, which are also buried at the site. Other materials buried at the site in large quantities are solid cyanide, a substance known as C5, 6, paint sludge, asbestos, pesticides, mercury, and arsenic. Considerable evidence was adduced to show that these and other substances deposited at the site are extremely toxic to human beings. Some of the adverse reactions which could result from exposure to these materials are pulmonary diseases, cancer, brain damage, and birth defects.

P#10. The general geologic profile of the site shows a surface layer of about 10 feet of loess (wind-blown silt and clay material), under which lies 40 to 65 feet of glacial till. In the till material there is a thin sand layer of a few inches to approximately two feet. Some ground water has been *10 found in the sand layer. All trenches dug at the site have between 10 to 15 feet of glacial till below them. The glacial till is reported to be very dense and is not very permeable. Thus liquids do not travel through it quickly.

P#11. Permeability studies conducted before the site opened by John Mathes, a professional engineer hired by the defendant, indicate permeability results ranging from 7.4 X 10 -8 centimeters per second to 1.2 X 10 -8 centimeters per second (cm/sec.). (The larger the negative exponent is, the less permeable the soil. E. g., a finding of 10 -8 cm/sec. indicates that the soil is less permeable than would a reading of 10 -4 cm/sec.) After the site opened, Mathes took permeability samples from or near the bottoms of the trenches that had been dug. His second set of results ranged from 1.4 X 10 -7 cm/sec. to .9 X 10 -7 cm/sec.

P#12. Dr. James Williams, an engineering geologist with the Missouri Geology and Land Survey, also made permeability findings on behalf of the defendant from samples taken from the site after it opened. Dr. Williams' results ranged from 7 X 10 -6 cm/sec. to 1 X 10 -7 cm/sec. Dr. Williams testified on cross-examination that the general permeability of the site is considered to be greater than 1 X 10 -8 cm/sec. and that he would not expect the average permeability of the soil to be as low as that used for samples.

P#13. In the interim between the opening of the site and the time of trial, the IEPA adopted a suggested permeability standard of 1 X 10 -8 cm/sec. for hazardous-waste landfills.

P#14. Subsidence of the earth underneath the site is another contention raised by the plaintiffs to support their thesis that the site is unsafe and is therefore an enjoinable nuisance. Dr. Nolan Augenbaugh testified extensively at trial. Dr. Augenbaugh took pictures of the area from an airplane as well as at ground level. During his testimony, he pointed out where subsidence occurred in the pictures he had taken. Dr. Augenbaugh stated that he had observed subsidence *11 in a wheat field on the Wilbur Sawyer farm on June 17, 1977. Dr. Augenbaugh also testified that a subsidence basin lies to the northeast of the disposal site. The pictures also indicate, according to Dr. Augenbaugh, fractures in the ground. One picture depicts a fault, which, Dr. Augenbaugh explained, is a "fracture where there's been differential movement of the two blocks. One block has been moved more than the other block." Sawyer, the farmer, told Dr. Augenbaugh the cracks had begun to appear approximately two months before, which would have been spring 1977. Several of these subsidences and fractures are located approximately one-half mile from the western boundary of the lower part of the disposal site. Dr. Augenbaugh testified that, in his opinion, subsidence can and will occur at the disposal site. Further, that ruptures in the earth would occur which, like an open pipe, would act as conduits for artesian water to reach the trenches, thereby contaminating the water.

P#15. Dr. Augenbaugh was recalled to testify on rebuttal. He testified that on March 22, 1978, he returned to the Sawyer farm. With the use of a backhoe, Dr. Augenbaugh had a trench dug across the subsidence cracks which he had observed earlier. When the digging was completed, there was a trench nine feet long and approximately three feet wide, with a maximum depth of a little over eight feet. Photographs were taken and slides prepared of the operation at the site. As the trench was being dug, water began to seep into the trench at a depth of approximately 4 to 41/2 feet. Dr. Augenbaugh testified that the water flowed from subsidence fractures which were below the surface of the ground. Dr. Augenbaugh then poured some green dye into a surface fracture which was located approximately 10 feet away from the trench. The green dye entered the trench through two openings within 25 minutes.

P#16. Thomas O. Glover, a mining engineer and liason officer with the United States Bureau of Mining, Department *12 of the Interior, also testified regarding subsidence. Glover defined subsidence as the settling of the ground, due to the diminution of the underground support structure, and either the pillars pushing into the fine clay bottom below the coal system, or the roof fracturing immediately above the coal seam and continuing to the surface. He stated that subsidence normally can be expected to appear, on the average, 40 years after a mine has closed down. Glover never visited the instant disposal site, but he had examined the information relative to Superior Mine No. 4 and he had witnessed subsidences many times in the field over the course of 27 years as a mining engineer. Glover offered the opinion that there is a possibility of subsidence wherever coal is mined and underground support is removed.

P#17. Several of the defendant's expert witnesses, James Douglas Andrews, the designer of the site and a consulting engineer for the defendant, John A. Mathes, an engineer, Steven Hunt, a geologist with the Illinois State Geological Survey (ISGS), and Paul B. DuMontelle, an engineering geologist with ISGS and coordinator of environmental geology for the Survey, testified in summary that there would be subsidence at the site, but that it would not be deep, would close in a short time, and could be repaired by means of engineering techniques.

P#18. Another of plaintiffs' witnesses, Dr. Arthur Zahalsky, offered the opinion that an "explosive interaction," resulting in chemical explosions, fires, or emissions of poisonous gases, will occur at the site. Dr. Zahalsky is a professor of biochemistry and head of the laboratory of biochemical parasitology at Southern Illinois University at Edwardsville. He testified in essence that if sufficient oxygen could reach the buried chemicals, and he believed it could, then an explosive interaction of unknown date of occurrence, magnitude, and duration is likely. Moreover, Dr. Zahalsky testified that it is unknown what *13 interactions might occur when the waste materials combine after the deterioration of the steel containers and paper bags.

P#19. The defendant challenged Dr. Zahalsky's opinion during cross-examination and requested him to diagram the precise chemical formula which would result in an explosive interaction. Dr. Zahalsky testified that a precise formula could not be diagrammed. He stated that the defendant's trench logs indicate that several of the chemical wastes have flash points less than 80 degrees Fahrenheit. Zahalsky reviewed the trench logs and gave examples of chemicals, such as paranitroaniline, which is a strong oxidizing agent and may be explosive, and also paint sludge, which has a flash point of less than 80 degrees Fahrenheit, which could result in a chemical fire. Dr. Zahalsky offered one scenario in which acidic chlorinated degreasers would interact with waste phenolic, releasing the phenolics so that the flash point would be achieved, thereby setting off the paint sludges which, in turn, would set off paint wastes, which would achieve the temperature sufficient for the ignition and combustion of liquid PCBs. All of these materials are deposited together in trench No. 3.

P#20. Finally, considerable testimony was adduced, much of it conflicting, as to dust, odors, and spills of chemical waste which have occurred in the village. Various residents testified that dust emanating from the site blew toward their houses. Also, odors which caused burning eyes, running noses, headaches, nausea, and shortness of breath were mentioned in testimony. The odors themselves were said to resemble, among other things, fertilizer, insecticide, and burning rubber. There was further testimony that the dust and odors interfered with the witnesses' ability to use their yards for gardening or other recreational uses. The defendant presented witnesses who denied that the disposal site was the source of any odors, and that the *14 odors resulted from the local practices of openly burning refuse and dumping sewage into a nearby creek.

P#21. There was testimony that trucks carrying the waste materials to the disposal site via Wilson Avenue, the main street of the village, sometimes spilled toxic liquids onto the street. The evidence is undisputed, both from the defendant's receiving reports and testimony from IEPA inspectors, that many drums arrived on the site leaking waste materials. Also, Sam Campagna, defendant's site manager, testified that he heard that a drum had once been dropped into a trench rather than stacked using a drum handler. He did not know whether rumors that this practice persisted were true or not, but he had ordered that such a practice cease.

P#22. The defendant has raised several issues on appeal: (1) whether the finding of the circuit and appellate courts that the waste-disposal site is a prospective nuisance is contrary to the manifest weight of the evidence; (2) whether those courts applied the wrong legal standard in finding that the waste-disposal site constitutes a prospective nuisance; (3) whether the circuit and appellate courts erred in failing to balance the equities, either in finding a prospective nuisance or in fashioning relief; (4) whether the courts erred in failing to defer to, or to otherwise weigh, the role of the IEPA, the United States Environmental Protection Agency (USEPA), and the Illinois State Geological Survey (ISGS); (5) whether the courts erred in finding that plaintiffs have no adequate remedy at law; (6) whether the courts erred in ordering a mandatory injunction; and, finally, (7) whether the courts' decisions constituted a taking of property without due process of law.

P#23. We conclude that the evidence in this case sufficiently establishes by a preponderance of the evidence that the chemical-waste-disposal site is a nuisance both presently and prospectively. The defendant does not challenge the *15 fact that the spillage from improperly contained chemical waste, the odors, and the dust created by the site constitute a present interference with the right of the plaintiffs to enjoy and use their property. Thus, we will not belabor this point.

P#24. The defendant points out three areas where, it argues, the trial court made erroneous findings of fact. The defendant refers to: (1) Dr. Arthur Zahalsky's opinion testimony concerning an explosive interaction and Dr. Stephen Hall's testimony which concurred in that opinion; (2) evidence concerning soil permeability; and, (3) infiltration of water into the trenches, and of migration out of the defendant's trenches of chemical waste either through the "bathtub effect" or subsidence.

P#25. We have reviewed the extensive record compiled in this case. While it is true that the defendant vigorously challenged the evidence concerning an explosive interaction, permeability, and infiltration and migration due to subsidence, the defendant has not overcome the natural and logical conclusions which could be drawn from the evidence. Findings of fact made by the trial court will not be set aside unless they are contrary to the manifest weight of the evidence. John Calnan Co. v. Talsma Builders, Inc. (1977), 67 Ill.2d 213, 218, 10 Ill.Dec. 242, 367 N.E.2d 695; Kenny Construction Co. v. Metropolitan Sanitary District (1971), 52 Ill.2d 187, 196, 288 N.E.2d 1.

P#26. Defendant argues that Dr. Zahalsky and Dr. Hall are unqualified to render opinions concerning an explosive interaction occurring in the trenches. Dr. Zahalsky is a professor of biochemistry at Southern Illinois University at Edwardsville, the holder of a doctorate in that discipline, and has been active in his field since 1967. Dr. Hall is an associate professor of science and technology in the Department of Chemistry at Southern Illinois University at Edwardsville. He was awarded a doctorate in inorganic and analytical chemistry in 1967, as well as a master's *16 degree in environmental health. While working on that master's degree, his second, Dr. Hall studied toxicology, a course dealing with the health effects of chemicals, and took courses on air pollution and occupational health and safety as affected by chemicals in the work environment. Currently, Dr. Hall teaches a course in industrial toxicology at the University.

P#27. Over a limited objection by the defendant, the court qualified Dr. Hall as an expert in the fields of industrial toxicology, analytical, organic and inorganic chemistry, occupational hygiene, and environmental health.

P#28. Defendant placed several experts on the stand to refute the conclusions of Drs. Zahalsky and Hall. These experts testified that the fire-retardant properties of some of the chemicals would prevent chemical fires, that the gases predicted by Dr. Hall due to the mixing of chemicals would not occur, and that other chemical reactions predicted by Dr. Hall would not occur.

P#29. The defendant particularly relies upon the opinion of Dr. Raymond D. Harbison, a professor of pharmacology at Vanderbilt University, a toxicologist and consultant to the USEPA on toxic-waste handling. Dr. Harbison offered the opinion that the instant site is the most advanced scientific landfill in this country, and that the inventory system and the "absolute confinement" of the materials to the site render the interaction of the chemicals an impossibility.

P#30. At bottom, Dr. Harbison's opinion is premised upon his belief that the materials at the site will be sufficiently confined so that they will not pose a threat to the health or lives of the residents of the village. Dr. Harbison's opinions were discounted by the trial court, however, due to the substantial evidence which shows that the soil is more permeable than originally thought; that there is migration of water out of the trenches; and that there is subsidence in the area. Moreover, Dr. Harbison's opinion *17 must be further discounted due to his erroneous statement that the waste materials will be sufficiently confined since "there is no ground water to be contaminated anyway below the particular site." Dr. Harbison later amended that statement to say there was no "usable water supply below the site" in terms of volume. This statement is also erroneous and also ignores evidence that the ground water would flow from beneath the site, thereby transporting any contamination into Cahokia Creek and could eventually flow into the Mississippi River. Thus we will not overturn the trial court's findings on this issue. They are amply supported by the manifest weight of the evidence.

P#31. The defendant next contends that the appellate and circuit courts misinterpreted the permeability tests admitted into evidence. It is argued that permeability coefficients are but one factor in determining the permeability of soil. We agree, but the fact remains that the defendant placed a good deal of emphasis on the tests conducted by John Mathes and Dr. Williams, which show that the soil at the site is more permeable than the IEPA suggested standard of 1 X 10 -8 cm/sec. These courts also relied upon the testimony of Dr. Williams, defendant's witness, that the soil was probably even more permeable than indicated in the tests. Based on this evidence the trial court was correct in finding that the permeable nature of the soil, as demonstrated by the coefficients, as one of several factors, poses a threat of migration of chemical waste away from the disposal site. That finding will not be disturbed.

P#32. The defendant also contends that the trial court's finding that subsidence warrants closing of the site is erroneous. The defendant argues that, assuming arguendo that subsidence would occur at the site, it could be counteracted by engineering techniques. This issue becomes complicated by the fact that the IEPA adopted *18 a regulation providing that Class I disposal sites (i. e., chemical-waste-disposal sites), must be secure without engineering. The USEPA, however, has recently adopted regulations to require all landfill sites to establish containment-engineering systems to detect and prevent migration of chemicals. (45 Fed.Reg. 33,239-42 (May 19, 1980).) Moreover, the General Assembly has, since the inception of this suit, passed a statute prohibiting the placement of a hazardous-waste-disposal site above a shaft or tunneled mine. Section 21(g) of the Environmental Protection Act provides:

"No person shall:

(g) Locate a hazardous waste disposal site above an active or inactive shaft or tunneled mine or within 2 miles of an active fault in the earth's crust. In counties of population less than 225,000 no hazardous waste disposal site shall be located (1) within 11/2 miles of the corporate limits as defined on June 30, 1978, of any municipality without the approval of the governing body of the municipality in an official action; or (2) within 1000 feet of an existing private well or the existing source of a public water supply measured from the boundary of the actual active permitted site and excluding existing private wells on the property of the permit applicant.

The provisions of this subsection do not apply to publicly-owned sewage works or the disposal or utilization of sludge from publicly-owned sewage works. " (Ill.Rev.Stat.1979, ch. 1111/2, par. 1021(g).)

The instant disposal site is above an inactive tunneled mine lying partly within the corporate limits of the village of Wilsonville. Without an express statutory provision stating an act is to have retroactive effect, it can only be applied prospectively. (Stigler v. City of Chicago (1971), 48 Ill.2d 20, 24, 268 N.E.2d 26; People ex rel. Schmidt v. Yerger (1961), 21 Ill.2d 338, 344, 172 N.E.2d 753; 2 A. Sutherland, Statutory Construction sec. 41.04, at 252 (1973).) Thus, the defendant cannot be thought to be in violation of the foregoing provision. *19 The fact remains, however, that the instant site, which is intended to be permanent, is located above an inactive tunneled mine.

P#33. Moreover, Dr. Nolan Augenbaugh testified at great length, supported by many photographs, of the considerable subsidence which has already occurred near the site. In Dr. Augenbaugh's opinion, subsidence will occur at the site itself. The defendant's experts testified that any subsidence would be negligible and shallow and would not present a threat to health or life. Dr. Augenbaugh refuted this testimony. He stated that subsidence would permit chemical-waste materials to seep into the ground water. In addition, Dr. Augenbaugh testified that subsidence would create a "bathtub effect" by permitting water to get into the trenches, eventually rise to the surface, overflow, and contaminate the ground around the site. We think the circuit court was fully justified in giving more weight to Dr. Augenbaugh's well-documented opinion than to the opinions of defendant's experts. We will not disturb that finding.

P#34. Another assignment of error raised by defendant is that the circuit court should have allowed its motion to strike the opinion testimony of Drs. Zahalsky and Hall because of lack of a foundation for their opinions, lack of qualifications, and lack of evidence that any intermixing of chemicals would occur.

P#35. We again are constrained to disagree with the defendant's characterization of the testimony adduced at trial. Dr. Zahalsky and Dr. Hall testified that oxidizing channels caused by root systems and subsidence of the earth would permit air to reach the chemical-waste materials. Defendant's own site manager testified that the 55-gallon drums and paper bags used to transport the materials to the site were not intended to and would not contain the materials forever. There was evidence in fact that several of the drums were rusting, leaking, and spilling when they arrived *20 at the site and that others were rolled over the edge of the trenches. Furthermore, photographs taken of the site and admitted into evidence show that the individual drums were not uniformly separated by several feet of clay. Moreover, Dr. Zahalsky, as recognized by the circuit court, is fully qualified in the field of biochemistry, and Dr. Hall is qualified as a chemist and toxicologist. They both testified to possible reactions caused by the intermixing of certain chemicals. They both also stated the reactions were not certainties but that, with the given flashpoints of certain chemicals, the fact that oxygen could reach the waste materials and the highly volatile nature of some of the chemical-waste materials, in their opinions, based upon a reasonable degree of scientific certainty, it was entirely possible that an "explosive interaction" in the form of fires, gaseous emissions, or explosions could occur at the site. While defendant's expert witnesses disputed these opinions and referred to fire-retardant properties of some chemicals, or the unavailability of ambient temperatures due to lack of oxygen, we are unable to say that Drs. Zahalsky's and Hall's opinions were wrong and the other experts were right. Drs. Zahalsky's and Hall's opinions are at least as plausible as defendant's experts, are based on explicit examples of possible chemical reactions, are buttressed by the two doctors' qualifications, and are supported by evidence concerning conditions at the site which indicate intermixing could occur. The trial court was correct in denying the motion to strike.

P#36. As the defendant candidly admits about its next assigned error, it cannot prove that 13 persons did not smell odors or see dust emanating from the site. Therefore, it cannot argue that the court's finding based on this evidence was contrary to the manifest weight of the evidence.

The defendant does argue, however, that evidence of dust and odors does not justify ordering closure of the site. Less restrictive relief must be ordered instead. We agree, of *21 course, that dust and odors alone do not justify the relief which has been ordered in this case. "Whether smoke, odors, dust or gaseous fumes constitute a(n) (enjoinable) nuisance depends on the peculiar facts presented by each case." (City of Chicago v. Commonwealth Edison Co. (1974), 24 Ill. App.3d 624, 631-32, 321 N.E.2d 412, wherein it was held that "no unreasonable or substantial injury" was established so as to warrant enjoining the defendant from operating its plant (24 Ill. App.3d 624, 633, 321 N.E.2d 412).) But, when the dust and odors the trial court found to be present at the site are considered together with the other evidence indicating that the air, water, and earth in and around the site will become contaminated, the trial court's relief is not excessive.

P#37. The same is true of defendant's argument that the evidence of spillage from trucks as they were driven through the village does not warrant closure of the site. Evidence of spillage is simply an additional reason the circuit court ordered the site closed. Whether spillage alone would justify closure is not before us.

P#38. The trial court herein concluded that defendant's chemical-waste-disposal site constitutes both a private and a public nuisance. Professor Prosser has defined a private nuisance as "a civil wrong, based on a disturbance of rights in land" (Prosser, Torts sec. 86, at 572 (4th ed. 1971)), and a public nuisance as "an act or omission 'which obstructs or causes inconvenience or damage to the public in the exercise of rights common to all Her Majesty's subjects.' " (Prosser, Torts sec. 88, at 583 (4th ed. 1971) quoting, Stephen, General View of the Criminal Law of England 105 (1890); City of Chicago v. Festival Theatre Corp. (1980), 88 Ill.App.3d 216, 223, 43 Ill.Dec. 341, 410 N.E.2d 341.) Prosser has also quoted the following, more precise definition of a public nuisance: " 'A common or public nuisance is the doing of or the failure to do something that injuriously affects the safety, health or morals of the public, or works *22 some substantial annoyance, inconvenience or injury to the public.' " (Prosser, Torts sec. 88, at 583 n.29 (4th ed. 1971), quoting, Commonwealth v. South Covington & Cincinnati Street Ry. Co. (1918), 181 Ky. 459, 463, 205 S.W. 581, 583.) It is generally conceded that a nuisance is remediable by injunction or a suit for damages. See Belmar Drive-In Theatre v. Illinois State Toll Highway Com. (1966), 34 Ill.2d 544, 546, 216 N.E.2d 788.

P#39. The defendant herein argues that "(e)ven if some or all of plaintiffs' evidence is deemed believable, the findings of the courts below that (defendant's) conduct constitutes a prospective nuisance must be reversed for failure to * * * balance the reasonableness and utility of the defendant's conduct, the harm to the plaintiff, and the general societal policy toward risk-taking before (a court may) find an actionable nuisance present." The defendant continues that the law of Illinois requires that the circuit court engage in a balancing process before reaching a conclusion that the waste disposal site presents a prospective nuisance. The appellate court appears to have agreed with the defendant that the trial court did not engage in a balancing process:

> "The record in the case on appeal indicates that the trial court acknowledged the need for the landfill facility and the substantial investment defendant had made in it but stated in its memorandum opinion, 'The court will not balance public benefit or public inconvenience against the individual right,' thus, apparently refusing to engage in the balancing." (77 Ill.App.3d 618, 638, 33 Ill.Dec. 163, 396 N.E.2d 552.)

P#40. We do not agree, however, with the foregoing characterization of the trial court's statement. The trial court's statement is a direct quotation from Wente v. Commonwealth Fuel Co. (1908), 232 Ill. 526, 533, 83 N.E. 1049. There, this court affirmed a decree in equity which enjoined the defendant from piling its coal against the plaintiff's building and from operating its coal hopper in the manner in which it had *23 previously been operated. This court said:

> "The business of the defendant is a necessary one and it is not a nuisance per se, but if a business is offensive to such a degree as to materially interfere with ordinary physical comfort, measured, not by the standard of persons of delicate sensibilities and fastidious habits, but by the habits and feelings of ordinary people, and the damages are of a nature which cannot be adequately compensated for in an action at law, a court of equity will grant an injunction. In such a case the court will not balance public benefits or public inconvenience against the individual right. (Seacord v. People, 121 Ill. 623 (13 N.E. 194).)"

P#41. It is reasonably clear that this court and the circuit court meant that where individual rights are unreasonably interfered with, the public benefit from a particular facility will not outweigh the individual right, and the facility's use will be enjoined or curtailed. Such a conclusion presupposes a balancing process with the greater weight being given to the individual's right to use and enjoy property over a public benefit or convenience from having a business operate at a particular location. In such an instance, the individual's right to noninterference takes precedence.

P#42. Moreover, the trial court did engage in a balancing process, as is made clear by the following excerpt from the trial court's memorandum opinion.

"It is the opinion of the Court that the state of the law is such that nuisance cannot be justified on the ground of necessity, pecuniary interest, convenience or economic advantage.

P#43. The Court understands as does counsel that there is a need for disposal of industrial hazardous wastes. However, where disposal of wastes create a nuisance said disposal site may be closed through legal action.

P#44. Substantial sums of money have been expended by the defendant in developing and operating the Earthline site at Wilsonville. Not only is the site convenient to nearby industries *24 but it is a profit producer for the defendant. All of these elements are relevant to our economic system but notwithstanding the same it is the opinion of the Court that nuisances cannot be justified on such grounds when we have substantial injury to individual rights, community rights, substantial damage to human beings and other living things.

P#45. The Court recognizes that in time of war or great national emergency the creation of a nuisance may be legally allowed and/or authorized by statute. Such is not the situation before the Court in this cause.

P#46. Whether or not a business is useful or necessary or whether or not it contributes to the welfare and/or prosperity of the community are elements to be considered in a serious manner but said elements are not determinative as to whether or not the operation is a nuisance.

P#47. The importance of an industry to the wealth and prosperity of an area does not as a matter of law give to it rights superior to the primary or natural rights of citizens who live nearby. However, such matters may be considered and have been in this case.

P#48. It is the opinion of the Court that trifling annoyances or inconveniences of an operation will not give the character of a nuisance to a business that is useful and necessary to society.

P#49. A significant inquiry is was the business established and then persons moved into the business area after it was established and subsequent thereto the business operation moved in and now complaints are made by the citizens who were located in the area before the business was so located. It is the opinion of the Court that if a business is located in a certain area before complainants moved into the area and if the complainants come to the nuisance this may constitute a defense or operate as an estoppel. A person cannot place himself in a position where you suffer and then complain. In this case the defendant established its chemical waste landfill near the area where persons of the Village had resided for many years. Complaints came from residents many of whom lived in the area long before the industrial waste disposal site was ever established.

P#50. An industrial waste disposal site in and adjacent to a village means that the hazardous waste disposal operation is near or next to homes, families children, youth, middle *25 aged and old people sick people, well people sensitive persons and anxious and fearful persons. The location of a business has significance in reference to being a nuisance or not being a nuisance." (Emphasis added.)

P#51. We think the foregoing indicates that the trial court did carefully engage in a balancing process between the site's social utility and the plaintiffs' right to enjoy their property and not suffer deleterious effects from chemical wastes. Accordingly, the defendant's argument that the trial court did not balance the equities in this case is without merit.

P#52. The defendant's next contention is that the courts below were in error when they failed to require a showing of a substantial risk of certain and extreme future harm before enjoining operation of the defendant's site. We deem it necessary to explain that a prospective nuisance is a fit candidate for injunctive relief. Prosser states: "Both public and private nuisances require some substantial interference with the interest involved. Since nuisance is a common subject of equity jurisdiction, the damage against which an injunction is asked is often merely threatened or potential; but even in such cases, there must be at least a threat of a substantial invasion of the plaintiff's interests." (Prosser, Torts sec. 87, at 577 (4th ed. 1971).) The defendant does not dispute this proposition; it does, however, argue that the trial court did not follow the proper standard for determining when a prospective nuisance may be enjoined. The defendant argues that the proper standard to be used is that an injunction is proper only if there is a "dangerous probability" that the threatened or potential injury will occur. (See Restatement (Second) of Torts sec. 933(1), at 561, comment b (1979).) The defendant further argues that the appellate court looked only at the potential consequences of not enjoining the operation of the site as a nuisance and not at the likelihood of whether harm would occur. The defendant assigns error on this basis.

P#53. We agree with the defendant's statement of the law, *26 but not with its urged application to the facts of this case. Again, Professor Prosser has offered a concise commentary. He has stated that "(o)ne distinguishing feature of equitable relief is that it may be granted upon the threat of harm which has not yet occurred. The defendant may be restrained from entering upon an activity where it is highly probable that it will lead to a nuisance, although if the possibility is merely uncertain or contingent he may be left to his remedy after the nuisance has occurred." (Prosser, Torts sec. 90, at 603 (4th ed. 1971).) This view is in accord with Illinois law. (People ex rel. Difanis v. Futia (1978), 56 Ill.App.3d 920, 926, 15 Ill.Dec. 184, 373 N.E.2d 530; Fink v. Board of Trustees (1966), 71 Ill.App.2d 276, 281-82, 218 N.E.2d 240.) In Fink the plaintiff sought to enjoin construction of a dam and also the discharge of sewage effluent in a watercourse which flowed past plaintiffs' property. Construction of the dam was not enjoined, but the discharge of effluent was prospectively enjoined. The court stated:

> "While, as a general proposition, an injunction will be granted only to restrain an actual, existing nuisance, a court of equity may enjoin a threatened or anticipated nuisance, where it clearly appears that a nuisance will necessarily result from the contemplated act or thing which it is sought to enjoin. This is particularly true where the proof shows that the apprehension of material injury is well grounded upon a state of facts from which it appears that the danger is real and immediate. While care should be used in granting injunctions to avoid prospective injuries, there is no requirement that the court must wait until the injury occurs before granting relief." (71 Ill.App.2d 226, 281-82, 218 N.E.2d 240.)

P#54. We agree.

P#55. In this case there can be no doubt but that it is highly probable that the chemical-waste-disposal site will bring *27 about a substantial injury. Without again reviewing the extensive evidence adduced at trial, we think it is sufficiently clear that it is highly probable that the instant site will constitute a public nuisance if, through either an explosive interaction, migration, subsidence, or the "bathtub effect," the highly toxic chemical wastes deposited at the site escape and contaminate the air, water, or ground around the site. That such an event will occur was positively attested to by several expert witnesses. A court does not have to wait for it to happen before it can enjoin such a result. Additionally, the fact is that the condition of a nuisance is already present at the site due to the location of the site and the manner in which it has been operated. Thus, it is only the damage which is prospective. Under these circumstances, if a court can prevent any damage from occurring, it should do so.

P#56. The defendant next asserts that error occurred in the courts below when they failed to defer to the IEPA and the USEPA, as well as when they failed to give weight to the permits issued by the IEPA. This assertion has no merit, however, because the data relied upon by the IEPA in deciding to issue a permit to the defendant were data collected by the defendant, data which have been proved at trial to be inaccurate. In particular, defendant's experts concluded that any subsidence at the site would be negligible. The IEPA (as well as the USEPA) adopted this inaccurate conclusion in deciding to issue a permit to the defendant.

P#57. We also disagree with the defendant that since the plaintiffs could seek review from the IEPA's decision to grant permits to the defendant through the Pollution Control Board they have an adequate remedy at law and are unable to obtain relief in a court of equity. First, the plaintiffs are not seeking a review of the issuance of permits. The plaintiffs seek to enjoin a nuisance, a matter which is properly brought in a court of equity. This court *28 has stated that jurisdiction exists in the circuit court "to abate public nuisances which may endanger the general welfare." (People ex rel. Scott v. Janson (1974), 57 Ill.2d 451, 460, 312 N.E.2d 620.) Thus, the trial court has subject matter jurisdiction to decide the issues raised herein, and to award appropriate equitable relief.

P#58. The next issue we consider is whether the trial court erroneously granted a permanent injunction. The defendant argues first that the courts below granted injunctive relief without proof that the alleged injury is both substantial and certain to occur. We have already addressed this question in discussing whether relief may be granted for a prospective nuisance. We will not unduly prolong this already lengthy opinion with duplicative discussion. The second argument raised is that the courts below did not balance the equities in deciding to enjoin the defendant from continuing to operate the waste-disposal site. Defendant cites Harrison v. Indiana Auto Shredders Co. (7th Cir. 1975), 528 F.2d 1107, for the proposition that the court must balance the relative harm and benefit to the plaintiff and defendant before a court may enjoin a nuisance. (528 F.2d 1107, 1109.) A balancing process is implicit in the following statements made by this court in Haack v. Lindsay Light & Chemical Co. (1946), 393 Ill. 367, 373, 375, 66 N.E.2d 391:

> "It is equally clear that the rule in this State and generally, is, and should be, that even though a right has been established in law, a court of equity will not, as a matter of course, interpose by injunction but will consider all the circumstances, the consequences of such action and the real equity of the case.
>
> To entitle one to injunctive relief he must establish, as against the defendant, an actual and substantial injury and not merely a technical inconsequential *29 wrong entitling him to nominal damages, only. To warrant the allowance of the writ of injunction it must clearly appear that some act has been done or is threatened against the plaintiff which will produce an irreparable injury to him. (Cleveland v. Martin, 218 Ill. 73 (75 N.E. 772); Girard v. Lehigh Stone Co., 280 Ill. 479 (117 N.E. 698); Dunn v. Youmans, 224 Ill. 34 (79 N.E. 321); Springer v. Walters, 139 Ill. 419 (28 N.E. 761).) As this court observed in Klumpp v. Rhoads, 362 Ill. 412 (200 N.E. 153) 'If the damages are of a nature which cannot be adequately compensated for in a suit at law, equity will afford relief by injunction. On the other hand, lawful and useful business may not be stopped on account of trifling or imaginary annoyances which do not constitute real injury.' " (393 Ill. 367, 375, 66 N.E.2d 391.)

P#59. We would add that an injunction should be reasonable and should only be as broad as is essential to safeguard the rights of the plaintiff. Toushin v. City of Chicago (1974), 23 Ill.App.3d 797, 804, 320 N.E.2d 202.

P#60. In Harrison, an auto shredder operated its business in a residential neighborhood in Indianapolis. There was considerable testimony from nonexperts that the shredder created too much noise, vibration, and air pollution in the forms of dust and debris. The defendant shredder company defended on the ground that while difficulties in starting up the operation had occurred, it had taken steps, and would do whatever further was necessary, to abate the nuisance. Several experts testified that the noise, vibration, and pollution were well within permissible State and local standards. After a 30-day trial, the court issued a permanent injunction ordering the shredder to cease operations and awarded permanent and punitive damages to the plaintiffs for the diminution in value of their property. The trial court conceded that the shredder performed a "very real social function" in disposing of and recycling old automobiles, but concluded that the machine ought *30 to be somewhere else. (528 F.2d 1107, 1119.) The court of appeals agreed that the shredder's effect upon the quality of life in the neighborhood entitled the plaintiffs to some form of equitable relief and damages. The court did not, however, view the complete cessation of operations as appropriate to the facts presented. The court stated:

> "Reasonableness is the standard by which the court should fashion its relief in ordinary nuisance cases, Meeks v. Woods, 66 Ind.App. 594, 118 N.E. 591 (1918), and reasonableness is also the appropriate standard for relief from environmental nuisance. Ordinarily a permanent injunction will not lie unless (1) either the polluter seriously and imminently threatens the public health or (2) he causes non-health injuries that are substantial and the business cannot be operated to avoid the injuries apprehended. Thus the particular situation facts of each pollution nuisance case will determine whether a permanent injunction should be issued." (528 F.2d 1107, 1123.)

P#61. The court concluded in Harrison that since the defendant was not in violation of any relevant zoning standards, and since the shredder did not pose an imminent hazard to the public health, the defendant should not be prevented from continuing to operate. The court then ordered that the defendant be permitted a reasonable time to "launder its objectionable features." 528 F.2d 1107, 1125.

P#62. This case is readily distinguishable for the reason that the gist of this case is that the defendant is engaged in an extremely hazardous undertaking at an unsuitable location, which seriously and imminently poses a threat to the public health. We are acutely aware that the service provided by the defendant is a valuable and necessary one. We also know that it is preferable to have chemical-waste-disposal sites than to have illegal dumping in rivers, streams, and deserted areas. But a site such as defendant's, *31 if it is to do the job it is intended to do, must be located in a secure place, where it will pose no threat to health or life, now, or in the future. This site was intended to be a permanent disposal site for the deposit of extremely hazardous chemical-waste materials. Yet this site is located above an abandoned tunneled mine where subsidence is occurring several years ahead of when it was anticipated. Also, the permeability-coefficient samples taken by defendant's experts, though not conclusive alone, indicate that the soil is more permeable at the site than expected. Moreover, the spillage, odors, and dust caused by the presence of the disposal site indicate why it was inadvisable to locate the site so near the plaintiff village.

P#63. Therefore, we conclude that in fashioning relief in this case the trial court did balance relative hardship to be caused to the plaintiffs and defendant, and did fashion reasonable relief when it ordered the exhumation of all material from the site and the reclamation of the surrounding area. The instant site is akin to Mr. Justice Sutherland's observation that "Nuisance may be merely a right thing in a wrong place like a pig in the parlor instead of the barnyard." Village of Euclid v. Ambler Realty Co. (1926), 272 U.S. 365, 388, 47 S.Ct. 114, 118, 71 L.Ed. 303, 311, quoted in 2 J. Dooley, Modern Tort Litigation sec. 31.15, at 225 (1977).

P#64. We are also cognizant of amicus USEPA's suggestion in its brief and affidavits filed with the appellate court which urge that we remand to the circuit court so that alternatives to closure of the site and exhumation of the waste materials may be considered. The USEPA states: "Heavy equipment may damage drums, releasing wastes and possibly causing gaseous emissions, fires, and explosions. Repackaging and transporting damaged drums also risks releasing wastes. Workers performing the exhumation face dangers from contact with or inhalation of wastes; these risks cannot be completely eliminated with protective *32 clothing and breathing apparatus. Nearby residents may also be endangered." It is ironic that the host of horribles mentioned by the USEPA in support of keeping the site open includes some of the same hazards which the plaintiffs have raised as reasons in favor of closing the site.

P#65. The USEPA continues that while it is not suggesting a specific alternative remedy to closure, possible alternative remedies exist: "A proper cap of low permeability can ensure that little or no rain water can infiltrate the site, and thus that little leachate will be formed. Leachate-collection sumps can also be installed to remove whatever leachate is formed. Ground water monitoring can generally detect any migration of waste constituents, and counterpumping of contaminated ground water (or other measures) can protect against further migration."

P#66. We note, however, that the USEPA does not suggest how the location of the disposal site above an abandoned tunneled mine and the effects of subsidence can be overcome. Instead, the USEPA refers to a report admitted into evidence at trial, which was prepared by a technical evaluation team from the USEPA. The team's report had a limited scope. It only "compares and relates the technical aspects of the facility for disposal of PCB's to the EPA proposed regulations." The team visited the site on June 8, 1977, and discussed the site with defendant's personnel. Extensive technical data were provided to the team by defendant, the IEPA, ISGS, and other sources during the site visit and over the next several months, but the team itself did not collect any soil or water samples for analysis. Thus the team used the same data in reaching its conclusion as were used during the trial by defendant. The team noted the following points:

> "(1) The glacial till which lies under the site is quite dense and essentially massive (permeability 10 -8 cm/sec.)."
> This finding was effectively refuted at trial.
> *33 "(2) The potential for mine subsidence under the site as reported by the ISGS is negligible."
> Dr. Augenbaugh's studies, which the circuit court gave more weight, directly contradicted this finding.
> "(3) The 14 groundwater and the 3 surface water sampling points around the site are sufficient to detect any contamination of the sand layer or of the surface drainage channels (analyses to date indicate no change in the amounts or types of contaminants compared to those measured from samples taken before the site began accepting waste)."
> As previously stated, some of the sampling points are a considerable distance apart, thereby allowing for the possibility that contamination could occur and be undetected. Moreover, though the defendant states that it could easily establish a containment trench to catch any waste migration, since the IEPA does not have such a requirement, the defendant did not build a containment trench. Indeed, IEPA regulations require that Class I disposal sites, such as the instant one, must be secure without the use of containment-engineering techniques. Since the inception of this case, however, the USEPA has adopted regulations which require containment trenches at all chemical-waste-disposal sites.

P#67. Finally, Sam Campagna, defendant's former site manager, testified at trial that no test had, as yet, been taken from the samples to detect whether cyanide was present in the monitoring wells, and that, during the quarterly sampling, tests were conducted to detect certain chemicals only. Thus, some chemicals could be present for several quarters before tests would reveal their presence.

> "(4) The operation of the site, as demonstrated to the (team) considers those precautions necessary to assure that both the public and the environment are protected.
> (5) The site, at the time of the visit, was in good order and the site housekeeping procedures appear adequate."
> *34 These findings are in conflict with the defendant's own delivery reports and other evidence adduced at trial which show that many of the drums were brought to the site in a rusting and leaking condition. Also, the evidence of spillage on the streets of Wilsonville, and of rolling drums into trenches instead of carefully lowering them in, fly in the face of the team's report.

"(6) The segregation of PCBs from solvents as practiced by (defendant) will cause the PCBs to be nearly immobile (PCB travel times will be at least 10 to 100 times longer than even the least mobile heavy metals)."

P#68. Dr. Hall challenged this finding when he testified that PCBs would be dissolved in the organic solvent components of the paint sludges deposited in trenches Nos. 2, 3, and 4. Moreover, Robert A. Griffin, an associate geochemist with the ISGS, reported to the USEPA that although PCBs are "immobile in soil materials, including pure sand, when leached with water," when "the mobility of PCB's were tested using organic solvents (e. g. carbon tetrachloride, methylene chloride, methanol, and acetone), using the same experimental conditions as on the aqueous solvent tests, the PCB's were found to be highly mobile." Griffin went on to say that as long as PCBs were not disposed in the same trenches with organic compounds that would make PCBs soluble, the possibility of migration of PCBs was nil. Clearly, this precaution has not been followed by the defendant.

P#69. Finally, the USEPA's own regulations governing disposal of PCBs, which became effective November 19, 1980, contain the following:

"High temperature incineration is the primary disposal method for PCBs. This disposal method is the only technique that will result in the destruction of PCBs and prevent the eventual escape of the chemical to the environment. Properly operated chemical waste landfills may provide an element of security for the containment of PCBs *35 for long periods of time, but the ultimate fate of PCBs using this method is unknown.

All PCB chemical substances, PCB mixtures, PCB articles, and PCB containers are to be disposed of by high temperature incineration with the following exceptions:

(A) PCB transformers * * *

(B) Until July 1, 1979, approved chemical waste landfills may be used for the disposal of non-liquid PCB mixtures * * *

(C) Small PCB compactors that are used in private housing units * * *. (42 Fed.Reg. 26,566 (1977).)

Therefore, the PCBs contained at defendant's site are in violation of USEPA regulations presently in effect, even though it is true that these regulations are not strictly enforced by the USEPA.

P#70. The point is that the USEPA is asking this court to remand this cause to the circuit court on the basis of evidence which the trial court has previously considered and discounted in favor of the plaintiffs' evidence. We see no point in doing so. The circuit court carefully weighed the evidence adduced throughout the 104-day trial, balanced the relative hardship to the plaintiffs and defendant of permitting the site to continue to operate, or closing it down, and reached the conclusion which is strongly supported by the record, that the site's dangers outweigh its utility. Moreover, it needs to be remembered, as the trial judge pointed out, that the nuisance in this case came to the village. (See Prosser, Torts sec. 91, at 611 (4th ed. 1971).) The residents of Wilsonville have a right to enjoy and use their property without being unreasonably interfered with by the defendant's hazardous-waste site. Also, there is evidence in the record that representatives of the defendant told the village board, in response to a question from the water works commissioner, that no toxic materials would be buried at the site, when the truth is precisely the opposite. We view these factors as additional reasons why *36 defendant's conduct is inequitable and why plaintiffs are entitled to a permanent injunction. We conclude therefore that the relief fashioned by the trial court is reasonable under the precise facts of this case and will not be disturbed.

P#71. The defendant raises another point that the courts below refused to consider the practicability of exhuming and moving the wastes deposited at the site. Our reading of the opinions of the trial and appellate courts indicates the contrary. Serious consideration was given to available remedies; and it was concluded that exhumation of the materials and reclamation of the site is the best and safest alternative. Additionally, the defendant "concedes" in its reply brief filed with this court that it is possible to excavate the site and haul the materials elsewhere. It disputes, however, the technical and scientific reasonableness of doing so.

P#72. First, many of these materials have already been transported once from Dittmer, Missouri, where they were illegally dumped and had destroyed all vegetation for a square mile, to Wilsonville. So it is possible to transport these materials. Second, since the trial court has decided that the likelihood exists that great harm will be done if the materials are not moved, it seems only reasonable that the materials must be taken somewhere safer than where they are now deposited. It is the defendant's responsibility to make certain the exhumation is performed in a careful manner.

P#73. Finally, the defendant argues that the decisions of the courts below constitute sudden changes in State law and, as such, deprive the defendant of its property without due process of law. (See Hughes v. Washington (1967), 389 U.S. 290, 298, 88 S.Ct. 438, 443, 19 L.Ed.2d 530, 536 (Stewart, J., concurring).) We disagree; the principles of law applied in this case are neither new, unreasonable, nor unpredictable. Manifestly, a party cannot expect to operate *37 a site in the manner and in the location the defendant has chosen and expect to be immune from liability for creating a public nuisance. Defendant's argument has no merit in this case.

P#74. Accordingly, for all the reasons stated, the judgments of the circuit and appellate courts are affirmed and the cause is remanded to the circuit court to enable it to retain jurisdiction to supervise the enforcement of its order. See Hake v. People (1907), 230 Ill. 174, 196, 82 N.E. 561; Melbourne Corp. v. City of Chicago (1979), 76 Ill.App.3d 595, 611, 31 Ill.Dec. 914, 394 N.E.2d 1291.

P#75. Affirmed and remanded.

RYAN, Justice, concurring:

While I agree with both the result reached by the majority and the reasoning employed supporting the opinion, I wish to add a brief comment. In response to the defendant's argument that the trial court failed to apply the proper standard for determining when a prospective nuisance may be enjoined, the majority concluded that the court had in fact applied the correct rule as set out in Fink v. Board of Trustees (1966), 71 Ill.App.2d 276, 218 N.E.2d 240. I am concerned that the holding of Fink, quoted by the majority (86 Ill.2d at 26, 55 Ill.Dec. at ––, 426 N.E.2d at 836), may be an unnecessarily narrow view of the test for enjoining prospective tortious conduct in general. Any injunction is, by its very nature, the product of a court's balancing of competing interests, with a result equitably obtained. Prosser, in discussing the law of nuisance, quoted by the majority (86 Ill.2d at 26, 55 Ill.Dec. at ––, 426 N.E.2d at 836), states:

> "(I)f the possibility (of harm) is merely uncertain or contingent (the plaintiff) may be left to his remedy after the nuisance has occurred." Prosser, Torts sec. 90, at 603 (4th ed. 1971).

Prosser thus recognizes that there are cases in which the possibility of inflicting harm is slight and where the plaintiff may be left to his remedy at law. However, I believe that there are situations where the harm that is *38 potential is so devastating that equity should afford relief even though the possibility of the harmful result occurring is uncertain or contingent. The Restatement's position applicable to preventative injunctive relief in general is that "(t)he more serious the impending harm, the less justification there is for taking the chances that are involved in pronouncing the harm too remote." (Restatement (Second) of Torts sec. 933, at 561, comment b (1979).) If the harm that may result is severe, a lesser possibility of it occurring should be required to support injunctive relief. Conversely, if the potential harm is less severe, a greater possibility that it will happen should be required. Also, in the balancing of competing interests, a court may find a situation where the potential harm is such that a plaintiff will be left to his remedy at law if the possibility of it occurring is slight. This balancing test allows the court to consider a wider range of factors and avoids the anomalous result possible under a more restrictive alternative where a person engaged in an ultrahazardous activity with potentially catastrophic results would be allowed to continue until he has driven an entire community to the brink of certain disaster. A court of equity need not wait so long to provide relief.

Although the "dangerous probability" test has certainly been met in this case, I would be willing to enjoin the activity on a showing of probability of occurrence substantially less than that which the facts presented to this court reveal, due to the extremely hazardous nature of the chemicals being dumped and the potentially catastrophic results.

CASE STUDY II: SPUR INDUSTRIES, INC. V. DEL E. WEBB DEV. CO., 494 P. 2D 700 (ARIZ. 1972)

Note the location of the properties involved in this dispute on the maps in *Study Questions for Spur,* at the end of this case study and on the Companion Website, at http://www.environmentallaw-teach.org/. The dispute concerns properties west of Phoenix, Arizona. Read the *Spur v. Del Webb* opinion, which is printed in this chapter after the *Study Questions*, and in the *Companion.* As you read, notice the paragraph numbering, color code the paragraphs, if that helps you to organize the information, and focus on how the material in each paragraph fits into one of the rubrics for a brief as indicated below. The brief structure below is the same as in *Boomer, Whalen,* and *Wilsonville.*

1. Heading

2. Facts

3. Procedural History

4. Legal Issues

5. Holding or Decision

6. Reasoning

7. Dissenting Opinions

As opinions go, this one is well-organized and logical. In the paragraph 1, Vice Chief Justice of the Arizona Supreme Court provides some procedural history and then clearly states the two central legal issues in this action. Del Webb sues Spur Industries for creating a nuisance by operating a cattle feedlot close to its new development of homes in Sun City. The trial court has enjoined Spur and required the closing and cleanup of the cattle feedlot. The two legal issues before the court are:

a) whether it is equitable for a feedlot operation to be closed as a result of an action taken by a residential home developer when the feedlot was lawful and operating before the residential homes were built and became a nuisance only after the homes were built?

b) whether, if the feedlot can be enjoined, it is then proper for the residential home developer to pay the cost of moving the feedlot because the developer "came to the nuisance?"

Paragraphs 2-8 of the opinion contain the essential facts for this case. The two maps (Exhibits A and B) are important. We learn that this area was primarily agricultural and remained so after the development of the senior citizen community of Youngtown was built in 1954. In 1956, the cattle feedlots were developed and by 1959, there were 35 acres of feedlots with 6,000-7,000 head of cattle. Also in 1959, Del Webb purchased 20,000 acres of farmland and began developing Sun City. In 1960, Spur bought the feedlots from the previous owners and, by 1962, it had completed an expansion program that increased the feedlot acreage to 114 with between 20,000 and 30,000 head of cattle. Exhibit A (1962), is shown below with the author's annotations. Exhibit B (also shown below with the author's annotations) shows that Del Webb had expanded its property holdings north of Peoria Avenue, and most significantly, between Peoria and Olive Avenues bringing the Del Webb property adjacent to the Spur feedlots. According to testimony, in 1963, Del Webb recognized that "sales resistance became so great that the parcels were difficult if not impossible to sell" and the property between Peoria and Olive had not been developed because of this sales resistance. The court states that in 1967, "Del Webb filed its original complaint alleging that in excess of 1300 lots in the southwest portion were unfit for development for sale as residential lots because of the operation of the Spur feedlot."

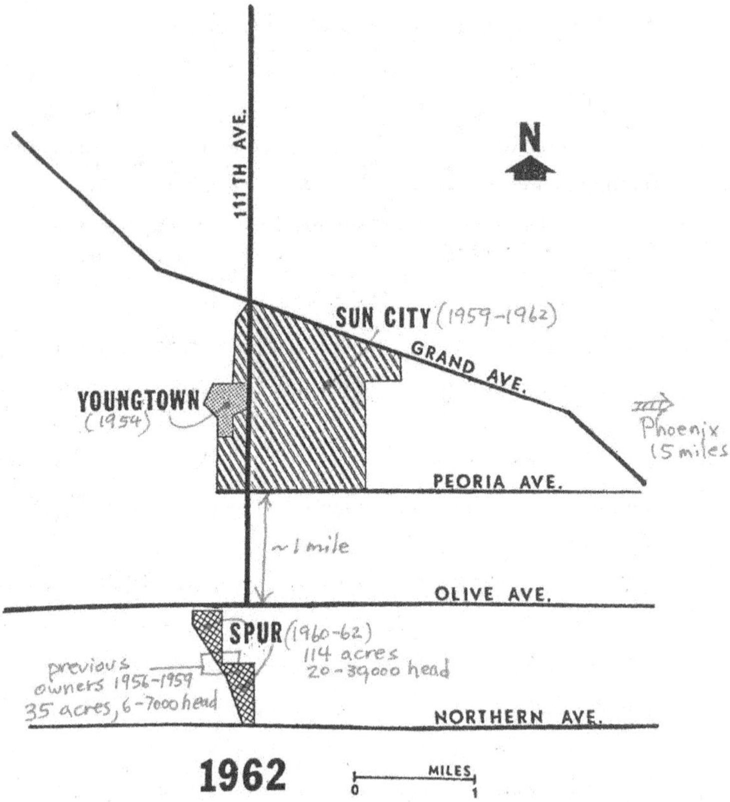

EXHIBIT A

Curiously, we learn in paragraph 9 of the opinion that Del Webb, a private corporation, has filed a public nuisance intentional tort. The citizens or municipal government of Youngtown and Sun City are not parties to this lawsuit. Later we will learn why Del Webb has the standing to sue in public nuisance.

Paragraphs 12-17 of the opinion deal with legal issue #1 – "May Spur Be Enjoined?" Paragraph 12 of the opinion discusses the difference between private and public nuisance, and paragraph 13 discusses the balancing of the equities in the determination of a remedy for private or public nuisance. "Where the injury is slight, the remedy… lies in an action for damages rather than one for an injunction" and then, citing *Boomer v. Atlantic Cement Co.*, the court states that "some courts have held in the 'balancing of conveniences' cases, that damages may be the sole remedy." Using this logic, the court states that the residents of Youngtown, where the nuisance is a minor inconvenience," would be entitled to damages but not injunctive relief. On the other hand, Arizona's highest court has "no difficulty, however, in agreeing with the conclusion of the trial court that Spur's operation was an enjoinable public nuisance as far as the people in the southern portion of Del Webb's Sun City were concerned." In support of this conclusion, the court then quotes

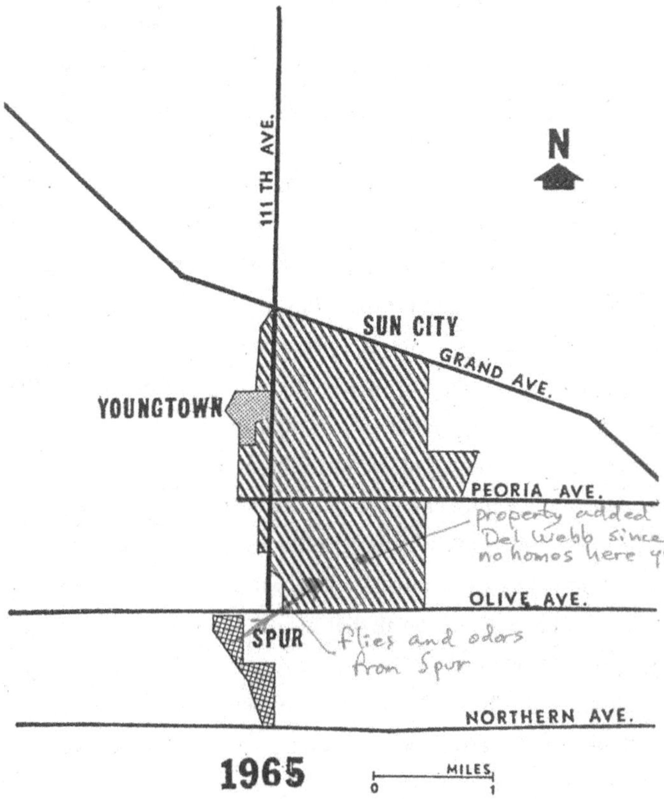

EXHIBIT B

Arizona State law with regard to public nuisance in paragraph 15, and then in paragraph 16, quotes a persuasive authority of a previous Arizona case that says: "[a] business which is not per se a public nuisance may become such by being carried on at a place where the health, comfort, or convenience of a populous neighborhood is affected." "Per se" means by itself.

Paragraph 17 of the opinion states that "it is clear that as to the citizens of Sun City, the operation of Spur's feedlot was both a public and private nuisance. They could have maintained an action to abate the nuisance." Individual citizens of Wilsonville (unlike those in *Boomer*) did not sue in private nuisance. Del Webb's standing is also addressed here. The court states that "Del Webb having shown special injury in the loss of sales, had a standing to bring suit to enjoin the nuisance." According to the Second Restatement of Torts, the test for standing in a public nuisance action is that the member of the public "suffered harm of a kind different from that suffered by other members of the public exercising the right common to the general public that was the subject of the interference." This is a somewhat arcane legal standard but, in the state of Arizona and in the majority of other states, a private corporation may sue in public nuisance if its injury is different from that experienced by the public.

Legal question #2 – "Must Del Webb Indemnify Spur?" – is addressed in paragraphs 18-26 of the opinion. "Indemnify" means to compensate the injured party for their loss, in this case for the cost of closing down the feedlot operation, reclaiming the site and then opening another feedlot elsewhere.

Paragraph 18 of the opinion emphasizes that "courts have long recognized a special responsibility to the public when acting as a court of equity." Quoting from *American Jurisprudence* (2nd ed.) the court states: "[c]ourts of equity may, and frequently do, go much further both to give and withhold relief in furtherance of the public interest than they are accustomed to go when only private interests are involved." *American Jurisprudence* is a persuasive secondary source, an encyclopedia of the U. S. law. It is a hybrid source written by practitioners for practitioners containing brief legal explanations filled with relevant law references. Paragraph 19 of the opinion adds the caveat that the court is also "concerned with protecting the operator of a lawfully, albeit noxious, business from the result of a knowing and willful encroachment by others near his business."

Paragraph 20 of the opinion describes "coming to the nuisance" cases: property owners who purchase property and "knowingly came into a neighborhood reserved for industrial or agricultural endeavors [...] may not have relief." Recall that in both the *Boomer* and *Wilsonville* opinions the court indicated that Boomer et al. as well as the citizens of Wilsonville were already there as property owners or residents and, thus, did not "come to the nuisance." The paragraph ends with a long quote about how residential developers avoid taxes and zoning laws by buying property beyond municipal boundaries and therefore outside the area in which the municipality's zoning regulations and real estate taxes apply. The suggestion is that this quote applies to Del Webb. The paragraph ends with the statement that if Webb were "the only party injured, we would feel justified in holding that the doctrine of 'coming to the nuisance' would have been a bar to the relief asked for by Webb."

Paragraph 22 of the opinion quotes from a Massachusetts opinion that: "[t]he law of nuisance affords no rigid rule to be applied in all instances. It is elastic. It undertakes to require only that which is fair and reasonable under all the circumstances." Both the *Boomer* and *Wilsonville* cases are prime examples of cases showing there are no "rigid rules" for nuisance, but the equities must be balanced in all cases.

Paragraph 23 of the opinion suggests that *Spur* case will also prove to have a novel solution. "Spur is required to move not because of any wrongdoing on the part of Spur, but because of a proper and legitimate regard for the courts for the rights and interests of the public." Continuing this thought in paragraph 24, the court states that "it does not equitably or legally follow, however, that Webb, being entitled to the injunction, is then free of any liability to Spur if Webb has in fact been the cause of the damage Spur has sustained." Finally, in paragraph 25 the court concludes that "[h]aving brought people to the nuisance to the foreseeable detriment of Spur, Webb must indemnify Spur for a reasonable amount of the cost of moving or shutting down."

Paragraph 26 of the opinion contains the order of the court. The case is sent back to the trial court for determination of the compensation that Webb must pay Spur.

To clarify, paragraph 27 of the opinion, the injunction against Spur, was affirmed but the lower courts' refusal to force Del Webb to indemnify Spur was reversed.

Miscellaneous Issues

The Court stated that "as to the citizens of Sun City, Spur's feedlot was both a public and private nuisance. They could have successfully maintained an action to abate the nuisance." *Spur Industries*, 494 P.2d at 706. Indeed, over 400 homeowners sued Spur for damages, but Spur successfully sued Del Webb so that Del Webb would have to compensate Spur for any damages that it might have to pay to individual homeowners in private nuisance tort actions. Additionally, on remand, Del Webb reached a settlement with Spur for $1 million plus the cost of relocating the cattle feedlot. (See, *Telephone conversation with L. Dennis Marlowe, plaintiff's counsel (Mar. 13, 1985)*, as mentioned in Jeff L. Lewin, Compensated Injunctions and the Evolution of Nuisance Law, 71 Iowa L. Rev. 775, 832 (1986)).

Public nuisance would seem to provide major possibilities for environmental tort actions. The problem is standing. A homeowner in Sun City could not sue in public nuisance because they would not have a "special injury," an injury different in kind as well as degree from the rest of the neighborhood. This is not true in every state, so precedent in any particular state would have to be examined to determine if the special injury rule is in force. Lawsuits to test such a rule might be useful while other states may provide more opportunity for a citizen to sue on behalf of the public.

Study Questions for *Spur Industries*

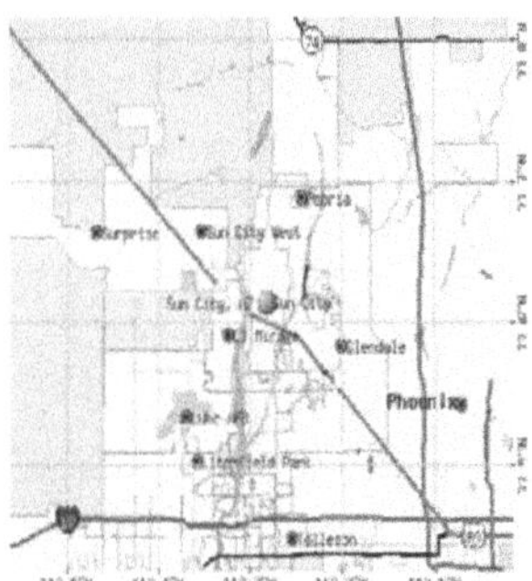

http://www.city-data.com/city/Sun-City-Arizona.html

Sun City, Arizona and picture of Del Webb

1. What are the facts in *Spur v. Del Webb Development Co.*? What was the original cause of action at the trial court level? Who were the plaintiff and defendant at the trial court level in *Spur*? What were the elements of this cause of action? What are the two issues the court addressed?

2. What is standing? Was it *Spur* or *Del Webb* (the plaintiff or the defendant) that had to convince the court that it had standing? What was the issue regarding standing? How was it resolved?

3. Define the concept of coming to the nuisance. Is coming to the nuisance a defense or a cause of action? If the plaintiff can raise it, then it is a cause of action. If the defendant can raise it, then it is an affirmative defense. Did *Del Webb* or *Spur* come to the nuisance? Explain.

Cattle feedlot, https://www.farmsanctuary.org/learn/factory-farming/dairy/

4. How does the trial court's holding differ from the Arizona Supreme Court's holding?

Spur Industries (Court Opinion)

108 Ariz. 178

Supreme Court of Arizona, In Banc.

SPUR INDUSTRIES, INC., AN ARIZONA CORPORATION FORMERLY SPUR FEEDING CO., AN ARIZONA CORPORATION, APPELLANT AND CROSS-APPELLEE,

v.

DEL E. WEBB DEVELOPMENT CO., AN ARIZONA CORPORATION, APPELLEE AND CROSS-APPELLANT.

No. 10410.

|

March 17, 1972.

|

Rehearing Denied April 18, 1972.

Synopsis

Action was brought by real estate developer to enjoin cattle feeding operation. The Superior Court of Maricopa County, Cause No. C-207029, Kenneth C. Chatwin, J., entered a decree from which cross-appeals were taken. The Supreme Court, Cameron, V.C.J., held, inter alia, that where defendant commenced cattle feeding operations in agricultural area well outside boundaries of any city and subsequently real estate developer purchased land nearby and commenced an extensive retirement community development, developer was entitled to enjoin the cattle feeding operation as a nuisance but it was required to indemnify cattle feeder for the reasonable cost of moving or shutting down.

Affirmed in part, reversed in part and remanded.

Attorneys and Law Firms
*179 Snell & Wilmer, by Mark Wilmer, and John Lundin, Phoenix, for appellant and cross-appellee.
L. Dennis Marlowe, Tempe, for appellee and cross-appellant.
Opinion

CAMERON, Vice Chief Justice.

P#1. From a judgment permanently enjoining the defendant, Spur Industries, Inc., from operating a cattle feedlot near the plaintiff Del E. Webb Development Company's Sun City, Spur appeals. Webb cross-appeals. Although numerous issues are raised, we feel that it is necessary to answer only two questions. They are:

> 1. Where the operation of a business, such as a cattle feedlot is lawful in the first instance, but becomes a nuisance by reason of a nearby residential area, may the feedlot operation be enjoined in an action brought by the developer of the residential area?
>
> 2. Assuming that the nuisance may be enjoined, may the developer of a completely new town or urban area in a previously agricultural area be required to indemnify the operator of the feedlot who must move or cease operation because of the presence of the residential area created by the developer?

P#2. *180 The facts necessary for a determination of this matter on appeal are as follows. The area in question is located in Maricopa County, Arizona, some 14 to 15 miles west of the urban area of Phoenix, on the Phoenix-Wickenburg Highway, also known as Grand Avenue. About two miles south of Grand Avenue is Olive Avenue which runs east and west. 111th Avenue runs north and south as does the Agua Fria River immediately to the west. See Exhibits A and B below.

P#3. *181 Farming started in this area about 1911. In 1929, with the completion of the Carl Pleasant Dam, gravity flow water became available to the property located to the west of the Agua Fria River, though land to the east remained dependent upon well water for irrigation. By 1950, the only urban areas in the vicinity were the agriculturally related communities of Peoria, El Mirage, and Surprise located along Grand Avenue. Along 111th Avenue, approximately one mile south of Grand Avenue and 1 1/2 miles north of Olive Avenue, the community of Youngtown was commenced *182 in 1954. Youngtown is a retirement community appealing primarily to senior citizens.

P#4. In 1956, Spur's predecessors in interest, H. Marion Welborn and the Northside Hay Mill and Trading Company, developed feed-lots, about 1/2 mile south of Olive Avenue, in an area between the confluence of the usually dry Agua Fria and New Rivers. The area is well suited for cattle feeding and in 1959, there were 25 cattle feeding pens or dairy operations within a 7 mile radius of the location developed by Spur's predecessors. In April and May of 1959, the Northside Hay Mill was feeding between 6,000 and 7,000 head of cattle and Welborn approximately 1,500 head on a combined area of 35 acres.

P#5. In May of 1959, Del Webb began to plan the development of an urban area to be known as Sun City. For this purpose, the Marinette and the Santa Fe Ranches, some 20,000 acres of farmland, were purchased for $15,000,000 or $750.00 per acre. This price was considerably less than the price of land located near the urban area of Phoenix, and along with the success of Youngtown was a factor influencing the decision to purchase the property in question.

P#6. By September 1959, Del Webb had started construction of a golf course south of Grand Avenue and Spur's predecessors had started to level ground for more feedlot area. In 1960, Spur purchased the property in question and began a rebuilding and expansion program extending both to the north and south of the original facilities. By 1962, Spur's expansion program was completed and had expanded from approximately 35 acres to 114 acres. See Exhibit A above.

P#7. Accompanied by an extensive advertising campaign, homes were first offered by Del Webb in January 1960 and the first unit to be completed was south of Grand Avenue and approximately 2 1/2 miles north of Spur. By 2 May 1960, there were 450 to 500 houses completed or under construction. At this time, Del Webb did not consider odors from the Spur feed pens a problem and Del Webb continued to develop in a southerly direction, until sales resistance became so great that the parcels were difficult if not impossible to sell. Thomas E. Breen, Vice President and General Manager of the housing division of Del Webb, testified at deposition as follows:

> 'Q Did you ever have any discussions with Tony Cole at or about the time the sales office was opened south of Peoria concerning the problem in sales as the development came closer towards the feed lots?
>
> 'A Not at the time that that facility was opened. That was subsequent to that.
>
> 'Q All right, what is it that you recall about conversations with Cole on that subject?
>
> 'A Well, when the feed lot problem became a bigger problem, which, really, to the best of my recollection, commenced to become a serious problem in 1963, and there was some talk about not developing that area because of sales resistance, and to my recollection we shifted-we had planned at that time to the eastern portion of the property, and it was a consideration.
>
> 'Q Was any specific suggestion made by Mr. Cole as to the line of demarcation that should be drawn or anything of that type exactly where the development should cease?
>
> 'A I don't recall anything specific as far as the definite line would be, other than, you know, that it would be advisable to stay out of the southwestern portion there because of sales resistance.

'Q And to the best of your recollection, this was in about 1963?

'A That would be my recollection, yes.

'Q As you recall it, what was the reason that the suggestion was not *183 adopted to stop developing towards the southwest of the development?

'A Well, as far as I know, that decision was made subsequent to that time.

'Q Right. But I mean at that time?

'A Well, at that time what I am really referring to is more of a long-range planning than immediate planning, and I think it was the case of just trying to figure out how far you could go with it before you really ran into a lot of sales resistance and found a necessity to shift the direction.

'Q So that plan was to go as far as you could until the resistance got to the point where you couldn't go any further?

'A I would say that is reasonable, yes.'

P#8. By December 1967, Del Webb's property had extended south to Olive Avenue and Spur was within 500 feet of Olive Avenue to the north. See Exhibit B above. Del Webb filed its original complaint alleging that in excess of 1,300 lots in the southwest portion were unfit for development for sale as residential lots because of the operation of the Spur feedlot.

P#9. Del Webb's suit complained that the Spur feeding operation was a public nuisance because of the flies and the odor which were drifting or being blown by the prevailing south to north wind over the southern portion of Sun City. At the time of the suit, Spur was feeding between 20,000 and 30,000 head of cattle, and the facts amply support the finding of the trial court that the feed pens had become a nuisance to the people who resided in the southern part of Del Webb's development. The testimony indicated that cattle in a commercial feedlot will produce 35 to 40 pounds of wet manure per day, per head, or over a million pounds of wet manure per day for 30,000 head of cattle, and that despite the admittedly good feedlot management and good housekeeping practices by Spur, the resulting odor and flies produced an annoying if not unhealthy situation as far as the senior citizens of southern Sun City were concerned. There is no doubt that some of the citizens of Sun City were unable to enjoy the outdoor living which Del Webb had advertised and that Del Webb was faced with sales resistance from prospective purchasers as well as strong and persistent complaints from the people who had purchased homes in that area.

P#10. Trial was commenced before the court with an advisory jury. The advisory jury was later discharged and the trial was continued before the court alone. Findings of fact and conclusions of law were requested and given. The case was vigorously contested, including special actions in this court on some of the matters. In one of the special actions before this court, Spur agreed to, and did, shut down its operation without prejudice to a determination of the matter on appeal. On appeal the many questions raised were extensively briefed.

P#11. It is noted, however, that neither the citizens of Sun City nor Youngtown are represented in this lawsuit and the suit is solely between Del E. Webb Development Company and Spur Industries, Inc.
MAY SPUR BE ENJOINED?

P#12. The difference between a private nuisance and a public nuisance is generally one of degree. A private nuisance is one affecting a single individual or a definite small number of persons in the enjoyment of private rights not common to the public, while a public nuisance is one affecting the rights enjoyed by citizens as a part of the public. To constitute a public nuisance, the nuisance must affect a considerable number of people or an entire community or neighborhood. City of Phoenix v. Johnson, 51 Ariz. 115, 75 P.2d 30 (1938).

P#13. Where the injury is slight, the remedy for minor inconveniences lies in an action for damages rather than in one for an injunction. Kubby v. Hammond, 68 Ariz. 17, 198 P.2d 134 (1948). Moreover, *184 some courts have held, in the 'balancing of conveniences' cases, that damages may be the sole remedy. See Boomer v. Atlantic Cement Co., 26 N.Y.2d 219, 309 N.Y.S.2d 312, 257 N.E.2d 870, 40 A.L.R.3d 590 (1970), and annotation comments, 40 A.L.R.3d 601.

P#14. Thus, it would appear from the admittedly incomplete record as developed in the trial court, that, at most, residents of Youngtown would be entitled to damages rather than injunctive relief.

P#15. We have no difficulty, however, in agreeing with the conclusion of the trial court that Spur's operation was an enjoinable public nuisance as far as the people in the southern portion of Del Webb's Sun City were concerned.

s 36-601, subsec. A reads as follows:

> 's 36-601. Public nuisances dangerous to public health

'A. The following conditions are specifically declared public nuisances dangerous to the public health:

'1. Any condition or place in populous areas which constitutes a breeding place for flies, rodents, mosquitoes and other insects which are capable of carrying and transmitting disease-causing organisms to any person or persons.'

P#16. By this statute, before an otherwise lawful (and necessary) business may be declared a public nuisance, there must be a 'populous' area in which people are injured:

'* * * (I)t hardly admits a doubt that, in determining the question as to whether a lawful occupation is so conducted as to constitute a nuisance as a matter of fact, the locality and surroundings are of the first importance. (citations omitted) A business which is not per se a public nuisance may become such by being carried on at a place where the health, comfort, or convenience of a populous neighborhood is affected. * * * What might amount to a serious nuisance in one locality by reason of the density of the population, or character of the neighborhood affected, may in another place and under different surroundings be deemed proper and unobjectionable. * * *.' MacDonald v. Perry, 32 Ariz. 39, 49-50, 255 P. 494, 497 (1927).

P#17. It is clear that as to the citizens of Sun City, the operation of Spur's feedlot was both a public and a private nuisance. They could have successfully maintained an action to abate the nuisance. Del Webb, having shown a special injury in the loss of sales, had a standing to bring suit to enjoin the nuisance. Engle v. Clark, 53 Ariz. 472, 90 P.2d 994 (1939); City of Phoenix v. Johnson, supra. The judgment of the trial court permanently enjoining the operation of the feedlot is affirmed.

MUST DEL WEBB INDEMNIFY SPUR?

P#18. A suit to enjoin a nuisance sounds in equity and the courts have long recognized a special responsibility to the public when acting as a court of equity:

s 104. Where public interest is involved.

'Courts of equity may, and frequently do, go much further both to give and withhold relief in furtherance of the public interest than they are accustomed to go when only private interests are involved. Accordingly, the granting or withholding of relief may properly be dependent upon considerations of public interest. * * *.' 27 Am.Jur.2d, Equity, page 626.

P#19. In addition to protecting the public interest, however, courts of equity are concerned with protecting the operator of a lawfully, albeit noxious, business from the result of a knowing and willful encroachment by others near his business.

P#20. In the so-called 'coming to the nuisance' cases, the courts have held that the residential *185 landowner may not have relief if he knowingly came into a neighborhood reserved for industrial or agricultural endeavors and has been damaged thereby:

> 'Plaintiffs chose to live in an area uncontrolled by zoning laws or restrictive covenants and remote from urban development. In such an area plaintiffs cannot complain that legitimate agricultural pursuits are being carried on in the vicinity, nor can plaintiffs, having chosen to build in an agricultural area, complain that the agricultural pursuits carried on in the area depreciate the value of their homes. The area being Primarily agricultural, and opinion reflecting the value of such property must take this factor into account. The standards affecting the value of residence property in an urban setting, subject to zoning controls and controlled planning techniques, cannot be the standards by which agricultural properties are judged.
>
> 'People employed in a city who build their homes in suburban areas of the county beyond the limits of a city and zoning regulations do so for a reason. Some do so to avoid the high taxation rate imposed by cities, or to avoid special assessments for street, sewer and water projects. They usually build on improved or hard surface highways, which have been built either at state or county expense and thereby avoid special assessments for these improvements. It may be that they desire to get away from the congestion of traffic, smoke, noise, foul air and the many other annoyances of city life. But with all these advantages in going beyond the area which is zoned and restricted to protect them in their homes, they must be prepared to take the disadvantages.' Dill v. Excel Packing Company, 183 Kan. 513, 525, 526, 331 P.2d 539, 548, 549 (1958). See also East St. Johns Shingle Co. v. City of Portland, 195 Or. 505, 246 P.2d 554, 560-562 (1952).

And:

> '* * * a party cannot justly call upon the law to make that place suitable for his residence which was not so when he selected it. * * *.' Gilbert v. Showerman, 23 Mich. 448, 455, 2 Brown 158 (1871).

P#21. Were Webb the only party injured, we would feel justified in holding that the doctrine of 'coming to the nuisance' would have been a bar to the relief asked by Webb, and, on the other hand, had Spur located the feedlot near the outskirts of a city and had the city grown toward the feedlot, Spur would have to suffer the cost of abating the nuisance as to those people locating within the growth pattern of the expanding city:

> 'The case affords, perhaps, an example where a business established at a place remote from population is gradually surrounded and becomes part of a populous center, so that a business which formerly was not an interference with the rights of others has become so by the encroachment

of the population * * *.' City of Ft. Smith v. Western Hide & Fur Co., 153 Ark. 99, 103, 239 S.W. 724, 726 (1922).

P#22. We agree, however, with the Massachusetts court that:

> 'The law of nuisance affords no rigid rule to be applied in all instances. It is elastic. It undertakes to require only that which is fair and reasonable under all the circumstances. In a commonwealth like this, which depends for its material prosperity so largely on the continued growth and enlargement of manufacturing of diverse varieties, 'extreme rights' cannot be enforced. * * *.' Stevens v. Rockport Granite Co., 216 Mass. 486, 488, 104 N.E. 371, 373 (1914).

P#23. There was no indication in the instant case at the time Spur and its predecessors located in western Maricopa County that a new city would spring up, full-blown, alongside the feeding operation and that the developer of that city would ask the court to order Spur to move because of the new *186 city. Spur is required to move not because of any wrongdoing on the part of Spur, but because of a proper and legitimate regard of the courts for the rights and interests of the public.

P#24. Del Webb, on the other hand, is entitled to the relief prayed for (a permanent injunction), not because Webb is blameless, but because of the damage to the people who have been encouraged to purchase homes in Sun City. It does not equitable or legally follow, however, that Webb, being entitled to the injunction, is then free of any liability to Spur if Webb has in fact been the cause of the damage Spur has sustained. It does not seem harsh to require a developer, who has taken advantage of the lesser land values in a rural area as well as the availability of large tracts of land on which to build and develop a new town or city in the area, to indemnify those who are forced to leave as a result.

P#25. Having brought people to the nuisance to the foreseeable detriment of Spur, Webb must indemnify Spur for a reasonable amount of the cost of moving or shutting down. It should be noted that this relief to Spur is limited to a case wherein a developer has, with foreseeability, brought into a previously agricultural or industrial area the population which makes necessary the granting of an injunction against a lawful business and for which the business has no adequate relief.

P#26. It is therefore the decision of this court that the matter be remanded to the trial court for a hearing upon the damages sustained by the defendant Spur as a reasonable and direct result of the granting of the permanent injunction. Since the result of the appeal may appear novel and both sides have obtained a measure of relief, it is ordered that each side will bear its own costs.

P#27. Affirmed in part, reversed in part, and remanded for further proceedings consistent with this opinion.
HAYS, C.J., STRUCKMEYER and LOCKWOOD, JJ., and UDALL, Retired Justice.
All Citations
108 Ariz. 178, 494 P.2d 700, 4 ERC 1052, 53 A.L.R.3d 861, 2 Envtl. L. Rep. 20,390

CASE STUDY III: BORLAND V. SANDERS LEAD CO., INC., 369 SO. 2D 523 (ALA. 1979)

Note the location of the Sanders Lead Company (still in existence) along Henderson Highway in Troy, Alabama on the maps in *Study Questions for Borland* available on the Companion Website, at http://www.environmentallaw-teach.org/, and in this chapter. Read the *Borland v. Sanders Lead* opinion, which is printed in this chapter after the *Study Questions*, and in the *Companion*. As you read, notice the paragraph numbering, color code the paragraphs, if that helps you to organize the information, and focus on how the material in each paragraph fits into one of the rubrics for a brief as indicated below. The brief structure below is the same as in *Boomer*, *Whalen*, *Wilsonville*, and *Spur.*

1. Heading

2. Facts

3. Procedural History

4. Legal Issues

5. Holding or Decision

6. Reasoning

7. Dissenting Opinions

In paragraph 1 of the opinion, we learn that this is a trespass tort action. Our previous cases (*Boomer, Wilsonville,* and *Spur*) have all been private or public nuisance cases. If a single phrase or word could be used to describe the cases we have examined so far, for *Boomer* it would be "balancing the equities," for *Wilsonville* it would be "prospective nuisance," and for *Spur,* it would be "coming to the nuisance." For *Borland,* though there are a number of issues, the main issue would be "trespass." In the trial court the case was heard *ore tenus*, that is, it was presented orally to a judge without a jury. In a *bench trial*, the judge acts as the finder-of-fact as well as presiding over the trial and making determinations as to substantive and procedural law. Because parties have a constitutional right to a jury trial, a bench trial occurs only when both parties agree. We learn that the trial court ruled for Sanders Lead Co. The Alabama Supreme Court states that "we reverse and remand for a new trial." There is no record of another trial, so it is likely that the parties settled. In the end, the Borlands, the "Appellants," were winners while the Sanders Lead Co., "Appellee," was the loser.

The elements of a *prima-facia case* of trespass according to *Borland* are: 1) the plaintiff is the property owner whose right was violated by the trespass, 2) the defendant's action caused the trespass, and 3) the defendant acted with general intent. The main issue, in this case, is issue number 1. Paragraphs 2-5 of the opinion provides the relevant facts. In 1968, the Sanders Lead Co. opened a lead battery recovery factory to recycle the lead plates, sulphuric acid, and plastics from dead batteries. The smelter used to melt the lead plates was built on Henderson Highway just across the street from the 159 acres of woodland and farmland owned by the Borlands. The Borlands raised cattle and grew almond trees and other crops. The Court discusses the "baghouse," a building containing large fabric bags through which the hot exhaust from the smelter passes. The bags filter out particles in the exhaust, much of which is lead. The exhaust gases must pass through two cooling systems on the way to the baghouse. This is to prevent extremely hot gases from burning the filter bags. This is indeed what happened on two occasions where the bags caught fire, releasing smoke and particulates into the atmosphere. Sanders claimed that the baghouse removed 99% of the lead particulates, but the Borlands dispute this. In any case, the Borlands' claim that they have been impacted by the 1% of lead particulates that leaks through in addition to the releases of lead particulates during fires and malfunctions. They claim that their property has been damaged by lead particulates and sulfoxide deposits.

Paragraph 6 of the opinion informs us that "there is a presumption in favor of findings of fact made by the trial court since it hears the disputed evidence *ore tenus*" but "this rule has never precluded the Court from reversing a case where the trial court erroneously applies the principles of law involved." Paragraphs 8 and 9 describe the two major errors made by the trial court that were the basis of its (erroneous) holding.

The first error is contained in the trial court's final decree that states that the Borlands' land "is significantly increased in value due to its proximity to the lead plant and has a much higher value as a commercial property rather than residential or farm property," and that this is one of the reasons that the court determined that the "plaintiffs [could] not recover of the defendant." In paragraph 10, the Court introduces the second error with regard to the *Alabama Air Pollution Control Act,* but then switches back to the appreciation of the value of the Borlands' property and states that such "rule, in effect, would permit private condemnation which, unquestionably, is impermissible." It is not until paragraph 30 that the Court explains that appreciation in the value of farm or residential property because of the proximity of a newly developed industry would allow industries to "have absolute control over the use of another's property" and "it overlooks the fact that the appreciation factor is totally unrelated to the wrongful acts complained of."

The second error is a variation of the "permit defense" often used by industrial polluters in court. The defendant argues that they have complied with all the relevant air pollution statutes and are, therefore, shielded from liability from polluting the Borlands' property. The trial court agreed. In paragraph 11, the court quotes from the *Alabama Air Pollution Control Act*: "[t] hat nothing in this section shall be construed to limit or abrogate any private remedies now available to any person for...restitution for damage resulting therefrom." Referring to this quote from the *Alabama Air Pollution* statute, paragraph 12 states: "Alabama law clearly provides an appropriate remedy for Plaintiffs who have been directly injured by the deleterious effects of pollutants created by another party's acts." Nevertheless, this statutory authority to sue is not required since environmental torts allow plaintiffs injured by the same harms regulated by statute to maintain their cause of action and to sue, recover damages, and seek equitable relief. All defendants in our previous cases (Atlantic Cement Co., SCA Services, and Spur Industries) had complied with all applicable environmental statutes, but this did not shield them from a verdict of liability. Like *Borland,* these previous cases were intentional torts. This means that if the defendants created the conditions (cement dust in the air, toxic wastes dumped in pits, or flies and smells from cattle feces), in negligence torts, it must be proven that the defendant failed to act as a reasonable person to someone to whom a duty of care is owed as required by law under the circumstances. Defendants may introduce evidence that they complied with relevant statutes as an affirmative defense against a finding of negligence.

Paragraphs 13-37 of the opinion explain the nature of trespass. First, the court compares and contrasts private nuisance and trespass. The significance of this discussion comes, as we shall see, from the fact that this opinion provides the "modern view" of trespass.

In paragraphs 13 and 14, the court cites *Rushing v. Hooper-McDonald,* a previous Alabama Supreme Court case, which quotes from Restatement 2d of Torts: "[i]n order that there may be a trespass under the rule stated in this Section, it is not necessary that the foreign matter should be thrown directly and immediately upon the other's land. It is enough that an act is done with knowledge that it will to a substantial certainty result in the entry of foreign matter." "Knowingly" in this case does not mean that someone has dumped foreign matter in a particular spot because they know that it will eventually move onto another's realty (real estate or the land

and the buildings on it) in a willful and malicious way, but only that they intended to dump the foreign matter and therefore, they intended the natural consequences of this act whether they thought about this result or not.

In paragraphs 16-20, the court discusses the importance of an Oregon Supreme Court case, *Martin v. Reynolds Metal,* because this case was "remarkably similar to the present case" in that "an aluminum reduction plant caused certain fluoride compounds in the form of gases and particulates, invisible to the naked eye, to become airborne and settle on Plaintiff's property, rendering it unfit for raising livestock." The defendants in *Martin* argued that "there had not been a sufficient invasion of Plaintiff's property to constitute trespass" and that "at most, Defendant's acts constituted a nuisance." In paragraph 15, we learn that the *Martin* Court "pointed out that trespass and nuisance are separate torts for the protection of different interests invaded – trespass protecting the possessor's interest in exclusive possession of property and nuisance protecting the interest in use and enjoyment," and also noted "that the same conduct on the part of a defendant may, and often does, result in actionable invasion of both interests."

Paragraph 7 of the opinion discusses the evolution of the trespass tort from the English "common law forms of action" where trespass to land occurred when the "injury was both direct and substantial." From this evolved a "dimensional test" (analogous to the "dangerous probability" test in *Wilsonville*) that held that "[i]f the intruding agent could be seen by the naked eye, the intrusion was considered a trespass. If the agent could not be seen, it was considered indirect and less substantial, hence, a nuisance."

In paragraphs 18 and 19, we learn that the *Martin* Court "rejected the dimensional test and substituted in its place a force and energy test, stating" that "we may define trespass as an intrusion which invades the possessor's protected interest in exclusive possession, whether that intrusion is by visible or invisible pieces of matter or by energy which can be measured only by the mathematical language of the physicist."

The next paragraphs discuss *the force and energy* test where the Oregon Court agreed that the vibrations and concussions from a blasting operation constituted a trespass. Alabama case law rejects the idea that shock waves of energy from blasting constitute a trespass, but this rejection was based on a proof of negligence so that the Alabama Court indicates that it will await an appropriate case to decide on the issue of intentional trespass and shock waves of energy.

Paragraph 22 begins with the statement: "[h]aving shown trespass and nuisance are not always mutually exclusive remedies, we do not wish to intimate that there is no longer a distinction in the two remedies." This is a confusing statement. Where a plaintiff can prove all of the required elements of trespass or nuisance, the court will return a verdict of liability. If a nuisance or trespass is found after trial, a remedy is then considered. The appropriate remedy may be damages, an injunction, or both.

The following paragraphs continue with a discussion of another Oregon case, *Wilson v. Parent,* where the defendant was accused of making "vile and obscene gestures toward her [the plaintiff] and directed vile, obscene and profane language at her." While the complaint alleged a nuisance, the court spent time considering whether this offense would pass the force and energy test and could be considered a trespass as well. The conclusion was that the damage "was not the result of the intensity of the light and noise, but, instead, of its unique nature, i.e., the obnoxious meanings communicated by the words and gestures." Furthermore, "[t]he facts in *Wilson* represent a *de minimis* invasion of the interest of possession, but a substantial invasion to the interest of use and enjoyment."

Paragraph 24 introduces another *de minimis* principle, specifically, that of "*de minimis non curat lex* – the law does not concern itself with trifles." This to assuage the minds of those who could see in this Court's ruling a situation where "every property owner in this State would have a cause of action against any neighboring industry which emitted particulate matter into the atmosphere or even a passing motorist, whose exhaust emissions come to rest on another's property."

Paragraphs 25-29 provide a "restatement and summary of the principles involved" in the modern theory of trespass defined by the force and energy test. One such principle is that "whether an invasion of a property interest is a trespass or a nuisance does not depend upon whether the intruding agent is 'tangible' or 'intangible.' Instead, an analysis must be made to determine the interest interfered with. If the intrusion interferes with the right to exclusive possession of property, the law of trespass applies. If the intrusion is to the interest in use and enjoyment of property, the law of nuisance applies. As previously observed...trespass and nuisance are not necessarily mutually exclusive." Paragraph 26 is dicta (i.e., extraneous material which is merely informative or explanatory).

Paragraph 27 provides a summary of the elements of a trespass cause of action. The plaintiff must prove "1) an invasion affecting an interest in the exclusive possession of his property; 2) an intentional doing of the act which results in the invasion; 3) reasonable foreseeability that the act done could result in an invasion of the plaintiff's possessory interest; and 4) substantial damage to the *res.*" Following the earlier Latin trivia, here is another example. *Res* means *thing* (in this case, property). There are really three distinct elements of trespass because elements two and three above describe an intentional tort where the defendant intends to do the act and is responsible for the reasonably foreseeable consequences whether he wanted them to happen or not. Paragraph 28 is dicta. Paragraph 29 reemphasizes the distinction between a nuisance and a trespass and the elements needed to prove a trespass in court.

Paragraphs 30-37 (the end of the opinion) cover the issue of damages for an actionable trespass. Paragraph 30 dismisses as irrelevant the defendant's argument that plaintiff's property increased in value:

Paragraph 31 states "that the measure of damages in trespass cases is the difference between the value of the land before and after the trespass." The court reaffirms that appreciation has no relevance in this determination, and indicates that "if the 'before and after' rule of damages applies, then, the value is not determined based on best and highest use of the property, but on the owner's desired or previous use." Paragraph 32 adds that the "before and after" rule is subservient to the "underlying proposition" that the "plaintiff is ordinarily entitled to an amount which will compensate him for actual damages sustained."

Paragraph 33 adds that "Alabama has long accepted the dichotomy between permanent and continuous trespass." Quoting from another Alabama case, the court states that: "where the trespass is a continuing one, and not of that class of permanent appropriations, to be assessed for all time at once, there may be successive actions for each continuance of the trespass." In the case of the Borlands' property the court says in paragraph 35: "[i]f the injury is permanent, damages may be recovered or all time- past, present and future. The measure of damages means the difference in the fair market value of the property before and after the trespass, based on the plaintiff's use of the property." Paragraph 36 adds that "if the nature of the injury is continuous... the plaintiff can recover for the use of his property" and "any damages for future loss must be recovered in a later action if and when a subsequent trespass occurs." Thus, the Alabama Court would allow temporary damages for a continuous trespass. While the court did not determine whether the trespass was continuous, it seems clear that the smelter would be depositing particles of lead continuously.

Miscellaneous Issues

It is clear, given the modern theory of trespass and the force and energy test, that Boomer could have sued in trespass. If he had done so, would this have allowed him to avoid the *Whalen* precedent? Furthermore, the Alabama court would allow temporary damages for a continuous trespass and allow the plaintiffs to maintain their cause of action in the future. The New York Court of Appeals reversed temporary damages for the continuous deposition of cement particles on the Boomers and others and replaced this remedy with permanent damages, one recovery based on the theory of a "servitude on the land."

The *Borland* case has expanded the use and theory of trespass torts and its possible use in environmental torts, but the history is uneven with various states ruling differently from the Alabama Supreme Court. The article on "Damages from Pesticide Spray Drift under Trespass Law" from *Ecology Law Currents* provides an excellent summary of these twists and turns in environmental tort jurisprudence.

Study Questions for Borland

Be sure to understand the <u>*new concepts*</u> introduced by this case, which continue to be both in italics, and underlined. Start with our Glossary. If you cannot find a definition there, use a dictionary.

1. What are the elements of trespass here?

2. What is the <u>procedural history</u>? Why is Sanders Lead Company the <u>appellee?</u>

3. What are the facts of this case? Be sure to note the relationship of plaintiffs' and defendant's property and the activities carried out on each property. What is a <u>*baghouse*</u>? According to the plaintiffs, what has caused the harm they experience?

A "bag house"

http://infohalifax.tk/hocis/lithium-batterien-recycling-qoc.php

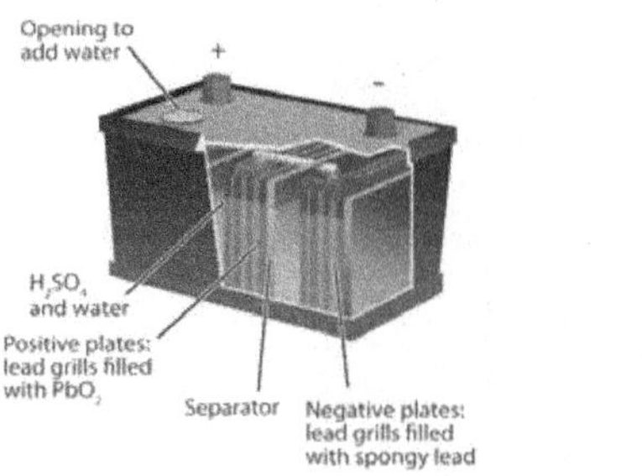

https://chem.libretexts.org/Bookshelves/Introductory_Chemistry/Book%3A_Beginning_Chemistry_(Ball)/14%3A_Oxidation_and_Reduction/14.4%3A_Applications_of_Redox_Reactions_-_Voltaic_Cells

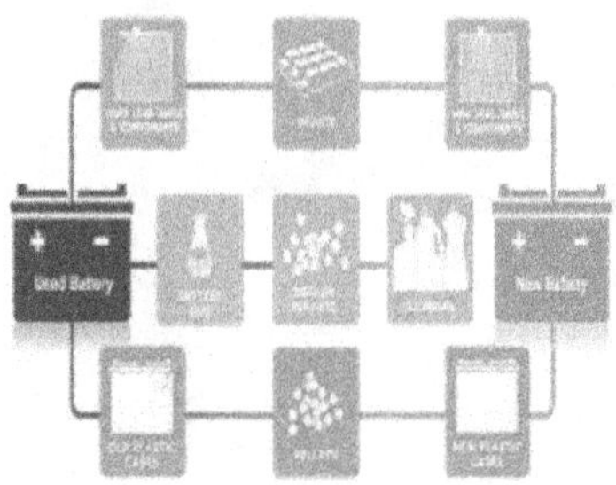

<u>https://www.mpoweruk.com/recycling.htm</u>

4. The trial court made two major mistakes: one concerning Alabama law and one concerning <u>*appreciation*</u>. Describe these mistakes. What is the <u>*permit defense*</u>? What is <u>*private condemnation*</u>?

Rotary furnace for smelting lead, https://myportelizabeth.co.za/how-to-dispose-of-your-used-car-battery/21956

5. What is the significance of *Rushing v. Hoper-McDonald*? What is a case of *first impression*? What is *realty*? How is this consistent with RESTATEMENT, 2D, TORTS, §158?

6. Why did the plaintiffs in *Martin v. Reynolds-Metals* sue in trespass? What are *non-possessory injuries to land*? What is the difference between a nuisance tort and a trespass tort according to the *Martin* court?

ROTARY FURNACE FOR SMELTING LEAD https://myportelizabeth.co.za/how-to-dispose-of-your-used-car-battery/21956

7. Are *Rushing* and *Martin* both Alabama cases? What gives the *Martin* case special significance?

8. The *Martin* court rejected the *dimensional test* and substituted the *force and energy test*. Explain what both of these tests do to determine *trespassory invasion.* Restate the *Martin* court's definition of trespass.

9. Explain the connection between de *minimus non curat lex* and a *real and substantial invasion of a protected interest*. Is this an example of *judicial line-drawing*? Explain.

10. What determines whether a *real and substantial invasion of a protected interest* is a trespass or a nuisance? Are nuisance and trespass mutually exclusive? Explain.

11. What are *nominal damages*? When will they be awarded in Alabama? What does it mean to say that nominal damages will support *punitive damages*? If this case stands as precedent, will nominal damages be awarded in trespass cases in the future?

12. What are the elements of trespass in Alabama? Is this different from the *modern theory* of trespass? What represents *res*?

LEAD AND POLYPROPYLENE MATERIALS FROM CAR BATTERIES
https://www.eldan-recycling.com/en-us/lead-and-polypropylene-materials-car-batteries

Borland (Court Opinion)

369 SO.2D 523

SUPREME COURT OF ALABAMA.

J. H. BORLAND, SR. AND SARAH M. BORLAND

V.

SANDERS LEAD COMPANY, INC., A CORPORATION.

77-283.

|

FEB. 9, 1979.

|

REHEARING DENIED APRIL 6, 1979.

Synopsis

Owners of agricultural land sued lead company to recover for damage to their agricultural property by allegedly dangerous accumulation of lead particulates and sulfoxide deposits. The Circuit Court, Pike County, Terry L. Butts, J., rendered judgment for lead company, and landowners appealed. The Supreme Court, Jones, J., held that: (1) compliance with Alabama Air Pollution Control Act did not shield defendant from liability for damages caused by pollutants emitted from its smelter; (2) fact that because of its proximity to the lead plant plaintiffs' property had a higher value as commercial property than as residential or farm property did not bar recovery; (3) if an intrusion interferes with right to exclusive possession of property, the law of trespass applies but if the intrusion is to the interest in use and enjoyment, the law of nuisance applies; (4) for an indirect invasion to amount to an actionable trespass there must be an interference with plaintiff's exclusive possessory interest; (5) general rule that measure of damages is difference between value of the land before and after the trespass is subservient to underlying theory of damages, i. e., that plaintiff is entitled to an amount which will compensate him for actual damages sustained, and (6) a distinction exists between permanent and continuous trespass.

Reversed and remanded.

Attorneys and Law Firms

***525** Jack Crenshaw of Crenshaw, Minor & Carr, Montgomery, for appellants.

N. J. Cervera of Cervera & Yancey, and Oliver W. Brantley of Brantley & Calhoun, Troy, for appellee.

Opinion

JONES, Justice.

P#1. This appeal involves the right of a property owner, in an action for trespass, to recover damages for pollution of his property. The case was tried Oretenus to the trial Judge without a jury, and judgment was rendered for the Defendant. We reverse and remand for a new trial.

P#2. J. H. Borland, Sr., and Sarah M. Borland, Appellants, own approximately 159 acres of land, located just south of Troy, Alabama, on Henderson Road. On this property, Appellants raise cattle, grow several different crops, and have a large pecan orchard.

P#3. In 1968, the Appellee, Sanders Lead Company, started an operation for the recovery of lead from used automobile batteries. This operation is conducted on property just east of the Borlands' property across Henderson Road. The Appellee's smelter was placed on the west edge of their property, that part nearest to the Appellants' property. The smelter is used to reduce the plates from used automobile batteries. It is alleged by Appellants that the smelting process results in the emission of lead particulates and sulfoxide gases.

P#4. It is undisputed that Appellee installed a filter system, commonly known as a "bag house," to intercept these lead particulates which otherwise would be emitted into the atmosphere. The "bag house" is a building containing fiber bags. The smoke emitting from the furnace is passed through two cooling systems before passing through the "bag house" so that the fiber bags will not ***526** catch fire. If properly installed and used, an efficient "bag house" will recover over 99% Of the lead emitted. On two occasions, the cooling system at Appellee's smeltering plant has failed to function properly, resulting in the "bag house's" catching fire on both occasions. There is a dispute as to the efficiency of Appellee's "bag house" throughout its operation.

P#5. Appellants allege that, because of the problems with the "bag house," their property has been damaged by a dangerous accumulation of lead particulates and sulfoxide deposits on their property.

Admittedly, this is an Ore tenus case and the law is well settled that, in such cases, this Court is precluded from altering a lower court's findings unless those findings are clearly erroneous. Donnelly v. Doak, 346 So.2d 414 (Ala.1977). It is equally true, however, that this rule has never precluded this Court from reversing a case where the trial court erroneously applies the principles of law involved. Babcock v. Smith, 285 Ala. 557, 234 So.2d 573 (1970); St. Clair Industries, Inc. v. Harmon's Pipe & Fitting Co., 282 Ala. 466, 213 So.2d 201 (1968).

P#6. As stated by the Court of Civil Appeals in the very recent case of Alabama Farm Bureau Mutual Ins. Co., Inc. v. Davis, 354 So.2d 15 (Ala.Civ.App.1978):

> "(I)n cases of this nature there is a presumption in favor of findings of fact made by the trial court since it hears the disputed evidence ore tenus. This presumption precludes our reversal of the trial court's judgment unless it is determined to be plainly and palpably wrong. . . . (T)his presumption is not applicable in situations where the trial judge takes an erroneous view of the law as applied to the facts . . . ." (Emphasis added.)

P#7. It is our opinion that the trial Judge has misapplied the law in this case.

P#8. In the trial Court's final decree, it is stated:

> "Any court Is bound by the applicable laws in any case. In any society operating under manmade Law there is inherent the possibility that The law will provide no appropriate remedy for grievances no matter how strongly the equitable conscience of the court and/or a community may feel the need for action." (Emphasis in the original.)

P#9. Furthermore, the trial Court held:

> "It is the opinion of the court that the plaintiffs not recover of the defendant. The court would comment that there is ample evidence (even from the testimony of plaintiff, J. H. Borland) that his land is significantly increased in value due to its proximity to the lead plant and has a much higher value as commercial property rather than residential or farm property . . . ."

P#10. It is apparent from a further reading of the final decree that the trial Court was under the mistaken impression that compliance with the Alabama Air Pollution Control Act shielded the Defendant from liability for damages caused by pollutants emitting from its smelter. This is not the law in this State. Furthermore, the trial Court incorrectly applied the law of this State in concluding that, because there was evidence showing that the Plaintiffs' farm had increased in value as industrial property, due to its proximity to the lead plant, Plaintiffs could not recover of the Defendant. Such a rule, in effect, would permit private condemnation, which, unquestionably, is impermissible. A discussion of the applicable rule of damages appears later in this opinion.

P#11. The Alabama Air Pollution Control Act is codified at s 22-28-1, Et seq., Alabama Code 1975. s 22-28-23, Alabama Code 1975, specifically provides:

(N)othing in this section shall be construed to limit or abrogate any private remedies now available to any person for the alleviation, abatement, control, correction or prevention of air pollution Or restitution for damage resulting therefrom. (Emphasis added.)

P#12. Alabama law clearly provides an appropriate remedy for Plaintiffs who have been directly injured by the deleterious effects of pollutants created by another party's acts.

P#13. *527 In Rushing v. Hooper-McDonald, Inc., 293 Ala. 56, 300 So.2d 94 (1974), this Court held, in a case of first impression, that a trespass need not be inflicted directly on another's realty, but may be committed by discharging foreign polluting matter at a point beyond the boundary of such realty. Rushing specifically held that a trespass is committed by one who knowingly discharges asphalt in such a manner that it will in due course invade a neighbor's realty and cause harm.

P#14. In Rushing, this Court cited with approval Restatement, Second, Torts, s 158, and particularly emphasized a portion of the Comments under this section, which recites:

> " 'In order that there may be a trespass under the rule stated in this Section, it is not necessary that the foreign matter should be thrown directly and immediately upon the other's land. It is enough that an act is done with knowledge that it will to a substantial certainty result in entry of foreign matters.' "

P#15. Rushing further cited with approval the case of Martin v. Reynolds Metals Co., 221 Or. 86, 342 P.2d 790, cert. denied, 362 U.S. 918, 80 S.Ct. 672, 4 L.Ed.2d 739 (1959). In Martin, a case remarkably similar to the present case, the Plaintiffs sought recovery from the Defendant, aluminum company, for trespass. The Plaintiffs in Martin alleged that the operation by Defendants of an aluminum reduction plant caused certain fluoride compounds in the form of gases and particulates, invisible to the naked eye, to become airborne and settle on Plaintiffs' property, rendering it unfit for raising livestock. Plaintiffs in the present case allege that the operation of Defendant's lead reduction plant causes an emission of lead particulates, and SO 2, invisible to the naked eye, which emissions have settled on their property, making it unsuitable for raising cattle or growing crops.

P#16. The Defendants in Martin contended that there had not been a sufficient invasion of Plaintiffs' property to constitute trespass, but, at most, Defendant's acts constituted a nuisance. This would have allowed the Defendants to set up Oregon's two-year statute of limitations applicable to non-possessory injuries to land rather than Oregon's six-year statute for trespass to land.

P#17. The Martin Court pointed out that trespass and nuisance are separate torts for the protection of different interests invaded trespass protecting the possessor's interest in exclusive possession of property and nuisance protecting the interest in use and enjoyment. The Court noted, and we agree, that the same conduct on the part of a defendant may, and often does, result in the actionable invasion of both interests.

P#18. The confusion surrounding trespass and nuisance is due in a large part to the influence of common law forms of action. The modern action for trespass to land stemmed inexorably from the common law action for trespass which lay when the injury was both direct and substantial. Nuisance, on the other hand, would lie when injuries were indirect and less substantial. See Winfield, Nuisance as a Tort, 4 Camb.L.J., 189, 201-06 (1931). A fictitious "dimensional" test arose, which obviated the necessity of determining whether the intrusion was "direct" and "substantial." If the intruding agent could be seen by the naked eye, the intrusion was considered a trespass. If the agent could not be seen, it was considered indirect and less substantial, hence, a nuisance. See, e. g., 1 Harper & James, Torts, s 1.23 (1946) (where the dimensional or the tangible/intangible test is included in an earlier definition of trespass and nuisance).

P#19. In Martin v. Reynolds, supra, the Court stated:

> ". . . The defendant asks us to take account of the difference in size of the physical agency through which the intrusion occurs and relegate entirely to the field of nuisance law certain invasions which do not meet the dimensional test, whatever that is."

P#20. The Martin Court rejected the dimensional test and substituted in its place a force and energy test, stating:

> "The view recognizing a trespassory invasion where there is no 'thing' which can ***528** be seen with the naked eye undoubtedly runs counter to the definition of trespass expressed in some quarters. 1 Restatement, Torts s 158, Comment H (1934); Prosser, Torts s 13 (2d Ed. 1955). It is quite possible that in an earlier day when science had not yet peered into the molecular and atomic world of small particles, the courts could not fit an invasion through unseen physical instrumentalities into the requirement that a trespass can result only from a Direct invasion. But in this atomic age even the uneducated know the great and awful force contained in the atom and what it can do to a man's property if it is released. In fact, the now famous equation E=mc 2 has taught us that mass and energy are equivalents and that our concept of 'things' must be reframed. If these observations on science in relation to the law of trespass should appear theoretical and unreal in the abstract, they become very practical and real to the possessor of land when the unseen force cracks the foundation of his house. The force is just as real if it is

chemical in nature and must be awakened by the intervention of another agency before it does harm.

"If, then, we must look to the character of the instrumentality which is used in making an intrusion upon another's land we prefer to emphasize the object's energy or force rather than its size. Viewed in this way we may define trespass as an intrusion which invades the possessor's protected interest in exclusive possession, whether that intrusion is by visible or invisible pieces of matter or by energy which can be measured only by the mathematical language of the physicist.

"We are of the opinion, therefore, that the intrusion of the fluoride particulates in the present case constituted a trespass."

P#21. In deciding what acts constitute a trespass, the Oregon Supreme Court cited earlier cases recognizing that a trespass is committed by a defendant's blasting operation when the vibrations and concussions to earth and air cause damage to the plaintiff's property. Admittedly, as the Appellee contends, Alabama case law rejects the theory that mere concussion caused by blasting operations constitutes a trespass. Coalite, Inc. v. Aldridge, 285 Ala. 137, 229 So.2d 539 (1969). Coalite requires proof of negligence where a defendant's blasting operation causes injury to the plaintiffs' property, unless rocks or debris actually invade the confines of the plaintiffs' land.

P#22. Judicial restraint compels us to await the appropriate case, in an adversary setting, to address any reconsideration of the trespass/negligence dichotomy presented by Coalite. Suffice it to say that here we are not dealing with a vibration/concussion case. Moreover, it is clear from a thorough reading of Martin that the reliance by the Oregon Supreme Court on the trespass theory of the earlier blasting case was not essential to the Martin holding that deposits of fluoride particulates constituted a trespass upon the plaintiffs' land.

P#23. Having shown trespass and nuisance are not always mutually exclusive remedies, we do not wish to intimate that there is no longer a distinction in the two remedies. Indeed, this distinction is evident in the case of Wilson v. Parent, 228 Or. 354, 365 P.2d 72 (1961). There, Plaintiff alleged that her son-in-law, who resided on adjoining property, made vile and obscene gestures toward her and directed vile, obscene and profane language at her. The Plaintiff framed her complaint in nuisance, but a significant portion of the opinion was devoted to the question of whether the intrusions were trespasses.

P#24. The Wilson Court stated:

"(T)he judiciary, though not composed of atomic scientists, fully recognize that dust, smoke, invisible gas, light and sound, and atomic fallout, are propelled over and across the lands of another and sometimes rest thereon, but it seems Reasonably obvious that the ether waves moving from the hands of the defendant to the eyes of the plaintiff and the sound waves from his vocal cords to her ears do not constitute trespass to land, even though the damage caused by them be ***529** far more than de minimis." (Emphasis added.)

P#25. This conclusion is "Reasonably obvious " only when it is realized that the damage in Wilson was not the result of the intensity of the light and noise, but, instead, of its unique nature, i. e., the obnoxious meanings communicated by the words and gestures. Note, 19 Okla.L.Rev. 117 (1966). The facts in Wilson represent a De minimis invasion to the interest of possession, but a substantial invasion to the interest of use and enjoyment.

It might appear, at first blush, from our holding today that every property owner in this State would have a cause of action against any neighboring industry which emitted particulate matter into the atmosphere, or even a passing motorist, whose exhaust emissions come to rest upon another's property. But we hasten to point out that there is a point where the entry is so lacking in substance that the law will refuse to recognize it, applying the maxim De minimis non curat lex the law does not concern itself with trifles. In the present case, however, we are not faced with a trifling complaint. The Plaintiffs in this case have suffered, if the evidence is believed, a real and substantial invasion of a protected interest.

P#26. Although we view this decision as an application, and not an extension, of our present law of trespass, we feel that a brief restatement and summary of the principles involved in this area would be appropriate. Whether an invasion of a property interest is a trespass or a nuisance does not depend upon whether the intruding agent is "tangible" or "intangible." Instead, an analysis must be made to determine the interest interfered with. If the intrusion interferes with the right to exclusive possession of property, the law of trespass applies. If the intrusion is to the interest in use and enjoyment of property, the law of nuisance applies. As previously observed, however, the remedies of trespass and nuisance are not necessarily mutually exclusive.[8]

P#27. While the direct/indirect analysis of the nature of the intrusion is not a valid method of determining trespass vis-a-vis nuisance, this analysis must be made in order to determine the elements necessary to prove trespass. If the intrusion is direct, then, under our present law,

8 Indeed, because of the comprehensive language of our nuisance statute (s 6-5-120), conduct which rises to the level of trespass to land, generally speaking, would support a nuisance action; the converse, however, is not necessarily true.

actual damages need not be shown; nominal damages may be awarded and this will support punitive damages. This is true whether the intrusion is intentional or unintentional.[9]

P#28. Under the modern theory of trespass, the law presently allows an action to be maintained in trespass for invasions that, at one time, were considered indirect and, hence, only a nuisance. In order to recover in trespass for this type of invasion (i. e., the asphalt piled in such a way as to run onto plaintiff's property, or the pollution emitting from a defendant's smoke stack, such as in the present case), a plaintiff must show 1) an invasion affecting an interest in the exclusive possession of his property; 2) an intentional doing of the act which results in the invasion; 3) reasonable foreseeability that the act done could result in an invasion of plaintiff's possessory interest; and 4) substantial damages to the Res.

P#29. A further clarification of our nuisance/indirect trespass dichotomy is appropriate at this point. In the traditional sense, the law of nuisance applies where the invasion results in no substantial damage to the Res, but where there is interference with the use and enjoyment of one's property. ***530** The classic cases of the barking dog, the neighboring bawdy house, noise, smoke, fumes, or obnoxious odors generally invoke the doctrine of the law of nuisance. These intrusions do not typically result in any actionable damage to the Res ; the injury caused by such acts usually results in a diminution of the use value of the property causally related to the harmful conduct made the basis of the claim.

P#30. We emphasize that these intrusions are not relegated to the nuisance remedy simply because of their indirect nature; rather, they do not constitute a trespass because all of the requisite elements of trespass to land are not present. For an indirect invasion to amount to an actionable trespass, there must be an interference with plaintiff's exclusive possessory interest; that is, through the defendant's intentional conduct, and with reasonable foreseeability, some substance has entered upon the land itself, affecting its nature and character, and causing substantial actual damage to the Res. For example, if the smoke or polluting substance emitting from a defendant's operation causes discomfort and annoyance to the plaintiff in his use and enjoyment of the property, then the plaintiff's remedy is for nuisance; but if, as a result of the defendant's operation, the polluting substance is deposited upon the plaintiff's property, thus interfering with his exclusive possessory interest by causing substantial damage to the Res, then the plaintiff may seek his remedy in trespass, though his alternative remedy in nuisance may co-exist.

---

9 We note that a number of jurisdictions have adopted the so-called "modern view" that when the trespass is nondeliberate (unintentional), damages need not be awarded where the trespass causes no actual injury. See 75 Am.Jur.2d Trespass, s 49, at 43. This Court to date, has not accepted this so-called "modern view." The issue whether actual damages must be shown where the trespass is unintentional is not before this Court on this appeal. We leave any reconsideration of this point to a later case where the issue is directly presented.

P#31. On remand, the issue of the proper measure of damages will undoubtedly arise. In its final decree, the trial Court held that the Plaintiffs' property had increased in value as commercial property due to its proximity to the Defendant's lead plant; therefore, Plaintiffs were not allowed to recover of the Defendant. As noted earlier, such a rule would allow industries, as here, to have absolute control over the use of another's property. This clearly is not the rule for measuring damages in trespass cases. Moreover, it overlooks the fact that the appreciation factor is totally unrelated to the wrongful acts complained of.

P#32. It is often stated that the measure of damages in trespass cases is the difference between the value of the land before and after the trespass. In Alabama Power Company v. Thompson, 250 Ala. 7, 32 So.2d 795, 9 A.L.R.2d 974 (1947), this Court followed the general rule and pointed out that the adaptability of the property for a special purpose affecting its value is an element for the consideration of the jury in assessing damages. Similarly, the fact that Plaintiffs have used their property for a particular purpose (and may have no desire to sell their property at the higher commercial value) is an element to be considered in determining damages. It seems clear that if the "before and after" rule of damages applies, then, the value is not determined based on the best and highest use of the property, but on the owner's desired or previous use.

P#33. We note, however, that this may not be a case where the damages are to be based on the difference in value before and after the trespass. This rule is subservient to the underlying proposition for measuring damages in trespass cases: The Plaintiff is ordinarily entitled to an amount which will compensate him for actual damages sustained. Thomas v. Bank of Hurtsboro, 243 Ala. 658, 11 So.2d 370 (1942). In 75 Am.Jur.2d, Trespass s 51, it is stated:

> "No hard and fast principles can be laid down for the measurement of damages in this class of cases. Generally, the rules to be applied depend upon whether or not the injury is permanent or temporary in character. As is the rule generally, in the case of permanent injury, the recovery must include all damages, both past and future. The proper measure of damages is the difference between the value of the realty before the injury and its value after the injury, except where there is a total destruction, when the owner is entitled to recover the entire value.
>
> "As to temporary injuries, the authorities are not in agreement as to the proper rule generally for their computation. Some courts have applied the rule in actions *531 of trespass that the cost of restoring the property to its former condition is the proper measure of damages for a temporary injury thereto when this is less than the diminution of the market value of the whole property by reason of the injury, but where the cost of restoration is more than the diminution in the market value, the latter is generally the true measure of damages. In general, the measure of damages for wrongfully depriving the plaintiff of the use of his property is the rental value or

> the reasonable value of the use of the property during the time he is deprived thereof. Thus for a wrongful ouster of the plaintiff from a portion of his farm, damages may be awarded equal to the difference in the rental value of the farm with and without such portion." (Emphasis ours.)

P#34. Alabama has long accepted the dichotomy between permanent and continuous trespass, along with the factual distinctions incident to a determination of the appropriate measure of damages. In Louisville & Nashville Railroad Co. v. Higginbotham, 153 Ala. 334, 44 So. 872 (1907), it is stated:

> "And where the trespass is a continuing one, and not of that class of permanent appropriations, to be assessed for all time at once, there may be successive actions for each continuance of the trespass."

P#35. In Thomas v. Bank of Hurtsboro, supra, the Court held that where the trespass put the plaintiff out of possession the measure of damages was the amount that would compensate for use and occupation (i. e., fair rental value).

P#36. In conclusion, in determining the amount of damages recoverable by a plaintiff whose property has been trespassed upon, the law is flexible and the rule simple: What will compensate the plaintiff for the injury he has received? In a case such as the present one, it must first be determined whether the alleged intrusion is of a permanent nature or of a continuing nature. If the injury is permanent, damages must be recovered for all time past, present and future. The measure of damages means the difference in the fair market value of the property before and after the trespass, based on the plaintiff's use of the property or adaptability of the property to a particular use prior to the trespass.

P#37. If the nature of the injury is continuous (i. e., during the tenure of the trespass), the plaintiff can recover for the use of his property or its fair rental value. (Also, plaintiff may be able to recover the cost of restoration if this, plus rental value, is less than the diminution in value.) Any damages for future loss must be recovered in a later action if and when a subsequent trespass occurs.

P#38. Additionally, as pointed out in Rushing, supra, plaintiffs are entitled to recover for the loss to personal property if the loss is proximately caused by the trespass.

P#39. REVERSED AND REMANDED.
All the Justices concur.

CASE STUDY IV: BRANCH V. W. PETROLEUM, INC., 657 P.2D 267 (UTAH, 1982)

Note the location of the Utah properties involved in this dispute on the maps in *Study Questions for Branch v. Western Petroleum,* on the Companion Website at http://www.environmentallaw-teach.org/. Read the *Branch opinion,* which is printed in this chapter after the *Study Questions,* and in the *Companion.* As you read, notice the paragraph numbering, color code the paragraphs, if that helps you to organize the information, and focus on how the material in each paragraph fits into one of the rubrics for a brief as indicated below. The brief structure below is the same as in *Boomer, Whalen, Wilsonville, Spur,* and *Borland.*

1. Heading

2. Facts

3. Procedural History

4. Legal Issues

5. Holding or Decision

6. Reasoning

7. Dissenting Opinions

Branch is a private nuisance tort, the elements of which are: 1) proof of harm (the nuisance), 2) proof of causation, and 3) strict liability. There are significant causation issues, but the main issue in *Branch* is the holding that strict liability applies.

In paragraph 1 of the opinion, we learn that Branches alleged that the wastewaters disposed of by Western Petroleum had percolated into the groundwater system and contaminated the culinary water in their wells. The jury answered questions presented by the court in "special interrogatories, finding, inter alia" (among other things) that Western Petroleum was liable for contaminating the wells. In the remedy phase of the trial, the jury awarded $8,050 for contamination of the wells and $700 for trespass (to be explained later), $10,000 for "mental suffering, discomfort and annoyance," and $13,000 in punitive damages. We learn that the "jury, over objection, was instructed on the theory of negligence." Presumably the plaintiffs were the ones to object. In any case, "the trial court entered judgment on the basis of strict liability," though damages for mental suffering were not allowed.

Much like in *Wilsonville*, Western Petroleum appeals and paragraph 2 enumerates a host of errors made by the trial court. These include: 1) that negligence, not strict liability, is the only valid legal theory on which judgment can be sustained, and 2) that the court erred in not instructing on proximate cause, in percentage of negligence and contamination attributable to the Branches, in improper selection of the "jury venire" (i.e., the group of individuals from which the jury is selected), and, finally, in the award of punitive damages without a showing of "willful and malicious" behavior. The Branches also cross-appealed contending that the "court erred in striking the jury award for mental suffering, discomfort, and annoyance." This is why this Supreme Court of Utah case is *Branch v. Western Petroleum* as opposed to *Western Petroleum v. Branch.*

Paragraphs 3-8 provide the relevant facts found at the trial court level. In 1976, the Branches purchased 21 acres on which there was a well that produced water used for culinary purposes. Their property was at an elevation that was 200-300 feet lower than the adjacent property owned by Western Petroleum. The well had been used since 1929 by the prior owners who ran a dairy operation. Two months after purchasing the property, the Branches noticed that the well water began to taste bad and smell like petroleum products. In one instance, polluted water from Western's disposal pit overflowed and ran downhill causing damage to food stored in the Branches' basement. After many rabbits and chickens died, presumably from consuming this water, the water was tested and found unfit for use. The Branches then began buying water and having it trucked to their farm. They even drilled a new well, but that well became unusable after a few months.

Paragraph 6 begins with the Branches requesting that Western Petroleum stop dumping formation water into the disposal pit. Western Petroleum refused to stop dumping its formation water into the disposal pit unless the Branches compensated them. Western did agree to build another pond to prevent wastewaters from overflowing onto the Branches' property. Western was careless and built part of the pond directly on property owned by the Branches. Western allowed trucks to drive on the Branches' property and to spray polluted water directly onto lands owned by the Branches, causing additional damage. Paragraph 7 outlines the family difficulties, mental anguish, and frustration that the Branches experienced because they were unable to use their well water

Paragraph 8 describes Western Petroleum's lack of knowledge about state laws regulating the dumping of petroleum drilling formation waters into open pits and, that even when Western Petroleum became aware of these laws, Western Petroleum did not seek to obtain permits for their disposal ponds.

Paragraphs 9-12 discuss the role of expert witnesses in determining causation; that is, that Western Petroleum's dumping was the proximate cause of contaminated groundwater that flowed to the Branches' wells. Mr. Ferris, the expert witness for Western Petroleum, admits that the petroleum formation waters dumped into the pits contaminated the surface aquifer, but that the Branches' wells obtain water from a deeper aquifer called the Duchesne Formation. Mr. Montgomery, the expert witness for the Branches, testified that joints or fractures connect the contaminated surface aquifer to the Duchesne Formation and provide a conduit for contamination. As in *Wilsonville*, the plaintiffs' expert was considered more reliable; and the jury, in response to the special interrogatories, found that Western Petroleum was "negligent...in dumping formation waters in its evaporation pit" and that this was "a cause of the pollution of the water" in the plaintiffs' wells.

The central legal question of *Branch v. Western Petroleum* is stated at the beginning of paragraph 13: "[t]he major substantive dispute is whether the trial court erred in entering judgment against Western on the basis of strict liability for pollution of the Branches' wells." There is confusion since Western Petroleum argued that "other states have based liability for pollution of subterranean waters on negligence, nuisance, or trespass." Nuisance and trespass are actionable torts for which verdicts of liability are common. Negligence is not an actionable tort but is, instead, a theory of defendant's conduct, like that of intent or strict liability. Western contends "the only accepted theory upon which this case could be based is negligence" because the "Branches failed to allege nuisance or trespass." This argument makes no sense because this case is, from an analytical point of view, a strict liability nuisance action.

Paragraph 14 enumerates the various potential theories of liability for pollution and one of these is strict liability. The list of theories is somewhat muddled. To be clear, in order to be found liable there must be proof of harm (nuisance or trespass, for instance, proof of causation, and proof of defendant's state of mind or conduct—negligence, intent, or strict liability). The Court reviews Utah state law in Paragraphs 15 and 16, finding that groundwater is "subject to the maxim that one may not use his land so as to pollute percolating waters to the injury of another." Because Utah is "one of the most arid states in the union, the protection of the purity of the water is of critical importance, and the legislature has enacted laws for the protection of both surface and subterranean waters." A section of Utah state law is then quoted: "Absent a permit, U.C.A., 1953, §73-14-5 made it 'unlawful for any person to discharge a pollutant into waters of the state...'" Western Petroleum failed to obtain a permit. Evidence at the trial court indicates that when Western was informed of this requirement, it ignored its obligation to obtain the proper permits. Hence, their actions were "unlawful," but it's not clear if Western Petroleum faced any consequences from Utah state officials for failing to obtain a permit. Paragraphs 17 and 18 are devoted to the central issue, strict liability. "The landmark case of *Rylands v. Fletcher*" is notable because it "held that one who uses his land in an unnatural way and thereby creates a dangerous condition or engages in abnormal activity may be strictly liable for injuries resulting from that condition or activity." Whether a condition or activity is considered abnormal is defined in terms of whether the condition or activity is unduly dangerous or inappropriate to the place where it is maintained. *Rylands v. Fletcher* is a landmark case because it has been used successfully in strict liability cases in many states as persuasive authority. In these cases, strict liability evolved from being originally limited to "ultra-hazardous activities" to being applicable to "abnormally dangerous activities." This is a significant shift, lowering the plaintiff's burden of proof.

To support its application, the court uses two persuasive secondary sources: a treatise (Prosser's Law of Torts), and the *Restatement (Second) of Torts,* which states:

> **Section 4. STRICT LIABILITY**
>
> The Restatement 2d of Torts, §519 provides that:
>
> (1) One who carries on an abnormally dangerous activity is subject to liability for harm to the person, land or chattels of another resulting from the activity, although he has exercised the utmost care to prevent such harm.
>
> (2) Such strict liability is limited to the kind of harm, the risk of which makes the activity abnormally dangerous.
>
> §520 lists the factors to be used when determining what constitutes an abnormally dangerous activity:
>
> In determining whether an activity is abnormally dangerous, the following factors are to be considered:
>
> (a) Whether the activity involves a high degree of risk of some harm to the person, land, or chattels of others;
>
> (b) Whether the gravity of the harm which may result from it is likely to be great;
>
> (c) Whether the risk cannot be eliminated by the exercise of reasonable care;
>
> (d) Whether the activity is not a matter of common usage;
>
> (e) Whether the activity is inappropriate to the place where it is carried on; and
>
> (f) The value of the activity to the community.

Paragraph 19 is devoted to a discussion of nuisance torts. "Nuisance law also protects property interests from non-trespassory invasions." It is important to remember the distinctions between nuisance and trespass discussed in *Borland v. Sanders Lead.* As the Rhode Island Supreme Court stated in *Wood v. Picillo*: "[d]istinguished from negligence liability, liability in nuisance is predicated upon unreasonable injury rather than upon unreasonable conduct....Thus, plaintiffs may recover in nuisance despite the otherwise non-tortious nature of the conduct which creates the injury." In a negligence nuisance, harm (to the use and enjoyment of property) and causation have been proven; but, in addition, unreasonable conduct must also have been proven. In *Boomer* as well as *Wilsonville,* and *Spur,* both private and public nuisances were proven but the basis of the conduct responsible for the harm was shown to be intentional. Here in *Branch,* the tort is nuisance, and the defendant's culpability is proven under a theory of strict liability.

In addition to a long reasoning involving the issue of strict liability that was first addressed in paragraph 14, and then further detailed in paragraphs 17-18 and 21-28, the Court also addresses what other courts have called the "permit defense." In paragraph 2 it states that "it is of no consequence that a business which causes a nuisance is a lawful business." This, of course, was evident in *Boomer, Wilsonville,* and *Spur.* But it might be added that Western Petroleum did not act lawfully.

The "grounds for holding Western strictly liable for the pollution of the Branches' well" are presented in paragraph 21. The Court states: "[f]irst, the facts of the case support application of the rule of strict liability because the ponding of the toxic formation water in an area adjacent to the Branches' wells constituted an abnormally dangerous and inappropriate use of the land in light of its proximity to the Branches' property and was unduly dangerous to the Branches' use of their well water." The court then cites several cases using the rule introduced in *Rylands v. Fletcher* as persuasive authority. One case, in particular, *Atlas Chemical Industries Inc. v. Anderson,* is given special attention in paragraph 22. The Utah Supreme Court writes: "[a] n industrial polluter can and should assume the costs of pollution as a cost of doing business rather than charge the loss to a wholly innocent party." Further, the Court quotes: "[t]he costs of injuries resulting from pollution must be internalized by industry as a cost of production and borne by consumers and shareholders, or both, and not by the injured individual." While this is a significant general conclusion about the costs of pollution and the role of the courts, it does not directly bear on the specific reasoning for holding Western Petroleum strictly liable.

Paragraph 24 states that: "[t]he judgment of the trial court may also be sustained on the alternative doctrine of nuisance per se," that is, literally, nuisance by or in itself. Returning to the unlawful behavior of Western Petroleum in failing to obtain the required permits, the Court adds: "[w]hen the conditions giving rise to a nuisance are also a violation of a statutory prohibition, these conditions constitute a nuisance per se."

Paragraph 25 clarifies the previous statement that *Branch* involves a strict liability, nuisance tort. The Court states: "[w]e are aware that a nuisance theory was not presented to the trial court. Usually we will not consider on appeal a theory not presented to the trial court. However, nuisance per se is in reality just another term for strict liability. Furthermore, we may affirm a trial court's decision on proper grounds even though different than those relied upon by the trial court." So, the nuisance theory survives and is what should have been presented by the Branches' attorneys in the trial court. Paragraph 27 records the court ruling upholding the trial court's holding: "the trial court properly ruled that Western was strictly liable for the damage which it caused the Branches." This is true, despite the fact that a nuisance theory was not presented. The court then dismisses several of the issues raised by Western Petroleum, stating that: "[s]ince liability was properly based on strict liability, the failure of the trial court to give instructions on comparative negligence and proximate cause was not an error." Further, the "issue of actual causation was decided in favor of the Branches, and there was no issue of proximate causation to be decided." If there were any questions about the application of all three theories of civil liability, in paragraph 28, the court concludes: "the findings were sufficient as to all the factual issues."

Section III (paragraphs 29-32) focuses on the remedy. First, it addresses Western Petroleum's contention that "the trial court should have reduced the damages awarded for pollution of the wells by the percentage of pollution found by the jury to have been caused by other parties or conditions" (paragraph 29). Then, it moves to agents of the pollution, the contaminants, whose amount was well "above the safe level of 500 part per million." The contamination above that level caused the whole injury, and as to that, Western was legally responsible."

Section IV (paragraphs 33-36) addresses Western Petroleum's contention that "the trial was defective on the ground that the jury venire was improperly chosen because those who wanted to go elk hunting were excused." Recall that the jury venire is the pool of individuals from which the jury will be selected. The next and final sections (paragraphs 37-44) address the appeal of the amount of punitive damages awarded and the favorable verdict for Branches' mental suffering.

Miscellaneous Issues - Internalization of the Externalities

In *Branch*, the Utah Supreme Court writes: "[a]n industrial polluter can and should assume the costs of pollution as a cost of doing business rather than charge the loss to a wholly innocent party." Further, the Court quotes from *Atlas Chemical*: "[t]he costs of injuries resulting from pollution must be internalized by industry as a cost of production and borne by consumers and shareholders, or both, and not by the injured individual." This raises the important issue of the internalization of the costs of pollution externalized (placed on society and the environment) by the polluters.

For companies, pollution that can be externalized without penalty or bad publicity is good for the "bottom line" or profit. It is useful to look at environmental tort actions through the prism of how well the result internalized the externalities. Let us compare the internalization of the externalities in *Boomer*, *Wilsonville*, *Spur*, and *Borland*.

Oscar Boomer sued in private nuisance for damage to his property. He did not sue for harm to his health for breathing the cement dust. It is very expensive and scientifically difficult to provide proof of causation where a plaintiff alleges harm to his health. The cost (both property and health damage) of the cement dust pollution to residents (those not party to the lawsuit) is not accounted for in *Boomer*. The only internalizing effect was the ~$185,000 in damages paid by the Atlantic Cement Co. So, internalization of the externalities is very limited.

In *Wilsonville*, injunctions were issued and SCA Services had to remove all the toxic wastes and restore the site at a cost of about $5 million. The residents of Wilsonville also sued in private nuisance and recovered about $2.5 million (divided among ~600 residents and property owners). Thus, nearly all of the externalities were internalized. Of course, all that toxic waste, including PCBs, had to go somewhere, hopefully to a more secure site. *Spur* was ordered to move its cattle feedlots and all of the foul odors and flies were removed from Sun City. Because Del Webb came to the nuisance by expanding its development of Sun City, it was ordered to pay Spur to move its operations. This is perhaps a novel decision by the court, but in the end, most of the externalities were internalized. The foul odors, flies, and water pollution were moved elsewhere.

The internalization of the externalities in *Borland* was (like *Boomer*) very limited. Yes, damages were paid to the Borlands for the harmful effects of lead particulates; but the total harmful effects of lead pollution (both to other properties, human health, and environmental impacts) were not accounted for.

The Branches received both compensatory and punitive damages for the contamination of their wells, but the cost of cleaning up the disposal site and the long-term groundwater contamination of the Branches' property, as well as other properties, was not internalized.

Of course, Boomer and other local residents, the Borlands, and the Branches may not have been concerned with harm to other residents or the environment. Del Webb was only concerned with public health because of their lost sales, and while the noxious odors and flies were moved elsewhere, the more significant impact of pathogens and nutrients on local waterways never became an issue.

In order to stop pollution, the polluter must assume the cost of pollution prevention. This may affect the bottom line as well as competitiveness in the world marketplace. Because pollution can increase profits and competitiveness, there is a built-in motivation to pollute. This dilemma was beautifully delineated in Garret Hardin's essay "The Tragedy of the Commons" (see the Companion Website at http://www.environmentallaw-teach.org/). Of course, regulations and penalties imposed on polluters by environmental statutes have had a major impact on the internalization of the externalities. Still, we are living the tragedy of the commons. All we need to do is realize the nature and extent of groundwater contamination of brownfields and Superfund sites, or of the impact of the global changes in the chemistry of the atmosphere.

Study Questions for *Branch*

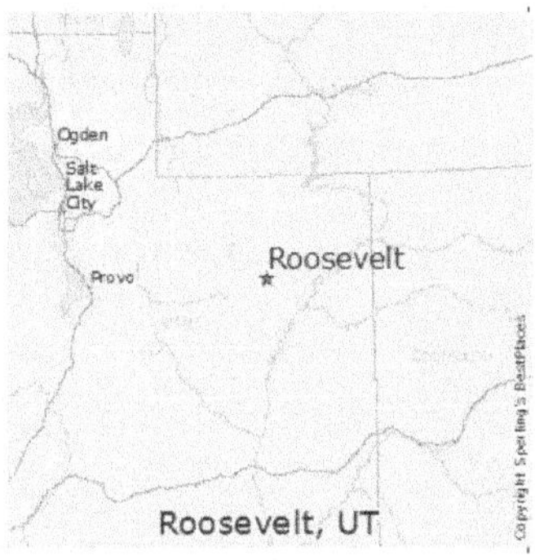

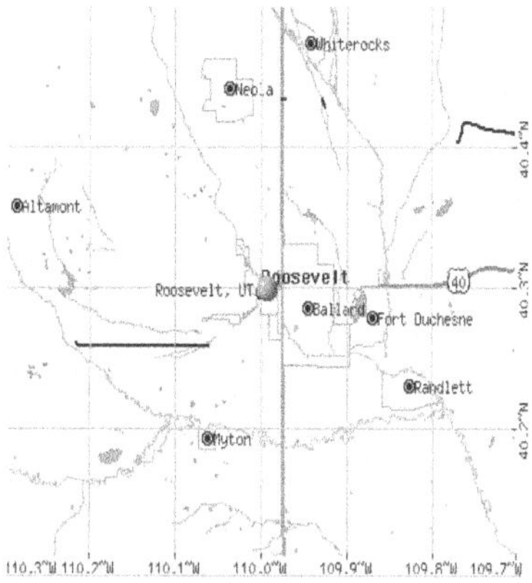

https://www.rooseveltcity.com/

Western bought 40 acres of land north of Roosevelt, Utah in December of 1975.

1. What are the elements of nuisance as raised in *Branch*?

2. Describe the important facts for this case. Did Branch come to the nuisance? Explain.

3. What was the procedural history?

4. What was the role of expert witnesses?

Main Street in Roosevelt Utah, https://www.rooseveltcity.com/_

5. Draw the hydrogeologic conditions showing groundwater contamination for *Branch v. Western Petroleum*?

6. The *Branch* court made two key decisions, one of which was on the elements and the other, regarding the remedy. Describe both of these two key decisions and the reasoning for each.

Moqui Indian trading Post, Roosevelt, Utah, 1976
https://thebookshelfofemilyj.com/2013/04/10/ethnocentrism-in-the-indian-in-the-cupboard/

Branch **(Court Opinion)**

657 P.2D 267

SUPREME COURT OF UTAH.

LLOYD BRANCH AND JEANNE BRANCH, PLAINTIFFS AND RESPONDENTS,

V.

WESTERN PETROLEUM, INC., DEFENDANT AND APPELLANT.

NO. 17178.

|

NOV. 8, 1982.

Synopsis

Property owner sued adjoining owners for pollution of plaintiffs' culinary water wells caused by percolation of oil well formation waters which defendant had ponded on its property. The Fourth District Court, Duchesne County, J. Robert Bullock, J., rendered judgment for plaintiffs on jury verdicts, and appeal and cross appeal were taken. The Supreme Court, Stewart,

J., held that: (1) defendant could be held liable either on theory of strict liability or under doctrine of nuisance per se; (2) it was of no consequence that defendant was conducting a wholly legitimate business; (3) since injury was not total amount of contaminants in the well, which contained high amount of natural contaminants, but rather amount of contaminants above safe level of 500 parts per million no reduction of damages was required where defendant was legally responsible for contamination above the safe level; (4) punitive damages were properly awarded; and (5) damages were recoverable from mental suffering, discomfort and annoyance.

Affirmed in part and remanded in part.

Attorneys and Law Firms

Gayle F. McKeachnie, Clark B. Allred, Vernal, for defendant and appellant.
George E. Mangan, Herbert W. Gillespie, Roosevelt, for plaintiffs and respondents.

Opinion

STEWART, Justice:

P#1. The Branches, the plaintiff property owners, sued for damages for the pollution of their culinary water wells caused by percolation of defendant Western Petroleum Inc.'s formation waters (waste waters from oil wells containing various chemical contaminants) into the subterranean water system that feeds the wells. A jury answered questions to special interrogatories, finding, inter alia, that the formation waters had contaminated plaintiffs' two wells and awarded damages of $8,050 for pollution of the well water, $700 for trespass, $10,000 for "mental suffering, discomfort and annoyance," and $13,000 punitive damages. The jury, over objection, was instructed on the theory of negligence; however, the trial court entered judgment on the basis of strict liability for the above amounts, except that damages for mental suffering, discomfort, and annoyance were disallowed.

P#2. Western appeals, arguing that the trial court erred in awarding damages for pollution of the wells on the basis of strict liability. It contends that negligence is the only valid legal theory upon which the judgment can be sustained and that the trial court erred (1) in not instructing on proximate cause; and (2) in not directing the jury to find the percentage of negligence attributable to each party as required by the Utah Comparative Negligence Act, U.C.A., 1953, § 78-27-38. Western also complains of the trial court's failure to reduce damages by the percentage of pollution "caused by other parties or conditions"; an improper selection of the jury venire; and the award of punitive damages without a showing that defendant's actions were willful and malicious. No attack is made on the judgment of $700 for trespass. On a cross-appeal, the Branches contend that the court erred in striking the jury award for mental suffering, discomfort, and annoyance.

I.

P#3. In December 1975, Western purchased forty acres of land in a rural area north of Roosevelt, Utah, which had previously been used as a gravel pit. Western used the property solely for the disposal of formation water, a waste water produced by oil wells while drilling for oil. Formation water contains oil, gas and high concentrations of salt and chemicals, making it unfit for culinary or agricultural uses. The formation water was transported by truck from various oil-producing sites and emptied into the disposal pit with the intent that the toxic water would dissipate through evaporation into the air and percolation into the ground. Alternative sites for disposing of the water were available to Western, but at a greater expense.

P#4. In 1976, the Branches purchased a parcel of property immediately adjacent to, and at an elevation of approximately 200 to 300 feet lower than, Western's property. The twenty-one acre parcel had on it a "diligence" well, which had been in existence since 1929, some outbuildings, and a home. After acquiring the property, the Branches made some $60,000 worth of improvements to the home and premises. Prior owners of the property used the water from the well for a grade A dairy and later a grade B dairy. Both dairy operations required that the water be approved for fitness and purity by appropriate state agencies. The Branches, as had all prior owners since 1929, used water from the diligence well for culinary purposes. The water from the diligence well was described as being sweet to the taste and of a high quality until December of 1976.

P#5. Two months after purchasing the property, the Branches noticed that the well water began to take on a peculiar taste and had the distinctive smell of petroleum products. Soap added to the water would no longer form suds. They observed that polluted water from Western's disposal pit was running onto the surface of the Branches' property and, on one occasion, reached their basement, causing damage to food stored there. After testing the diligence well water and finding it unfit for human consumption, and after their rabbits and one hundred chickens had died, apparently from the polluted water, the Branches began trucking water to their property from outside sources. In November, 1977, the Branches dug an additional well south of their home. Water from the new well was tested and found safe for culinary purposes. But after a few months, the new well also ceased producing potable water, and on advice of the State Health Department, the Branches ceased using the new well for culinary purposes and hauled water to their property almost until the time of trial.

P#6. The Branches requested Western to cease dumping formation water in the disposal pit, but Western refused unless the Branches would post a bond to cover the costs. Western did, however, agree to build a pond on its property to contain the escaping surface water and prevent it from flowing onto the Branches' land. In doing so, Western failed to establish the proper boundary line and built part of the pond on the Branches' land. After the Branches hired a surveyor to establish that Western had built the pond on their land, Western built another containing pond on its own property. The pond, however, was only partially successful in preventing the run-off onto the Branches' land from the disposal pit. Western caused additional damage by permitting its trucks to enter the Branches' property for the purpose of pumping out the containment ponds. When the discharge nozzles on the trucks were left open, polluted water was sprayed directly onto the Branches' land.

P#7. As a consequence of the unavailability of culinary water in her home, plaintiff Jeanne Branch returned to her original home in Colorado for a three or four month period so that she could "pull herself together." During this time, Lloyd Branch made weekly trips to and from Colorado to be with his family and otherwise tried to keep in contact with his wife on the telephone while he maintained his contracting business in Roosevelt.

P#8. Western's agents admitted that they did not know, and made no attempt to ascertain, what state law was with respect to permitting formation waters to seep or percolate into subsurface waters. Even after Western became aware of the laws relative to dumping, it still took no affirmative action to obtain approval of its ponds.

P#9. At trial the major issue was whether and how Western's formation waters caused the pollution of the Branches' wells. Western's expert, Mr. Ferris, a private geologist with approximately two years professional experience in the Rocky Mountain area, and the Branches' expert, Mr. Montgomery, a state geologist who had spent nine years working for the Utah Division of Water Resources, agreed that the subsurface waters consist of shallow groundwater and a deeper aquifer known as the Duchesne Formation. The Duchesne Formation produces the culinary water which is tapped by the Branches' wells. The two experts also agreed that formation water in the disposal pit was percolating into the subsurface waters, but they disagreed on whether the polluted waters had merely entered the shallow groundwaters or had percolated down into the Duchesne Formation.

P#10. Ferris maintained that the formation water only entered the shallow groundwater and did not penetrate to the Duchesne Formation. He concluded that the formation water could have entered the Branches' original well only through cracks in the well casing at the level of the shallow groundwaters. He further testified that none of Western's polluted water entered the Branches' new well because there were no cracks in its casing. In addition, Ferris testified that since the shallow groundwaters were naturally contaminated and unfit for human use, Western's additional pollutants were of no consequence to the Branches. The new well, according to Ferris, contained naturally poor, although useable, water from the Duchesne Formation.

P#11. Montgomery, testifying for the Branches, admitted that the Duchesne Formation water was of relatively poor quality and contained many natural contaminants. However, he stressed that the natural contaminants were not sufficient to cause the well water to fall below the standards set by the Public Health Service for acceptable human use. He stated that the waters from Western's disposal water percolated below the shallow groundwater and through natural joints and cracks into the deeper Duchesne Formation, where it entered both of the Branches' wells and made them unfit for human use.

P#12. The jury obviously considered Montgomery the more convincing of the two experts. It found, in response to special interrogatories, that "defendant's use of the evaporation pit for the dumping of formation water [was] a cause of the pollution of the water in plaintiffs' [wells]," and that Western caused 66 percent of the pollution in Branches' original well and 52 percent of the pollution in the new well. The rest of the pollution was found to be caused by other unspecified "parties or conditions." The jury also found that Western was "negligent ... in dumping formation waters in its evaporation pit," and had also committed a "trespass upon plaintiffs' land ... other than the claimed pollution of [the] wells."

II.

P#13. The major substantive dispute is whether the trial court erred in entering judgment against Western on the basis of strict liability for pollution of the Branches' wells. Western argues that other states have based liability for pollution of subterranean waters on either negligence, nuisance, or trespass, and that since the Branches failed to allege nuisance or trespass, "the only accepted theory upon which this case could be based is negligence."[10] Therefore, according to Western, the trial court erred in entering judgment on the basis of strict liability. Western further submits that since the court did not instruct the jury on proximate cause and comparative negligence, the judgment cannot stand. The Branches, on the other hand, take the position that Western created an abnormally dangerous condition by collecting contaminated water on its land for the purpose of having it seep or percolate into the groundwater and that, therefore, the law of strict liability controls.

---

10 Defendant relies on the following authorities: General Crude Oil Co. v. Aiken, 162 Tex. 104, 344 S.W.2d 668 (1961); Ross v. Fink, Okl., 378 P.2d 1011 (1963); Turner v. Big Lake Oil Co., 128 Tex. 155, 96 S.W.2d 221 (1936); United Fuel Gas Co. v. Sawyers, Ky., 259 S.W.2d 466 (1953); Annot., 38 A.L.R.2d 1265, 1268 (1954); and Annot., 39 A.L.R.3d 910, 921 (1971).

P#14. This Court has not heretofore had occasion to consider the legal principles which govern liability for the pollution of subterranean waters by industrial wastes. Our survey of cases from other states and of legal scholars indicates that a variety of legal theories have been relied on. The theories that have been employed include negligence, private nuisance, public nuisance, negligent nuisance, nuisance without negligence, intentional nuisance, absolute nuisance, trespass, and strict liability. Davis, *Groundwater Pollution: Case Law Theories for Relief,* 39 Mo.L.Rev. 117 (1974); Annot., Landowner's Right to Relief Against Pollution of His Water Supply by Industrial or Commercial Waste, 39 A.L.R.3d 910 (1971); Annot., Liability for Pollution of Subterranean Waters, 38 A.L.R.2d 1265 (1954). *See generally* Atlas Chemical Industries, Inc. v. Anderson, Tex.Civ.App., 514 S.W.2d 309 (1974), *aff'd,* 524 S.W.2d 681 (1975). The variety of approaches reflects numerous considerations, such as the general hydrological conditions in the state; the relative significance of promoting industrialization compared with the importance of promoting conservation of water; the nature of the particular state's water law; and, in particular, whether the doctrine of correlative rights applies to the use of water resources. *See* Davis, *Groundwater Pollution, supra,* at 119–37.

P#15. In England under the common law, percolating water was considered part of the freehold and subject to private ownership. In American law it is generally recognized that a landowner has no absolute right to pollute percolating waters. Annot., 38 A.L.R.2d at 1267. In this state, a landowner has no such absolute right because percolating waters belong to the people of the state. J.J.N.P. v. State of Utah, 655 P.2d 1133, No. 17183, Utah, (filed September 22, 1982). For that reason, ***273** and because percolating waters are migratory and the rights of the landowners to those waters are correlative, § 73–5–1, such waters are subject to the maxim that one may not use his land so as to pollute percolating waters to the injury of another. Annot., 38 A.L.R.2d at 1267.

P#16. As Utah is one of the most arid states in the union, the protection of the purity of the water is of critical importance, and the Legislature has enacted laws for the protection of both surface and subterranean waters.[11] U.C.A., 1953, § 26–11–8 (Supp.1981); § 40–6–5; § 76–10–801;

11 Section 73–14–1, in effect at the time this case was tried, expressed the policy of the State with regard to pollution:

Pollution of waters—Public policy of state. Whereas the pollution of the waters of this state constitutes a menace to public health and welfare, creates public nuisances, is harmful to wildlife, fish and aquatic life, and impairs domestic, agricultural, industrial, recreational and other legitimate beneficial uses of water, and whereas such pollution is contrary to the best interests of the state and its policy for the conservation of the water resources of the state, it is hereby declared to be the public policy of this state to conserve the waters of the state and to protect, maintain and improve the quality thereof for public water supplies, for the propagation of wildlife, fish and aquatic life, and for domestic, agricultural, industrial, recreational and other legitimate beneficial uses; to provide that no waste be discharged into any waters of the state without first being given the degree of treatment necessary to protect the legitimate beneficial uses of such waters; to provide for the prevention, abatement and control of new or existing water pollution; to place first in priority those control measures directed toward elimination of pollution which creates hazards to the public health; to give reasonable consideration to the economic impact of water pollution control on industry including agriculture in the state; and to co-operate with other agencies of the state, agencies of other states and the federal government in carrying out these objectives.

§ 76-10-802; § 76-10-803(1)(d). Absent a permit, U.C.A., 1953, § 73-14-5[12] made it unlawful for any person to discharge a pollutant into waters of the state or to cause pollution as defined in section 73-14-2(a) which constitutes a menace to public health and welfare, or is harmful to wildlife, fish or acquatic life, or impairs domestic, agricultural, industrial, recreational or other beneficial uses of water, or to place or cause to be placed any wastes in a location where there is probable cause to believe they will cause pollution.

P#17. Two doctrines have developed in the common law to provide a remedy to a private landowner for nontrespassory injuries caused by another. The landmark case of *Rylands v. Fletcher,* 3 H. & C. 774, 159 Eng.Rep. 737 (1865), rev'd in *Fletcher v. Rylands,* L.R. 1 Ex. 265 (1866), aff'd in *Rylands v. Fletcher,* L.R. 3 H.L. 330 (1868), held that one who uses his land in an unnatural way and thereby creates a dangerous condition or engages in an abnormal activity may be strictly liable for injuries resulting from that condition or activity. Whether a condition or activity is considered abnormal is defined in terms of whether the condition or activity is unduly dangerous or inappropriate to the place where it is maintained. W. Prosser, Law of Torts § 78, at 506 (4th ed. 1971). That doctrine was the genesis of § 519 of the Restatement of Torts (1939), which, however, limited strict liability to "ultrahazardous activities." Prosser, *supra,* at 512.

P#18. Although *Rylands v. Fletcher* was initially rejected by a number of states, its influence has been substantial in the United States. According to the latest edition of Dean Prosser's treatise on torts, only seven American jurisdictions have rejected the rule of that case, while some thirty jurisdictions have essentially approved the rule. *Id.* at 509. Indeed, the strict liability rule of the Restatement of Torts was broadened in § 519 of the Restatement (Second) of Torts by making it applicable to "abnormally dangerous activities."

P#19. Nuisance law also protects property interests from nontrespassory invasions. Unlike most other torts, it is not centrally concerned with the nature of the conduct causing the damage, but with the nature and relative importance of the interests interfered with or invaded. The doctrine of nuisance "has reference to the interests invaded, to the damage or harm inflicted, and not to any particular kind of action or omission which has lead to the invasion." W. Prosser, *supra,* § 87 at 73-75. Since it is not the nature of one's conduct that generally is essential to an action for nuisance, a person whose interests have been invaded may have a claim for relief based both on nuisance and on the nature of the conduct producing the damage. *See* Cities

Chapter 14 of Title 73 was repealed and replaced by the Utah Water Pollution Control Act, § 26-11-1 et seq. in 1981. Laws of Utah 1981, Ch. 126.

12 As stated *supra* note 2, Chapter 14 of Title 73 was replaced by the Water Pollution Control Act, § 26-11-1 et seq. Section 26-11-8 of that act is similar to repealed § 73-14-5.

Service Oil Co. v. Merritt, Okl., 332 P.2d 677, 684 (1958); Wood v. Picillo, R.I., 443 A.2d 1244 (1982). As the court in *Wood* stated:

> The essential element of an actionable nuisance is that persons have suffered harm or are threatened with injuries that they ought not have to bear. Citizens for Preservation of Waterman Lake v. Davis, R.I., 420 A.2d 53, 59 (1980). Distinguished from negligence liability, liability in nuisance is predicated upon unreasonable injury rather than upon unreasonable conduct. Braun v. Iannotti, 54 R.I. 469, 471, 175 A. 656, 657 (1934). Thus, plaintiffs may recover in nuisance despite the otherwise nontortious nature of the conduct which creates the injury.

Id. at 1247. *Accord,* Vincent v. Salt Lake County, Utah, 583 P.2d 105 (1978); Mowrer v. Ashland Oil & Refining Co., 518 F.2d 659 (7th Cir.1975).

P#20. It is of no consequence that a business which causes a nuisance is a lawful business. *Mowrer v. Ashland Oil & Refining Co., supra,* at 661. The production of formation water is a natural and necessary incident to the business of producing oil and gas. A business such as Western, which collects and disposes of formation water, conducts a wholly legitimate business. But that does not give it a license to dispose of waste in a manner that for practical purposes appropriates the property of others by making it impossible for them to use water which they are entitled to use. North Point C.I. Co. v. Utah & Salt Lake Canal Co., 16 Utah 246, 52 P. 168 (1898).

P#21. There are two separate, although somewhat related, grounds for holding Western strictly liable for the pollution of the Branches' wells. First, the facts of the case support application of the rule of strict liability because the ponding of the toxic formation water in an area adjacent to the Branches' wells constituted an abnormally dangerous and inappropriate use of the land in light of its proximity to the Branches' property and was unduly dangerous to the Branches' use of their well water. Several cases on comparable facts have applied strict liability due to the abnormal danger of polluting activity. For example, Mowrer v. Ashland Oil & Refining Co., Inc., 518 F.2d 659 (7th Cir.1975), applied strict liability to the leakage of crude oil and salt water into a fresh water well; Yommer v. McKenzie, 255 Md. 220, 257 A.2d 138 (1969), applied the same rule to the seepage of gasoline from an underground tank into an adjoining landowner's well; Cities Service Co. v. Florida, Fla.App., 312 So.2d 799 (1975), applied strict liability to the escape of phosphate slime into a creek and river. See also Bumbarger v. Walker, 193 Pa.Super. 301, 164 A.2d 144 (1960) (strict liability for well pollution caused by defendant's mine blasting). See generally Clark-Aiken Co. v. Cromwell-Wright Co., 367 Mass. 70, 323 N.E.2d 876 (1975) (strict liability applied to escape of impounded water); Indiana Harbor Belt Railroad Co. v. American Cynamid Co., 517 F.Supp. 314 (N.D.Ill.1981) (strict liability applied to spillage of toxic chemical that resulted in property damage and pollution of water supply); W. Prosser, supra, § 78 at

512–13 and cases there cited.[13] See also Atlas Chemical Industries, Inc. v. Anderson, Tex.Civ. App., 514 S.W.2d 309 (1974), aff'd 524 S.W.2d 681 (1975), where the Texas court, distinguishing a case relied upon by Western, Turner v. Big Lake Oil Co., 128 Tex. 155, 96 S.W.2d 221 (1936), held the defendant strictly liable for polluting surface streams with industrial wastes.[14] The strict liability rule of *Rylands v. Fletcher* was held to apply to pollution cases "in which the defendant has set the substance in motion for escape, such as the discharge of the harmful effluent or the emission of a harmful gas or substance."[15] *Atlas Chemical, supra,* at 314.

P#22. In concluding that strict liability should govern in that case, the court in *Atlas Chemical* reasoned that the common law rules of tort liability in pollution cases "should be in conformity with the public policy of this state as declared by the Legislature in the Texas Water Code ...." *Id.* at 315.[16] The court also found support for the rule of strict liability in the policy consideration that an industry should not be able to use its property in such a way as to inflict injury on the property of its neighbors because to do so would result in effect in appropriating the neighbor's property to one's own use. An industrial polluter can and should assume the costs of pollution as a cost of doing business rather than charge the loss to a wholly innocent party. The court in *Atlas Chemical* stated:

---

13 For cases applying various theories with differing results see Davis, *Groundwater Pollution: Case Law Theories for Relief,* 39 Mo.L.Rev. 117 (1974).

14 The Texas court was of the opinion that if the escape of the pollution was unintentional then the governing law is negligence, not strict liability. In non-pollution cases, this Court has not required that a nuisance action be based on negligence. Vincent v. Salt Lake County, Utah, 583 P.2d 105 (1978); Sanford v. University of Utah, 26 Utah 2d 285, 488 P.2d 741 (1971).

15 Even if Western did not know that the formation water would enter the aquifer and cause damage to plaintiffs' wells, it could have determined the likelihood of that consequence. As Professor Davis has stated:

> A polluter should not be absolved from liability just because he may not be able to anticipate the movement of the polluted groundwater he created. This defense should not be recognized for several reasons. First, the hydrology of groundwater movement is much better understood now than it was when many of the early groundwater pollution cases were decided. Even though precise mapping of groundwater movement in any particular location is still expensive, it is within the reach of any major waste producer which proposes to inject wastes underground. Disposal wells need porous formations for successful waste injection and the appropriate hydrologic tests would insure a successful injection well. Therefore, persons deliberately disposing of wastes underground ought to be required to act in accordance with the information gained by such testing regarding the movement of the injected wastes and their probable effects on neighboring groundwater uses. If they do not make such tests, they should be charged with the information they would have gained had they made them. Second, it is generally known now that liquids placed on the ground will seep into the soil and may enter the body of groundwater percolating beneath the surface. Persons causing groundwater pollution in ways, other than by deliberate underground disposal, should be charged with such knowledge and should not be insulated from liability for groundwater pollution by claiming that they know nothing more about groundwater movement than was known in 1843 when *Acton v. Blundell* was decided. Although a particular polluter might still legitimately claim he could not predict particular injurious consequences of his activity, he can no longer claim legitimately that the polluting material vanished from the earth once it seeped beneath the surface. He knows it will go somewhere. Such a defense to nuisance liability is not recognized in surface watercourse and air pollution cases. Groundwater pollution cases should not recognize it either.
>
> Pollution of a groundwater aquifer may have pervasive effects both in terms of territorial extent and duration. With reliance on our groundwater supplies increasing, the old court-made rules concerning groundwater pollution are no longer adequate.

Davis, *supra* note 3, at 145–46. See also Wood v. Picillo, R.I., 443 A.2d 1244, 1249 (1982).

16 The holding of the court in Atlas Chemical was limited to uses in which the discharge of pollutants was intentional. In the instant case, the discharge was also intentional.

P#23. We know of no acceptable rule of jurisprudence which permits those engaged in important and desirable enterprises to injure with impunity those who are engaged in enterprises of lesser economic significance. The costs of injuries resulting from pollution must be internalized by industry as a cost of production and borne by consumers or shareholders, or both, and not by the injured individual.

Id. at 316.

P#24. We think these reasons adequately support application of the rule of strict liability in this case.

P#25. The judgment of the trial court may also be sustained on the alternative doctrine of nuisance per se. The pollution of underground water has been held a nuisance by a number of courts. Pollard v. Land West, Inc., 96 Idaho 274, 526 P.2d 1110 (1974); Cities Service Oil Co. v. Merritt, Okl., 332 P.2d 677 (1958); Wood v. Picillo, R.I., 443 A.2d 1244 (1982); Watson v. Great Lakes Pipeline Co., 85 S.D. 310, 182 N.W.2d 314 (1970); Haveman v. Beulow, 36 Wash.2d 185, 217 P.2d 313 (1950); see generally 39 A.L.R.3d at 922; 38 A.L.R.2d at 1285. When the conditions giving rise to a nuisance are also a violation of a statutory prohibition, those conditions constitute a nuisance per se, and the issue of the reasonableness of the defendant's conduct and the weighing of the relative interests of the plaintiff and defendant is precluded because the Legislature has, in effect, already struck the balance in favor of the innocent party. Defendant's violation of § 73–14–5 (See § 26–11–8 for corresponding current provision) and § 76–10–801 removed the issue of the reasonableness of its conduct compared with the nature of the injury inflicted from consideration in this case. The declaration of the Legislature is conclusive, and its determination will not be second guessed. Harmison v. City of Lewistown, 153 Ill. 313, 38 N.E. 628 (1894); City of Chicago v. Shaynin, 258 Ill. 69, 101 N.E. 224 (1913); Eccles v. Ditto, 23 N.M. 235, 167 P. 726 (1917); W. Prosser, supra, § 87 at 582–83. The result for practical purposes is the same as strict liability.

P#26. We are aware that a nuisance theory was not presented to the trial court. Usually we will not consider on appeal a theory not presented to the trial court. However, nuisance per se is in reality just another term for strict liability. Furthermore, we may affirm a trial court's decision on proper grounds even though different than those relied upon by the trial court. Jesperson v. Jesperson, Utah, 610 P.2d 326 (1980); Allphin Realty, Inc. v. Sine, Utah, 595 P.2d 860 (1979).

P#27. In sum, the trial court properly ruled that Western was strictly liable for the damage which it caused the Branches. Since liability was properly based on strict liability, the failure of the trial court to give instructions on comparative negligence and proximate cause was not error. Contributory negligence is neither a defense to a nuisance action, Mowrer v. Ashland

Oil & Refining Co. Inc., 518 F.2d 659 (1975), nor to an action based on strict liability. The issue of actual causation was decided in favor of the Branches, and there was no issue of proximate causation to be decided.

P#28. We have already noted that the jury in this case was instructed, over the Branches objection, on a theory of negligence and that the jury's findings did not cover all the issues under a negligence theory. Nevertheless, the findings were sufficient as to all the factual issues under the law of nuisance per se and strict liability.

III.

P#29. Western also contends that the trial court should have reduced the damages awarded for the pollution of the wells by the percentage of pollution found by the jury to have been caused by other parties or conditions.

P#30. It is conceded by the Branches that the water in the area contains a high level of natural contaminants, although not so high as to make the water unsafe or unpotable. Federal health standards established 500 parts of solids per million as the highest safe level for the water. Based on the latest chemical tests that were conducted, the Branches' diligence well contained 980 parts of solids per million and the new well 920 parts of solids per million. The jury found that Western was responsible for 66 per cent of the solids in the diligence well and 52 per cent of the solids in the second well.

P#31. The amount of contaminants in the diligence well attributable to Western, therefore, was 646.8 parts per million, leaving approximately 333 parts per million attributable to either natural or other causes. As for the new well, Western was responsible for 478.4 parts per million of the contaminants, ***277** and the remaining 441 parts were attributable to either natural or other causes. Thus, without the pollution caused by Western, the level of contaminants in both wells would have been within the limits of the federal safety standards. In other words, but for Western's pollution, the wells would have been useable.

P#32. Contrary to the implication of Western's argument, the injury to the Branches was not the total amount of contaminants in each well; it was rather the amount of contaminants above the safe level of 500 parts per million. The contamination above that level caused the whole injury, and as to that, Western was legally responsible.

IV.

P#33. Western also contends that the trial was defective on the ground that the jury venire was improperly chosen because those who wanted to go elk hunting were excused. Section 78–46–16(1) requires that a challenge to jury selection be made "[w]ithin seven days after the moving party discovered, or by the exercise of diligence could have discovered the grounds therefore, and in any event before the trial jury is sworn to try the case ...."

P#34. Western contends that it was not aware of the improper action prior to the time the jury was sworn and therefore was unable to file a motion challenging the selection of the jury within the statutory time period. Upon learning of the removal of those prospective jurors who desired to go elk hunting, Western filed with the trial court a motion requesting a new trial or a hearing to determine whether the jury selection was proper. The motion was denied, and no hearing was held.

P#35. Western's objection is not well taken. There are no affidavits indicating how many prospective jurors were excused or why Western did not find out about the facts sooner. We think the defect should have been discovered in the exercise of due diligence before the commencement of the trial as required by the statute.

P#36. Even assuming that the challenge was timely raised, § 78–46–16(2) requires a "substantial failure to comply with this act" and a showing that an "actual and substantial injustice and prejudice has resulted or will result to a party in consequence of the failure" to comply. Applying this latter requirement, Western's contention of prejudicial error fails. The jury panel was comprised of four males and four females. It consisted of a superintendent of schools, a highway patrolman, a former deputy sheriff (currently a Department of Transportation employee), a farmer-rancher, a county recorder, a high school secretary, and two housewives. There is nothing in the record to suggest that the prospective jurors who were excused were drawn from any particular religious, cultural, racial, sexual, or socio-economic class. Nor is there anything to suggest that the excluded group represented a belief or conviction, not otherwise represented on the panel, which was more sympathetic to the interests of Western. Since there is no reason to suppose the elimination of a few elk hunters from the panel skewed the composition of the jury panel in any manner, and since the jury was passed for cause, there is no basis for finding prejudicial error.

V.

P#37. Western's final contention on its appeal challenges the award of punitive damages. It argues that punitive damages are appropriate only when willful and malicious conduct is shown and that the court erred in including the phrase "reckless indifference and disregard" in its instruction on punitive damages. However, in Terry v. Zions Cooperative Mercantile Institution, Utah, 605 P.2d 314 (1979), this Court held that punitive damages may be awarded when one acts with reckless indifference and disregard of the law and his fellow citizens:

> This presumed malice or malice in law does not consist of personal hate or ill will of one person towards another but rather refers to that state of mind which is reckless of law and of the legal rights of the citizens in a person's conduct toward that citizen.... In such cases malice in ***278** law will be implied from unjustifiable conduct which causes the injury complained of or from a wrongful act intentionally done without cause or excuse.

Id. at 327. *See also First Security Bank v. J.B.J. Feedyards, 653 P.2d 591 (1982).*

P#38. The evidence in this case meets that standard. Western discharged the waste water into the disposal pit intending that it seep into and percolate through the soil. Thus, the pollution of the percolating waters was willful and carried out in disregard of the rights of the Branches. Moreover, Western compounded the Branches' problems by its trespass on their land, the spraying of waste water over their land and the failure to comply with state law. In addition, Western continued its dumping activities even after the pollution of the diligence well. The punitive damage award was adequately supported by evidence of reckless indifference toward, and disregard of, the Branches' rights.

P#39. Furthermore, there is no merit to Western's contention that the award of punitive damages was excessive and influenced by passion or prejudice rather than reason. The jury was properly instructed that the purpose of exemplary damages is to deter defendant and others from engaging in similar conduct. In *Terry v. Zion's Cooperative Mercantile Institution, supra,* this Court stated:

P#40. The purpose of a punitive or exemplary damage award is not to compensate the party harmed but rather to punish the wrongdoer, to deter him from similar acts in the future, and to provide fair warning to others similarly situated that such conduct is not tolerated.

Due to the purposes underlying the award of punitive damages many factors contribute in determining their appropriate measure.... The jury in its original decision or the court in its review of that decision must also consider the particular nature of the defendant's acts, the probability of those acts being repeated in the future, and the relative wealth of the particular defendant.

605 P.2d at 328. See also Nash v. Craigco, Inc., Utah, 585 P.2d 775, 778 (1978). The award of punitive damages is a matter in the first instance for the discretion of the jury, and the award was not excessive in relation to actual damages in either our view or the view of the trial judge whose judgment we accord considerable weight because of his first hand knowledge of the evidence in the case.

VI.

P#41. The jury returned a verdict in favor of the Branches for mental suffering, discomfort and annoyance in the amount of $10,000. During the trial, the court dismissed the claim for such damages on the ground that "emotional distress and anxiety and upset concerning the matter is not compensible, per se. It may be in connection with exemplary, punitive damages. I don't know. But per se, there isn't a separate cause of action for that. And I grant your motion." Notwithstanding that ruling, the trial judge reconsidered, and at the conclusion of the trial, submitted a special interrogatory on the amount of damage suffered by the Branches as a result of "emotional distress, discomfort and annoyance." In response to that interrogatory, the jury found damages in the amount of $10,000. The trial judge initially entered judgment for that amount, but then struck that part of the judgment apparently on the ground that such damages could be recoverable, if at all, only under the doctrine of Samms v. Eccles, 11 Utah 2d 289, 358 P.2d 344 (1961). Samms dealt with the independent tort of intentional infliction of emotional distress, not with a nuisance case, and is therefore clearly inapplicable to this case.

P#42. It has, however, long been recognized that "a plaintiff may recover damages for personal inconvenience, annoyance and discomfort caused by the existence of a nuisance." Wade v. Fuller, 12 Utah 2d 299, 302, 365 P.2d 802, 805 (1961). See also Pollard v. Land West Inc., 96 Idaho 274, 526 P.2d 1110 (1974); Edwards v. Talent Irrigation District, 280 Or. 307, 570 P.2d 1169 (1977); 58 Am.Jur.2d Nuisances § 124 and § 125 (1971) (citing cases awarding damages for mental distress).

P#43. Admittedly, damages for inconvenience, annoyance, discomfort and mental distress are not capable of precise calculation, although those elements may reflect direct, immediate, and real injury. In this case the jury had evidence before it to justify the award of substantial damages of the type under consideration. The Branches testified to the emotional distress caused Jeanne Branch which culminated in her leaving her husband for a period of three or four months. In addition to that, the Branches were forced to truck water onto their property and to take numerous other steps to counter the nuisance created by Western.

P#44. For the foregoing reasons, we affirm the judgment of the trial court in all respects except with respect to the striking of the award of damages for mental distress, annoyance, and discomfort and remand for the re-entry of that award in the amount specified by the jury.

HALL, C.J., and OAKS and HOWE, JJ., concur.
DURHAM, J., does not participate herein.

Chapter 9 – Toxic Torts and A Civil Action

The purpose of this short chapter is to provide insight and materials for teaching and learning about toxic torts which have an environmental impact. Perhaps the best lawsuit to learn about toxic torts is the case of *Anne Anderson, et al. v. W.R. Grace and Beatrice Foods*, 628 F.Supp. 1219 (E.D. Mass.1986). This lawsuit involves a gripping story described by Jonathan Harr in his book A Civil Action. It was one of the first nationally publicized landmark toxic tort cases. *Anderson* involved the toxic chemical contamination of groundwater and two city wells by large and powerful corporations. The plaintiffs claimed that these toxic chemicals in the water supply had caused leukemia, deaths, and other serious illnesses.

Starting in the mid-1960s residents of Woburn, Massachusetts became aware that many children in a small neighborhood served by these two wells had contracted leukemia. This was a classic "cancer cluster," a geographic area with a much higher-than-normal rate of cancer. Led by Anne Anderson, the mother of Jimmy Anderson who had contracted leukemia and died, a grassroots movement developed eventually leading to a class-action lawsuit. The plaintiffs in this lawsuit were seven families, all of whom had children with leukemia and five of whom had died.

Recall from Chapter 6 that the "elements of a lawsuit are the constituent parts that the plaintiffs must prove in order for a jury or a judge sitting as finder-of-fact to find the defendant liable. There are three basic elements for a civil suit: a) proof of harm; b) proof of causation; and, c) proof of fault." The assault on the environment by the release and dumping of toxic wastes became an important issue in the 1970s. With the publicity surrounding the toxic wastes at Love Canal in New York, the Valley of the Drums in Kentucky, and many other similar toxic spills, the federal government responded by passing the *Toxic Substances Control Act in 1976* and the *Comprehensive Environmental Response, Compensation, and Liability Act, or Superfund Act of 1980 (C.E.R.C.L.A.).* Toxic torts, however, were the only way for persons harmed by the release of these toxic substances to hold liable the responsible parties and receive compensation. The scale of toxic tort lawsuits can vary dramatically from the release of a single toxic compound that harms a single person to the exposure of a multitude of people by the release of toxins on a large scale. The exposures may be acute or may occur over a long period of time. Mass tort exposure cases are particularly complicated, largely because causation is so difficult to prove and also because of issues of civil procedure.

While there were many toxic compounds found in the two wells in Woburn, trichloroethylene (TCE) received the headlines. The complexity of proving causation involved proving (by the preponderance of the evidence) that W.R. Grace and Beatrice used and dumped TCE into the environment so that it entered the groundwater system. The plaintiffs then had to prove that this contaminated groundwater moved to the wells and not in another direction. Next, they had to show when molecules of TCE from the responsible parties were dumped, and that these molecules had enough time to travel to the wells and expose people who used that water. Finally, they had to prove that it was TCE that substantially contributed to (or caused) the leukemias and other illnesses. None of this is trivial. At the start of the trial there was little or no evidence to show that TCE caused any illnesses and, in addition, the wells were contaminated with dozens of other toxic compounds. While the discovery by the Commonwealth of Massachusetts that the wells were severely contaminated, and the groundwater evidence developed by the E.P.A. provided the plaintiffs with the basis for a lawsuit, the critical timing element was lacking. Eventually, the Woburn aquifer became one of the most studied groundwater systems on the planet, and substantial medical evidence was developed showing the harms that the plaintiffs suffered from TCE. The development of this evidence cost well over a million dollars. The trial came to an end when Beatrice was removed from the case, and W.R. Grace settled with the plaintiffs. The trial did demonstrate that a dedicated attorney (Jan Schlichtmann) and his associates, as well as families traumatized by exposure to toxic chemicals, could challenge two powerful corporations with deep pockets and their attorneys, and achieve substantial success. The lawsuit also produced national publicity raising awareness of the harms to human health from improper disposal of toxic wastes.

The case also showed that proof of causation is the central issue in toxic tort lawsuits. This is because in toxic tort cases, the causation is not proximate (or next to) the harm. Unlike a man shooting someone with a gun, in toxic torts, the cause is remote and often hidden. Toxins released into the environment often follow invisible and unknown pathways through the air and water or via subterranean channels. Toxic chemicals may interact with other chemicals in the environment in complex ways. In addition, subtle but devastating harm often does not immediately manifest itself in an observable illness. There are often lengthy latent periods.

Finally, chronic low-level exposure is not well understood for specific toxins. Who knew at the beginning of the *Woburn* trial that exposure to TCE would not only be from drinking the water but also from breathing vapors during showers and baths and, especially for children taking baths, via dermal absorption directly through the skin into the bloodstream?

As mentioned, issues of civil procedure further complicate toxic tort trials. While the *Woburn* case was settled out of court, significant motions were resolved in *Anderson v. W.R. Grace & Co.*, 628 F. Supp. 1219 (E.D. Mass. 1986). See Ch. 10 - *Toxic Tort and Civil Action* folder on the Companion Website, at http://www.environmentallaw-teach.org/. All the documents of the case including the elaborate history of civil procedure can be found in A Documentary Companion to A Civil Action by Lewis Grossman, Robert G. Vaughn, and Jonathan Harr. In fact, this tome has been used as the basis for courses in federal civil procedure classes in law schools. In addition, A Guide to the Reading of Jonathan Harr's A Civil Action by Peter Bower, as well as many other related teaching and learning materials can be found in the Ch. 10 - *Toxic Tort and Civil Action* folder on the Companion Website at http://www.environmentallaw-teach.org/.

A treasure trove of dynamic teaching materials can be found in the massive library of materials available at *Science in the Courtroom: The Woburn Toxic trial* (https://serc.carleton.edu/woburn/index.html). The Seattle University School of Law has produced a series of three videos, including interviews with all the participants in the *Woburn* trial called LESSONS FROM WOBURN: THE UNTOLD STORIES, THE RULES OF CIVIL PROCEDURE, CONDUCT AND SETTLEMENT. A guide to these videos is also available. These can be found at:

https://law.seattleu.edu/centers-and-institutes/films-for-justice-institute/lessons-from-woburn

We used A CIVIL ACTION as a springboard for an *Internal Memorandum of Law* writing exercise, for which students assume the role of the *Woburn* town attorney and are asked to advise the city council on the advisability of initiating a lawsuit for the contamination of the town's wells. It is reproduced at the end of this chapter.

Finally, there are a host of resources that document other prominent mass toxic tort trials. These include:

1. Agent Orange on Trial: Mass Toxic Disasters in the Courts by Peter H. Schuck documents the class action lawsuit filed against the chemical industry by over 2 million former soldiers exposed to Agent Orange during the Vietnam War. Agent Orange was used as part of the campaign by the U.S. military to defoliate the jungle and leave the Viet Cong and North Vietnamese without forest cover. The toxic compounds in Agent Orange (including dioxin) were shown to cause cancers, birth defects, and a host of other serious illnesses. The long, dramatic, and complex legal struggle ended with a settlement of $180 million. This became the Agent Orange Settlement Fund, which was dispersed to Vietnam veterans in need of assistance. The Fund closed in 1997 when all of its assets had been used. Of course, the hundreds of thousands of Vietnamese exposed to this chemical warfare agent were never compensated. For more information, see the U.S. Department of Veteran Affairs statement in the Ch. 10 - *Toxic Tort and Civil Action* folder on the Companion Website, at http://www.environmentallaw-teach.org/.

2. The Pulitzer prize-winning Toms River: A Story of Science and Salvation by Dan Fagin documents the use of the Toms River in New Jersey as the private dumping ground for several large chemical companies including Ciba Specialty Chemicals and Union Carbide. These companies also buried thousands of leaking drums in open pits. The class action lawsuit was filed against these companies by 69 families of children who were victims of a cancer cluster proven to be caused by water pollution. The lawsuit was settled out of court, of course with no admission of guilt. See "Families Settle for Childhood Cancer Claims in Toms River, N.J." in the Ch. 10 - *Toxic*

Tort and Civil Action folder on the Companion Website at http://www.environmentallaw-teach.org/.

3. Justice Downwind: America's Atomic Testing Program in the 1950s by Howard Ball documents the U.S. atomic testing program of the 1950s at the Nevada Test Site, the childhood leukemias and the other cancers and ailments suffered by the "downwinders" (largely members of Mormon communities of Nevada and Utah) who were exposed to radioactive fallout, and the lawsuit against the federal government that followed. In *Irene Allen et al. v. United States*, 588 F. Supp. 247 (D. Utah 1984), *rev'd*, 816 F.2d 1417 (10th Cir. 1987), Judge Bruce S. Jenkins of the Utah District Court (10th Circuit) Central Division wrote an astounding opinion. It goes on for over 200 pages and is both a textbook on nuclear physics, nuclear bombs, the biological effects of radiation, as well as a searing indictment of the willfully negligent behavior of federal government officials who knowingly doused these communities with radiation and then lied about doing so and about the effects of nuclear fallout on the people. While this opinion was a vindication for the all those plaintiffs and their families, the case was appealed, and the Appellate Court in *Irene Allen* overturned the District Court decision on sovereign immunity grounds using the discretionary function. The U.S. Supreme Court, in *Allen v. U.S.*, 484 U.S. 1004 (1988), refused to grant certiorari. These opinions can be found in the Ch. 10 - *Toxic Tort and Civil Action* folder on the Companion Website at http:// www.environmentallaw-teach.org/. An interview with Judge Bruce S. Jenkins about this case can be seen at http://www.10thcircuithistory.org/blog/2015/8/26/kued-interview-with-senior-judge-bruce-s-jenkins-of-utah. Eventually, the Federal Cancer Compensation fund was created by Congress, and the "Downwinders," Nuclear Weapons Workers, Uranium Workers, Nevada Test Site Workers, and Atomic Veterans had some recognition and compensation for the harms they suffered. See the Cancer Benefits Center at http://www.nevadatestsite.info/.

4. While there is no book on the subject, attorney Robert A. Billot brought suit on behalf of victims exposed to releases of perfluorooctanoic acid (PFOA) used in the manufacture of Teflon by Dupont in Parkersburg, PA. Dupont dumped thousands of tons of C-8 waste, PFOA-contaminated sludge into unlined pits and nearby landfills contaminating local water supplies (See, *Leach v. E.I. Du Pont de Nemours & Co.*, 01-C-608, 2002 WL 1270121, at *5 (W. Va. Cir. Apr. 10, 2002). Dupont was aware of the dangers of PFOA exposure. However, it kept this information secret and denied having such knowledge. *Leach* was a mass toxic tort suit was filed on behalf of the local residents exposed to PFOA-contaminated water. Over 3500 individual suits were eventually settled out of court for nearly $700 million. Though slow to respond, the E.P.A., using the Toxic Substances Control Act, filed a lawsuit against DuPont for concealing evidence about the dangers of PFOA. Again, the case was settled out of court for $16.5 million, the largest ever E.P.A. settlement at that time. An excellent article is *The Lawyer Who Became DuPont's*

Worst Nightmare, at https://www.nytimes.com/2016/01/10/magazine/the- lawyer-who-became-duponts-worst-nightmare.html.

A CIVIL ACTION: AN INTERNAL MEMORANDUM OF LAW FOR THE CITY OF WOBURN. LEGAL WRITING EXERCISE

1. Read A CIVIL ACTION by Jonathan Harr. Assume that you are an intern in the office of the attorney working for the municipality of Woburn. Just before the events that unfold in the chapter entitled "Facher's Plea," the City Council has asked your firm to prepare a memorandum of law for their review. As an intern, you have received very specific instructions. You are to examine the feasibility of filing a public nuisance, intentional tort against W.R. Grace and Beatrice asking for an injunction and damages.

2. Examine the elements of this particular civil action. What evidence exists to support your claim? Summarize what you must prove in order to win your case. In what court will you file your complaint? What kind of damages will you seek? What will be the purpose of your request for an injunction? What difficulties do you expect to encounter both legally and with your particular clients?

3. Be specific, be brief, and be organized in your typewritten reply of 800-1000 words. Use the format for the internal memorandum of law given to you and discussed in class.

Chapter 10 - The Endangered Species Act of 1973

In this book, you have the opportunity to see how an entire area of law was created, and how it has since evolved. Starting as judge-made law, environmental law is today heavily statutory. The bulk of this book is represented by what is viewed as one of the formative environmental law statutes. You now have the necessary tools to understand its normative value and thus its social, political, and economic implications, and also how to research its provisions if necessary.

THE ENDANGERED SPECIES ACT OF 1973

The ENDANGERED SPECIES ACT OF 1973 (E.S.A.), was approved on December 28, 1973. It received a pubic law number identifier, and it is cited as Public Law 93–205. Because it was published in Volume 87 of the STATUTES AT LARGE, STARTING AT PAGE 88, it is also cited as 87 Stat. 88. The E.S.A. has known multiple amendments. They are all added in its codified version, starting with 16 U.S.C. §1531 et seq.

Thus, when you research the E.S.A., you go to the STATUTES AT LARGE if you want to read the historical, original version of the Act. If you want to read the binding, current version of the E.S.A, you will need to go to the UNITED STATES CODE.

The E.S.A. is a unique and revolutionary statute. When it was passed, there was no other law like it. The protections that the E.S.A. provides for endangered and threatened species are indeed radical and include:

1) powerful prohibitions;

2) far-reaching mandates; and

3) provisions for citizen standing and participation.

If you want to read the statute as it was passed by Congress in 1973, go to Govinfo.gov, or directly to https://www.govinfo.gov/content/pkg/STATUTE-87/pdf/STATUTE-87-Pg884.pdf. If you want to read the codified version of the E.S.A., again, go to Govinfo.gov., and find its provisions from the UNITED STATES CODE's page, at https://www.govinfo.gov/app/collection/uscode, or go to Cornell University's Govinfo mirror site, at https://www.law.cornell.edu/uscode/text/16/chapter-35. This is not the official version, but an authoritative version for educational purposes. An html version of the official 2017 version of the Act is available on the Companion

Website and at the end of this chapter. The most recent official version of the U.S.C. is dated 2017, which means it contains all the amendments from 1973 until 2017.

While reading the codified version of the statute, become familiar with the organization of this statute and its fifteen sections:

§ 1531 - Congressional findings and declaration of purposes and policy - available at https://www.govinfo.gov/content/pkg/USCODE-2017-title16/pdf/USCODE-2017-title16-chap35-sec1531.pdf.
§ 1532 – Definitions - available at https://www.govinfo.gov/content/pkg/USCODE-2017-title16/pdf/USCODE-2017-title16-chap35-sec1532.pdf.
§ 1533 - Determination of endangered species and threatened species - available at https://www.govinfo.gov/content/pkg/USCODE-2017-title16/pdf/USCODE-2017-title16-chap35-sec1533.pdf.
§ 1534 - Land acquisition - available at https://www.govinfo.gov/content/pkg/USCODE-2017-title16/pdf/USCODE-2017-title16-chap35-sec1534.pdf.
§ 1535 - Cooperation with States – available at https://www.govinfo.gov/content/pkg/USCODE-2017-title16/pdf/USCODE-2017-title16-chap35-sec1535.pdf.
§ 1536 - Interagency cooperation – available at https://www.govinfo.gov/content/pkg/USCODE-2017-title16/pdf/USCODE-2017-title16-chap35-sec1536.pdf.
§ 1537 - International cooperation – available at https://www.govinfo.gov/content/pkg/USCODE-2017-title16/pdf/USCODE-2017-title16-chap35-sec1537.pdf.
§ 1537a - Convention implementation – available at https://www.govinfo.gov/content/pkg/USCODE-2017-title16/pdf/USCODE-2017-title16-chap35-sec1537a.pdf.
§ 1538 - Prohibited acts – available at https://www.govinfo.gov/content/pkg/USCODE-2017-title16/pdf/USCODE-2017-title16-chap35-sec1538.pdf.
§ 1539 – Exceptions – available at https://www.govinfo.gov/content/pkg/USCODE-2017-title16/pdf/USCODE-2017-title16-chap35-sec1539.pdf.
§ 1540 - Penalties and enforcement – available at https://www.govinfo.gov/content/pkg/USCODE-2017-title16/pdf/USCODE-2017-title16-chap35-sec1540.pdf.
§ 1541 - Endangered plants – available at https://www.govinfo.gov/content/pkg/USCODE-2017-title16/pdf/USCODE-2017-title16-chap35-sec1541.pdf.
§ 1542 - Authorization of appropriations – available at https://www.govinfo.gov/content/pkg/USCODE-2017-title16/pdf/USCODE-2017-title16-chap35-sec1542.pdf.
§ 1543 - Construction with Marine Mammal Protection Act of 1972 – available at https://www.govinfo.gov/content/pkg/USCODE-2017-title16/pdf/USCODE-2017-title16-chap35-sec1543.pdf.
§ 1544 - Annual cost analysis by Fish and Wildlife Service – available at https://www.govinfo.gov/content/pkg/USCODE-2017-title16/pdf/USCODE-2017-title16-chap35-sec1544.pdf.

First Section: Declaration of Purposes and Policy (§ 1531)

Because courts carefully study and use legislative intent to interpret the meaning of a statute, a close reading of 16 U.S.C. § 1531 is essential. In the statement of "Findings," it is important to note in subsection four (4) that "the United States has pledged itself as a sovereign state in the international community to conserve to the extent practicable the various species of fish or wildlife and plants facing extinction, pursuant to" six named treaties and agreements. The most important of these is (a)(4)(F) the *Convention on International Trade in Endangered Species of Wild Fauna and Flora* (CITES). As we shall see, these treaties and agreements, especially CITES, have a special place in the E.S.A.

In 16 U.S.C. § 1531(b) it is stated that the "purposes of this chapter are to provide a means whereby the ecosystems upon which endangered species and threatened species depend may be conserved, to provide a program for the conservation of such endangered species and threatened species, and to take such steps as may be appropriate to achieve the purposes of the treaties and conventions set forth in subsection (a) of this section." This statement of congressional intent has three important elements. First, conventions are made a national imperative. Second, conservation of habitat is made a priority. Third, achieving the goals set forth in international treaties less obvious, but most importantly, the words "conserve" and "conservation" are specifically used. The significance of these words can be more fully appreciated by turning to 16 U.S.C. § 1532(3), which reads:

> The terms "conserve," "conserving," and "conservation" mean to use and the use of all methods and procedures which are necessary to bring any endangered species or threatened species to the point at which the measures provided pursuant to this chapter are no longer necessary. Such methods and procedures include, but are not limited to, all activities associated with scientific resources management such as research, census, law enforcement, habitat acquisition and maintenance, propagation, live trapping, and transplantation, and, in the extraordinary case where population pressures within a given ecosystem cannot be otherwise relieved, may include regulated taking.

Section 1531(c) declares that it is "the policy of Congress that all Federal departments and agencies shall seek to conserve endangered species and threatened species and shall utilize their authorities in furtherance of the purposes of this chapter." This reinforces the statement of "purposes" by mandating with an affirmative command ("shall") that the whole administrative apparatus of the federal government shall "conserve," that is, shall "use of all methods and procedures which are necessary to bring any endangered species or threatened species to the point at which the measures provided pursuant to this chapter are no longer necessary." This is a powerful mandate and we will see in *TVA v. Hill* (discussed below) just how the courts interpret this mandate and define the true meaning of the E.S.A.

Second Section: Definitions (§1532)

While we may think that if we read English, we can read any text written in English, legal literature is here to prove us wrong. For instance, the E.S.A. has its own meaning of a person. According to 16 U.S.C. § 1532 – Subsection (13):

> the term "person" means an individual, corporation, partnership, trust, association, or any other private entity; or any officer, employee, agent, department, or instrumentality of the Federal Government, of any State, municipality, or political subdivision of a State, or of any foreign government; any State, municipality, or political subdivision of a State; or any other entity subject to the jurisdiction of the United States.

This definition is perhaps a bit of a surprise. A person is (for the purposes of the E.S.A.) not just an individual. While this definition is found in many other statutes, this example demonstrates the critical importance of reading the definitions contained in a statute.

In fact, we will see that the meaning of a term used in a statute is often the basis of a lawsuit, and such lawsuits determine the meaning of the statute of which they are a part. It is important to note that 16 U.S.C. § 1533 – "Determination of endangered species and threatened species" is critical because, in order to benefit from the protection of the E.S.A., a species must first be listed as endangered or threatened. The listing process, participation in this process by "persons" (as defined by the E.S.A.), and the lawsuits this process generates will be discussed in detail later on in *Carlton v. Babbitt.*

Section 1532(8) defines the term "fish or wildlife" as "any member of the animal kingdom, including without limitation, any mammal, fish, bird (including any migratory, nonmigratory, or endangered bird for which protection is also afforded by treaty or other international agreement), amphibian, reptile, mollusk, crustacean, arthropod or other invertebrate, and includes any part, product, egg, or offspring thereof, or the dead body or parts thereof." It is important to note that § 1538(a)(1) does not include plants but does include any and all parts of the life cycles of "fish and wildlife." Moreover, E.S.A. protections include any bird protected by treaty or international agreement.

Sixth Section: Far Reaching Mandate (§1536)

Section 1536, blandly entitled "Interagency cooperation," contains far-reaching mandates for the federal government. Subsection (a)(1) states that "all other Federal agencies shall, in consultation with and with the assistance of the Secretary, utilize their authorities in furtherance of the purposes of this chapter by carrying out programs for the conservation of endangered species and threatened species listed pursuant to section 1533 of this title." This is a strong statement given the affirmative mandate "shall" and the definition of conservation previously discussed. Far more important, however, is 16 U.S.C. §1536(a)(2) that states:

> Each Federal agency shall, in consultation with and with the assistance of the Secretary, insure that any action authorized, funded, or carried out by such agency (hereinafter in this section referred to as an "agency action") is not likely to jeopardize the continued existence of any endangered species or threatened species or result in the destruction or adverse modification of habitat of such species which is determined by the Secretary, after consultation as appropriate with affected States, to be critical, unless such agency has been granted an exemption for such action by the Committee pursuant to subsection (h) of this section. In fulfilling the requirements of this paragraph each agency shall use the best scientific and commercial data available.

This subsection mandates that all federal "agency actions" are not likely to jeopardize the continued existence of any endangered or threatened species or result in the destruction or adverse modification of habitat of such species as determined by the Secretary. This is a sweeping, far-reaching mandate that extends the power of the E.S.A. onto private property. Any private property owner who needs a federal permit for construction must now confront several sections of the E.S.A., including the "no take" clause. In addition, for the first time in history, a federal law confronts habitat destruction, the main cause of extinction of species. The ability of "critical habitat" designation to extend onto private property provides the endangered species important, additional protection. Designation of critical habitat will be discussed when we cover 16 U.S.C. § 1533 – "Determination of endangered species and threatened species" in *Palila v. Hawaii.* Moreover, "agency actions" include all federal projects or state and local government projects with federal money. Section 1536(a)(2) is all-encompassing. *TVA v. Hill,* for instance, involves the construction of a federal dam by a federally owned corporation.

Ninth Section: Powerful Prohibitions (§ 1538)

The E.S.A. prohibitions refer to "any person subject to the jurisdiction of the United States." So, before we discuss what is prohibited, we need to understand who is affected by the E.S.A. prohibitions. What is a "person"? As we remember, §1532 contained the definition of a person.

Section 1538(a)(1)(A) makes it "unlawful" to import or export listed species. "Import" is further defined in § 1532(10) to mean "to land on, bring into, or introduce into, or attempt to land on, bring into, or introduce into, any place subject to the jurisdiction of the United States, whether or not such landing, bringing, or introduction constitutes an importation within the meaning of the customs laws of the United States." Section 1538(a)(1)(B) and (C) makes it unlawful to "take any such species within the United States or the territorial sea of the United States," or to "take any such species upon the high seas." Refer to § 1532(19) in which we learn that the "term 'take' means to harass, harm, pursue, hunt, shoot, wound, kill, trap, capture, or collect, or to attempt to engage in any such conduct." Later in *Palila v. Hawaii,* we will learn how the meaning of "harm" in the definition of "take" was litigated and defined by case law. "*High seas,*" in maritime law, means that part of the open ocean that is not part of a country's territorial *waters.*

Section 1538(a)(1)(D)(E) and (F) further protect endangered and threatened species by making it unlawful for any person to "possess, sell, deliver, carry, transport, or ship, by any means whatsoever, any such species taken in violation of subparagraphs (B) and (C)," to "deliver, receive, carry, transport, or ship in interstate or foreign commerce, by any means whatsoever and in the course of a commercial activity, any such species," or to sell or offer for sale in interstate or foreign commerce any such species. In *U.S. v. Billie,* we will examine the penalties and prosecution of an individual that killed ("took"), possessed, and transported a Florida panther, an endangered species. See §1532(9) for the definition of "foreign commerce."

Section 1538(a)(1)(G) makes it unlawful for any person to "violate any regulation pertaining to such species or to any threatened species of fish or wildlife listed pursuant to section 1533 of this title and promulgated by the Secretary pursuant to authority provided by this chapter." The "Secretary" is defined in 16 U.S.C. § 1532(15) as "the Secretary of the Interior or the Secretary of Commerce as program responsibilities are vested pursuant to the provisions of Reorganization Plan Numbered 4 of 1970; except that with respect to the enforcement of the provisions of this chapter and the Convention which pertain to the importation or exportation of terrestrial plants, the term also means the Secretary of Agriculture." The "Convention" is CITES. The Reorganization Plan No. 4 consolidated the environmental responsibilities previously spread out in a number of disparate agencies into the newly created E.P.A. and National Oceanic and Atmospheric Administration (NOAA), which is part of the Department of Commerce. Other environmental responsibilities were consolidated into existing agencies, such as the Department of Interior. The Fish and Wildlife Service (FWS), an agency within the Department of Interior, is responsible for carrying out the E.S.A. for animals and plants that live on the land mass of the United States (see https://www.fws.gov/endangered/index.html). The National Marine Fisheries Service (NMFS), an agency within NOAA that is within the Department of Commerce, is responsible for carrying out the E.S.A. for animals and plants that live in the territorial waters of the United States (see https://www.fisheries.noaa.gov). The NMFS also manages efforts under the Marine Mammal Protection Act (MMPA).

Section 1538(a)(2) provides prohibitions to protect listed plant species. Subsection (2)(A) makes it unlawful to import and export such species, and subsections (2)(C) and (2)(D) make it unlawful to "deliver, receive, carry, transport, or ship in interstate or foreign commerce, by any means whatsoever and in the course of a commercial activity, any such species" and "sell or offer for sale in interstate or foreign commerce any such species." Subsection (2)(B) makes it unlawful to "remove and reduce to possession any such species from areas under Federal jurisdiction; maliciously damage or destroy any such species on any such area" and also makes it a federal offense to violate any State law and "remove, cut, dig up, or damage or destroy" plants listed under the E.S.A. This, of course, is a major limitation of the E.S.A. Endangered and threatened plants are protected only on federal lands. In 2018, thirty-two states had laws to protect endangered and threatened plant species.

State laws only partially fill the void for plants, and while providing support for endangered and threatened animals, these laws are generally weaker than the federal protections set forth in the E.S.A. Like the federal E.S.A., state laws do not protect plants on private property. Two states do not have any protection for endangered species. Only 18 states have laws that protect all federally-listed species. Citizens are not allowed to petition for listing or delisting of a species in 30 states, 38 states have no laws for designating critical habitat, and recovery planning is only required in 2 states. Clearly, there is ample room for citizen participation to adopt or even go beyond the federal E.S.A.

The prohibitions enumerated in 16 U.S.C. § 1538(a)(1) and (2) are amplified in 16 U.S.C. § 1538(c) in which CITES is incorporated into the E.S.A. by making it "unlawful for any person subject to the jurisdiction of the United States to engage in any trade in any specimens contrary to the provisions of the Convention, or to possess any specimens traded contrary to the provisions of the Convention, including the definitions of terms in article I thereof." The rest of this subsection and the remaining subsections of § 1538 provide the requirements that must be met if any species listed in CITES is to be imported into the United States. For instance, African elephant ivory may be imported but only if its provenance can be certified with the required recordkeeping.

The revolutionary significance of § 15 38 is two-fold. First, it closes down the U. S. market for the worldwide trade in endangered or threatened species. Before the E.S.A., the U.S. was an important market for the international trade of endangered species. Indeed, there are approximately 6000 species of animals and 30,000 species of plants protected against over-exploitation through international trade by CITES. Of course, trade in endangered species continues throughout the world, especially in less-developed countries, but the U.S.'s ban has provided important relief. Second, the "no-take" and other provisions of 16 U.S.C. § 1538(a)(1) protect endangered and threatened fish and wildlife in the U.S. that are not a significant part of the trade in listed U.S. species. These legal barriers are further strengthened by the civil and criminal penalties attached to the violation of these protections.

Third and Eleventh Sections: CITIZEN STANDING AND PARTICIPATION (§§ 1533-1540)

Finally, the third reason that the E.S.A. is so unique and powerful is because the E.S.A. stands for citizen involvement. For instance, 16 U.S.C. § 1533 enables "interested person[s]" to petition the Secretary to add a species to the endangered or threatened lists and to revise a critical habitat designation." Again, a number of notification and other prerequisites are required.

The E.S.A. provides an important avenue for citizen participation with 16 U.S.C. § 1540(g) – "Citizen suits." This provision states:

> (1) Except as provided in paragraph (2) of this subsection any person may commence a civil suit on his own behalf—
>
> (A) to enjoin any person, including the United States and any other governmental instrumentality or agency (to the extent permitted by the eleventh amendment to the Constitution), who is alleged to be in violation of any provision of this chapter or regulation issued under the authority thereof; or
>
> (B) to compel the Secretary to apply, pursuant to section 1535(g)(2)(B)(ii) of this title, the prohibitions set forth in or authorized pursuant to section 1533(d) or 1538(a)(1)(B) of this title with respect to the taking of any resident endangered species or threatened species within any State; or
>
> (C) against the Secretary where there is alleged a failure of the Secretary to perform any act or duty under section 1533 of this title which is not discretionary with the Secretary.

These lawsuits fall within the general jurisdiction of federal district courts, without regard to the amount in controversy or the citizenship of the parties. In any civil suit commenced under subparagraph (B), the district court shall compel the Secretary to apply the prohibition sought if the court finds that the allegation that an emergency exists is supported by substantial evidence. Before a citizen suit can be initiated there are some notification and other requirements that must be met. These requirements are described in subsequent subsections of the E.S.A.

The next sections will help you understand the checks and balances the judiciary exercises over the legislative body within the context of E.S.A. litigation. Each case added meaning in factual context to the E.S.A. statutory provisions. You do not know the meaning of a statute unless you find a case that applies it to a particular controversy. In the process, you will continue to hone your skills of reading cases, now with an added challenge of incorporating a legislative text. To see if you understood the material, try to answer the questions in How Case Law Defines a Statute – Legal Exercise.

Tennessee Valley Authority v. Hiram Hill et al. – 437 U.S. 153 (1978)

One of finest examples of how case law defines the meaning of a statute is the landmark case *Tennessee Valley Authority v. Hiram Hill et al.* – 437 U.S. 153 (1978), hereafter, *TVA v. Hill.* This decision gave the E.S.A. its "teeth." Agencies often interpret sections of a statute without dispute, but, where there is dispute; case law always defines the statute. Every rule-making, adjudication, or agency decision that is challenged in court allows the Court to give the statute and its rules and regulations their real meaning. Similarly, the provisions of the Constitution are interpreted by courts and defined by case law. Note the location of the Tellico Dam and the Little Tennessee River on the maps in the *Study Questions for TVA v. Hill* on the Companion Website, at http://www.environmentallaw-teach.org/. You will also find images and commentary on the snail darter and the dam itself. Print out or read online the *TVA v. Hill* opinion of Chief Justice Burger from https://supreme.justia.com/cases/federal/us/437/153/. As you read, use the technique taught to you in Chapter 8, color-coding, or numbering the paragraphs, so it becomes easier for you to note how the information fits the rubrics of case-briefing, also mentioned below. Unlike in the previous chapter, we will pin-cite to the official version of the case, 437 U.S. 153, available from https://supreme.justia.com/cases/federal/us/437/153/.

1. Heading

2. Facts

3. Procedural History

4. Legal Issues

5. Holding or Decision

6. Reasoning

7. Dissenting Opinions

Right at the beginning, Chief Justice Burger presented the two legal issues: 1) whether the Court could enjoin (issue an injunction to stop) the construction of a dam that was 95% completed because impoundment of waters behind the dam would eliminate the last known population of snail darters, an endangered fish, and, 2) whether congressional appropriations for construction of the dam after the E.S.A. became the law of the land constituted a repeal of the E.S.A. for this particular federal project (437 U. S. 156).

Next, the Justice presents the history, context, and essential facts of this case. We learn that Little Tennessee's lower 33 miles contain "clear, free-flowing waters." *Id.* It is in this area that the Tennessee Valley Authority, party to this litigation, and a federally owned public corporation for which Congress allocated funds, started the construction of the Tellico Dam in 1967. The dam would convert "the river's shallow, fast-flowing waters into a deep reservoir" (*Id.* at. 157). The National Environmental Protection Act (N.E.P.A.) saga in the political and legal fight by landowners, farmers, Cherokee Indians, conservationists, fishermen, and concerned citizens to save the last free-flowing waters of Little Tennessee helps us understand what is at stake in this case. Furthermore, we are introduced to the snail darter, which was discovered in the Little Tennessee River during this time in 1973 (*Id.* at 158), when the E.S.A. was enacted. As part of the facts, we learn that the snail darter requires shallow, free-flowing, oxygenated waters. Shallow waters allow sunlight to reach bottom gravel and allow the growth of periphyton, the primary source of food for the foraging snails that are the main source of food for the aptly named snail darter. The dam would eliminate the habitat required by the snail darter and exterminate the remaining population of 10-15,000 snail darters. So, this information provides an in-depth explanation of the ecological issues that would be created by the completion of the Tellico Dam.

The significance of the ecological concerns relating to the completion of the Tellico Dam are emphasized by footnote 9: "'Critical habitat' means any air, land, or water area (exclusive of those existing man-made structures or settlements which are not necessary to the survival and recovery of a listed species) and constituent elements thereof, the loss of which would appreciably decrease the likelihood of the survival and recovery of a listed species or a distinct segment of its population. The constituent elements of critical habitat include, but are not limited to: physical structures and topography, biota, climate, human activity, and the quality and chemical content of land, water, and air. Critical habitat may represent any portion of the present habitat of a listed species and may include additional areas for reasonable population expansion." As we shall see in *Palila v. Hawaii,* this definition, codified at 50 C.F.R. § 402.02, is later removed in favor of another definition.

Following the best structure of legal writing, upon introducing the facts, the Justice introduced the law: 16 U.S.C. §1536(a)(2) mandating that the Secretary "shall ...insure" that all federal agency actions do not "jeopardize the continued existence of any endangered species or threatened species or result in the destruction or adverse modification of habitat of such species which is determined by the Secretary, after consultation as appropriate with affected States, to be critical."

The snail darter is that type of species. A petition for listing the snail darter as an endangered species was submitted and approved in 1975. The snail darter's survival depends on the preservation of the lower 33 miles of the Little Tennessee River as its "critical habitat" (*Id.* at 162). The TVA's attempt to transplant the snail darter to another river ecosystem tributary in the Tennessee River was still ongoing, so the court was still asked to decide between either the eradication of a species or the halt of the dam construction.

The Court explains the added difficulty of its position: Congress passed a bill appropriating $29 million for the construction of the Tellico Dam and that the House Committee on Appropriations issued a statement that the dam "should be completed as promptly as possible" (*Id.* at 164). In these Congressional forums, the TVA also presented its position that the E.S.A. "did not prohibit the completion of a project authorized, funded, and substantially constructed before the Act was passed."

Next, we learn more about the procedural history and the rationales for the District Court's and Court of Appeal's decisions as well as more factual and historical context. We learn that the respondents, the plaintiffs in the original action (*Hill v. TVA,* 419 F. Supp. 753 (E.D. Tennessee, 1976)), filed a lawsuit in the District Court of the Northern Division of Tennessee "seeking to enjoin the completion of the dam and impoundment of the reservoir on the ground that those actions would violate the Act by directly causing the extinction of the species *Percina (imostoma) tanasi.*" (*Id.*). There had been administrative and legislative hearings, and the District Court dismissed the complaint and denied the "requested relief" (an injunction). While the District Court did find that impoundment of water behind the dam would make it "highly probable" the snail darter would become extinct, the District Court balanced the equities, finding (*Id.,* at 166) that the dam was nearly complete and thus, granting an injunction would mean the loss of tens of millions of dollars. Meanwhile, Congress had continued to appropriate funds for the dam even after the discovery of an endangered snail darter, and that "a federal project becomes so near completion and so incapable of modification that a court of equity should not apply a statute long after inception of the project to produce an unreasonable result" (*Id.*).

The absurdity of the District Court's imagined result is then described. Its trial decision was appealed to the Court of Appeals for the Sixth Circuit in Cincinnati. Certiorari was eventually granted by the Court of Appeals for the Sixth Circuit.

While this litigation was undergoing, Congress passed the TVA's budget, providing funding for the Tellico Dam, and a Senate Committee issued a statement that the E.S.A. did not prevent the completion of the dam and that requested its "prompt" completion.

The procedural history of *TVA v. Hill* continues with the Court of Appeals, *Hill v. TVA,* 549 F.2d 1064 (6th Cir. 1977), which reversed the lower court's decision and issued an injunction, stopping the completion of the dam on the grounds of a "blatant statutory violation" (*Id.* at 168). TVA was ordered to halt "all activities incident to the Tellico Project which may destroy or modify the critical habitat of the snail darter." Ominously, as we shall see, the Court of Appeals provided the only solution for TVA, stating that the injunction would stand unless Congress exempted Tellico from compliance with the Act or the snail darter ceased to be endangered (or its critical habitat materially redefined).

The Court of Appeals found a "prima facie case" (the Latin equivalent for "the allegations are sufficient on their face") of the "blatant ...violation of Section 7 the Act" (Sect. 7 is codified as 16 U.S.C. § 1536). The Court of Appeals found the balancing necessary for the District Court's holding was untenable. It could not "balance the worth of an endangered species against the value of an ongoing public works measure" (*Id.* at 169). The Court of Appeals found that previous expenditures on the construction of the dam were "irrelevant in calculating the social and economic costs attributable to the disappearance of a unique form of life." It is not the responsibility of the Court to balance "how many dollars must be invested before the value of a dam exceeds that of the endangered species." The Court of Appeals also thought that statements by Congressional Committees in support of funding and building the dam were irrelevant when considering the "proper application of an existing statute" and that the only "relevant legislation was the Act itself, '[t]he meaning and spirit' of which was 'clear on its face.'" Thus, the only balancing of the equities the Court of Appeal would consider was one that would clearly require protecting endangered species and make sure that no federal agency actions jeopardized its continued existence. As a result, an injunction was the only recourse. The Supreme Court granting certiorari ends the procedural history discussion.

By the time the case reached the United States Supreme Court, the Secretary of the Interior pursuant to the E.S.A. had already "declared the snail darter an endangered species whose critical habitat would be destroyed by creation of the Tellico Dam" (*Id.,* at 172). That decision was not under review, as the Court stated that "no judicial review of the Secretary's determinations has ever been sought and hence the validity of his actions is not open to review in this Court" (*Id.*).

By now we know the facts, the law, the issues, and the procedural history of *TVA v. Hill.* The holding is provided immediately with "[f]or the reasons stated hereinafter, we hold that both questions must be answered in the affirmative" (*Id.* at 172).

The essential reasoning for the determination that TVA's action violated the E.S.A. is presented as it follows:

> One would be hard pressed to find a statutory provision whose terms were any plainer than those in § 7 of the Endangered Species Act. Its very words affirmatively command all federal agencies 'to *insure* that actions *authorized, funded,* or *carried out* by them do not *jeopardize* the continued existence' of an endangered species or '*result* in the destruction or modification of habitat of such species. 16 U.S.C. § 1536 (1976 ed.) (Emphasis added.) (*Id.* at 173).

This language admits of no exception. Nonetheless, petitioner urges, as do the dissenters, that the Act cannot reasonably be interpreted as applying to a federal project which was well under way when Congress passed the Endangered Species Act of 1973. To sustain that position, however, we would be forced to ignore the ordinary meaning of plain language. It has not been shown, for example, how TVA can close the gates of the Tellico Dam without 'carrying out' an action that has been 'authorized' and 'funded' by a federal agency. Nor can we understand how such action will '*insure*' that the snail darter's habitat is not disrupted. Accepting the Secretary's determinations, as we must, it is clear that TVA's proposed operation of the dam will have precisely the opposite effect, namely the *eradication* of an endangered species. (*Id.*).

Now that the issue of whether the actions of TVA violated the E.S.A. has been resolved, the Court moves to determining a remedy. The Court begins with a discussion of legislative intent with the conclusion that the language, history, and structure of the legislation under review here indicates "'beyond doubt that Congress intended endangered species to be afforded the highest of priorities'" (*Id.* at 174). The legislative history of the E.S.A. is discussed next. There are many quotes from congressional hearings and reports, all expressing concern about the extinction of any species, about the threat of habitat destruction, and about the need to prevent these losses. In furtherance of these goals, the Court targets the definition of "conserve" that is specifically defined to mean

> 'to use and the use of *all methods and procedures which are necessary* to bring *any endangered species or threatened species* to the point at which the measures provided pursuant to this chapter are no longer necessary. §1532(2). (Emphasis added.) (*Id.* at 180).

The Court also emphasizes the significance of § 7 (§ 7 was codified at § 1536) and of the citizen suit provision to force compliance (Sections 1540(c)& (g)) to initiate listing of endangered and threatened species (Sect. 1533(c)(2)). Next, the Court notes the change in language from the earlier version of the E.S.A. in which federal agencies were to protect endangered species "'*insofar as is practicable and consistent with the[ir] primary purposes*'" (*Id.* at 181).

This language is purposefully omitted in the 1973 E.S.A. and replaced with language that "'*requires* the Secretary and the heads of all other Federal departments and agencies to use their authorities in order to carry out programs for the protection of endangered species, and it further *requires* that those agencies take *the necessary action* that will *not jeopardize* the continuing existence of endangered species or result in the destruction of critical habitat of those species.'" These changes have produced language that is mandatory. The Court next elaborates on the mandatory language in the E.S.A.

The crux of the issue of determining a remedy and the result of balancing the equities evolves around "the plain language of the Act, buttressed by its legislative history, shows clearly that Congress viewed the value of endangered species as 'incalculable" (*Id.* at 187). The Court could not balance the loss of a sum certain -- even $100 million -- against a congressionally declared "incalculable value." So, in balancing the "incalculable" value of endangered species against anything else, endangered species always win.

The "exceptions to the statute's broad sweep" address the issue of implied repeal. The Court dismissed the claim because that statements of congressional committees were made pursuant to the mistaken belief that the E.S.A. did not apply and that the E.S.A. was not "in any respect amended or repealed." Paragraph 58 includes the important statement that "[t]here is nothing in the appropriations measures, as passed, which states that the Tellico Project was to be completed irrespective of the requirements of the Endangered Species Act." The important implication is that Congress could have made the Tellico Dam project exempt from the E.S.A., but it never did. Next, the Court disfavors repeals by implication, and citing precedent states that the "doctrine disfavoring repeals by implication applies with full vigor when . . . the subsequent legislation is an *appropriations* measure," and then citing both House and Senate rules that specifically prohibit implied repeal.

The Court further explains the discretionary nature of equitable relief and the how balancing the equities works: "Congress has spoken in the plainest of words, making it abundantly clear that the balance has been struck in favor of affording endangered species the highest of priorities" (*Id.* at 194). The Court upholds the appellate decision. Justices Blackmun and Powell dissented.

The End Game

In the E.S.A. cases that are analyzed next, it will be clear that the decision in *TVA v. Hill* has determined the meaning of the statute by setting a precedent, an astounding line-in-the-sand, that has given the protection of endangered and threatened species the highest of priorities, so much so, that any balancing in equitable decision-making always falls on the side of the endangered or threatened species. As perhaps the top landmark case of environmental law, it is a precedent that has stood the test of time.

TVA v. Hill was decided in June of 1978. Even before this decision, pork-barrel politicians, who were scared that another endangered species could upset their plans for federal projects in their districts or state, began developing legislation that would create a committee within the E.S.A. with the power to exempt a particular federal project or action from the mandates of § 1536(a)(2).

On Nov. 10, 1978, the 95th Congress passed Public law 95-632 that created the "Endangered Species Committee," and President Carter signed the amendment into law. Open your copy of the E.S.A. and turn to §1536(e). The purpose of this Committee as stated in subsection (e)(2) is to "review any application submitted to it pursuant to this section and determine... whether or not to grant an exemption from the requirements of subsection (a)(2) of this section for the action set forth in such application." Section (e)(3) states that "[t]he Committee shall be composed of seven members as follows:

(A) The Secretary of Agriculture.

(B) The Secretary of the Army.

(C) The Chairman of the Council of Economic Advisors.

(D) The Administrator of the Environmental Protection Agency.

(E) The Secretary of the Interior.

(F) The Administrator of the National Oceanic and Atmospheric Administration.

(G) The President....shall appoint one individual from each affected state, as determined by the "Secretary of Interior."

The application for an exemption (subsection g) can be initiated by a "Federal agency, the Governor of the State in which an agency action will occur, if any, or a permit or license applicant may apply to the Secretary for an exemption for an agency action of such agency." The procedures that must be followed are outlined in subsections (g) and (h). In order for the exemption to be granted, five out of the seven members of the Endangered Species Committee (ESC) must vote in favor of the exemption (subsection (h)(1)). The Committee's "determination on the record" must demonstrate that:

"(i) there are no reasonable and prudent alternatives to the agency action;

(ii) the benefits of such action clearly outweigh the benefits of alternative courses of action consistent with conserving the species or its critical habitat, and such action is in the public interest;

(iii) the action is of regional or national significance; and

(iv) neither the Federal agency concerned nor the exemption applicant made any irreversible or irretrievable commitment of resources prohibited by subsection (d).

Subsection (d) warns that "the Federal agency and the permit or license applicant shall not make any irreversible or irretrievable commitment of resources with respect to the agency action which has the effect of foreclosing the formulation or implementation of any reasonable and prudent alternative measures which would not violate subsection (a)(2) of this section." This subsection was included because, in spite of repeated warnings that the Tellico Dam project would violate the E.S.A., the TVA and the federal government spent funds in a relentless pursuit of their desired project. If an exemption is granted, subsection (h)(1)(B) requires the implementation of a "reasonable mitigation and enhancement measures, including, but not limited to, live propagation, transplantation, and habitat acquisition and improvement, as are necessary and appropriate to minimize the adverse effects of the agency action upon the endangered species, threatened species, or critical habitat concerned." Attempts to transplant the snail darter started well before this amendment became part of the E.S.A. and, as we shall see, plays a particular role in the end-game.

The E.S.C. was otherwise known as the "God Squad" because it was delegated the authority to determine that a federal action or project was more important than species extinction. The E.S.C. convened for the first time to deliberate about granting an exemption for the completion of the Tellico Dam. In January of 1979, the Committee voted unanimously to reject the exemption. The reasons were economic, rather than based ecologically on habitat destruction and the extinction of an endangered species. What the farmers, Cherokees, concerned citizens, fishermen, lawyers, economists, and scientists of the anti-Tellico coalition and the Association for the Preservation of the Little Tennessee River had been saying all along was verified. The Tellico Dam was a pork-barrel boondoggle for which 200 farmers had land condemned for a real estate development scheme that was abandoned two years before the final Supreme Court decision. Land condemnations had been fought in court. The same federal district court judge who would later rule for the TVA in the District Court case summarily dismissed all complaints. Farmers and their families were evicted, their farms burned and bulldozed, and the rich, valley farm soils were flooded. The flooding would cover and destroy ancient towns, religious sites, and burial mounds of the Cherokee nation and obliterate the last 33 miles of a wild and scenic river of unique value to white-water enthusiasts, fishermen, and lovers of nature. The river-based development plan proposed by these citizens as an alternative to the Tellico Dam project was considered by the E.S.C. to be far more economically beneficial to regional residents than the TVA dam project. After the unanimous vote to reject the Tellico exemption, Secretary of the Interior Cecile Andrus said, "I hate to see the snail darter get the credit for stopping a project that was ill-conceived and uneconomic in the first place." Charles Schultze, Chairman of the Council of Economic Advisors, said, "[h]ere is a project that is 95% complete, and if one takes the cost of finishing it against the total project benefits and does it properly, it doesn't pay, which says something about the original design." This high-level God Squad considered the actual merits of the Tellico Dam project and compared them to alternative plans prepared by local citizens and concluded that the citizen plans would have been overwhelmingly more beneficial. It would seem that the snail darter and the wild and scenic 33 miles at the end of the Little Tennessee River now had a chance for survival. It had been demonstrated that the citizens' plan to farm the rich agricultural lands, preserve the archaeological history of the Cherokee, provide fishing and swift river kayaking and canoeing, enhance tourism, and, in addition, save the snail darter from extinction, was the most economical and ecologically sound plan.

Before we consider the ultimate fate of the snail darter and the plan to save Little Tennessee, it is important to note that the E.S.C. has met only two other times since its inception. At the same time that the E.S.C. considered the Tellico Dam exemption, it considered an exemption for the Grayrocks Dam on the Laramie River in Wyoming. The dam was to be built to supply cooling waters for a large coal-fired power plant. The problem was that the dam would reduce the already critical amount of water available to the marshlands of the Platte River downstream, and these marshlands had been designated as a critical habitat for the endangered whooping crane. The state of Nebraska sued in federal court under the E.S.A. and obtained an injunction preventing the construction of the dam. This injunction further aggravated members of Congress, who pushed harder and successfully created the E.S.C. The state of Nebraska and a consortium of power companies engaged in negotiations and were able to come to an agreement that allowed construction of the dam in return for the purchase of a new whooping crane habitat and a plan to maintain proper water supply to the Platte marshlands. The E.S.C. granted the Grayrocks Dam exemption along with a detailed and extensive mitigation plan for the whooping crane.

The last time the E.S.C. met concerned logging and the northern spotted owl. Again, this started with a lawsuit, *Seattle Audubon Soc. v. Evans,* 771 F. Supp. 1081 (W.D. Wash. 1991), *aff'd sub nom. Seattle Audubon Socy. v. Evans,* 952 F.2d 297 (9th Cir. 1991) (1991). In *Evans,* the court ordered stoppage of logging on federal lands in the Pacific Northwest because of the threat to the northern spotted owl that requires large areas of old-growth forest to survive. The Bureau of Land Management (B.L.M.) filed a petition for an exemption with the E.S.C. In May of 1992, the E.S.C. granted an exemption, but limited the number of tracts of virgin forest that the B.L.M. could sell. This exemption was overturned in federal court because of an illegal procedure. Negotiations between the B.L.M. and environmentalists eventually led to the creation of the Forest Management Ecosystem Team, created by President Clinton. The Team created a plan under which logging was allowed to continue at a limited rate while 10 million acres of old-growth forest were set aside for the spotted owl. While the focus of this chapter is the E.S.A., the lawsuit that initiated this prolonged struggle between loggers, environmentalists, the courts, and the government involved the National Forest Management Act, and is a good example of the many statutes protecting wildlife and habitat (see Chapter 11) that support and expand habitat and protection of endangered or threatened wildlife and plants.

After the ruling of the E.S.C., the TVA, however, continued its assault on the Supreme Court decision, the citizens' plan for redevelopment of the Little Tennessee Valley, and the snail darter. Senator Howard Baker (R-TN), with other members of the Tennessee delegation assisting in the House, were able to surreptitiously place an amendment into an appropriations bill in committee without the general knowledge of Congress. This amendment exempted the Tellico Dam from the E.S.A. and provided the last bit of funding needed to close the dam to the Little Tennessee River. While there was resistance and debate on the Senate and House floors when the bill came to a vote, the bill passed and President Carter, while expressing his reservations, signed the bill into law. The TVA closed the gates a month later and began flooding the valley. All of the estimated 20-25,000 snail darters in the Little Tennessee River have since perished. Nevertheless, due to transplantation efforts, several small populations have survived in other watersheds of the Tennessee River, and the status of the snail darter has been downgraded from endangered to threatened. This was a devastating blow to those who had struggled to preserve the Little Tennessee River and a sad lesson in conniving pork-barrel politics and vindictiveness.

Miscellaneous Commentary and Other Issues

You may wonder how the TVA was able to push through Congress such an overwhelmingly flawed project. This is a good time to introduce to you the so-called *Iron Triangle* and its ability to produce what is known as *pork-barrel projects*. The *Iron Triangle* is a symbiotic relationship between members of Congress, especially those on appropriations committees, government agency bureaucrats, and special interest lobby groups. Each group performs a mutually beneficial service for the other that often results in *pork-barrel projects*, typically federal funding for government programs or projects that is sent to the local district or state of the appropriation committee member, but often particularly benefiting major campaign contributors or companies who will carry out the program or project. A good example would be a defense contractor who provides support for his state's Senator, who sits on the Senate Defense Appropriations Subcommittee, with both the defense contractor and the Senator having contacts within the Department of Defense. Members of the Department of Defense and defense contractors move freely move back and forth to further the incestuous relationship. Favors are given, and money is allocated, often hundreds of millions, even billions, of dollars.

The TVA had the influence and support of the Tennessee delegation of Senators and Congressmen, including Senator Baker, and had longstanding connections to the appropriations committees during decades of dam-building. Their influence reached into the Department of Interior when the snail darter became an issue. Money was allocated without any review of the actual project. Later the media overwhelmingly described the story as a bunch of extremist environmentalists who were using the snail darter as an excuse to obstruct a much-needed hydroelectric dam project. The true nature of this pork-barrel boondoggle, including the fact that this dam produced no electricity, was not revealed until later.

TVA v. Hill remains a landmark decision because it stills maintains its power, though threats to the E.S.A. continually rear their head in Congress. The saga of how a coalition of farmers, concerned citizens, scientists, Cherokees, and lawyers produced the *TVA v. Hill* decision is richly instructive because it also tells the story of the building of the modern environmental movement, a movement that grew out of many struggles similar to Overton Park, Scenic Hudson, and the Tellico Dam.

The best sources of detailed information in the struggle to save the Little Tennessee River and the snail darter, and the political and legal struggle ending with *TVA v. Hill* are:

1) The Snail Darter and the Dam: How Pork-Barrel Politics Endangered a Little Fish and Killed a River by Zygmunt J.B. Plater (Yale University Press 2013) and the website http://bcm.bc.edu/issues/fall_2013/features/ fish-tale.html, and,

2) The Snail Darter Case: TVA versus the Endangered Species Act by Kenneth M. Murchison (Univ. Press of Kansas 2007).

In *TVA v. Hill,* The Supreme Court described the Endangered Species Act as "the most comprehensive legislation for the preservation of endangered species ever enacted by any nation" (437 U.S. 176). This leads to another question you may wonder after reading the case: What forces in American society made it possible to pass a statute like the E.S.A.? This question has to do with the evolution of the environmental movement in the U.S.A., as well as the developing understanding of why endangered species and their ecosystems and biodiversity are so important.

Clearly, the Iron Triangle and the pork-barrelists did not understand the power of the E.S.A. and the threat that endangered and threatened species posed for their projects. See, e.g., Pork Barrel Politics; Rivers and Harbors Legislation, 1947-1968 by John A. Ferejohn (Stanford Univ. Press, 1974). So, while the E.S.A. passed Congress without raising eyebrows, the struggle that preceded *TVA v. Hill* and, of course, the decision itself, caught everyone's attention. Then the Iron Triangle and pork-barrel politicians felt the threat and went into action, but, in spite of the God Squad, were not successful in pushing through Congress anything that really weakened the E.S.A. The forces that defeated the reactionary attack on the E.S.A. are the same forces that made it a reality in the first place.

Of course, it is important to remember that none of these forces would have been expressed without our vibrant evolving representative democracy, its Constitution and Bill of Rights, later Amendments to the CONSTITUTION, and our strong belief in the Four Freedoms. As the activists involved with the *TVA v. Hill* victory have demonstrated:

> "Democracy is not something that you believe in, or something that you hang your hat on. It's something that you do, you participate. Without participation, democracy crumbles and fails. If you participate, you win, and the future is yours." - Abbie Hoffman, radical activist *(1936 - 1989).*

Study Questions for TVA v. Hill

1. Provide the pertinent facts and procedural history of this case. What was the cause of action and requested remedy at the trial court level? What was the most important fact in this case?

2. Was TVA responsible for violating the E.S.A.? What was the reasoning behind this decision?

3. What was the second issue faced by the Court? Did the Court balance the equities in coming to this decision? Explain.

4. How did case law define the E.S.A.?

5. What happened to the Tellico Dam? How did this come about?

6. What is the "God Squad?" Why was it created? Has it served its purpose?

Palila v. Hawaii Dept. of Land and Nat. Resources, 649 F. Supp. 1070 (D. Haw. 1986) (PALILA II)

Note the location of the island of Hawaii. Review the *Study Questions for Palila v. Hawaii* on the Companion Website. You will also find images and commentary on the critical habitat for the Palila, the importance of mamane forest, and further information about Palila recovery efforts. Read *Palila v. Hawaii,* 649 F. Supp 1070 (PALILA II) from Court Listener, a Free Law Project, https://www.courtlistener.com/opinion/1631621/palila-v-hawaii-dept-of-land-natural-resources/. PALILA II was aff'd in 852 F.2d 1106 (9th Cir. 1988). It refers to PALILA I, 471 F.Supp. 985 (D. Hawaii 1979), which is available at https://www.courtlistener.com/opinion/1805278/palila-v-hawaii-dept-of-land-natural-resources/. To pin cite, use the headlines of each case, and the paragraphs thereafter. As you read, focus on how the information in each paragraph fits into the rubrics for a brief below.

1. Heading

2. Facts

3. Procedural History

4. Legal Issues

5. Holding or Decision

6. Reasoning

7. Dissenting Opinions

Note that PALILA II is brought on behalf of the Palila bird by the Sierra Club, Audubon Society, and Alan Zeigler against the Hawaii Department of Land Resources, its chairman, and various rifle, archery, and sportsmen's clubs. The lawsuit is brought under 16 U.S.C. § 1540(g) "Citizen suits" wherein (1) "any person may commence a civil suit" and in (1)(A) "to enjoin any person... who is alleged to be in violation of any provision of the chapter..." Standing is, therefore, not an issue.

The first paragraph of PALILA II following the name of the Senior District Judge, Samuel P. King, who wrote the opinion, briefly describes the controversy at hand, that between the interests of the mouflon sheep hunters on the slopes of Mauna Kea and those of the endangered bird species Palila, which makes its home there, or more exactly—whether the mouflon sheep are harming the Palila—resulting in an illegal taking. Paragraph 2 describes *Palila v. Hawaii Dept. of Land and Nat. Resources*, 471 F. Supp. 985 (D. Haw. 1979), aff'd, 639 F.2d 495 (9th Cir. 1981), now generally referred to as PALILA I. PALILA II, which was brought in the same court before the same judge, alleged harm to the Palila bird by feral sheep and goats, but not by mouflon sheep.

In PALILA I, Judge Samuel King "found that the feral sheep and goats were harming the Palila in violation of E.S.A. and "ordered the State of Hawaii to remove all feral sheep and goats from the critical habitat of the Palila." Paragraphs 3 and 4 of PALILA II address a mouflon sheep study that became the basis for the PALILA II litigation. The plaintiffs in PALILA II sought a mandatory injunction "requiring the State of Hawaii to remove all mouflon sheep from the critical habitat of the Palila." The legal question before the court "is whether the mouflon sheep are 'harming' the Palila." "Harming," as we shall see, is part of the definition of "take." Section 1538(a)(1)(b) of the E.S.A. strictly prohibits "taking" endangered species.

The "Factual Background" is presented in paragraphs 5-13. Paragraphs 5-7 provide historical background for the Palila, which was discovered on the island of Hawaii in 1879. Palila is endemic (native) to Hawaii and is found on the "upper slopes" of Mauna Kea, but its present range is about 10% of its historical range. The shrinkage of its range was "largely due to habitat destruction from grazing ungulates (hoofed mammals)." PALILA I is mentioned again with emphasis on the destruction of the mamane forest (upon which the Palila is dependent). Paragraph 8 indicates that Palila was listed as an endangered species in 1967. (See 50 C.F.R. § 17.11 in the Palila folder on the Companion Website, at http://www.environmentallaw- teach.org/). In paragraph 13, we learn that a critical habitat was designated for the Palila in 1977 (see 50 C.F.R. § 17.95 below). This habitat circles Mauna Kea in a band from elevations of 6600 to 9400 feet. Note that Mauna Kea, a dormant volcano, reaches over two-and-a-half miles above sea level. This band contains the remaining Palila population and essentially coincides with the remaining mamane forest that makes up the Palila's critical habitat. Paragraphs 9 and 10 discuss the actual number of Palila birds. In 1979 (at the time of the PALILA I decision) there were only approximately 1500 Palila birds, a dangerously low number. Footnote 7 gives recent population figures for the Palila birds. The population of Palila birds had fluctuated (see Footnote #7) to approximately 2200 birds that have remained at a "static" level making the bird still "biologically endangered" because "the bird had not experienced any significant 'upward trend.'" Paragraph 11 expands on why the mamane forest is Palila's obligate habitat: it provides a preferred food (mamane seed pods, flowers, buds, and leaves, as well as berries of the naio tree) and shelter for nesting and reproduction. Paragraph 12 expands on the altitudinal and seasonal variations in the mamane forest to which the Palila has adapted.

Species		Historic Range	Vertebrate population where endangered or threatened	Status	When listed	Critical habitat	Special rules
Common name	Scientific name						
Kingfisher, Guam Micronesian	*Halcyon cinnamomina cinnamomina.*	West Pacific Ocean—U.S.A. (Guam).	......do	E	156	NA	NA
Kite, Cuba hook-billed	*Chondrohierax uncinatus wilsonii*	West Indies—Cuba	......do	E	3	NA	NA
Kite, Everglade snail	*Rostrhamus sociabilis plumbeus*	U.S.A. (FL), Cuba	U.S.A. (FL)	E	1	17.95(b)	NA
Kite, Grenada hook-billed	*Chondrohierax uncinatus mirus*	West Indies—Grenada	Entire	E	3	NA	NA
Kokako (wattlebird)	*Callaeas cinerea*	New Zealand	......do	E	3	NA	NA
Lark, Raso	*Alauda razae*	Atlantic Ocean—Raso Island (Cape Verde).	......do	E	571	NA	NA
Macaw, glaucous	*Anodorhynchus glaucus*	Paraguay, Uruguay, Brazil	......do	E	15	NA	NA
Macaw, indigo	*Anodorhynchus leari*	Brazil	......do	E	15	NA	NA
Macaw, little blue	*Cyanopsitta spixii*	......do	......do	E	15	NA	NA
Magpie-robin, Seychelles (thrush)	*Copsychus sechellarum*	Indian Ocean—Seychelles Islands.	......do	E	3	NA	NA
Malimbe, Ibadan	*Malimbus ibadanensis*	Nigeria	......do	E	571	NA	NA
Malkoha, red-faced (cuckoo)	*Phaenicophaeus pyrrhocephalus*	Sri Lanka (=Ceylon)	......do	E	3	NA	NA
Mallard, Mariana	*Anas oustaleti*	West Pacific Ocean—U.S.A. (Guam, Mariana Islands).	......do	E	23	NA	NA
Megapode, Maleo	*Macrocephalon maleo*	Indonesia (Celebes)	......do	E	3	NA	NA
Megapode, Micronesian (=La Perouse's).	*Megapodius laperouse*	West Pacific Ocean—Palau Islands, U.S.A. (Mariana Islands).	......do	E	3	NA	NA
Millerbird, Nihoa (old world warbler).	*Acrocephalus familiaris kingi*	U.S.A. (HI)	......do	E	1	NA	NA
Monarch, Tinian (old world flycatcher).	*Monarcha takatsukasae*	West Pacific Ocean—U.S.A. (Mariana Islands).	......do	T	3, 261	NA	NA
Moorhen, Hawaiian common	*Gallinula chloropus sandvicensis*	U.S.A. (HI)	......do	E	1	NA	NA
Moorhen, Mariana common	*Gallinula chloropus guami*	West Pacific Ocean—U.S.A. (Guam, Tinian, Saipan, Pagan).	......do	E	156	NA	NA
Murrelet, marbled	*Brachyramphus marmoratus marmoratus.*	U.S.A. (AK, CA, OR, WA), Canada (B.C.).	U.S.A. (CA, OR, WA)	T	479	17.95(b)	NA
Nightjar, Puerto Rican	*Caprimulgus noctitherus*	U.S.A. (PR)	Entire	E	6	NA	NA
Nukupu'u (honeycreeper)	*Hemignathus lucidus*	U.S.A. (HI)	......do	E	1, 2	NA	NA
Nuthatch, Algerian	*Sitta ledanti*	Algeria	......do	E	571	NA	NA
'O'o, Kauai (honeyeater)	*Moho braccatus*	U.S.A. (HI)	......do	E	1	NA	NA
Ostrich, Arabian	*Struthio camelus syriacus*	Jordan, Saudi Arabia	......do	E	3	NA	NA
Ostrich, West African	*Struthio camelus spatzi*	Spanish Sahara	......do	E	3	NA	NA
'O'u (honeycreeper)	*Psittirostra psittacea*	U.S.A. (HI)	......do	E	1	NA	NA
Owl, Anjouan scops	*Otus rutilus capnodes*	Indian Ocean—Comoro Island	......do	E	3	NA	NA
Owl, giant scops	*Mimizuku (=Otus) gurneyi*	Philippines—Marinduque and Mindanao Island.	......do	E	15	NA	NA
Owl, Madagascar red	*Tyto soumagnei*	Madagascar	......do	E	401	NA	NA
Owl, Mexican spotted	*Strix occidentalis lucida*	U.S.A. (AZ, CO, NM, TX, UT), Mexico.	Entire	T	494	17.95(b)	NA
Owl, northern spotted	*Strix occidentalis caurina*	U.S.A. (CA, OR, WA), Canada (B.C.).	......do	T	393	17.95(b)	NA
Owl, Seychelles scops	*Otus magicus (=insularis) insularis.*	Indian Ocean—Seychelles Islands.	......do	E	3	NA	NA
Owlet, Morden's	*Otus ireneae*	Kenya	......do	E	3	NA	NA
Oystercatcher, Canarian black	*Haematopus meadewaldoi*	Atlantic Ocean—Canary Islands	......do	E	571	NA	NA
Palila (honeycreeper)	*Loxioides bailleui*	U.S.A. (HI)	......do	E	1	17.95(b)	NA
Parakeet, blue-throated (=ochre-marked).	*Pyrrhura cruentata*	Brazil	......do	E	3	NA	NA
Parakeet, Forbes'	*Cyanoramphus auriceps forbesi*	New Zealand	......do	E	3	NA	NA
Parakeet, golden	*Aratinga guarouba*	Brazil	......do	E	15	NA	NA
Parakeet, golden-shouldered	*Psephotus chrysopterygius*	Australia	......do	E	3	NA	NA
Parakeet, Mauritius	*Psittacula echo*	Indian Ocean—Mauritius	......do	E	3	NA	NA
Parakeet, Norfolk Island	*Cyanoramphus cookii (=novaezelandiae c.).*	Australia (Norfolk Island)	......do	E	401	NA	NA
Parakeet, orange-bellied	*Neophema chrysogaster*	Australia	......do	E	4	NA	NA
Parakeet, paradise	*Psephotus pulcherrimus*	......do	......do	E	4	NA	NA
Parakeet, scarlet-chested	*Neophema splendida*	......do	......do	E	4	NA	NA
Parakeet, turquoise	*Neophema pulchella*	......do	......do	E	3	NA	NA
Parrot, Bahaman or Cuban	*Amazona leucocephala*	West Indies—Cuba, Bahamas, Caymans.	......do	E	3, 15	NA	NA
Parrot, ground	*Pezoporus wallicus*	Australia	......do	E	6	NA	NA
Parrot, imperial	*Amazona imperialis*	West Indies—Dominica	......do	E	3	NA	NA
Parrot, night (=Australian)	*Geopsittacus occidentalis*	Australia	......do	E	3	NA	NA
Parrot, Puerto Rican	*Amazona vittata*	U.S.A. (PR)	......do	E	1	NA	NA
Parrot, red-browed	*Amazona rhodocorytha*	Brazil	......do	E	3	NA	NA
Parrot, red-capped	*Pionopsitta pileata*	......do	......do	E	15	NA	NA
Parrot, red-necked	*Amazona arausiaca*	West Indies—Dominica	......do	E	50	NA	NA
Parrot, red-spectacled	*Amazona pretrei pretrei*	Brazil, Argentina	......do	E	15	NA	NA
Parrot, red-tailed	*Amazona brasiliensis*	Brazil	......do	E	401	NA	NA
Parrot, Seychelles lesser vasa	*Coracopsis nigra barklyi*	Indian Ocean—Seychelles (Praslin Island).	......do	E	571	NA	NA
Parrot, St. Vincent	*Amazona guildingii*	West Indies—St. Vincent	......do	E	3	NA	NA
Parrot, St. Lucia	*Amazona versicolor*	West Indies—St. Lucia	......do	E	3	NA	NA
Parrot, thick-billed	*Rhynchopsitta pachyrhyncha*	Mexico, U.S.A. (AZ, NM)	Mexico	E	3	NA	NA
Parrot, vinaceous-breasted	*Amazona vinacea*	Brazil	Entire	E	15	NA	NA
Parrotbill, Maui (honeycreeper)	*Pseudonestor xanthophrys*	U.S.A. (HI)	......do	E	1	NA	NA
Pelican, brown	*Pelecanus occidentalis*	U.S.A (Carolinas to TX, CA, OR, WA), West Indies, coastal Central and South America.	Entire, except U.S. Atlantic coast, FL, AL.	E	2, 3, 171	NA	NA
Penguin, Galapagos	*Spheniscus mendiculus*	Ecuador (Galapagos Islands)	Entire	E	3	NA	NA
Petrel, Hawaiian dark-rumped	*Pterodroma phaeopygia sandwichensis.*	U.S.A. (HI)	......do	E	1	NA	NA
Petrel, Madeira	*Pterodroma madeira*	Atlantic Ocean—Madeira Island	......do	E	571	NA	NA
Petrel, Mascarene black	*Pterodroma aterrima*	Indian Ocean—Mauritius (Reunion Island).	......do	E	571	NA	NA
Pheasant, bar-tailed	*Syrmaticus humiae*	Burma, China	......do	E	3	NA	NA
Pheasant, Blyth's tragopan	*Tragopan blythii*	Burma, China, India	......do	E	3	NA	NA
Pheasant, brown eared	*Crossoptilon mantchuricum*	China	......do	E	3	NA	NA
Pheasant, Cabot's tragopan	*Tragopan caboti*	......do	......do	E	3	NA	NA
Pheasant, cheer	*Catreus wallichii*	India, Nepal, Pakistan	......do	E	401	NA	NA
Pheasant, Chinese monal	*Lophophorus lhuysii*	China	......do	E	3	NA	NA
Pheasant, Edward's	*Lophura edwardsi*	Vietnam	......do	E	3	NA	NA
Pheasant, Elliot's	*Syrmaticus ellioti*	China	......do	E	15	NA	NA

PALILA *(Psittirostra bailleui)*

Hawaii. An area of land, water, and airspace on the island of Hawaii, Hawaii County, with the following components: (1) The State of Hawaii Mauna Kea Forest Reserve, except (a) that portion above the 10,000 foot contour line, (b) that portion south of the Saddle Road (State Highway 20), (c) lands owned by the United States in the Pohakuloa Training Area north of the Saddle Road (State Highway 20) established by Executive Order 1719 (Parcel 6, State of Hawaii Tax Map Key 4-4-16, Third Division), (d) that portion (Parcel 10, Kaohe IV, State of Hawaii Tax Map Key 4-4-16, Third Division) lying north of the Saddle Road (State Highway 20) and south of the Power Line Road; (2) that portion of the State of Hawaii Kaohe Game Management Area (Parcel 4, State of Hawaii Tax Map Key 4-4-15, Third Division) to the north and east of the Saddle Road (State Highway 20); (3) that portion of the Upper Waikii Paddock (Parcel 2, State of Hawaii Tax Map Key 4-4-15, Third Division) northeast of the Saddle Road (State Highway 20); (4) that portion of the lands of Humuula between Puu Kahinahina and Kole lying southeast of the Mauna Kea Forest Reserve fence (portions of Parcels 2, 3, and 7, State of Hawaii Tax Map Key 3-8-1, Third Division) which are included in the State conservation district.

NOTE: Map follows:

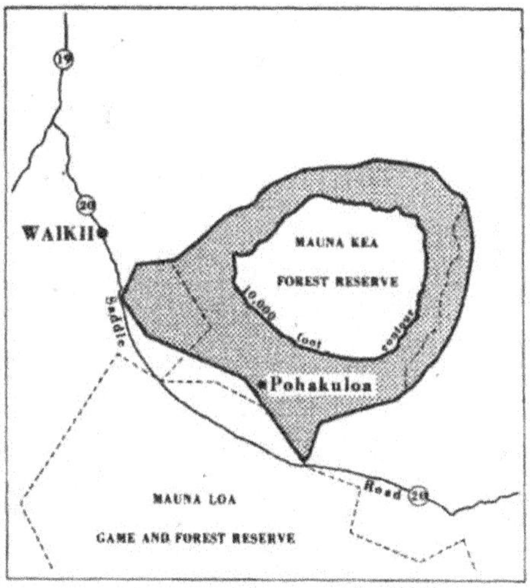

50 C.F.R. §17.95 - The diameter of the circular band is approximately 12 miles.

Paragraphs 14 and 15 summarize the situation with the mouflon sheep. Like the feral sheep and goats that were the subject of PALILA I, the mouflon sheep are an invasive species and were introduced as a game animal in the early 1960s. Most significantly, the "defendant Department of Land and Natural Resources presently maintains the mouflon population for sport-hunting purposes within the Mauna Kea Game Management Area. (This state game management area happens to include most of the Palila's critical habitat.)" Most of the approximately 500 mouflon sheep lived within the Palila's critical habitat.

The next section, entitled "The Law," contains the applicable statute, E.S.A. 16 U.S.C. § 1532(5), and regulatory provisions about harm, 46 F.R. 29, 490 and 54, 748 (The *Palila* was already listed as an endangered species with a respectively designated habitat). At that time, E.S.A. 16 U.S.C. § 1532(5) stated,

> (A) The term "critical habitat" for a threatened or endangered species means—
>
> (i) the specific areas within the geographical area occupied by the species, at the time it is listed in accordance with the provisions of section 1533 of this title, on which are found those physical or biological features (I) essential to the conservation of the species and (II) which may require special management considerations or protection; and
>
> (ii) specific areas outside the geographical area occupied by the species at the time it is listed in accordance with the provisions of section 1533 of this title, upon a determination by the Secretary that such areas are essential for the conservation of the species.
>
> (B) Critical habitat may be established for those species now listed as threatened or endangered species for which no critical habitat has heretofore been established as set forth in subparagraph (A) of this paragraph.
>
> (C) Except in those circumstances determined by the Secretary, critical habitat shall not include the entire geographical area which can be occupied by the threatened or endangered species.

As we have already noted in our discussion of *TVA v. Hill*, this particular definition no longer exists and was superseded by a definition in 50 C.F.R. § 424.02 that, in turn, was also eliminated in 2011 because "these terms are defined in the [Endangered Species] Act, and the existing regulatory definitions do not add meaning to the terms." Paragraph 16 ends with a statement of the law that is central to this case, that is, Sect. 1538(a)(1)(B) which "makes it unlawful for any person to 'take' an endangered species." Further, the E.S.A. defines "take" in Section 1532(19) to mean to "harass, harm, pursue, hunt, shoot, wound, kill, trap, capture, or collect or to attempt to engage in any such conduct."

Because the central issue, in this case, is whether the mouflon sheep are harming the Palila resulting in an illegal taking, paragraph 17 refers to the definition of harm in 50 C.F.R. § 17.3 as an act which actually kills or injures wildlife. Such act may include significant habitat modification or degradation where it actually kills or injures wildlife by significantly impairing essential behavioral patterns, including breeding, feeding or sheltering.

In paragraph 18, the court states that, with regard to the Palila, it understands the meaning of harm to be activities that significantly modify or degrade the habitat, resulting in actual injury to the wildlife species.

This would include activities that significantly impair essential behavior patterns to the extent that there is an actual negative impact or injury to the endangered species, threatening its continued existence or recovery (649 F. Supp. 1075).

The meaning of "actual injury" is at the core of this decision. The court adds here that an actual injury includes activities that have an "actual negative impact," not just those activities that drive the bird toward extinction, but also those activities threatening its "recovery."

The next paragraphs are grouped under the heading "The Secretary's Redefinition of Harm." The court foreshadows its reasoning in paragraphs 20-27 by stating that the Secretary's amended regulations regarding the definition of harm "did not embody a substantial change in the previous definition" and that "both the original and amended definitions state that 'harm' may include significant habitat destruction that injures protected wildlife." Nevertheless, we learn in paragraph 20 that defendants argue that the definition of "harm" requires a showing of "actual injury," a body count that shows an actual decline in the numbers of Palila.

Paragraph 21 informs us that all the expert witnesses, including those hired by the defendant, agree that the "mouflon sheep are presently degrading the mamane forest, that this degradation is irreversible because it is suppressing the forest's regeneration, that Palila depend on the mamane for their existence, and that continued degradation could drive the Palila into extinction." The defendant's argument that the impact of the mouflon sheep on the mamane forest is only "potential" (as opposed to "actual") is farcical and will be discussed later along with specific details of mouflon impact.

Paragraphs 22 and 23 elucidated the meaning of "harm," which does not require death to individual members of the species; nor does it require a finding that habitat degradation is presently driving the species further toward extinction. Furthermore, taking is defined as habitat destruction that prevents the recovery of the species by affecting essential behavioral patterns. The court cites *TVA v. Hill* in which the Supreme Court held that it is "beyond doubt that Congress intended endangered species to be afforded the highest priorities" and emphasizes the conservation and preservation of ecosystems by referring to § 1531(b) "Purposes" –

> to provide a means whereby the ecosystems upon which endangered species and threatened species depend may be conserved, to provide a program for the conservation of such endangered species and threatened species.

Paragraphs 24-27 discuss the Secretary of the Interior's attempt to amend the definition of "harm." Paragraph 24 reiterates that the definition of harm found in 50 C.F.R. § 17.3 was in effect at the time of the PALILA I decision (and still in effect today). Paragraph 26 states that, in response to the PALILA I decision, many opposed the Secretary's proposed redefinition of "harm." In fact, the legal memorandum authored by the acting Deputy Assistant Secretary for Fish and Wildlife and Parks proposed the redefinition of "harm" to "prevent the result reached in PALILA I." While the Secretary did propose amended language for the definition of harm that required "actual death or injury to individual species members," there was enormous resistance during the period of comment required by the A.P.A. for proposed regulations that the Secretary back-tracked and the redefinition of harm finally promulgated "stresses the critical link between habitat modification and injury to the species." As a result, injury does not require a finding of "death to individual species members." More importantly, the court emphasizes that the Palila is hovering at or near the critical population mark. This situation made it both biologically and legally endangered. Thus, the court concluded that if the habitat modification prevents the population from recovering, then this causes injury to the species and should be actionable under E.S.A.

Paragraph 28 begins an important, in-depth discussion of the foregone conclusion that the mouflon sheep and the Palila could not share one habitat, but had to be separated. Paragraphs 28-30 reiterate the findings of PALILA I with regard to how feral sheep and goats damage and destroy the mamane forest and ends with the question (notwithstanding the title of this section) of whether the mouflon sheep "have a similar negative impact on the mamane and the Palila."

Paragraphs 31-36 are grouped under heading, "Impacts of Mouflon on Mamane and on Palila." Mamane is the favorite food of the mouflon sheep. They eat the seed pods, leaves, and stems, but more importantly, the seedlings and basal shoots that are the source of mamane regeneration. The mouflon sheep also strip and eat the bark of the mamane. The negative impact of this overgrazing is revealed the most at the timber line (the highest altitude on Mauna Kea where mamane can grow) where the trees are most vulnerable. There is also a "browse line" evident in the mamane forest. A browse line is a two-dimensional flat surface like a tree haircut created by over-eating from underneath revealing the highest branches that the mouflon sheep can reach. Footnote 35 provides the best and starkest evidence of mamane destruction. "Exclosures" are fenced areas that exclude the mouflon sheep. "The land outside the exclosure is devoid of mamane, littered with snags, has no regeneration and is nearly barren of vegetation." Snags are dead trees, usually a solitary main stem without any branches. Inside the exclosure there are "numerous mamane, a healthy understory, and vigorous growth."

Visit the *Study Questions for Palila* in the Palila folder on the Companion Website, at http://www.environmentallaw-teach.org/, to view images of an exclosure on Mauna Kea. "The contrast between the vegetation inside the exclosure, which has been protected from grazing, and outside is dramatic." In addition to grazing, and not mentioned here, is the destructive effect of the trampling of ungulate hooves causing soil erosion and root damage with no possibility of regeneration. Finally, the court adds: "[e]ither the mouflon sheep will further degrade the mamane ecosystem, thus decreasing the remaining Palila habitat and further depressing the Palila population. Or, at best, the mouflon will merely slow or prevent the recovery of the mamane forest, suppressing the available food supply and nesting sites for Palila, and thus preventing the Palila population from expanding toward recovery." Using this reasoning, the Court concludes in paragraph 37 that, if the mouflon sheep are allowed to remain on Mauna Kea, "the Palila population will not recover to the point where it can be removed from the Endangered Species List." The remedy is provided: "[i]f the Palila is to have any hope of survival, the mouflon must be removed to give the mamane forest a chance to recover and expand." Again, more information will be provided in the Palila Recovery Plan, discussed later. Now that the court has provided its holding and remedy, paragraphs 38-43 discuss the "Inappropriateness of Multiple Use Approach," a plan by the Hawaii Department of Land Resources "to maintain a viable sport-hunting population of mouflon and to enhance the mamane ecosystem to encourage the survival of the Palila." Aside from the scientific uncertainties of this plan, and the fact that mamane regeneration takes over 25 years before mature trees develop, the main issue here is that "the Endangered Species Act does not allow a 'balancing' approach for multiple use considerations." In fact, it is not the E.S.A. that does not allow a 'balancing' of interests, but the precedent set in *TVA v. Hill.* So, once the court determines that the mouflon sheep are harming the Palila and causing a "take" prohibited by 16 U.S.C. § 1538(a)(1)(B), the Palila must be given the highest priority in fashioning a remedy. "Once this significant negative impact has been shown, the Act leaves no room for mixed use or other management strategies or policies."

The "Conclusion"—paragraphs 44-46—repeats the court's holding regarding the remedy and reasoning. The final order requires that "the mouflon sheep are to be removed from the critical habitat of the Palila on Mauna Kea." Because there has not been full compliance by the Hawaii Department of Land resources with the orders of PALILA I, the court requires that "the order shall be combined with my previous order of 1979 mandating the removal of the feral sheep and goats" and that the order require the "removal of the hybrid mouflon/feral sheep." Thus, this order requires the removal of all ungulates from the critical habitat of the Palila.

Miscellaneous Commentary and Other Issues

The meaning of "harm" was further litigated and strengthened in *Babbitt v. Sweet Home Chapter of Communities for a Great Oregon*, 515 U.S. 687 (1995). This opinion, as well as a brief of this opinion, can be found in the Palila folder on the Companion Website at http:// www.environmentallaw-teach.org/). The Supreme Court held that under the E.S.A., the Secretary of the Interior may define prohibited "harm" within the E.S.A. provision defining "take," broadly to include destruction of habitats and breeding grounds as well as directly injuring or killing protected animals. A brief search through the Code of Federal Regulations shows that the definition of harm found at 50 CFR § 17.3 (2019) is still good law:

> Harm in the definition of "take" in the Act means an act which actually kills or injures wildlife. Such act may include significant habitat modification or degradation where it actually kills or injures wildlife by significantly impairing essential behavioral patterns, including breeding, feeding or sheltering.

While 16 U.S.C. §1532(19) defines "take" to mean "to harass, harm, pursue, hunt, shoot, wound, kill, trap, capture, or collect, or to attempt to engage in any such conduct," "harass" is further defined by 50 CFR § 17.3 (2019):

> Harass in the definition of "take" in the Act [E.S.A.] means an intentional or negligent act or omission which creates the likelihood of injury to wildlife by annoying it to such an extent as to significantly disrupt normal behavioral patterns which include, but are not limited to, breeding, feeding, or sheltering. This definition, when applied to captive wildlife, does not include generally accepted:
>
> (1) Animal husbandry practices that meet or exceed the minimum standards for facilities and care under the Animal Welfare Act,
>
> (2) Breeding procedures, or
>
> (3) Provisions of veterinary care for confining, tranquilizing, or anesthetizing, when such practices, procedures, or provisions are not likely to result in injury to the wildlife.

This definition was litigated in the U.S. Court of Appeals for the Fourth Circuit in *Hill v. Coggins*, 867 F.3d 499 (5th Cir. 2017), but the arguments were confined to the exceptions to this definition. It is significant to note that the definition of "harass" does not refer to an "act" that "actually kills or injures wildlife;" it only requires an intentional act which creates the likelihood of injury.

Recovery Plans

Section 1533(f)—Recovery Plans—required the Secretary to develop and implement plans (hereinafter *recovery plans*) for the conservation and survival of endangered species and threatened species. Section 1533(f)(1)(B) specifies what constitutes such a plan.

Remember that conservation is defined in Sect. 1532(3) as "procedures which are necessary to bring any endangered species or threatened species to the point at which such measures are no longer necessary." The measures referred to in 16 U.S.C. §1532(3) include, but are not limited to, all activities associated with scientific resources management such as research, census, law enforcement, habitat acquisition and maintenance, propagation, live trapping, and transplantation, and, in the extraordinary case where population pressures within a given ecosystem cannot be otherwise relieved, may include regulated taking.

Thus, the goal of the E.S.A. is not just to provide protection for those species listed as endangered or threatened, but also to remove them from the list through a plan for recovery. For instance, as soon as the Palila became endangered, in 1977, the U.S. Fish and Wildlife Services created the *Palila Recovery Plan*, originally approved in 1978. A Palila recovery plan also exists at the state level (https://dlnr.hawaii.gov/wildlife/files/2013/09/Fact-sheet-palila.pdf, or https://pacificrimconservation.org/wp-content/uploads/2013/10/Palila.pdf).

So, who is working to make the Palila Recovery a reality? Footnote 39 of PALILA II refers to the efforts of the State of Hawaii (between 1979-1986): "[f]or example, the State has instituted a mamane replanting program that is meeting with some success. Since 1979, the State has planted over 6000 mamane trees on 70 acres of the critical habitat, and they have maintained nine fenced exclosures of 4.5 acres each. They have begun a fog drip project to capture moisture to encourage native vegetation. They are continuing efforts to fence the entire Palila critical habitat to keep feral sheep and other ungulates out and to improve their ability to manage the mouflon herd. In addition, they have removed some of the hunting restrictions on mouflon sheep, allowing more mouflon to be taken." These efforts have continued through the Mauna Kea Forest Restoration Project (see https://dlnr.hawaii.gov/restoremaunakea/) and the Department of Forestry and Wildlife of the Hawaii Department of Land and Natural Resources. Of course, the U.S. Fish and Wildlife Service plays an important role in endangered species recovery. See https://www.fws.gov/endangered/.

A number of environmental organizations, including the Audubon Society, the American Bird Conservancy, the Sierra Club, and many others, play a pivotal role by providing scientific expertise, volunteers, media specialists, attorneys, and political will. There are many dedicated people working behind the scenes on every aspect of the Recovery Plan for the Palila.

The Palila is not alone in its struggle for existence on the Hawaiian Islands. The NABCI State of the Birds Report *http://nabci-us.org/how-we-work/state-of-the-birds/* is produced annually and addresses these struggles. There is also a STATE OF THE BIRDS 2009, http://www.stateofthebirds.org/2009/habitats/hawaiian-birds, which states:

> More bird species are vulnerable to extinction in Hawaii than anywhere else in the United States. Before the arrival of humans, the Hawaiian Islands supported 113 bird species unique in the world, including flightless geese, ibis, rails, and 59 species of Hawaiian honeycreepers. Since humans arrived, 71 bird species have become extinct and 31 more are federally listed as threatened or endangered. Of these, 10 have not been seen in as long as 40 years and may be extinct. Humans have introduced many bird species from other parts of the world: 43% of 157 species are not native. Among land birds, 69% are introduced species.

The San Diego Zoo Global Wildlife Conservancy is another example of an organization devoted to the Palila and other Pacific birds, see, e.g., https://youtu.be/qiR2U6QGLCw. The Pacific Islands Fish and Wildlife Office of the U.S. Fish and Wildlife Service is (because of the E.S.A.) also deeply involved (see https://www.fws.gov/pacificislands/teslist.html).

Standing and Palila II

In *Hawaiian Crow v. Lujan*, 906 F.Supp. 549 (D. Hawai'i, 2017), the defendants argued that the Hawaiian Crow (a bird) did not have standing to sue. The Ninth Circuit granted the defendants' motion to dismiss and held that, "the plain language of *Fed. R. Civ. P.17(c)* and the E.S.A., *16 U.S.C. § 1540(g)* did not authorize the bird to sue. The bird was clearly neither a person as defined in the E.S.A., 16 U.S.C.S. § 1532(13), nor an infant or incompetent person under Fed. R. Civ. P.17(c)." Prior to this, many birds, like the Palila, were listed as plaintiffs without the issue of standing being raised. While this is more of a technical issue, it is clear that animals and plants should never have had standing as plaintiffs.

While there are other Hawaiian bird lawsuits in federal court, most Hawaiian bird litigation is brought under the state's endangered species act. For instance, the 2017 codification of the Hawaii environmental laws is available at https://law.justia.com/codes/hawaii/2017/title-12/chapter-195d/.

Critical Habitat

As we have seen in PALILA I and PALILA II, damage to critical habitat that produces a "take" of an endangered species will trigger corrective measures in court. The designation of critical habitat is a powerful tool for protecting and recovering endangered species and is often the key to an endangered species' survival. But, as of 2015, critical habitat has been designated for only 468 of 948 endangered or threatened plants and 319 of 1464 endangered and threatened animals. Of course, there is no possibility of critical habitat designation unless a species is listed as endangered or threatened. As we shall discuss later, there are thousands or species that should be listed but are not, and thus, a critical habitat cannot be designated for these species. The struggle to list species will be discussed next in *Carlton v. Babbitt*, 900 F. Supp. 526 (D.D.C. 1995). Per 16 U.S.C. §1533(a)(3)(A), public and private parks, nature preserves, sanctuaries, and the like play a crucial role in providing critical habitat for unlisted but endangered or threatened species. Further, in Sect. 1533(b)(2), the E.S.A. states that while the Secretary designates critical habitats, and makes revisions thereto, under subsection (a)(3) on the basis of the best scientific data available, the Secretary may also exclude any area from critical habitat if he determines that the benefits of such exclusion outweigh the benefits of specifying such area as part of the critical habitat. Thus, the critical habitat designations require consideration of the economic and national security impacts. There is no such balancing required for the listing of species as endangered or threatened. Additionally, 50 C.F.R. § 424.19 (2019)—Impact analysis and exclusions from critical habitat—states:

> (a) At the time of publication of a proposed rule to designate critical habitat, the Secretary will make available for public comment the draft economic analysis of the designation. The draft economic analysis will be summarized in the Federal Register notice of the proposed designation of critical habitat.
>
> (b) Prior to finalizing the designation of critical habitat, the Secretary will consider the probable economic, national security, and other relevant impacts of the designation upon proposed or ongoing activities. The Secretary will consider impacts at a scale that the Secretary determines to be appropriate, and will compare the impacts with and without the designation. Impacts may be qualitatively or quantitatively described.
>
> (c) The Secretary has discretion to exclude any particular area from the critical habitat upon a determination that the benefits of such exclusion outweigh the benefits of specifying the particular area as part of the critical habitat. In identifying those benefits, in addition to the mandatory consideration of impacts conducted pursuant to paragraph (b) of this section, the Secretary may assign the weight given to any benefits relevant to the designation of critical habitat. The Secretary, however, will not exclude any particular area if, based on the best scientific and commercial data available, the Secretary determines that the failure to designate that area as critical habitat will result in the extinction of the species concerned.

To what extent economic impacts should be considered in critical habitat designation for endangered species has generated significant litigation. In the Nov./Dec. 2015 issue of *Trends* (the American Bar Association newsletter covering environment, energy, and resources), we find discussion of the Ninth Circuit's opinion in *Building Industry Association of the Bay Area v. Department of Commerce*, 792 F3d 1027, 2015 (9th Cir. 2015): "The decision upholds the designation of more than 13,000 square miles (8.6 million acres) of critical habitat for the federally threatened green sturgeon. The decision holds that, under section 4(b)(2) of E.S.A., the NMFS has discretion with respect to how it will consider the economic impacts of designating critical habitat. The court also ruled that subsequent NMFS decisions not to carve out certain areas from previous designations are unreviewable. Finally, the court confirmed the longstanding rule that environmental review is not required for critical habitat designations under the National Environmental Policy Act (NEPA). The decision will give federal agencies more leeway in making critical habitat decisions." The E.S.A. defines critical habitat at §1532(5). The most important phrase in this subsection of the E.S.A. is "essential to the conservation of the species," and 16 U.S.C. § 1532(3) defines the term conservation to include:

> All methods and procedures which are necessary to bring any endangered species or threatened species to the point at which the measures provided pursuant to this chapter are no longer necessary. Such methods and procedures include, but are not limited to, all activities associated with scientific resources management such as research, census, law enforcement, habitat acquisition and maintenance, propagation, live trapping, and transplantation, and, in the extraordinary case where population pressures within a given ecosystem cannot be otherwise relieved, may include regulated taking.

Critical habitat must include all areas deemed important to a species' survival or recovery, including those areas where the species currently lives and other areas that were once part of its range or are needed for movement and migration. Section §1533(b)(6)(C) introduces the need for establishing methods designating such habitats, while the criteria for designating critical habitats are set forth at 50 C.F.R. § 424.12. The designation of a critical habitat is a complex process. Flow charts for this process can be found in the Palila folder of the Companion Website, at http://www.environmentallaw-teach.org/. These flow charts reveal the complicated decision-making procedures. While the decisions are made by the Fish and Wildlife Service or the National Marine Fisheries Service (often referred to as NOAA Fisheries Service), the role of non-governmental scientists and environmental organizations is crucial.

As previously quoted, 50 C.F.R. § 424.19(c) states that the Secretary will not exclude any particular area if, based on the best scientific and commercial data available, failure to designate that area as a critical habitat will result in the extinction. This statement is problematic in that it contradicts the definition of conservation. These regulations restrict the Secretary only when it comes to survival of the species, while the clearly legislated purpose of conservation is "the use of all methods and procedures which are necessary to bring any endangered species or threatened species to the point at which the measures provided pursuant to this chapter are no longer necessary." Recovery is the stated purpose of the E.S.A. Critical habitat is to be designated to provide those physical or biological features...essential to the conservation of the species."

Finally, both private and public property may be designated as critical habitats; however, if private property is designated as a critical habitat, this does not impose an obligation on the landowner to affirmatively aid in the conservation of the endangered species. The FWS and NMFS are required to ensure that developments on the designated critical habitats do not adversely affect the critical habitat. Moreover, developments on private land designated as critical habitats trigger critical habitat protection requirements only if the development needs a "federal action," such as permits and licenses, loans and funding, or other federal involvement.

Critical habitat issues continue to generate litigation, as in the case of *Markle Interests, v. U.S. Fish and Wildlife Serv.*, 827 F.3d 452 (5th Cir. 2016), *cert. granted sub nom. Weyerhaeuser Co. v. U.S. Fish and Wildlife Serv.*, 138 S. Ct. 924 (2018), and *vacated and remanded sub nom. Weyerhaeuser Co. v. U.S. Fish and Wildlife Serv.*, 17-71, 2018 WL 6174253 (U.S. Nov. 27, 2018). Here, the court focused on the habitat of the dusky gopher frog, which lives in open-canopied pine forests and breeds in isolated, ephemeral ponds. The Fifth Circuit Court of Appeals held that the FWS could designate suitable private property as a critical habitat, even though the dusky gopher frog had never inhabited portions of the property included within the designated critical habitat area. In reaching this conclusion, the Fifth Circuit notes that designating privately-held land as a critical habitat for an endangered species does not require the landowners to participate in conserving the endangered species. Designation of land as a critical habitat, therefore, does not require an owner of privately-held land to introduce an endangered species onto the land or to modify the land in any way. The Fifth Circuit also mentions that the FWS may extend the deadline for critical habitat designation if a critical habitat cannot be determined at the time of the species' listing. The Fifth Circuit reaffirms that "the objective of the E.S.A. is to enable endangered species not merely to survive, but to recover from their endangered or threatened status," yet the court points out that the E.S.A. "explicitly mandates 'consideration' of 'economic impact'" when listing an area as a critical habitat.

Study Questions for Palila II

1. Name the plaintiffs and defendants. Why is standing not an issue in this case?

2. Provide the pertinent facts and procedural history of this case. How does the mouflon sheep affect the mamane forest? What was the cause of action and requested remedy at the trial court level?

3. What is the meaning of "take" in the E.S.A.? Quote and cite the relevant section (s) you use to answer this question.

4. How is the meaning of "take" further expanded in 50 CFR 17.3? Why is 50 CFR 17.3 so important to the meaning of take?

5. Briefly state the issue and finding in *Palila v. Hawaii* and then explain how this case further defined the meaning of "take" in the E.S.A. and CFR.

6. Does the E.S.A. define "critical habitat"? Where is "critical habitat" defined? What is the definition? Would the finding of the court have been different if there had been no critical habitat designated for the Palila? Explain.

7. What is a Recovery Plan? Why is this required by the E.S.A.? Quote and cite the relevant section (s) you use to answer this question.

Carlton v. Babbitt, 900 F. Supp. 526 (D.D.C. 1995)

A number of environmental organizations and interested individuals sued the Secretary of the Interior and the United States Fish and Wildlife Service ("FWS"), inter alia, alleging that the FWS decision not to reclassify the grizzly bear population of the Selkirk ecosystem from "threatened" to "endangered" was arbitrary and capricious, contrary to law, or not adequately justified. To offer some contextual information about the grizzly bear, here are Robert Porter Allen's words:

> This is an animal that cannot compromise or adjust its way of life to ours. Could not by its very nature, could not even if we allowed it the opportunity, which we did not. For the grizzly bear there is no freedom but that of unbounded space, no life except its own. Without meekness, without a sign of humility, it has refused to accept our idea of what the world should be like. If we succeed in preserving the wild remnant that still survives, the glory will rest primarily on this bear whose stubborn vigor has kept it alive in the face of increasing and seemingly hopeless odds.

~Robert Porter Allen from the Frontispiece to Interagency Grizzly Bear Guidelines

After you read the decision available at Justia, https://law.justia.com/cases/federal/district-courts/FSupp/900/526/2262127/, review the *Study Questions for Carlton v. Babbitt* on the Companion Website. You will also find images and commentary on the grizzly bear. As you read *Carlton v. Babbitt*, note its organization with headings and subheadings. Download the decision or print it, color-code it, or number the paragraphs as you go and focus on how the information in each paragraph fits into the rubrics for a brief noted below:

1. Heading
2. Facts
3. Procedural History
4. Legal Issues
5. Holding or Decision
6. Reasoning
7. Dissenting Opinions

For efficiency, the lawsuits were consolidated, and referred to as *Carlton v. Babbit*, for Jasper Carlton, the president of the Biodiversity Legal Foundation at that time—Carlton passed away in 2015. These cases are important because they discuss the listing of endangered and threatened species and require us to examine the listing process. Without being listed as endangered or threatened, a species has none of the protections of the E.S.A. Because these cases were brought against the FWS, they were defended by an attorney from the Environmental and Natural Resources Division of the Department of Justice.

Paragraph 1, right below the name of the District Court Judge, Paul L. Friedman, states the cause of action, the judicial review of the Secretary's decision not to reclassify a particular grizzly bear population as endangered. The next five paragraphs contain the procedural history, the background history of the case. Five distinct populations of grizzly bears were classified by the FWS as threatened in 1975. The plaintiffs petitioned the FWS in 1991 to change the status of the so-called Selkirk and Cabinet/Yaak populations from threatened to endangered. Paragraph 3 establishes that, according to the E.S.A., the FWS has the authority to list endangered and threatened species. Definitions are provided for both. Significantly, the court adds that the definition of species in 16 U.S.C. § 1532(16) includes any "distinct population segment." Paragraph 4 states that according to § 1533(b)(3)(A), "any 'interested person' may petition the FWS to list, delist, or reclassify the status of a species."

The definition of a "person" was previously presented during the discussion of citizen suits at the beginning of this chapter. After receiving a petition, the FWS must then follow the process required by the E.S.A. and presented below. The FWS has 90 days to determine if "the petition provides 'substantial scientific or commercial information' indicating that the petition action is warranted." If the action requested is deemed "warranted" by the FWS, a formal status review of the species and of the requested action is then conducted. The specific factors to be considered in this review are also mandated by the E.S.A. and will be discussed in detail later. The FWS has one year to determine "whether the petitioned action is warranted, not warranted, or is warranted but precluded due to work on other pending listing proposals." This determination is to be "based 'solely on the best of the scientific and commercial data available.'" The reference to "commercial data" should not be understood to imply consideration of economic factors in this determination. Relevant commercial data, for instance, might include data on fishermen's catch of fish.

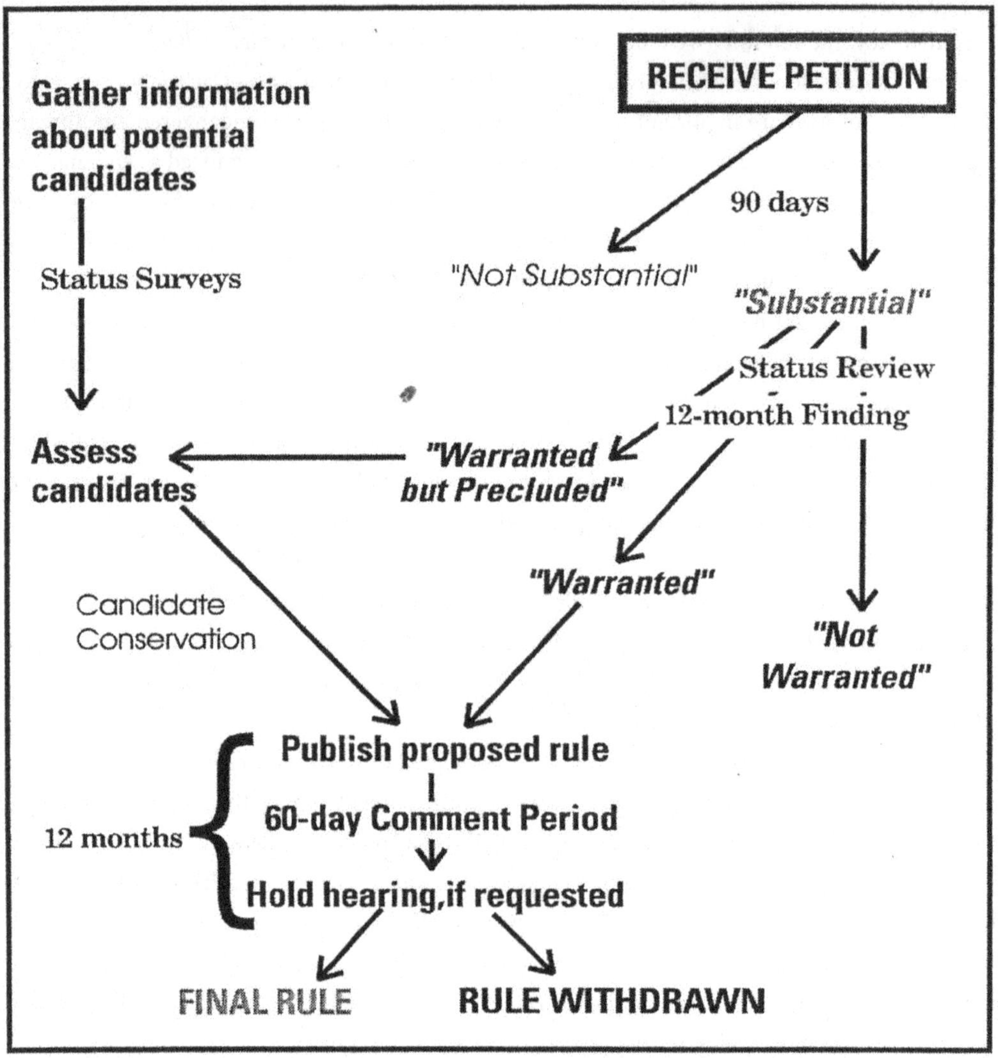

The flowchart above also shows that the FWS can "gather information about potential candidates," that is, a species, for listing, delisting, or reclassifying. If the action is deemed warranted, the species is moved to the "assess candidates" group, the same group that collects "warranted but precluded" actions. Candidates in this group must be reassessed each year to determine if the precluded designation is no longer required. Any warranted action then follows the procedures required by the APA for the creation of a new regulation. It should also be noted that all components of the foregoing process are made known because they are required to be published in the *Federal Register* (F.R.).

Paragraph 5 indicates that this process was followed for two distinct population segments of grizzly bears and that the FWS found that both petitions presented substantial evidence to warrant reclassification from threatened to endangered. In the subsequent formal status review, the FWS "determined that reclassification in the Selkirk ecosystem was not warranted and that reclassification in the Cabinet/Yaak ecosystem was warranted but precluded by work on other species having a higher priority listing." This reasoning behind this decision of the FWS was published in the F.R. See the *Carlton v. Babbitt* folder on the Companion Website for the "Twelve-Month Administrative Finding" in 50 F.R. 8250 (1993).

Paragraph 6 adds that the present lawsuit was initiated pursuant to the citizen suit provisions of the E.S.A. at 16 U.S.C. § 1540(g)(2), which requires plaintiffs *to serve* the defendants within a 60-day waiting period. This was done for each of the two bear populations at issue. On cross-motions for summary judgment by the defendants, the court consolidated the two civil actions.

Paragraphs 7 and 8 remind us of the standards for review previously described in Chapter 12. Review of agency actions is governed by the A.P.A, as codified in 5 U.S.C. § 706, and available at https://www.govinfo.gov/content/pkg/USCODE-2010-title5/pdf/USCODE-2010-title5-partI-chap7-sec706.pdf. It states:

> To the extent necessary to decision and when presented, the reviewing court shall decide all relevant questions of law, interpret constitutional and statutory provisions, and determine the meaning or applicability of the terms of an agency action. The reviewing court shall—
>
> (1) compel agency action unlawfully withheld or unreasonably delayed; and
>
> (2)hold unlawful and set aside agency action, findings, and conclusions found to be—
>
> (A) arbitrary, capricious, an abuse of discretion, or otherwise not in accordance with law;
>
> (B) contrary to constitutional right, power, privilege, or immunity;
>
> (C) in excess of statutory jurisdiction, authority, or limitations, or short of statutory right;
>
> (D) without observance of procedure required by law;
>
> (E) unsupported by substantial evidence in a case subject to sections 556 and 557 of this title or otherwise reviewed on the record of an agency hearing provided by statute; or
>
> (F) unwarranted by the facts to the extent that the facts are subject to trial de novo by the reviewing court.
>
> In making the foregoing determinations, the court shall review the whole record or those parts of it cited by a party, and due account shall be taken of the rule of prejudicial error.

The following two paragraphs introduce the standard of judicial review. In paragraph 7, the court cites subsections (A) and (D) of the above as relevant to this case. Paragraph 8 discusses the expertise of the FWS when noting that the "Court begins with a strong presumption in favor of upholding decisions of the FWS on the reclassification petitions." This is called the "deferential standard of review." Nevertheless, upon citing *Citizens to Preserve Overton Park v. Volpe*, the Court adds that it "must undertake a 'thorough, probing, in-depth review' of the agency's decision."

Paragraphs 9-27 discuss the distinct population segment of grizzly bears in the Selkirk ecosystem and are grouped together under the subheading "Selkirk Grizzly Bears." Paragraph 9 summarizes the findings of the FWS in the previously noted "12-Month Administrative Finding" that presumably supported its decision not to list this bear population as endangered. These findings include: a) that the only factor limiting population growth was human-caused mortality, which was described as decreasing; b) that survivorship, reproduction, and management programs were acceptable; and c) that the recovery zone for the Selkirk bears extends into Canada. All of these factors allowed the FWS to conclude that the Selkirk grizzlies were not endangered; that is, not in danger of extinction.

Paragraph 10 provides the factors required by the E.S.A. to be considered in any listing decision. Section 1533(a)(1) states:

> (1) The Secretary shall by regulation promulgated in accordance with subsection (b) determine whether any species is an endangered species or a threatened species because of any of the following factors:
>
> (A) the present or threatened destruction, modification, or curtailment of its habitat or range;
>
> (B) overutilization for commercial, recreational, scientific, or educational purposes;
>
> (C) disease or predation;
>
> (D) the inadequacy of existing regulatory mechanisms; or
>
> (E) other natural or manmade factors affecting its continued existence.

These factors are repeated at 50 C.F.R. § 424.11(c). These factors are important because they are repeated and examined in detail in this opinion.

Paragraph 11 follows these specific listing factors and summarizes the claims of the plaintiffs that: a) the Selkirk habitat is being destroyed and modified; b) poaching for bear parts, roadbuilding, mining, and timbering had caused direct and indirect overutilization of the grizzly species; c) grizzly bears face a high predation risk from humans; d) existing regulatory mechanisms have failed to reduce human-bear encounters; and e) the continued existence of this population segment is in danger because of low population numbers and low reproductive rates.

Defendants argue that they addressed all of these factors and, in paragraph 12, introduce a letter that more fully explains the FWS's reasoning. Plaintiffs argue that this letter "provides *post hoc rationalizations* for the FWS' otherwise deficient decision." This should sound familiar since the same issue was before the Supreme Court in *Citizens to Preserve Overton Park v. Volpe*. That case is cited here with a quote from the opinion that the "review of an agency's decision 'is to be based on the full administrative record that was before the [agency] at the time [it] made [its] decision.'" In paragraph 14, the court decided to allow the introduction of this letter because it did not "make new arguments or present new evidence," but merely "explains how the findings address each listing factor." Nevertheless, in paragraph 15 the court reveals some of the reasoning that will form the basis of its holding on the Selkirk grizzlies. While the letter "elucidates the agency's consideration of some of the five listing factors, it fails to demonstrate that the FWS fully and reasonably considered the others." In the case of human-caused mortality, the "letter actually undermines the bases for the decision of the FWS regarding the Selkirk grizzlies." Paragraph 16 begins an examination of the evidence provided by the FWS for each of the listing factors. With regard to the destruction or modification of the Selkirk grizzlies' habitat, the court found that the FWS had adequately explained that the Interagency Grizzly Bear Guidelines (see the *Carlton v. Babbitt* folder) "provide special grizzly bear habitat management areas within recovery zones and serve to 'accommodate conservation of grizzly bear habitat'" and that "additional land had been set aside as grizzly bear habitat," and timber extraction had been regulated to "minimize disturbance to the grizzlies." Discussion of listing factors "B" and "C" (overutilization and disease and predation) are combined in paragraphs 17, 18, and 19.

In both instances, the court finds that the "FWS has not sufficiently addressed whether there is overutilization of the Selkirk grizzly population . . . or whether the grizzly population is subject to disease and predation" (900 F. Supp. 532). The main issue is the allegation "that human-caused mortality is decreasing is not supported by the record" (*Id.*). After discussing the evidence of an increase in human-caused mortality, the court concludes that the agency failed to "explain the evidence which is available" or to make a "'rational connection between the facts found and the choice made.'" The court, therefore, holds that the "FWS must reconsider its findings and the available evidence regarding this issue."

Paragraphs 20 and 21 address the "inadequacy of existing regulatory mechanisms." The court found the evidence for the adequacy of the existing regulatory mechanisms insufficient because the FWS failed to properly consider human-caused mortality. The court reasoned that without an understanding of human-caused mortality it was impossible to determine if the existing "regulatory mechanisms" are inadequate and, further, that the FWS needed to provide a "more adequate explanation from the record to support its finding that the regulatory mechanisms are adequate."

The next five paragraphs are grouped under the heading "Other natural or manmade factors affecting the Selkirk grizzly's continued existence." The court finds that FWS has sufficiently addressed some, but not all, of the 'other natural or manmade factors affecting [the species] continued existence.'" The main "other factor" is the very small size of the Selkirk grizzly bear population (somewhere between 25 and 50 bears). The FWS provided no cogent analysis of population size even though it reported that the population was stable. In addition, the FWS did not address the issue of such a small population's vulnerability to extinction. Further, "the Court finds that the FWS could not properly support its finding that reproductive and survivorship rates are adequate without a better determination of the level or trend of human-caused mortality." In paragraph 25, the "plaintiffs assert that the low population makes the grizzlies more susceptible to sudden extinction from environmental stochasticity," that is, random events like fires, disease, or food availability. The defendants argued that the "contiguous Canadian ecosystem protects the Selkirk grizzlies from environmental and demographic stochasticity, as well as from inbreeding depression." While the court comes to no definitive conclusion, it states that while the "FWS considered the dangers of low population, its reliance on the contiguity of the Canadian ecosystem may require additional explanation." In paragraph 27, the court provides its holding, stating that the FWS "failed to fully explain the evidence that was available and drew conclusions that cannot be supported by the evidence on the record. Accordingly, the decision was arbitrary and capricious and must be remanded to the agency for further consideration."

The grizzly bears of the Cabinet/Yaak ecosystem are discussed paragraphs 28-39. While reclassification of the Cabinet/Yaak grizzlies from threatened to endangered was determined by the FWS to be warranted, such reclassification was also determined to be precluded "by work on other species having a higher priority for listing." Paragraph 29 refers to § 1533(b)(3)(B)(iii) of the E.S.A. that states:

> (I) The petitioned action is warranted, but that—
>
> (II) the immediate proposal and timely promulgation of a final regulation implementing the petitioned action in accordance with paragraphs (5) and (6) is precluded by pending proposals to determine whether any species is an endangered species or a threatened species, and
>
> (III) expeditious progress is being made to add qualified species to either of the lists published under subsection (c) and to remove from such lists species for which the protections of this chapter are no longer necessary, in which case the Secretary shall promptly publish such finding in the Federal Register, together with a description and evaluation of the reasons and data on which the finding is based.

The court adds that "this provision gives the agency discretion to direct its energy and resources to those species most in need of listing, reclassification or delisting" and that in the 1982 amendments to the E.S.A. that added this provision, Congress (in a House Conference report) stated that the "'listing process should utilize a scientifically based priority system to list and delist species, subspecies, and populations based on the degree of threat, and proceed in an efficient manner.'"

Paragraph 30 adds that in the following year the "FWS issued Priority Guidelines setting forth a scientifically based priority system for listing, reclassifying, and delisting species." (See 48 F.R. 43, 098 (1983), available in the Companion). The court adds that "through the Guidelines the FWS seeks to make the most appropriate use of the limited resources available to implement the Act." Listing endangered and threatened species is the most critical way to implement the Act. The immense backlog of species on the "warranted but precluded" candidates list and the appropriate use of the limited resources provided by Congress to implement the Act will be discussed later on.

In paragraphs 31 and 32, we learn that these "Priority Guidelines establish 12 priority categories" and that, according to this priority system, only species with a ranking of 1 or 2 could be listed and that the Cabinet/Yaak grizzlies had a ranking of six, which precluded their reclassification from threatened to endangered. In paragraphs 33 and 34, we learn that the plaintiffs "argue that the FWS abused its discretion" by "blindly" following the Guidelines and not using its discretion to think "outside-the-box" at the actual evidence available. The court agreed with the FWS. Most importantly, "the highest listing priority a particular grizzly bear population can receive is a three because various grizzly bear populations, including the Cabinet/Yaak grizzly bears, are listed as a subspecies." Moreover, the "Court concludes that the defendants adequately explained the manner in which they exercised their discretion in following the 1983 Policy Guidelines and provided adequate support for their application of the Guidelines to rank the Cabinet/Yaak grizzly."

Paragraphs 35-37 discuss the requirements of the E.S.A. "To properly invoke the warranted but precluded finding, the United Sates Fish and Wildlife Service (FWS) first must show that it is actively working on other pending proposals to determine whether any species is endangered or threatened. Second, it must demonstrate that it is, in fact, making expeditious progress in listing, reclassifying, or delisting other species. Third, it must publish its findings regarding whether it is making expeditious progress on other pending proposals." The court finds that the FWS "has failed to demonstrate" that it has met the first two of these "statutorily mandated requirements" and, further, that "there is no evidence that it has published findings in this regard." Thus, citing *Citizens to Preserve Overton Park v. Volpe*, there is no record that the court can use to determine whether the FWS has made "expeditious progress" as it had claimed.

Paragraphs 38 and 39 discuss the defendants' claims that 16 U.S.C. § 1533(b)(3)(B)(iii) "should be strictly construed to give the FWS discretion to deny listing to a species only if the agency is financially precluded from doing so." The Court responds by stating that the "plaintiffs ask the Court to read requirements into Section 1533(b)(3)(B)(iii) that do not appear in the language of the statute or its legislative history . . . Accordingly, the Court will not require the FWS to show that reclassifying the Cabinet-Yaak grizzlies is financially precluded." Having dismissed the financial issue, the Court summarizes its holding in paragraph 39 by stating that "the FWS must consider and support any finding that is made in accordance with the 1992 Guidelines and, if it maintains its warranted but precluded finding, it must show that it is making expeditious progress on other pending proposals."

Paragraphs 40-45 provide a summary of the court's two holdings: 1) its holding that the "reclassification of the Selkirk grizzly bear population as endangered is not warranted is arbitrary and capricious because defendants failed to sufficiently explain how they exercised their discretion with regard to the statutory listing factors and drew conclusions that cannot be supported by the evidence in the record," and 2) the court's holding that "defendant's decision that reclassification of the Cabinet/Yaak grizzly bear population as endangered is warranted but precluded is arbitrary and capricious because defendants have failed to supply the requisite reasoned analysis" in the record by publishing results showing it was making expeditious progress on other petitions. The court then gives the FWS 90 days to correct these shortcomings.

Miscellaneous Commentary and Other Issues

The FWS does correct the shortcomings that caused the arbitrary and capricious rulings and, thus, both the Selkirk and Cabinet/Yaak grizzly bear populations remain (to this day) threatened species. The recovery plans and present status of these and other grizzly bear populations can be found in the *Carlton v. Babbitt* folder on the Companion Website.

The current number of species of fungi, plants, and animals described by scientists in the U.S. is around 200,000. The number of species yet to be discovered and described in the U.S. is conservatively estimated to be 300,000-400,000. This is discussed in "A remarkable array: species diversity in the United States" (Stein, et al. 2000) in the book *Precious Heritage: The Status of Biodiversity in the United States.* Wilcove and Master (2005) (see the *Carlton v. Babbitt* folder on the Companion Website) estimate that only 15% of the known species in the U.S. have been sufficiently studied to determine whether they are threatened with endangerment. They also indicate that the actual number of species threatened with endangerment is easily ten times the number currently listed as threatened or endangered (i.e., 948 plants and 1464 animals).

Unless listed as endangered or threatened, a species has none of the protections of the E.S.A. The FWS and NMFS are limited by the funding provided by Congress and they must determine how to best allocate these resources. As a result, a struggle developed between the FWS/ NMFS and a number of environmental organizations because of the backlog of species that were warranted but precluded. These species had remained on the Candidates' list for years, even decades. Numerous court cases became costly and time-consuming. Negotiations with the FWS began and The Center for Biological Diversity (the descendant of the Biodiversity Legal Foundation and the legacy of Jasper Carlton who died in 2015) fought for and won a historic landmark legal agreement in 2011 with the FWS to move 757 imperiled species toward E.S.A. protections. The press release (8/12/11 - see the *Carlton v. Babbitt* folder on the Companion Website) from Center for Biological Diversity stated:

> A federal judge today approved a landmark legal agreement between the Center for Biological Diversity and the U.S. Fish and Wildlife Service requiring the agency to make initial or final

> decisions on whether to add hundreds of imperiled plants and animals to the federal endangered species list by 2018 …
>
> 'The court's approval today will allow this historic agreement to move forward, speeding protection for as many as 757 of America's most imperiled species,' said Noah Greenwald, endangered species director at the Center. 'The historic agreement gives species like the Pacific walrus, American wolverine and California golden trout a shot at survival.'
>
> The Center wrote scientific listing petitions and/or filed lawsuits to protect the 757 species as part of its decade-long campaign to safeguard 1,000 of America's most imperiled, least protected species. Spanning every taxonomic group, the species protected by the agreement include 26 birds, 31 mammals, 67 fish, 22 reptiles, 33 amphibians, 197 plants and 381 invertebrates.
>
> 'With approval of the agreement, species from across the nation will be protected,' said Greenwald. 'Habitat destruction, climate change, invasive species and other factors are pushing species toward extinction in all 50 states, and this agreement will help turn the tide.'
>
> Individual species included in the agreement include the walrus, wolverine, Mexican gray wolf, New England cottontail rabbit, three species of sage grouse, scarlet Hawaiian honeycreeper ('i'iwi), California golden trout and Rio Grande cutthroat trout – as well as 403 southeastern river-dependent species, 42 Great Basin springs nails and 32 Pacific Northwest mollusks.
>
> The agreement, formalized today with the judge's approval, was signed by the Center and the Fish and Wildlife Service on July 12. Already dozens of species have been proposed for listing, including the Miami blue butterfly, one of the rarest butterflies in the United States.
>
> While the agreement encompasses nearly all the species on the U.S. Fish and Wildlife Service's official list of 'candidates' for Endangered Species Act protection, two-thirds of the species in the agreement (499) are not on the list. This corresponds with the conclusion of numerous scientists and scientific societies that the extinction crisis is vastly greater than existing federal priority systems and budgets.

There is abundant information on the web on these issues. For instance, The Center for Biological Diversity's website at https://www.biologicaldiversity.org/ lists the rare plants and animals for which the Center has won protection. Also, the FWS has an Environmental Conservation Online System that gives the number of species listed as endangered or threatened for each year, https://ecos.fws.gov/ecp/. The data shows a seven-year national listing workplan, https://www.fws.gov/endangered/esa-library/pdf/Listing%207-Year%20Workplan%20Sept%202016.pdf.

Study Questions for Carlton v. Babbit

1. Who are the plaintiffs and defendants in this case? What are the basic facts and procedural history of this case? What was the cause of action?

2. Are distinct population segments of an endangered or threatened species protected? Explain, citing the appropriate section of the E.S.A.

3. What population segments were at issue here? What was the finding of the FWS regarding the reclassification of the Selkirk and Cabinet/Yak grizzlies from threatened to endangered?

4. Cite and briefly explain the relevant section of the Administrative Procedures Act (APA) that formed the basis for the judicial review obtained by the plaintiffs in *Carlton v. Babbit.* What is the "deferential standard of review," and how is this standard qualified by the precedent set in *Citizens to Preserve Overton Park v. Volpe*?

5. What are the "factors" that must be reviewed when considering listing changes? See 50 C.F.R. § 424.11(c).

6. What was the holding and reasoning regarding the Selkirk grizzlies?

7. What was the "negative finding" with regard to the Cabinet/Yak grizzly bear population that prompted the plaintiffs' lawsuit in *Carlton v. Babbitt*? What remedy did the plaintiffs seek?

8. Explain the judge's finding in the Cabinet/Yak portion of *Carlton v. Babbitt.* What was the remedy? How did this finding utilize the *Overton Park* case? The APA?

9. What was the end result of this lawsuit for these two population segments of grizzly bears?

10. What is the Candidates' List? What role has the Jasper Carlton Foundation and the Center for Biological Diversity played in listing new species as endangered?

United States of America v. James E. Billie, 667 F. Supp.1485 (S.D. Florida, 1987)

Read the opinion in U.S. v. Billie, on Justia, at https://law.justia.com/cases/federal/district-courts/FSupp/667/1485/2158741/. Review the *Study Questions for U.S. v. Billie* on the Companion Website, at http:// www.environmentallaw-teach.org/. You will also find images and commentary on the

Florida panther and Billie himself. As you read *U.S. v. Billie,* note its organization with headings and subheadings. Download the decision or print it, color-code it or number the paragraphs as you go and focus on how the information in each paragraph fits into the rubrics for a brief noted below:

1. Heading

2. Facts

3. Procedural History

4. Legal Issues

5. Holding or Decision

6. Reasoning

7. Dissenting Opinions

This case was heard by the U.S. District Court of the Southern District of Florida and is important for us as a vehicle to gain an understanding of how the E.S.A. is enforced. It is also significant because of the religious and First Amendment issues that are raised.

The first two paragraphs following the last name of the District Judge, Paine, introduce the procedural issues at hand in the motion to dismiss. However, they delineate the legal issues in the case in a confusing manner. Legal issue #1 is the validity (or in Billie's view, the invalidity) of the E.S.A.'s application "to acts without a commercial purpose on the Seminole Indian Reservation." This case involves hunting. Legal issue #2 involves the dismissal of the indictment ("information") for multiplicity (more than one charge for the same offense). Legal issue #3 asks whether the "possession count of the information violates his right to freedom of religion under the First Amendment." Issue #4 asks whether Billie had the requisite *mens rea* (state of mind to establish guilt). The issue of "selective prosecution on the basis of national origin" was eliminated when the court denied this motion at a pretrial hearing. Paragraph 3, titled, "Background," introduces the case: James Billie (the defendant) was charged in a two-count information with the taking and subsequent possession of a Florida panther, in violation of the E.S.A. These charges originate from 16 U.S.C. §1538—Prohibited acts, specifically, 16 U.S.C. § 1538(a)(1)(B) and 16 U.S.C. § 1538(a)(1)(D). Section 1540—Penalties and enforcement is added because § 1540(b)(1) involves criminal violations. The Florida panther is, of course, listed as endangered. James Billie is a member of the Seminole Indian Tribe, and all of the "acts complained of in the information were committed" three and one-half years earlier on the Big Cypress Seminole Indian Reservation.

Discussion of legal issue #1 begins in paragraph 4, the first under the heading "Applicability of Endangered Species Act to Seminole Indian Reservations." The critical question to be answered by the court is, given the plain language of the E.S.A., whether there was "Congressional intent to abrogate or modify his traditional right to hunt and fish on the reservation." The court does not find precedent in the Eleventh Circuit, so is bringing up persuasive cases from other circuits. The *Billie* court invokes the Eighth Circuit's *en banc* opinion in *Dion,* which held that the E.S.A. did not apply to Indians exercising non-commercial hunting rights on Indian land. However, it notes that *United States v. Dion,* 752 F.2d 1261 (8th Cir. 1985) was reversed by the Supreme Court, on grounds not related to the appellate court's finding on hunting rights and the E.S.A. The Supreme Court "expressly left unresolved the question of whether the Act abrogates Indian hunting rights" (667 F. Supp. 1487). The *en banc* decision (the full bench, that is, a panel of judges larger than that required to hear an appeal) is, therefore, persuasive (but not binding) authority for the Southern District of Florida in the Eleventh Circuit. Therefore, this is a question of first impression in the Eleventh Circuit.

In addressing legal issue #1, paragraphs 5 and 6 give information that has already been reviewed in previous opinions discussed in this chapter. Information on the historic and present range of the Florida panther can be found in the *U.S. v. Billie* folder on the Companion Website.

Paragraph 7 points to "several extraordinarily narrow exceptions to the Act's prohibitions." Of relevance to issue #1 is the fact that §1539—Exceptions, specifically subsection (e), allows that "Indians, Aleuts, or Eskimos residing in Alaska may take endangered or threatened species, but only such taking is for subsistence purposes" but such taking is "subject to such regulations as the Secretary may issue" subject to the Secretary's determination that such takings are to not materially and negatively affect the species. In spite of this special exception for Alaskan natives, no such exceptions are to be found in the E.S.A. for any other Indian tribe.

Paragraphs 8 and 9 discuss hunting rights on the Seminole Indian Reservation. The Supreme Court, while not ruling specifically on the E.S.A. and hunting rights, stated: "[a]s a general rule, Indians enjoy exclusive treaty rights to hunt and fish on lands reserved to them, unless such rights were clearly relinquished by treaty or have been modified by Congress" (*Menominee Tribe of Indians v. United States,* 391 U.S. 404). The Court adds that "although the Congress is empowered to abrogate Indian rights, its intent to do so must be clear and plain."

Paragraph 12 relies on the Supreme Court decision in *Puyallup Tribe, Inc. v. Department of Game,* 433 U.S. 165 (1977), that Indian treaty rights do not extend to the point of extinction. In *Puyallup Tribe,* the Supreme Court established that

> when the life of a steelhead is so precarious in a particular stream that all fishing should be banned until the species regains assurance of survival, the police power of the State is adequate

> to prevent the steelhead from following the fate of the passenger pigeon; and the Treaty does not give the Indians a federal right to pursue the last living steelhead until it enters their nets (391 U.S. 392).

In paragraphs 13 and 14, the Court cites *Northern Arapahoe Tribe v. Hodel,* 808 F.2d 741 (10th Cir. 1987) to illustrate "that Indian rights to hunt and fish are not absolute. Where conservation measures are necessary to protect endangered wildlife, the Government can intervene on behalf of other federal interests." Further in paragraph 15, the Court states: "[t]he Endangered Species Act is such a measure. Its general comprehensiveness, its nonexclusion of Indians, and the limited exceptions for certain Alaskan natives, *see supra* pt. II(A), demonstrate that Congress considered Indian interests, balanced them against conservation needs, and defined the extent to which Indians would be permitted to take protected wildlife." Supra means something discussed earlier or "above."

Paragraphs 16-18 address in a somewhat exhausting manner the legislative history and intent with regard to the "evidence that Congress intended to subject Indians to its prohibitions." In all of these paragraphs, the Court "infers" congressional intent from what was not passed or pursued. The Court examines testimony from the House (on a bill that wasn't passed) in which a subcommittee member asked for a list of endangered species on Indian lands. This list included the Florida panther. The subcommittee member asserts: "[s]tatements made by the Committee indicate its desire to prohibit American Indians from continuing such hunting or fishing, exemplifying a concern for the perile [sic] of our endangered species and the presumed inconsistency therewith in permitting American Indians to perhaps extinguish a species in the name of treaty rights."

Paragraphs 19 and 20 contain the basic reasoning for the court's holding on issue #1. "The legislative history must be considered along with the plain language of the Act. The narrow Alaskan exception, the inclusion of Indians within the Act's definition of 'person,' the Act's general comprehensiveness, and the evidence that the House committee desired to prohibit Indians from hunting and fishing protected species all provide 'clear evidence that Congress actually considered the conflict between its intended action on the one hand and Indian treaty rights on the other, and chose to resolve that conflict by abrogating the Indian rights." (*Dion,* 106 S.Ct. at 2216). Thus, "this court's conclusion that the Endangered Species Act applies to hunting by Indians on the Seminole reservations is based on both the character of their hunting rights and on the Act's abrogation of those rights. On-reservation hunting rights are not absolute when a species such as the Florida panther is in danger of extinction. To the extent that evidence of congressional abrogation of these rights is required, that standard has been met." When Congress passed the E.S.A., "it could not have intended that the Indians would have the unfettered right to kill the last handful of Florida panthers." Thus, the E.S.A. is valid and in full force when "applied to acts without a commercial purpose on the Seminole Indian Reservation."

Analysis of legal issue #4, Billie's *mens rea* or "the state of mind required for criminal violations of the Act," is found in paragraphs 21-27, and refers to 16 U.S.C. 1540—Penalties and enforcement. The Court then explains why the state only needs to prove general intent.

The distinction between general and specific intent is not addressed, though the distinction is central to the argument. Intent is a state of mind in which the person knows and desires the consequences of his or her act. Clearly, Billie intended to shoot the animal and to possess it. This, as Footnote 4 indicates, is general intent - the "defendant intended to do the proscribed act." Specific intent is essential for particular crimes, such as first-degree murder, which requires planning so that the crime is determined to be willful and premeditated. So, does the criminal taking of an endangered species require general or specific intent? Billie argues that "Congress must have meant something when it used the word 'knowingly.'" But the Court responds by indicating that "the legislative history of the Act indicates that Congress 'did not intend to make knowledge of the law an element' of a criminal violation." That is, ignorance of the law is no defense for Billie. Further, the Court states that "the word 'knowingly' means 'that the act was done voluntarily and intentionally and not because of mistake or accident.'" In addition, "such a definition comports with the general rule that criminal penalties attached to regulatory statutes intended to protect public health, safety, or welfare should be construed to effectuate their purpose." The Court's holding then follows: "Accordingly, the Government need prove only that the defendant acted with general intent when he shot the animal in question."

Paragraphs 24-27 discuss Billie's argument "that he could not have had the requisite *mens rea* to violate the Act because its applicability to on-reservation hunting by Indians was vague or highly debatable." Again, the Court turns to the Eighth Circuit decision in *Dion. Billie* uses the *Dion* decisions to "demonstrate that the Act's applicability to Indian land is so unclear that his intent to violate it could not be proved." Paragraph 25 begins with the important distinction that this "argument might be persuasive were intent to violate the law an element of the crime." Intent to violate the law should be understood to be a specific intent. The Court then states that "the statutes under which Billie has been charged require the Government to prove he acted not 'willfully' but 'knowingly'" and "the Eleventh Circuit pattern jury instructions specifically distinguish 'knowingly' from 'willfully,' which is defined as 'voluntarily and purposely, with the specific intent to do something the law forbids.'" And, finally, "because the Act applies to Indian lands, *see supra* pt. II, and does not require specific intent, the Government need not prove that Billie knew the Act applied to his on-reservation hunting in order to convict him."

Paragraphs 28-30 resolve issue #2 in which "Billie contends that the information must be dismissed for multiplicity, which is 'the charging of a single offense in more than one count.'" Billie was charged with two offenses: the taking; and the possession, carrying, and transportation of a Florida panther. The Court applies the *Blockburger* test: "where the same act or transaction constitutes a violation of two distinct statutory provisions, the test to be applied to determine whether there are two offenses or only one is whether each provision requires proof of an additional fact which the other does not." The prohibition against a "take" of an endangered species is set forth in 16 U.S.C. § 1538(a)(1)(B). The term "take" is specifically defined in 16 U.S.C. § 1532(19) and includes "shoot[ing], wound[ing], [or] kill[ing]" an endangered or threatened species. The prohibition against possessing, selling, delivering, carrying, transporting, or shipping is set out separately in 16 U.S.C. §1538(a)(1)(D). Both infractions require separate evidence and the evidence required for one offense has no bearing on the evidence required for the second offense. Hence, the Court held that the "motion to dismiss for multiplicity should be denied."

Paragraphs 31-45 deal at length with legal issue #3, "that the possession charge violates his right to freedom of religion under the First Amendment." Billie argues that "the Act is overbroad either on its face or as applied to him" and "the Act is unconstitutional because it sweeps within its ambit his constitutionally-protected practices."

Paragraphs 32 and 33 deal with "Facial Overbreadth." The Court cites a Supreme Court case—*Members of the City Council of the City of Los Angeles v. Taxpayers for Vincent,* 466 U.S. 789 (1984)—and states that a "statute is overbroad on its face if it is unconstitutional in every application or if it seeks to prohibit such a broad range of protected conduct that it is unconstitutional-ally overbroad." The Court then quotes from the opinion that for a determination of substantial overbreadth "'there must be a realistic danger that the statute itself will significantly compromise recognized First Amendment protections of parties not before the court for it to be facially challenged on overbreadth grounds.'" In paragraph 33 the Court reasons (again citing a Supreme Court decision) that "the possible constitutional applications of the Act are too numerous to conceive. The possibility that it might be unconstitutionally applied to certain religious practices does not render it void on its face where the remainder of the statute covers a whole range of easily identifiable and constitutionally proscribable conduct." Thus, the Court holds that the E.S.A. is not unconstitutionally overbroad and "Billie, therefore, must demonstrate that the Act is unconstitutional as applied to him."

Paragraph 34 begins the discussion of unconstitutional overbreadth as applied to Billie himself with the statement that "[n]ot all burdens on religion are unconstitutional." This is supported by the Supreme Court opinion in *Bowen v. Roy,* 476 U.S. 693 (1986). Quoting from *Cantwell v. Connecticut,* 310 U.S. 296 (1940), the Court adds that the "Free Exercise Clause 'embraces two concepts, - freedom to believe and freedom to act. The first is absolute but, in the nature of things, the second cannot be. Conduct remains subject to regulation for the protection of society.'" The Court, citing *United States v. Lee,* 455 U.S. 252 (1982), and giving several examples, states that "every practice an actor might classify as religious is not absolutely protected from governmental regulation."

In paragraph 35, the Court defines "unconstitutionally overbroad" under the E.S.A. The test has two prongs. "First, the law must regulate conduct rather than belief. Second, the law must have both a secular purpose and a secular effect" (*Grosz v. City of Miami Beach* 721 F.2d 729 (1983)). The Court finds that the government met the test. Drawing from the same opinion, the

Court "next 'faces the difficult task of balancing governmental interests against the impugned religious interest,'" and that this "'balance depends upon the cost to the Government of altering its activity to allow the religious practice to continue unimpeded versus the cost to the religious interest imposed by the Government activity.'"

In order to address the balancing of governmental interests against Billie's religious interests, paragraphs 37-40 emphasize that the Florida panther is endangered and its population is presently small and confined entirely to southern Florida where the Seminole Indian Reservation is located. Given the low population numbers and that the Recovery Plan for the Florida panther includes three distinct population centers (there were only two), allowing the hunting of the Florida panther for religious purposes would cause substantial harm.

In paragraph 41, "having assessed the governmental interest," the Court determines that it "must next balance it against the defendant's asserted religious interest in possessing" the Florida panther. In paragraph 42, we learn that the evidence consists largely of the testimony of Seminole medicine men who tell the Court "that panther parts are an important part of a medicine man's bundle. It is commonly known that panther claws and tails are used for different ailments, and a medicine man should have them on hand in case they are needed to minister to a particular illness." In paragraph 43, we learn that Billie testified that he is only a beginner in the practice of Seminole medicine and that "he had no thoughts regarding what he would do with the panther carcass after he shot it until the morning on which it was seized. At that time, it occurred to Billie that he could give it as a gift to a medicine man in order to humble himself. In bestowing such a high honor, Billie hoped that he would be able to learn more medicine."

In paragraph 44, the Court describes the standards that are used to balance the government's and Billie' religious interests. Citing another Supreme Court case, the Court quotes that "[t]o be protected by the Free Exercise Clause, a belief or practice must be 'rooted in religion.'" *Thomas v. Review Board of the Indiana Employment Security Division*, 450 U.S. 707 (1981). The Court then states that "where a party asserts, however, that otherwise lawful and secular governmental action should be prohibited, he must show a constitutionally cognizable infringement of a First Amendment right," *Sequoyah v. Tennessee Valley Authority*, 620 F.2d 1159 (1980) but it settled for a high standard of cognizant religious practice. The Court did not find that Billie had adequately shown that the possession of panther parts was central to the religious ceremony or ritual he practiced. Although there was testimony that panther parts were important to healing, after having viewed the witnesses, the panther parts were not essential.

In paragraph 45, the Court concludes that "the evidence has not adequately shown that Billie's religious interest in possessing panther parts should outweigh the compelling governmental interest in protecting the Florida panther." The Court holds that Billie's motion to dismiss the charges for overbreadth is denied and, thus, the government wins on all four issues.

Miscellaneous Commentary and Other Issues

In late August of 1987, a Federal District Court declared a mistrial in the prosecution that followed the decision in *U.S. v. Billie.* The deadlocked jury voted 7-5 for a not guilty verdict. It is important to note that Billie was originally arrested by state police and brought to trial in state court. Because Billie's attorney made counterclaims, the case was removed to the Federal District Court. The District Court judge did not permit any arguments about Billie's right to hunt on the Seminole Indian Reservation or about his First Amendment freedom of religion rights. The defense argued that Billie shot the panther on a dark night, that he only saw a pair of glowing eyes, and that the endangered Florida panther is difficult to distinguish from other cougar subspecies. The state and federal governments declined to retry Billie.

James Billie is an important member of the Seminole Indian Tribe and was chairman of the tribe for 27 years. He led the tribe in its successful landmark case before the Supreme Court in *Seminole Tribe of Florida v. Florida*, 517 U.S. 44 (1996). Billie had an early hardscrabble life in which he learned to catch and wrestle small alligators in tourist shows. Later he was attached to Special Commando Units of the Army during the Vietnam War. In addition, he was a musician and was nominated for a Grammy for his song BIG ALLIGATOR (or "Hal Pate Chobee" in Seminole), available at https://www.youtube.com/watch?v=jDl4U9ZiZzk.

Study Questions for U.S. v. Billie

1. What violations of the E.S.A. did Billie commit?

2. While there were several issues before the court, the main issue was whether the Endangered Species Act applied to hunting by Indians on the Seminole reservations. What was the Court's holding and reasoning on this issue?

3. Another issue considered by the Court was whether Billie had the requisite *mens rea* to commit a violation of the E.S.A. What is *mens rea*?

4. Explain the meaning of "knowingly' in Section 1540(b)(1) of the E.S.A. Cite a case as precedent for your argument. What is the difference between general and specific intent? What was the Court's holding and reasoning on the question of the requisite *mens rea*?

5. Who may commence a civil action for an alleged violation of the E.S.A.? A criminal action? Explain and cite any relevant statutory reference.

6. Can a person who knowingly violates the E.S.A be imprisoned? Explain and cite any reference.

7. Billie argued that his offenses should be dismissed because of "multiplicity." What does this mean? What is the *Blockburger* test and what did it have to do with the Court's holding and reasoning on this issue?

8. Billie also argued that the E.S.A. is unconstitutionally overbroad and violates his right to his religious beliefs. What does "overbroad" mean in this context? What did the Court rule and why, with regard to this issue?

STUDY QUESTIONS AND THE CODIFIED VERSION OF THE ENDANGERED SPECIES ACT, 16 U.S.C.§§ 1531 ET SEQ.

The E.S.A. protects endangered species with a three-pronged approach of powerful prohibitions, far reaching mandates, and citizen standing.

1. Explain the significance of *16 U.S.C.* § 1538 for the three-pronged approach.

2. What is CITES and how is it incorporated into *16 U.S.C.* § 1538?

3. Are plants and animals treated differently in *16 U.S.C.* § 1538? Explain.

4. Explain the significance of *16 U.S.C.* § 1536 and § 1540 for the three-pronged approach.

16 U.S.C.
United States Code, 2017 Edition
Title 16 - CONSERVATION
CHAPTER 35 - ENDANGERED SPECIES
Sec. 1531 - Congressional findings and declaration of purposes and policy
From the U.S. Government Publishing Office, www.gpo.gov

§1531. Congressional findings and declaration of purposes and policy

(a) Findings

The Congress finds and declares that—

(1) various species of fish, wildlife, and plants in the United States have been rendered extinct as a consequence of economic growth and development untempered by adequate concern and conservation;
(2) other species of fish, wildlife, and plants have been so depleted in numbers that they are in danger of or threatened with extinction;
(3) these species of fish, wildlife, and plants are of esthetic, ecological, educational, historical, recreational, and scientific value to the Nation and its people;
(4) the United States has pledged itself as a sovereign state in the international community to conserve to the extent practicable the various species of fish or wildlife and plants facing extinction, pursuant to—

(A) migratory bird treaties with Canada and Mexico;

(B) the Migratory and Endangered Bird Treaty with Japan;

(C) the Convention on Nature Protection and Wildlife Preservation in the Western Hemisphere;

(D) the International Convention for the Northwest Atlantic Fisheries;

(E) the International Convention for the High Seas Fisheries of the North Pacific Ocean;

(F) the Convention on International Trade in Endangered Species of Wild Fauna and Flora; and

(G) other international agreements; and

(5) encouraging the States and other interested parties, through Federal financial assistance and a system of incentives, to develop and maintain conservation programs which meet national and international standards is a key to meeting the Nation's international commitments and to better safeguarding, for the benefit of all citizens, the Nation's heritage in fish, wildlife, and plants.

(b) Purposes

The purposes of this chapter are to provide a means whereby the ecosystems upon which endangered species and threatened species depend may be conserved, to provide a program for the conservation of such endangered species and threatened species, and to take such steps as may be appropriate to achieve the purposes of the treaties and conventions set forth in subsection (a) of this section.

(c) Policy

(1) It is further declared to be the policy of Congress that all Federal departments and agencies shall seek to conserve endangered species and threatened species and shall utilize their authorities in furtherance of the purposes of this chapter.

(2) It is further declared to be the policy of Congress that Federal agencies shall cooperate with State and local agencies to resolve water resource issues in concert with conservation of endangered species.

(Pub. L. 93–205, §2, Dec. 28, 1973, 87 Stat. 884; Pub. L. 96–159, §1, Dec. 28, 1979, 93 Stat. 1225; Pub. L. 97–304, §9(a), Oct. 13, 1982, 96 Stat. 1426; Pub. L. 100–478, title I, §1013(a), Oct. 7, 1988, 102 Stat. 2315.)

16 U.S.C.
United States Code, 2017 Edition
Title 16 - CONSERVATION
CHAPTER 35 - ENDANGERED SPECIES
Sec. 1532 - Definitions
From the U.S. Government Publishing Office, www.gpo.gov

§1532. Definitions

For the purposes of this chapter—

(1) The term "alternative courses of action" means all alternatives and thus is not limited to original project objectives and agency jurisdiction.
(2) The term "commercial activity" means all activities of industry and trade, including, but not limited to, the buying or selling of commodities and activities conducted for the purpose of facilitating such buying and selling: *Provided, however,* That it does not include exhibition of commodities by museums or similar cultural or historical organizations.
(3) The terms "conserve", "conserving", and "conservation" mean to use and the use of all methods and procedures which are necessary to bring any endangered species or threatened species to the point at which the measures provided pursuant to this chapter are no longer necessary. Such methods and procedures include, but are not limited to, all activities associated with scientific resources management such as research, census, law enforcement, habitat acquisition and maintenance, propagation, live trapping, and transplantation, and, in the extraordinary case where population pressures within a given ecosystem cannot be otherwise relieved, may include regulated taking.
(4) The term "Convention" means the Convention on International Trade in Endangered Species of Wild Fauna and Flora, signed on March 3, 1973, and the appendices thereto.
(5)(A) The term "critical habitat" for a threatened or endangered species means—

(i) the specific areas within the geographical area occupied by the species, at the time it is listed in accordance with the provisions of section 1533 of this title, on which are found those physical or biological features (I) essential to the conservation of the species and (II) which may require special management considerations or protection; and

(ii) specific areas outside the geographical area occupied by the species at the time it is listed in accordance with the provisions of section 1533 of this title, upon a determination by the Secretary that such areas are essential for the conservation of the species.

(B) Critical habitat may be established for those species now listed as threatened or endangered species for which no critical habitat has heretofore been established as set forth in subparagraph (A) of this paragraph.

(C) Except in those circumstances determined by the Secretary, critical habitat shall not include the entire geographical area which can be occupied by the threatened or endangered species.

(6) The term "endangered species" means any species which is in danger of extinction throughout all or a significant portion of its range other than a species of the Class Insecta determined by the Secretary to constitute a pest whose protection under the provisions of this chapter would present an overwhelming and overriding risk to man.

(7) The term "Federal agency" means any department, agency, or instrumentality of the United States.

(8) The term "fish or wildlife" means any member of the animal kingdom, including without limitation any mammal, fish, bird (including any migratory, nonmigratory, or endangered bird for which protection is also afforded by treaty or other international agreement), amphibian, reptile, mollusk, crustacean, arthropod or other invertebrate, and includes any part, product, egg, or offspring thereof, or the dead body or parts thereof.

(9) The term "foreign commerce" includes, among other things, any transaction—

(A) between persons within one foreign country;

(B) between persons in two or more foreign countries;

(C) between a person within the United States and a person in a foreign country; or

(D) between persons within the United States, where the fish and wildlife in question are moving in any country or countries outside the United States.

(10) The term "import" means to land on, bring into, or introduce into, or attempt to land on, bring into, or introduce into, any place subject to the jurisdiction of the United States, whether or not such landing, bringing, or introduction constitutes an importation within the meaning of the customs laws of the United States.

(11) Repealed. Pub. L. 97–304, §4(b), Oct. 13, 1982, 96 Stat. 1420.

(12) The term "permit or license applicant" means, when used with respect to an action of a Federal agency for which exemption is sought under section 1536 of this title, any person whose

application to such agency for a permit or license has been denied primarily because of the application of section 1536(a) of this title to such agency action.

(13) The term "person" means an individual, corporation, partnership, trust, association, or any other private entity; or any officer, employee, agent, department, or instrumentality of the Federal Government, of any State, municipality, or political subdivision of a State, or of any foreign government; any State, municipality, or political subdivision of a State; or any other entity subject to the jurisdiction of the United States.

(14) The term "plant" means any member of the plant kingdom, including seeds, roots and other parts thereof.

(15) The term "Secretary" means, except as otherwise herein provided, the Secretary of the Interior or the Secretary of Commerce as program responsibilities are vested pursuant to the provisions of Reorganization Plan Numbered 4 of 1970; except that with respect to the enforcement of the provisions of this chapter and the Convention which pertain to the importation or exportation of terrestrial plants, the term also means the Secretary of Agriculture.

(16) The term "species" includes any subspecies of fish or wildlife or plants, and any distinct population segment of any species of vertebrate fish or wildlife which interbreeds when mature.

(17) The term "State" means any of the several States, the District of Columbia, the Commonwealth of Puerto Rico, American Samoa, the Virgin Islands, Guam, and the Trust Territory of the Pacific Islands.

(18) The term "State agency" means any State agency, department, board, commission, or other governmental entity which is responsible for the management and conservation of fish, plant, or wildlife resources within a State.

(19) The term "take" means to harass, harm, pursue, hunt, shoot, wound, kill, trap, capture, or collect, or to attempt to engage in any such conduct.

(20) The term "threatened species" means any species which is likely to become an endangered species within the foreseeable future throughout all or a significant portion of its range.

(21) The term "United States", when used in a geographical context, includes all States.

(Pub. L. 93–205, §3, Dec. 28, 1973, 87 Stat. 885; Pub. L. 94–359, §5, July 12, 1976, 90 Stat. 913; Pub. L. 95–632, §2, Nov. 10, 1978, 92 Stat. 3751; Pub. L. 96–159, §2, Dec. 28, 1979, 93 Stat. 1225; Pub. L. 97–304, §4(b), Oct. 13, 1982, 96 Stat. 1420; Pub. L. 100–478, title I, §1001, Oct. 7, 1988, 102 Stat. 2306.)

16 U.S.C.
United States Code, 2017 Edition
Title 16 - CONSERVATION
CHAPTER 35 - ENDANGERED SPECIES
Sec. 1533 - Determination of endangered species and threatened species
From the U.S. Government Publishing Office, www.gpo.gov

§1533. Determination of endangered species and threatened species

(a) Generally

(1) The Secretary shall by regulation promulgated in accordance with subsection (b) determine whether any species is an endangered species or a threatened species because of any of the following factors:

(A) the present or threatened destruction, modification, or curtailment of its habitat or range;

(B) overutilization for commercial, recreational, scientific, or educational purposes;

(C) disease or predation;

(D) the inadequacy of existing regulatory mechanisms; or

(E) other natural or manmade factors affecting its continued existence.

(2) With respect to any species over which program responsibilities have been vested in the Secretary of Commerce pursuant to Reorganization Plan Numbered 4 of 1970—

(A) in any case in which the Secretary of Commerce determines that such species should—

(i) be listed as an endangered species or a threatened species, or

(ii) be changed in status from a threatened species to an endangered species, he shall so inform the Secretary of the Interior; who shall list such species in accordance with this section;

(B) in any case in which the Secretary of Commerce determines that such species should—

(i) be removed from any list published pursuant to subsection (c) of this section, or

(ii) be changed in status from an endangered species to a threatened species, he shall recommend such action to the Secretary of the Interior, and the Secretary of the Interior, if he concurs in the recommendation, shall implement such action; and

(C) the Secretary of the Interior may not list or remove from any list any such species, and may not change the status of any such species which are listed, without a prior favorable determination made pursuant to this section by the Secretary of Commerce.

(3)(A) The Secretary, by regulation promulgated in accordance with subsection (b) and to the maximum extent prudent and determinable—

(i) shall, concurrently with making a determination under paragraph (1) that a species is an endangered species or a threatened species, designate any habitat of such species which is then considered to be critical habitat; and

(ii) may, from time-to-time thereafter as appropriate, revise such designation.

(B)(i) The Secretary shall not designate as critical habitat any lands or other geographical areas owned or controlled by the Department of Defense, or designated for its use, that are subject to an integrated natural resources management plan prepared under section 670a of this title, if the Secretary determines in writing that such plan provides a benefit to the species for which critical habitat is proposed for designation.

(ii) Nothing in this paragraph affects the requirement to consult under section 1536(a)(2) of this title with respect to an agency action (as that term is defined in that section).

(iii) Nothing in this paragraph affects the obligation of the Department of Defense to comply with section 1538 of this title, including the prohibition preventing extinction and taking of endangered species and threatened species.

(b) Basis for determinations

(1)(A) The Secretary shall make determinations required by subsection (a)(1) solely on the basis of the best scientific and commercial data available to him after conducting a review of the status of the species and after taking into account those efforts, if any, being made by any State or foreign nation, or any political subdivision of a State or foreign nation, to protect such species, whether by predator control, protection of habitat and food supply, or other conservation practices, within any area under its jurisdiction; or on the high seas.

(B) In carrying out this section, the Secretary shall give consideration to species which have been—

(i) designated as requiring protection from unrestricted commerce by any foreign nation, or pursuant to any international agreement; or

(ii) identified as in danger of extinction, or likely to become so within the foreseeable future, by any State agency or by any agency of a foreign nation that is responsible for the conservation of fish or wildlife or plants.

(2) The Secretary shall designate critical habitat, and make revisions thereto, under subsection (a)(3) on the basis of the best scientific data available and after taking into consideration the economic impact, the impact on national security, and any other relevant impact, of specifying any particular area as critical habitat. The Secretary may exclude any area from critical habitat if he determines that the benefits of such exclusion outweigh the benefits of specifying such area as

part of the critical habitat, unless he determines, based on the best scientific and commercial data available, that the failure to designate such area as critical habitat will result in the extinction of the species concerned.

(3)(A) To the maximum extent practicable, within 90 days after receiving the petition of an interested person under section 553(e) of title 5, to add a species to, or to remove a species from, either of the lists published under subsection (c), the Secretary shall make a finding as to whether the petition presents substantial scientific or commercial information indicating that the petitioned action may be warranted. If such a petition is found to present such information, the Secretary shall promptly commence a review of the status of the species concerned. The Secretary shall promptly publish each finding made under this subparagraph in the Federal Register.

(B) Within 12 months after receiving a petition that is found under subparagraph (A) to present substantial information indicating that the petitioned action may be warranted, the Secretary shall make one of the following findings:

(i) The petitioned action is not warranted, in which case the Secretary shall promptly publish such finding in the Federal Register.

(ii) The petitioned action is warranted, in which case the Secretary shall promptly publish in the Federal Register a general notice and the complete text of a proposed regulation to implement such action in accordance with paragraph (5).

(iii) The petitioned action is warranted, but that—

(I) the immediate proposal and timely promulgation of a final regulation implementing the petitioned action in accordance with paragraphs (5) and (6) is precluded by pending proposals to determine whether any species is an endangered species or a threatened species, and

(II) expeditious progress is being made to add qualified species to either of the lists published under subsection (c) and to remove from such lists species for which the protections of this chapter are no longer necessary, in which case the Secretary shall promptly publish such finding in the Federal Register, together with a description and evaluation of the reasons and data on which the finding is based.

(C)(i) A petition with respect to which a finding is made under subparagraph (B)(iii) shall be treated as a petition that is resubmitted to the Secretary under subparagraph (A) on the date of such finding and that presents substantial scientific or commercial information that the petitioned action may be warranted.

(ii) Any negative finding described in subparagraph (A) and any finding described in subparagraph (B)(i) or (iii) shall be subject to judicial review.

(iii) The Secretary shall implement a system to monitor effectively the status of all species with respect to which a finding is made under subparagraph (B)(iii) and shall make prompt use of the authority under paragraph 7 [1] to prevent a significant risk to the well being of any such species.

(D)(i) To the maximum extent practicable, within 90 days after receiving the petition of an interested person under section 553(e) of title 5, to revise a critical habitat designation, the Secretary shall make a finding as to whether the petition presents substantial scientific information indicating that the revision may be warranted. The Secretary shall promptly publish such finding in the Federal Register.

(ii) Within 12 months after receiving a petition that is found under clause (i) to present substantial information indicating that the requested revision may be warranted, the Secretary shall determine how he intends to proceed with the requested revision, and shall promptly publish notice of such intention in the Federal Register.

(4) Except as provided in paragraphs (5) and (6) of this subsection, the provisions of section 553 of title 5 (relating to rulemaking procedures), shall apply to any regulation promulgated to carry out the purposes of this chapter.

(5) With respect to any regulation proposed by the Secretary to implement a determination, designation, or revision referred to in subsection (a)(1) or (3), the Secretary shall—

(A) not less than 90 days before the effective date of the regulation—

(i) publish a general notice and the complete text of the proposed regulation in the Federal Register, and

(ii) give actual notice of the proposed regulation (including the complete text of the regulation) to the State agency in each State in which the species is believed to occur, and to each county, or equivalent jurisdiction in which the species is believed to occur, and invite the comment of such agency, and each such jurisdiction, thereon;

(B) insofar as practical, and in cooperation with the Secretary of State, give notice of the proposed regulation to each foreign nation in which the species is believed to occur or whose citizens harvest the species on the high seas, and invite the comment of such nation thereon;

(C) give notice of the proposed regulation to such professional scientific organizations as he deems appropriate;

(D) publish a summary of the proposed regulation in a newspaper of general circulation in each area of the United States in which the species is believed to occur; and

(E) promptly hold one public hearing on the proposed regulation if any person files a request for such a hearing within 45 days after the date of publication of general notice.

(6)(A) Within the one-year period beginning on the date on which general notice is published in accordance with paragraph (5)(A)(i) regarding a proposed regulation, the Secretary shall publish in the Federal Register—

(i) if a determination as to whether a species is an endangered species or a threatened species, or a revision of critical habitat, is involved, either—

(I) a final regulation to implement such determination,

(II) a final regulation to implement such revision or a finding that such revision should not be made,

(III) notice that such one-year period is being extended under subparagraph (B)(i), or

(IV) notice that the proposed regulation is being withdrawn under subparagraph (B)(ii), together with the finding on which such withdrawal is based; or

(ii) subject to subparagraph (C), if a designation of critical habitat is involved, either—

(I) a final regulation to implement such designation, or

(II) notice that such one-year period is being extended under such subparagraph.

(B)(i) If the Secretary finds with respect to a proposed regulation referred to in subparagraph (A)(i) that there is substantial disagreement regarding the sufficiency or accuracy of the available data relevant to the determination or revision concerned, the Secretary may extend the one-year period specified in subparagraph (A) for not more than six months for purposes of soliciting additional data.

(ii) If a proposed regulation referred to in subparagraph (A)(i) is not promulgated as a final regulation within such one-year period (or longer period if extension under clause (i) applies) because the Secretary finds that there is not sufficient evidence to justify the action proposed by the regulation, the Secretary shall immediately withdraw the regulation. The finding on which a withdrawal is based shall be subject to judicial review. The Secretary may not propose a regulation that has previously been withdrawn under this clause unless he determines that sufficient new information is available to warrant such proposal.

(iii) If the one-year period specified in subparagraph (A) is extended under clause (i) with respect to a proposed regulation, then before the close of such extended period the Secretary shall publish in the Federal Register either a final regulation to implement the determination or revision concerned, a finding that the revision should not be made, or a notice of withdrawal of the regulation under clause (ii), together with the finding on which the withdrawal is based.

(C) A final regulation designating critical habitat of an endangered species or a threatened species shall be published concurrently with the final regulation implementing the determination that such species is endangered or threatened, unless the Secretary deems that—

(i) it is essential to the conservation of such species that the regulation implementing such determination be promptly published; or

(ii) critical habitat of such species is not then determinable, in which case the Secretary, with respect to the proposed regulation to designate such habitat, may extend the one-year period specified in subparagraph (A) by not more than one additional year, but not later than the close of such additional year the Secretary must publish a final regulation, based on such data as may be available at that time, designating, to the maximum extent prudent, such habitat.

(7) Neither paragraph (4), (5), or (6) of this subsection nor section 553 of title 5 shall apply to any regulation issued by the Secretary in regard to any emergency posing a significant risk to the well-being of any species of fish or wildlife or plants, but only if—
(A) at the time of publication of the regulation in the Federal Register the Secretary publishes therein detailed reasons why such regulation is necessary; and
(B) in the case such regulation applies to resident species of fish or wildlife, or plants, the Secretary gives actual notice of such regulation to the State agency in each State in which such species is believed to occur.

Such regulation shall, at the discretion of the Secretary, take effect immediately upon the publication of the regulation in the Federal Register. Any regulation promulgated under the authority of this paragraph shall cease to have force and effect at the close of the 240-day period following the date of publication unless, during such 240-day period, the rulemaking procedures which would apply to such regulation without regard to this paragraph are complied with. If at any time after issuing an emergency regulation the Secretary determines, on the basis of the best appropriate data available to him, that substantial evidence does not exist to warrant such regulation, he shall withdraw it.

(8) The publication in the Federal Register of any proposed or final regulation which is necessary or appropriate to carry out the purposes of this chapter shall include a summary by the Secretary of the data on which such regulation is based and shall show the relationship of such data to such regulation; and if such regulation designates or revises critical habitat, such summary shall, to the maximum extent practicable, also include a brief description and evaluation of those activities (whether public or private) which, in the opinion of the Secretary, if undertaken may adversely modify such habitat, or may be affected by such designation.

(c) Lists

(1) The Secretary of the Interior shall publish in the Federal Register a list of all species determined by him or the Secretary of Commerce to be endangered species and a list of all species determined by him or the Secretary of Commerce to be threatened species. Each list shall refer to the species contained therein by scientific and common name or names, if any, specify with respect to each such species over what portion of its range it is endangered or threatened, and specify any critical habitat within such range. The Secretary shall from time to time revise each list published under the authority of this subsection to reflect recent determinations, designations, and revisions made in accordance with subsections (a) and (b).
(2) The Secretary shall—

(A) conduct, at least once every five years, a review of all species included in a list which is published pursuant to paragraph (1) and which is in effect at the time of such review; and
(B) determine on the basis of such review whether any such species should—

(i) be removed from such list;

(ii) be changed in status from an endangered species to a threatened species; or

(iii) be changed in status from a threatened species to an endangered species.

Each determination under subparagraph (B) shall be made in accordance with the provisions of subsections (a) and (b).

(d) Protective regulations

Whenever any species is listed as a threatened species pursuant to subsection (c) of this section, the Secretary shall issue such regulations as he deems necessary and advisable to provide for the conservation of such species. The Secretary may by regulation prohibit with respect to any threatened species any act prohibited under section 1538(a)(1) of this title, in the case of fish or wildlife, or section 1538(a)(2) of this title, in the case of plants, with respect to endangered species; except that with respect to the taking of resident species of fish or wildlife, such regulations shall apply in any State which has entered into a cooperative agreement pursuant to section 1535(c) of this title only to the extent that such regulations have also been adopted by such State.

(e) Similarity of appearance cases

The Secretary may, by regulation of commerce or taking, and to the extent he deems advisable, treat any species as an endangered species or threatened species even though it is not listed pursuant to this section if he finds that—
(A) such species so closely resembles in appearance, at the point in question, a species which has been listed pursuant to such section that enforcement personnel would have substantial difficulty in attempting to differentiate between the listed and unlisted species;
(B) the effect of this substantial difficulty is an additional threat to an endangered or threatened species; and
(C) such treatment of an unlisted species will substantially facilitate the enforcement and further the policy of this chapter.

(f) Recovery plans

(1) The Secretary shall develop and implement plans (hereinafter in this subsection referred to as "recovery plans") for the conservation and survival of endangered species and threatened species

listed pursuant to this section, unless he finds that such a plan will not promote the conservation of the species. The Secretary, in developing and implementing recovery plans, shall, to the maximum extent practicable—

(A) give priority to those endangered species or threatened species, without regard to taxonomic classification, that are most likely to benefit from such plans, particularly those species that are, or may be, in conflict with construction or other development projects or other forms of economic activity;

(B) incorporate in each plan—

(i) a description of such site-specific management actions as may be necessary to achieve the plan's goal for the conservation and survival of the species;

(ii) objective, measurable criteria which, when met, would result in a determination, in accordance with the provisions of this section, that the species be removed from the list; and

(iii) estimates of the time required and the cost to carry out those measures needed to achieve the plan's goal and to achieve intermediate steps toward that goal.

(2) The Secretary, in developing and implementing recovery plans, may procure the services of appropriate public and private agencies and institutions, and other qualified persons. Recovery teams appointed pursuant to this subsection shall not be subject to the Federal Advisory Committee Act.

(3) The Secretary shall report every two years to the Committee on Environment and Public Works of the Senate and the Committee on Merchant Marine and Fisheries of the House of Representatives on the status of efforts to develop and implement recovery plans for all species listed pursuant to this section and on the status of all species for which such plans have been developed.

(4) The Secretary shall, prior to final approval of a new or revised recovery plan, provide public notice and an opportunity for public review and comment on such plan. The Secretary shall consider all information presented during the public comment period prior to approval of the plan.

(5) Each Federal agency shall, prior to implementation of a new or revised recovery plan, consider all information presented during the public comment period under paragraph (4).

(g) Monitoring

(1) The Secretary shall implement a system in cooperation with the States to monitor effectively for not less than five years the status of all species which have recovered to the point at which the measures provided pursuant to this chapter are no longer necessary and which, in accordance with the provisions of this section, have been removed from either of the lists published under subsection (c).

(2) The Secretary shall make prompt use of the authority under paragraph 7[2] of subsection (b) of this section to prevent a significant risk to the well being of any such recovered species.

(h) Agency guidelines; publication in Federal Register; scope; proposals and amendments: notice and opportunity for comments

The Secretary shall establish, and publish in the Federal Register, agency guidelines to insure that the purposes of this section are achieved efficiently and effectively. Such guidelines shall include, but are not limited to—

(1) procedures for recording the receipt and the disposition of petitions submitted under subsection (b)(3) of this section;

(2) criteria for making the findings required under such subsection with respect to petitions;

(3) a ranking system to assist in the identification of species that should receive priority review under subsection (a)(1) of this section; and

(4) a system for developing and implementing, on a priority basis, recovery plans under subsection (f) of this section.

The Secretary shall provide to the public notice of, and opportunity to submit written comments on, any guideline (including any amendment thereto) proposed to be established under this subsection.

(i) Submission to State agency of justification for regulations inconsistent with State agency's comments or petition

If, in the case of any regulation proposed by the Secretary under the authority of this section, a State agency to which notice thereof was given in accordance with subsection (b)(5)(A)(ii) files comments disagreeing with all or part of the proposed regulation, and the Secretary issues a final regulation which is in conflict with such comments, or if the Secretary fails to adopt a regulation pursuant to an action petitioned by a State agency under subsection (b)(3), the Secretary shall submit to the State agency a written justification for his failure to adopt regulations consistent with the agency's comments or petition.

(Pub. L. 93–205, §4, Dec. 28, 1973, 87 Stat. 886; Pub. L. 94–359, §1, July 12, 1976, 90 Stat. 911; Pub. L. 95–632, §§11, 13, Nov. 10, 1978, 92 Stat. 3764, 3766; Pub. L. 96–159, §3, Dec. 28, 1979, 93 Stat. 1225; Pub. L. 97–304, §2(a), Oct. 13, 1982, 96 Stat. 1411; Pub. L. 100–478, title I, §§1002–1004, Oct. 7, 1988, 102 Stat. 2306, 2307; Pub. L. 108–136, div. A, title III, §318, Nov. 24, 2003, 117 Stat. 1433.)

16 U.S.C.
United States Code, 2017 Edition
Title 16 – CONSERVATION
CHAPTER 35 - ENDANGERED SPECIES
Sec. 1534 - Land acquisition
From the U.S. Government Publishing Office, www.gpo.gov

§1534. Land acquisition

(a) Implementation of conservation program; authorization of Secretary and Secretary of Agriculture

The Secretary, and the Secretary of Agriculture with respect to the National Forest System, shall establish and implement a program to conserve fish, wildlife, and plants, including those which are listed as endangered species or threatened species pursuant to section 1533 of this title. To carry out such a program, the appropriate Secretary—
(1) shall utilize the land acquisition and other authority under the Fish and Wildlife Act of 1956, as amended [16 U.S.C. 742a et seq.], the Fish and Wildlife Coordination Act, as amended [16 U.S.C. 661 et seq.], and the Migratory Bird Conservation Act [16 U.S.C. 715 et seq.], as appropriate; and
(2) is authorized to acquire by purchase, donation, or otherwise, lands, waters, or interest therein, and such authority shall be in addition to any other land acquisition authority vested in him.

(b) Availability of funds for acquisition of lands, waters, etc.

Funds made available pursuant to chapter 2003 of title 54 may be used for the purpose of acquiring lands, waters, or interests therein under subsection (a) of this section.

(Pub. L. 93–205, §5, Dec. 28, 1973, 87 Stat. 889; Pub. L. 95–632, §12, Nov. 10, 1978, 92 Stat. 3766; Pub. L. 113–287, §5(d)(32), Dec. 19, 2014, 128 Stat. 3267.)

16 U.S.C.
United States Code, 2017 Edition
Title 16 – CONSERVATION
CHAPTER 35 - ENDANGERED SPECIES
Sec. 1535 - Cooperation with States
From the U.S. Government Publishing Office, www.gpo.gov

§1535. Cooperation with States

(a) Generally

In carrying out the program authorized by this chapter, the Secretary shall cooperate to the maximum extent practicable with the States. Such cooperation shall include consultation with the States concerned before acquiring any land or water, or interest therein, for the purpose of conserving any endangered species or threatened species.

(b) Management agreements

The Secretary may enter into agreements with any State for the administration and management of any area established for the conservation of endangered species or threatened species. Any revenues derived from the administration of such areas under these agreements shall be subject to the provisions of section 715s of this title.

(c) Cooperative agreements

(1) In furtherance of the purposes of this chapter, the Secretary is authorized to enter into a cooperative agreement in accordance with this section with any State which establishes and maintains an adequate and active program for the conservation of endangered species and threatened species. Within one hundred and twenty days after the Secretary receives a certified copy of such a proposed State program, he shall make a determination whether such program is in accordance with this chapter. Unless he determines, pursuant to this paragraph, that the State program is not in accordance with this chapter, he shall enter into a cooperative agreement with the State for the purpose of assisting in implementation of the State program. In order for a State program to be deemed an adequate and active program for the conservation of endangered species and threatened species, the Secretary must find, and annually thereafter reconfirm such finding, that under the State program—
(A) authority resides in the State agency to conserve resident species of fish or wildlife determined by the State agency or the Secretary to be endangered or threatened;

(B) the State agency has established acceptable conservation programs, consistent with the purposes and policies of this chapter, for all resident species of fish or wildlife in the State which are deemed by the Secretary to be endangered or threatened, and has furnished a copy of such plan and program together with all pertinent details, information, and data requested to the Secretary;

(C) the State agency is authorized to conduct investigations to determine the status and requirements for survival of resident species of fish and wildlife;

(D) the State agency is authorized to establish programs, including the acquisition of land or aquatic habitat or interests therein, for the conservation of resident endangered or threatened species of fish or wildlife; and

(E) provision is made for public participation in designating resident species of fish or wildlife as endangered or threatened; or that under the State program—

(i) the requirements set forth in subparagraphs (C), (D), and (E) of this paragraph are complied with, and

(ii) plans are included under which immediate attention will be given to those resident species of fish and wildlife which are determined by the Secretary or the State agency to be endangered or threatened and which the Secretary and the State agency agree are most urgently in need of conservation programs; except that a cooperative agreement entered into with a State whose program is deemed adequate and active pursuant to clause (i) and this clause shall not affect the applicability of prohibitions set forth in or authorized pursuant to section 1533(d) of this title or section 1538(a)(1) of this title with respect to the taking of any resident endangered or threatened species.

(2) In furtherance of the purposes of this chapter the Secretary is authorized to enter into a cooperative agreement in accordance with this section with any State which establishes and maintains an adequate and active program for the conservation of endangered species and threatened species of plants. Within one hundred and twenty days after the Secretary receives a certified copy of such a proposed State program, he shall make a determination whether such program is in accordance with this chapter. Unless he determines, pursuant to this paragraph, that the State program is not in accordance with this chapter, he shall enter into a cooperative agreement with the State for the purpose of assisting in implementation of the State program. In order for a State program to be deemed an adequate and active program for the conservation of endangered species of plants and threatened species of plants, the Secretary must find, and annually thereafter reconfirm such finding, that under the State program—

(A) authority resides in the State agency to conserve resident species of plants determined by the State agency or the Secretary to be endangered or threatened;

(B) the State agency has established acceptable conservation programs, consistent with the purposes and policies of this chapter, for all resident species of plants in the State which are deemed

by the Secretary to be endangered or threatened, and has furnished a copy of such plan and program together with all pertinent details, information, and data requested to the Secretary;
(C) the State agency is authorized to conduct investigations to determine the status and requirements for survival of resident species of plants; and
(D) provision is made for public participation in designating resident species of plants as endangered or threatened; or that under the State program—

(i) the requirements set forth in subparagraphs (C) and (D) of this paragraph are complied with, and

(ii) plans are included under which immediate attention will be given to those resident species of plants which are determined by the Secretary or the State agency to be endangered or threatened and which the Secretary and the State agency agree are most urgently in need of conservation programs; except that a cooperative agreement entered into with a State whose program is deemed adequate and active pursuant to clause (i) and this clause shall not affect the applicability of prohibitions set forth in or authorized pursuant to section 1533(d) or section 1538(a)(1) of this title with respect to the taking of any resident endangered or threatened species.

(d) Allocation of funds

(1) The Secretary is authorized to provide financial assistance to any State, through its respective State agency, which has entered into a cooperative agreement pursuant to subsection (c) of this section to assist in development of programs for the conservation of endangered and threatened species or to assist in monitoring the status of candidate species pursuant to subparagraph (C) of section 1533(b)(3) of this title and recovered species pursuant to section 1533(g) of this title. The Secretary shall allocate each annual appropriation made in accordance with the provisions of subsection (i) of this section to such States based on consideration of—
(A) the international commitments of the United States to protect endangered species or threatened species;
(B) the readiness of a State to proceed with a conservation program consistent with the objectives and purposes of this chapter;
(C) the number of endangered species and threatened species within a State;
(D) the potential for restoring endangered species and threatened species within a State;
(E) the relative urgency to initiate a program to restore and protect an endangered species or threatened species in terms of survival of the species;
(F) the importance of monitoring the status of candidate species within a State to prevent a significant risk to the well being of any such species; and

(G) the importance of monitoring the status of recovered species within a State to assure that such species do not return to the point at which the measures provided pursuant to this chapter are again necessary.

So much of the annual appropriation made in accordance with provisions of subsection (i) of this section allocated for obligation to any State for any fiscal year as remains unobligated at the close thereof is authorized to be made available to that State until the close of the succeeding fiscal year. Any amount allocated to any State which is unobligated at the end of the period during which it is available for expenditure is authorized to be made available for expenditure by the Secretary in conducting programs under this section.

(2) Such cooperative agreements shall provide for (A) the actions to be taken by the Secretary and the States; (B) the benefits that are expected to be derived in connection with the conservation of endangered or threatened species; (C) the estimated cost of these actions; and (D) the share of such costs to be borne by the Federal Government and by the States; except that—

(i) the Federal share of such program costs shall not exceed 75 percent of the estimated program cost stated in the agreement; and

(ii) the Federal share may be increased to 90 percent whenever two or more States having a common interest in one or more endangered or threatened species, the conservation of which may be enhanced by cooperation of such States, enter jointly into an agreement with the Secretary.

The Secretary may, in his discretion, and under such rules and regulations as he may prescribe, advance funds to the State for financing the United States pro rata share agreed upon in the cooperative agreement. For the purposes of this section, the non-Federal share may, in the discretion of the Secretary, be in the form of money or real property, the value of which will be determined by the Secretary, whose decision shall be final.

(e) Review of State programs

Any action taken by the Secretary under this section shall be subject to his periodic review at no greater than annual intervals.

(f) Conflicts between Federal and State laws

Any State law or regulation which applies with respect to the importation or exportation of, or interstate or foreign commerce in, endangered species or threatened species is void to the extent that it may effectively (1) permit what is prohibited by this chapter or by any regulation which implements this chapter, or (2) prohibit what is authorized pursuant to an exemption or permit provided for in this chapter or in any regulation which implements this chapter. This chapter shall not otherwise be construed to void any State law or regulation which is intended to conserve migratory, resident, or introduced fish or wildlife, or to permit or prohibit sale of such fish or wildlife. Any State law or regulation respecting the taking of an endangered species or threatened species may be more restrictive than the exemptions or permits provided for in this chapter or in any regulation which implements this chapter but not less restrictive than the prohibitions so defined.

(g) Transition

(1) For purposes of this subsection, the term "establishment period" means, with respect to any State, the period beginning on December 28, 1973, and ending on whichever of the following dates first occurs: (A) the date of the close of the 120-day period following the adjournment of the first regular session of the legislature of such State which commences after December 28, 1973, or (B) the date of the close of the 15-month period following December 28, 1973.
(2) The prohibitions set forth in or authorized pursuant to sections 1533(d) and 1538(a)(1)(B) of this title shall not apply with respect to the taking of any resident endangered species or threatened species (other than species listed in Appendix I to the Convention or otherwise specifically covered by any other treaty or Federal law) within any State—
(A) which is then a party to a cooperative agreement with the Secretary pursuant to subsection (c) of this section (except to the extent that the taking of any such species is contrary to the law of such State); or
(B) except for any time within the establishment period when—
(i) the Secretary applies such prohibition to such species at the request of the State, or
(ii) the Secretary applies such prohibition after he finds, and publishes his finding, that an emergency exists posing a significant risk to the well-being of such species and that the prohibition must be applied to protect such species. The Secretary's finding and publication may be made without regard to the public hearing or comment provisions of section 553 of title 5 or any other provision of this chapter; but such prohibition shall expire 90 days after the date of its imposition unless the Secretary further extends such prohibition by publishing notice and a statement of justification of such extension.

(h) Regulations

The Secretary is authorized to promulgate such regulations as may be appropriate to carry out the provisions of this section relating to financial assistance to States.

(i) Appropriations

(1) To carry out the provisions of this section for fiscal years after September 30, 1988, there shall be deposited into a special fund known as the cooperative endangered species conservation fund, to be administered by the Secretary, an amount equal to 5 percent of the combined amounts covered each fiscal year into the Federal aid to wildlife restoration fund under section 669b of this title, and paid, transferred, or otherwise credited each fiscal year to the Sport Fishing Restoration Account established under 1016 of the Act of July 18, 1984.
(2) Amounts deposited into the special fund are authorized to be appropriated annually and allocated in accordance with subsection (d) of this section.

(Pub. L. 93–205, §6, Dec. 28, 1973, 87 Stat. 889; Pub. L. 95–212, Dec. 19, 1977, 91 Stat. 1493; Pub. L. 95–632, §10, Nov. 10, 1978, 92 Stat. 3762; Pub. L. 96–246, May 23, 1980, 94 Stat. 348; Pub. L. 97–304, §§3, 8(b), Oct. 13, 1982, 96 Stat. 1416, 1426; Pub. L. 100–478, title I, §1005, Oct. 7, 1988, 102 Stat. 2307.)

16 U.S.C.
United States Code, 2017 Edition
Title 16 – CONSERVATION
CHAPTER 35 - ENDANGERED SPECIES
Sec. 1536 - Interagency cooperation
From the U.S. Government Publishing Office, www.gpo.gov

§1536. Interagency cooperation

(a) Federal agency actions and consultations

(1) The Secretary shall review other programs administered by him and utilize such programs in furtherance of the purposes of this chapter. All other Federal agencies shall, in consultation with and with the assistance of the Secretary, utilize their authorities in furtherance of the purposes of this chapter by carrying out programs for the conservation of endangered species and threatened species listed pursuant to section 1533 of this title.
(2) Each Federal agency shall, in consultation with and with the assistance of the Secretary, insure that any action authorized, funded, or carried out by such agency (hereinafter in this section referred to as an "agency action") is not likely to jeopardize the continued existence of any endangered species or threatened species or result in the destruction or adverse modification of habitat of such species which is determined by the Secretary, after consultation as appropriate

with affected States, to be critical, unless such agency has been granted an exemption for such action by the Committee pursuant to subsection (h) of this section. In fulfilling the requirements of this paragraph each agency shall use the best scientific and commercial data available.
(3) Subject to such guidelines as the Secretary may establish, a Federal agency shall consult with the Secretary on any prospective agency action at the request of, and in cooperation with, the prospective permit or license applicant if the applicant has reason to believe that an endangered species or a threatened species may be present in the area affected by his project and that implementation of such action will likely affect such species.
(4) Each Federal agency shall confer with the Secretary on any agency action which is likely to jeopardize the continued existence of any species proposed to be listed under section 1533 of this title or result in the destruction or adverse modification of critical habitat proposed to be designated for such species. This paragraph does not require a limitation on the commitment of resources as described in subsection (d).

(b) Opinion of Secretary

(1)(A) Consultation under subsection (a)(2) with respect to any agency action shall be concluded within the 90-day period beginning on the date on which initiated or, subject to subparagraph (B), within such other period of time as is mutually agreeable to the Secretary and the Federal agency.
(B) In the case of an agency action involving a permit or license applicant, the Secretary and the Federal agency may not mutually agree to conclude consultation within a period exceeding 90 days unless the Secretary, before the close of the 90th day referred to in subparagraph (A)—

(i) if the consultation period proposed to be agreed to will end before the 150th day after the date on which consultation was initiated, submits to the applicant a written statement setting forth—

(I) the reasons why a longer period is required,

(II) the information that is required to complete the consultation, and

(III) the estimated date on which consultation will be completed; or

(ii) if the consultation period proposed to be agreed to will end 150 or more days after the date on which consultation was initiated, obtains the consent of the applicant to such period.

The Secretary and the Federal agency may mutually agree to extend a consultation period established under the preceding sentence if the Secretary, before the close of such period, obtains the consent of the applicant to the extension.

(2) Consultation under subsection (a)(3) shall be concluded within such period as is agreeable to the Secretary, the Federal agency, and the applicant concerned.

(3)(A) Promptly after conclusion of consultation under paragraph (2) or (3) of subsection (a), the Secretary shall provide to the Federal agency and the applicant, if any, a written statement setting forth the Secretary's opinion, and a summary of the information on which the opinion is based, detailing how the agency action affects the species or its critical habitat. If jeopardy or adverse modification is found, the Secretary shall suggest those reasonable and prudent alternatives which he believes would not violate subsection (a)(2) and can be taken by the Federal agency or applicant in implementing the agency action.
(B) Consultation under subsection (a)(3), and an opinion issued by the Secretary incident to such consultation, regarding an agency action shall be treated respectively as a consultation under subsection (a)(2), and as an opinion issued after consultation under such subsection, regarding that action if the Secretary reviews the action before it is commenced by the Federal agency and finds, and notifies such agency, that no significant changes have been made with respect to the action and that no significant change has occurred regarding the information used during the initial consultation.

(4) If after consultation under subsection (a)(2), the Secretary concludes that—
(A) the agency action will not violate such subsection, or offers reasonable and prudent alternatives which the Secretary believes would not violate such subsection;
(B) the taking of an endangered species or a threatened species incidental to the agency action will not violate such subsection; and
(C) if an endangered species or threatened species of a marine mammal is involved, the taking is authorized pursuant to section 1371(a)(5) of this title;
the Secretary shall provide the Federal agency and the applicant concerned, if any, with a written statement that—

(i) specifies the impact of such incidental taking on the species,

(ii) specifies those reasonable and prudent measures that the Secretary considers necessary or appropriate to minimize such impact,

(iii) in the case of marine mammals, specifies those measures that are necessary to comply with section 1371(a)(5) of this title with regard to such taking, and

(iv) sets forth the terms and conditions (including, but not limited to, reporting requirements) that must be complied with by the Federal agency or applicant (if any), or both, to implement the measures specified under clauses (ii) and (iii).

(c) Biological assessment

(1) To facilitate compliance with the requirements of subsection (a)(2), each Federal agency shall, with respect to any agency action of such agency for which no contract for construction has been entered into and for which no construction has begun on November 10, 1978, request of

the Secretary information whether any species which is listed or proposed to be listed may be present in the area of such proposed action. If the Secretary advises, based on the best scientific and commercial data available, that such species may be present, such agency shall conduct a biological assessment for the purpose of identifying any endangered species or threatened species which is likely to be affected by such action. Such assessment shall be completed within 180 days after the date on which initiated (or within such other period as is mutually agreed to by the Secretary and such agency, except that if a permit or license applicant is involved, the 180-day period may not be extended unless such agency provides the applicant, before the close of such period, with a written statement setting forth the estimated length of the proposed extension and the reasons therefor) and, before any contract for construction is entered into and before construction is begun with respect to such action. Such assessment may be undertaken as part of a Federal agency's compliance with the requirements of section 102 of the National Environmental Policy Act of 1969 (42 U.S.C. 4332).

(2) Any person who may wish to apply for an exemption under subsection (g) of this section for that action may conduct a biological assessment to identify any endangered species or threatened species which is likely to be affected by such action. Any such biological assessment must, however, be conducted in cooperation with the Secretary and under the supervision of the appropriate Federal agency.

(d) Limitation on commitment of resources

After initiation of consultation required under subsection (a)(2), the Federal agency and the permit or license applicant shall not make any irreversible or irretrievable commitment of resources with respect to the agency action which has the effect of foreclosing the formulation or implementation of any reasonable and prudent alternative measures which would not violate subsection (a)(2) of this section.

(e) Endangered Species Committee

(1) There is established a committee to be known as the Endangered Species Committee (hereinafter in this section referred to as the "Committee").

(2) The Committee shall review any application submitted to it pursuant to this section and determine in accordance with subsection (h) of this section whether or not to grant an exemption from the requirements of subsection (a)(2) of this section for the action set forth in such application.

(3) The Committee shall be composed of seven members as follows:

(A) The Secretary of Agriculture.

(B) The Secretary of the Army.

(C) The Chairman of the Council of Economic Advisors.
(D) The Administrator of the Environmental Protection Agency.
(E) The Secretary of the Interior.
(F) The Administrator of the National Oceanic and Atmospheric Administration.
(G) The President, after consideration of any recommendations received pursuant to subsection (g)(2)(B) shall appoint one individual from each affected State, as determined by the Secretary, to be a member of the Committee for the consideration of the application for exemption for an agency action with respect to which such recommendations are made, not later than 30 days after an application is submitted pursuant to this section.

(4)(A) Members of the Committee shall receive no additional pay on account of their service on the Committee.
(B) While away from their homes or regular places of business in the performance of services for the Committee, members of the Committee shall be allowed travel expenses, including per diem in lieu of subsistence, in the same manner as persons employed intermittently in the Government service are allowed expenses under section 5703 of title 5.

(5)(A) Five members of the Committee or their representatives shall constitute a quorum for the transaction of any function of the Committee, except that, in no case shall any representative be considered in determining the existence of a quorum for the transaction of any function of the Committee if that function involves a vote by the Committee on any matter before the Committee.
(B) The Secretary of the Interior shall be the Chairman of the Committee.
(C) The Committee shall meet at the call of the Chairman or five of its members.
(D) All meetings and records of the Committee shall be open to the public.

(6) Upon request of the Committee, the head of any Federal agency is authorized to detail, on a nonreimbursable basis, any of the personnel of such agency to the Committee to assist it in carrying out its duties under this section.
(7)(A) The Committee may for the purpose of carrying out its duties under this section hold such hearings, sit and act at such times and places, take such testimony, and receive such evidence, as the Committee deems advisable.
(B) When so authorized by the Committee, any member or agent of the Committee may take any action which the Committee is authorized to take by this paragraph.
(C) Subject to the Privacy Act [5 U.S.C. 552a], the Committee may secure directly from any Federal agency information necessary to enable it to carry out its duties under this section. Upon request of the Chairman of the Committee, the head of such Federal agency shall furnish such information to the Committee.

(D) The Committee may use the United States mails in the same manner and upon the same conditions as a Federal agency.
(E) The Administrator of General Services shall provide to the Committee on a reimbursable basis such administrative support services as the Committee may request.

(8) In carrying out its duties under this section, the Committee may promulgate and amend such rules, regulations, and procedures, and issue and amend such orders as it deems necessary.
(9) For the purpose of obtaining information necessary for the consideration of an application for an exemption under this section the Committee may issue subpenas for the attendance and testimony of witnesses and the production of relevant papers, books, and documents.
(10) In no case shall any representative, including a representative of a member designated pursuant to paragraph (3)(G) of this subsection, be eligible to cast a vote on behalf of any member.

(f) Promulgation of regulations; form and contents of exemption application

Not later than 90 days after November 10, 1978, the Secretary shall promulgate regulations which set forth the form and manner in which applications for exemption shall be submitted to the Secretary and the information to be contained in such applications. Such regulations shall require that information submitted in an application by the head of any Federal agency with respect to any agency action include, but not be limited to—
(1) a description of the consultation process carried out pursuant to subsection (a)(2) of this section between the head of the Federal agency and the Secretary; and
(2) a statement describing why such action cannot be altered or modified to conform with the requirements of subsection (a)(2) of this section.

(g) Application for exemption; report to Committee

(1) A Federal agency, the Governor of the State in which an agency action will occur, if any, or a permit or license applicant may apply to the Secretary for an exemption for an agency action of such agency if, after consultation under subsection (a)(2), the Secretary's opinion under subsection (b) indicates that the agency action would violate subsection (a)(2). An application for an exemption shall be considered initially by the Secretary in the manner provided for in this subsection, and shall be considered by the Committee for a final determination under subsection (h) after a report is made pursuant to paragraph (5). The applicant for an exemption shall be referred to as the "exemption applicant" in this section.
(2)(A) An exemption applicant shall submit a written application to the Secretary, in a form prescribed under subsection (f), not later than 90 days after the completion of the consultation process; except that, in the case of any agency action involving a permit or license applicant,

such application shall be submitted not later than 90 days after the date on which the Federal agency concerned takes final agency action with respect to the issuance of the permit or license. For purposes of the preceding sentence, the term "final agency action" means (i) a disposition by an agency with respect to the issuance of a permit or license that is subject to administrative review, whether or not such disposition is subject to judicial review; or (ii) if administrative review is sought with respect to such disposition, the decision resulting after such review. Such application shall set forth the reasons why the exemption applicant considers that the agency action meets the requirements for an exemption under this subsection.

(B) Upon receipt of an application for exemption for an agency action under paragraph (1), the Secretary shall promptly (i) notify the Governor of each affected State, if any, as determined by the Secretary, and request the Governors so notified to recommend individuals to be appointed to the Endangered Species Committee for consideration of such application; and (ii) publish notice of receipt of the application in the Federal Register, including a summary of the information contained in the application and a description of the agency action with respect to which the application for exemption has been filed.

(3) The Secretary shall within 20 days after the receipt of an application for exemption, or within such other period of time as is mutually agreeable to the exemption applicant and the Secretary—

(A) determine that the Federal agency concerned and the exemption applicant have—

(i) carried out the consultation responsibilities described in subsection (a) in good faith and made a reasonable and responsible effort to develop and fairly consider modifications or reasonable and prudent alternatives to the proposed agency action which would not violate subsection (a)(2);

(ii) conducted any biological assessment required by subsection (c); and

(iii) to the extent determinable within the time provided herein, refrained from making any irreversible or irretrievable commitment of resources prohibited by subsection (d); or

(B) deny the application for exemption because the Federal agency concerned or the exemption applicant have not met the requirements set forth in subparagraph (A)(i), (ii), and (iii).

The denial of an application under subparagraph (B) shall be considered final agency action for purposes of chapter 7 of title 5.

(4) If the Secretary determines that the Federal agency concerned and the exemption applicant have met the requirements set forth in paragraph (3)(A)(i), (ii), and (iii) he shall, in consultation with the Members of the Committee, hold a hearing on the application for exemption in accordance with sections 554, 555, and 556 (other than subsection (b)(1) and (2) thereof) of title 5 and prepare the report to be submitted pursuant to paragraph (5).

(5) Within 140 days after making the determinations under paragraph (3) or within such other period of time as is mutually agreeable to the exemption applicant and the Secretary, the Secretary shall submit to the Committee a report discussing—
(A) the availability of reasonable and prudent alternatives to the agency action, and the nature and extent of the benefits of the agency action and of alternative courses of action consistent with conserving the species or the critical habitat;
(B) a summary of the evidence concerning whether or not the agency action is in the public interest and is of national or regional significance;
(C) appropriate reasonable mitigation and enhancement measures which should be considered by the Committee; and
(D) whether the Federal agency concerned and the exemption applicant refrained from making any irreversible or irretrievable commitment of resources prohibited by subsection (d).

(6) To the extent practicable within the time required for action under subsection (g) of this section, and except to the extent inconsistent with the requirements of this section, the consideration of any application for an exemption under this section and the conduct of any hearing under this subsection shall be in accordance with sections 554, 555, and 556 (other than subsection (b)(3) of section 556) of title 5.
(7) Upon request of the Secretary, the head of any Federal agency is authorized to detail, on a nonreimbursable basis, any of the personnel of such agency to the Secretary to assist him in carrying out his duties under this section.
(8) All meetings and records resulting from activities pursuant to this subsection shall be open to the public.

(h) Grant of exemption

(1) The Committee shall make a final determination whether or not to grant an exemption within 30 days after receiving the report of the Secretary pursuant to subsection (g)(5). The Committee shall grant an exemption from the requirements of subsection (a)(2) for an agency action if, by a vote of not less than five of its members voting in person—
(A) it determines on the record, based on the report of the Secretary, the record of the hearing held under subsection (g)(4) and on such other testimony or evidence as it may receive, that—

(i) there are no reasonable and prudent alternatives to the agency action;

(ii) the benefits of such action clearly outweigh the benefits of alternative courses of action consistent with conserving the species or its critical habitat, and such action is in the public interest;

(iii) the action is of regional or national significance; and

(iv) neither the Federal agency concerned nor the exemption applicant made any irreversible or irretrievable commitment of resources prohibited by subsection (d); and

(B) it establishes such reasonable mitigation and enhancement measures, including, but not limited to, live propagation, transplantation, and habitat acquisition and improvement, as are necessary and appropriate to minimize the adverse effects of the agency action upon the endangered species, threatened species, or critical habitat concerned.

Any final determination by the Committee under this subsection shall be considered final agency action for purposes of chapter 7 of title 5.

(2)(A) Except as provided in subparagraph (B), an exemption for an agency action granted under paragraph (1) shall constitute a permanent exemption with respect to all endangered or threatened species for the purposes of completing such agency action—

(i) regardless whether the species was identified in the biological assessment; and

(ii) only if a biological assessment has been conducted under subsection (c) with respect to such agency action.

(B) An exemption shall be permanent under subparagraph (A) unless—

(i) the Secretary finds, based on the best scientific and commercial data available, that such exemption would result in the extinction of a species that was not the subject of consultation under subsection (a)(2) or was not identified in any biological assessment conducted under subsection (c), and

(ii) the Committee determines within 60 days after the date of the Secretary's finding that the exemption should not be permanent.

If the Secretary makes a finding described in clause (i), the Committee shall meet with respect to the matter within 30 days after the date of the finding.

(i) Review by Secretary of State; violation of international treaty or other international obligation of United States

Notwithstanding any other provision of this chapter, the Committee shall be prohibited from considering for exemption any application made to it, if the Secretary of State, after a review of the proposed agency action and its potential implications, and after hearing, certifies, in writing, to the Committee within 60 days of any application made under this section that the granting of any such exemption and the carrying out of such action would be in violation of an international treaty obligation or other international obligation of the United States. The Secretary of State shall, at the time of such certification, publish a copy thereof in the Federal Register.

(j) Exemption for national security reasons

Notwithstanding any other provision of this chapter, the Committee shall grant an exemption for any agency action if the Secretary of Defense finds that such exemption is necessary for reasons of national security.

(k) Exemption decision not considered major Federal action; environmental impact statement

An exemption decision by the Committee under this section shall not be a major Federal action for purposes of the National Environmental Policy Act of 1969 [42 U.S.C. 4321 et seq.]: Provided, That an environmental impact statement which discusses the impacts upon endangered species or threatened species or their critical habitats shall have been previously prepared with respect to any agency action exempted by such order.

(l) Committee order granting exemption; cost of mitigation and enhancement measures; report by applicant to Council on Environmental Quality

(1) If the Committee determines under subsection (h) that an exemption should be granted with respect to any agency action, the Committee shall issue an order granting the exemption and specifying the mitigation and enhancement measures established pursuant to subsection (h) which shall be carried out and paid for by the exemption applicant in implementing the agency action. All necessary mitigation and enhancement measures shall be authorized prior to the implementing of the agency action and funded concurrently with all other project features.
(2) The applicant receiving such exemption shall include the costs of such mitigation and enhancement measures within the overall costs of continuing the proposed action. Notwithstanding the preceding sentence the costs of such measures shall not be treated as project costs for the purpose of computing benefit-cost or other ratios for the proposed action. Any applicant may request the Secretary to carry out such mitigation and enhancement measures. The costs incurred by the Secretary in carrying out any such measures shall be paid by the applicant receiving the exemption. No later than one year after the granting of an exemption, the exemption applicant shall submit to the Council on Environmental Quality a report describing its compliance with the mitigation and enhancement measures prescribed by this section. Such a report shall be submitted annually until all such mitigation and enhancement measures have been completed. Notice of the public availability of such reports shall be published in the Federal Register by the Council on Environmental Quality.

(m) Notice requirement for citizen suits not applicable

The 60-day notice requirement of section 1540(g) of this title shall not apply with respect to review of any final determination of the Committee under subsection (h) of this section granting an exemption from the requirements of subsection (a)(2) of this section.

(n) Judicial review

Any person, as defined by section 1532(13) of this title, may obtain judicial review, under chapter 7 of title 5, of any decision of the Endangered Species Committee under subsection (h) in the United States Court of Appeals for (1) any circuit wherein the agency action concerned will be, or is being, carried out, or (2) in any case in which the agency action will be, or is being, carried out outside of any circuit, the District of Columbia, by filing in such court within 90 days after the date of issuance of the decision, a written petition for review. A copy of such petition shall be transmitted by the clerk of the court to the Committee and the Committee shall file in the court the record in the proceeding, as provided in section 2112 of title 28. Attorneys designated by the Endangered Species Committee may appear for, and represent the Committee in any action for review under this subsection.

(o) Exemption as providing exception on taking of endangered species

Notwithstanding sections 1533(d) and 1538(a)(1)(B) and (C) of this title, sections 1371 and 1372 of this title, or any regulation promulgated to implement any such section—
(1) any action for which an exemption is granted under subsection (h) shall not be considered to be a taking of any endangered species or threatened species with respect to any activity which is necessary to carry out such action; and
(2) any taking that is in compliance with the terms and conditions specified in a written statement provided under subsection (b)(4)(iv) shall not be considered to be a prohibited taking of the species concerned.

(p) Exemptions in Presidentially declared disaster areas

In any area which has been declared by the President to be a major disaster area under the Disaster Relief and Emergency Assistance Act [42 U.S.C. 5121 et seq.], the President is authorized to make the determinations required by subsections (g) and (h) of this section for any project for the repair or replacement of a public facility substantially as it existed prior to the disaster under section 405 or 406 of the Disaster Relief and Emergency Assistance Act [42 U.S.C. 5171 or 5172], and which the President determines (1) is necessary to prevent the recurrence of such a natural disaster and to reduce the potential loss of human life, and (2) to involve an emergency situation which does not allow the ordinary procedures of this section to be followed. Notwithstanding any other provision of this section, the Committee shall accept the determinations of the President under this subsection.

(Pub. L. 93–205, §7, Dec. 28, 1973, 87 Stat. 892; Pub. L. 95–632, §3, Nov. 10, 1978, 92 Stat. 3752; Pub. L. 96–159, §4, Dec. 28, 1979, 93 Stat. 1226; Pub. L. 97–304, §§4(a), 8(b), Oct. 13, 1982, 96 Stat. 1417, 1426; Pub. L. 99–659, title IV, §411(b), (c), Nov. 14, 1986, 100 Stat. 3741, 3742; Pub. L. 100–707, title I, §109(g), Nov. 23, 1988, 102 Stat. 4709.)

16 U.S.C.
United States Code, 2017 Edition
Title 16 – CONSERVATION
CHAPTER 35 - ENDANGERED SPECIES
Sec. 1537 - International cooperation
From the U.S. Government Publishing Office, www.gpo.gov

§1537. International cooperation

(a) Financial assistance

As a demonstration of the commitment of the United States to the worldwide protection of endangered species and threatened species, the President may, subject to the provisions of section 1306 of title 31, use foreign currencies accruing to the United States Government under the Food for Peace Act [7 U.S.C. 1691 et seq.] or any other law to provide to any foreign country (with its consent) assistance in the development and management of programs in that country which the Secretary determines to be necessary or useful for the conservation of any endangered species or threatened species listed by the Secretary pursuant to section 1533 of this title. The President shall provide assistance (which includes, but is not limited to, the acquisition, by lease or otherwise, of lands, waters, or interests therein) to foreign countries under this section under such terms and conditions as he deems appropriate. Whenever foreign currencies are available for the provision of assistance under this section, such currencies shall be used in preference to funds appropriated under the authority of section 1542 of this title.

(b) Encouragement of foreign programs

In order to carry out further the provisions of this chapter, the Secretary, through the Secretary of State, shall encourage—

(1) foreign countries to provide for the conservation of fish or wildlife and plants including endangered species and threatened species listed pursuant to section 1533 of this title;
(2) the entering into of bilateral or multilateral agreements with foreign countries to provide for such conservation; and
(3) foreign persons who directly or indirectly take fish or wildlife or plants in foreign countries or on the high seas for importation into the United States for commercial or other purposes to develop and carry out with such assistance as he may provide, conservation practices designed to enhance such fish or wildlife or plants and their habitat.

(c) Personnel

After consultation with the Secretary of State, the Secretary may—
(1) assign or otherwise make available any officer or employee of his department for the purpose of cooperating with foreign countries and international organizations in developing personnel resources and programs which promote the conservation of fish or wildlife or plants; and
(2) conduct or provide financial assistance for the educational training of foreign personnel, in this country or abroad, in fish, wildlife, or plant management, research and law enforcement and to render professional assistance abroad in such matters.

(d) Investigations

After consultation with the Secretary of State and the Secretary of the Treasury, as appropriate, the Secretary may conduct or cause to be conducted such law enforcement investigations and research abroad as he deems necessary to carry out the purposes of this chapter.
(Pub. L. 93–205, §8, Dec. 28, 1973, 87 Stat. 892; Pub. L. 96–159, §5, Dec. 28, 1979, 93 Stat. 1228; Pub. L. 110–246, title III, §3001(b)(1)(A), (2)(N), June 18, 2008, 122 Stat. 1820.)

16 U.S.C.
United States Code, 2017 Edition
Title 16 - CONSERVATION
CHAPTER 35 - ENDANGERED SPECIES
Sec. 1537a - Convention implementation
From the U.S. Government Publishing Office, www.gpo.gov

§1537a. Convention implementation

(a) Management Authority and Scientific Authority

The Secretary of the Interior (hereinafter in this section referred to as the "Secretary") is designated as the Management Authority and the Scientific Authority for purposes of the Convention and the respective functions of each such Authority shall be carried out through the United States Fish and Wildlife Service.

(b) Management Authority functions

The Secretary shall do all things necessary and appropriate to carry out the functions of the Management Authority under the Convention.

(c) Scientific Authority functions; determinations

(1) The Secretary shall do all things necessary and appropriate to carry out the functions of the Scientific Authority under the Convention.
(2) The Secretary shall base the determinations and advice given by him under Article IV of the Convention with respect to wildlife upon the best available biological information derived from professionally accepted wildlife management practices; but is not required to make, or require any State to make, estimates of population size in making such determinations or giving such advice.

(d) Reservations by the United States under Convention

If the United States votes against including any species in Appendix I or II of the Convention and does not enter a reservation pursuant to paragraph (3) of Article XV of the Convention with respect to that species, the Secretary of State, before the 90th day after the last day on which such a reservation could be entered, shall submit to the Committee on Merchant Marine and Fisheries of the House of Representatives, and to the Committee on the Environment and Public

Works of the Senate, a written report setting forth the reasons why such a reservation was not entered.

(e) Wildlife preservation in Western Hemisphere

(1) The Secretary of the Interior (hereinafter in this subsection referred to as the "Secretary"), in cooperation with the Secretary of State, shall act on behalf of, and represent, the United States in all regards as required by the Convention on Nature Protection and Wildlife Preservation in the Western Hemisphere (56 Stat. 1354, T.S. 982, hereinafter in this subsection referred to as the "Western Convention"). In the discharge of these responsibilities, the Secretary and the Secretary of State shall consult with the Secretary of Agriculture, the Secretary of Commerce, and the heads of other agencies with respect to matters relating to or affecting their areas of responsibility.

(2) The Secretary and the Secretary of State shall, in cooperation with the contracting parties to the Western Convention and, to the extent feasible and appropriate, with the participation of State agencies, take such steps as are necessary to implement the Western Convention. Such steps shall include, but not be limited to—

(A) cooperation with contracting parties and international organizations for the purpose of developing personnel resources and programs that will facilitate implementation of the Western Convention;

(B) identification of those species of birds that migrate between the United States and other contracting parties, and the habitats upon which those species depend, and the implementation of cooperative measures to ensure that such species will not become endangered or threatened; and

(C) identification of measures that are necessary and appropriate to implement those provisions of the Western Convention which address the protection of wild plants.

(3) No later than September 30, 1985, the Secretary and the Secretary of State shall submit a report to Congress describing those steps taken in accordance with the requirements of this subsection and identifying the principal remaining actions yet necessary for comprehensive and effective implementation of the Western Convention.

(4) The provisions of this subsection shall not be construed as affecting the authority, jurisdiction, or responsibility of the several States to manage, control, or regulate resident fish or wildlife under State law or regulations.

(Pub. L. 93–205, §8A, as added Pub. L. 96–159, §6(a)(1), Dec. 28, 1979, 93 Stat. 1228; amended Pub. L. 97–304, §5[(a)], Oct. 13, 1983, 96 Stat. 1421.)

16 U.S.C.
United States Code, 2017 Edition
Title 16 - CONSERVATION
CHAPTER 35 - ENDANGERED SPECIES
Sec. 1538 - Prohibited acts
From the U.S. Government Publishing Office, www.gpo.gov

§1538. Prohibited acts

(a) Generally

(1) Except as provided in sections 1535(g)(2) and 1539 of this title, with respect to any endangered species of fish or wildlife listed pursuant to section 1533 of this title it is unlawful for any person subject to the jurisdiction of the United States to—
(A) import any such species into, or export any such species from the United States;
(B) take any such species within the United States or the territorial sea of the United States;
(C) take any such species upon the high seas;
(D) possess, sell, deliver, carry, transport, or ship, by any means whatsoever, any such species taken in violation of subparagraphs (B) and (C);
(E) deliver, receive, carry, transport, or ship in interstate or foreign commerce, by any means whatsoever and in the course of a commercial activity, any such species;
(F) sell or offer for sale in interstate or foreign commerce any such species; or
(G) violate any regulation pertaining to such species or to any threatened species of fish or wildlife listed pursuant to section 1533 of this title and promulgated by the Secretary pursuant to authority provided by this chapter.

(2) Except as provided in sections 1535(g)(2) and 1539 of this title, with respect to any endangered species of plants listed pursuant to section 1533 of this title, it is unlawful for any person subject to the jurisdiction of the United States to—
(A) import any such species into, or export any such species from, the United States;
(B) remove and reduce to possession any such species from areas under Federal jurisdiction; maliciously damage or destroy any such species on any such area; or remove, cut, dig up, or damage or destroy any such species on any other area in knowing violation of any law or regulation of any State or in the course of any violation of a State criminal trespass law;
(C) deliver, receive, carry, transport, or ship in interstate or foreign commerce, by any means whatsoever and in the course of a commercial activity, any such species;
(D) sell or offer for sale in interstate or foreign commerce any such species; or

(E) violate any regulation pertaining to such species or to any threatened species of plants listed pursuant to section 1533 of this title and promulgated by the Secretary pursuant to authority provided by this chapter.

(b) Species held in captivity or controlled environment

(1) The provisions of subsections (a)(1)(A) and (a)(1)(G) of this section shall not apply to any fish or wildlife which was held in captivity or in a controlled environment on (A) December 28, 1973, or (B) the date of the publication in the Federal Register of a final regulation adding such fish or wildlife species to any list published pursuant to subsection (c) of section 1533 of this title: *Provided,* That such holding and any subsequent holding or use of the fish or wildlife was not in the course of a commercial activity. With respect to any act prohibited by subsections (a)(1)(A) and (a)(1)(G) of this section which occurs after a period of 180 days from (i) December 28, 1973, or (ii) the date of publication in the Federal Register of a final regulation adding such fish or wildlife species to any list published pursuant to subsection (c) of section 1533 of this title, there shall be a rebuttable presumption that the fish or wildlife involved in such act is not entitled to the exemption contained in this subsection.

(2)(A) The provisions of subsection (a)(1) shall not apply to—

(i) any raptor legally held in captivity or in a controlled environment on November 10, 1978; or

(ii) any progeny of any raptor described in clause (i); until such time as any such raptor or progeny is intentionally returned to a wild state.

(B) Any person holding any raptor or progeny described in subparagraph (A) must be able to demonstrate that the raptor or progeny does, in fact, qualify under the provisions of this paragraph, and shall maintain and submit to the Secretary, on request, such inventories, documentation, and records as the Secretary may by regulation require as being reasonably appropriate to carry out the purposes of this paragraph. Such requirements shall not unnecessarily duplicate the requirements of other rules and regulations promulgated by the Secretary.

(c) Violation of Convention

(1) It is unlawful for any person subject to the jurisdiction of the United States to engage in any trade in any specimens contrary to the provisions of the Convention, or to possess any specimens traded contrary to the provisions of the Convention, including the definitions of terms in article I thereof.

(2) Any importation into the United States of fish or wildlife shall, if—

(A) such fish or wildlife is not an endangered species listed pursuant to section 1533 of this title but is listed in Appendix II to the Convention,

(B) the taking and exportation of such fish or wildlife is not contrary to the provisions of the Convention and all other applicable requirements of the Convention have been satisfied,
(C) the applicable requirements of subsections (d), (e), and (f) of this section have been satisfied, and
(D) such importation is not made in the course of a commercial activity,
be presumed to be an importation not in violation of any provision of this chapter or any regulation issued pursuant to this chapter.

(d) Imports and exports

(1) In general
It is unlawful for any person, without first having obtained permission from the Secretary, to engage in business—
(A) as an importer or exporter of fish or wildlife (other than shellfish and fishery products which (i) are not listed pursuant to section 1533 of this title as endangered species or threatened species, and (ii) are imported for purposes of human or animal consumption or taken in waters under the jurisdiction of the United States or on the high seas for recreational purposes) or plants; or
(B) as an importer or exporter of any amount of raw or worked African elephant ivory.

(2) Requirements
Any person required to obtain permission under paragraph (1) of this subsection shall—
(A) keep such records as will fully and correctly disclose each importation or exportation of fish, wildlife, plants, or African elephant ivory made by him and the subsequent disposition made by him with respect to such fish, wildlife, plants, or ivory;
(B) at all reasonable times upon notice by a duly authorized representative of the Secretary, afford such representative access to his place of business, an opportunity to examine his inventory of imported fish, wildlife, plants, or African elephant ivory and the records required to be kept under subparagraph (A) of this paragraph, and to copy such records; and
(C) file such reports as the Secretary may require.

(3) Regulations
The Secretary shall prescribe such regulations as are necessary and appropriate to carry out the purposes of this subsection.

(4) Restriction on consideration of value or amount of African elephant ivory imported or exported

In granting permission under this subsection for importation or exportation of African elephant ivory, the Secretary shall not vary the requirements for obtaining such permission on the basis of the value or amount of ivory imported or exported under such permission.

(e) Reports

It is unlawful for any person importing or exporting fish or wildlife (other than shellfish and fishery products which (1) are not listed pursuant to section 1533 of this title as endangered or threatened species, and (2) are imported for purposes of human or animal consumption or taken in waters under the jurisdiction of the United States or on the high seas for recreational purposes) or plants to fail to file any declaration or report as the Secretary deems necessary to facilitate enforcement of this chapter or to meet the obligations of the Convention.

(f) Designation of ports

(1) It is unlawful for any person subject to the jurisdiction of the United States to import into or export from the United States any fish or wildlife (other than shellfish and fishery products which (A) are not listed pursuant to section 1533 of this title as endangered species or threatened species, and (B) are imported for purposes of human or animal consumption or taken in waters under the jurisdiction of the United States or on the high seas for recreational purposes) or plants, except at a port or ports designated by the Secretary of the Interior. For the purpose of facilitating enforcement of this chapter and reducing the costs thereof, the Secretary of the Interior, with approval of the Secretary of the Treasury and after notice and opportunity for public hearing, may, by regulation, designate ports and change such designations. The Secretary of the Interior, under such terms and conditions as he may prescribe, may permit the importation or exportation at nondesignated ports in the interest of the health or safety of the fish or wildlife or plants, or for other reasons, if, in his discretion, he deems it appropriate and consistent with the purpose of this subsection.
(2) Any port designated by the Secretary of the Interior under the authority of section 668cc–4(d) 'of this title, shall, if such designation is in effect on December 27, 1973, be deemed to be a port designated by the Secretary under paragraph (1) of this subsection until such time as the Secretary otherwise provides.

(g) Violations

It is unlawful for any person subject to the jurisdiction of the United States to attempt to commit, solicit another to commit, or cause to be committed, any offense defined in this section.

(Pub. L. 93–205, §9, Dec. 28, 1973, 87 Stat. 893; Pub. L. 95–632, §4, Nov. 10, 1978, 92 Stat. 3760; Pub. L. 97–304, §9(b), Oct. 13, 1982, 96 Stat. 1426; Pub. L. 100–478, title I, §1006, title II, §2301, Oct. 7, 1988, 102 Stat. 2308, 2321; Pub. L. 100–653, title IX, §905, Nov. 14, 1988, 102 Stat. 3835.)

16 U.S.C.
United States Code, 2017 Edition
Title 16 - CONSERVATION
CHAPTER 35 - ENDANGERED SPECIES
Sec. 1539 - Exceptions
From the U.S. Government Publishing Office, www.gpo.gov

§1539. Exceptions

(a) Permits

(1) The Secretary may permit, under such terms and conditions as he shall prescribe—
(A) any act otherwise prohibited by section 1538 of this title for scientific purposes or to enhance the propagation or survival of the affected species, including, but not limited to, acts necessary for the establishment and maintenance of experimental populations pursuant to subsection (j); or
(B) any taking otherwise prohibited by section 1538(a)(1)(B) of this title if such taking is incidental to, and not the purpose of, the carrying out of an otherwise lawful activity.
(2)(A) No permit may be issued by the Secretary authorizing any taking referred to in paragraph (1)(B) unless the applicant therefor submits to the Secretary a conservation plan that specifies—
(i) the impact which will likely result from such taking;
(ii) what steps the applicant will take to minimize and mitigate such impacts, and the funding that will be available to implement such steps;
(iii) what alternative actions to such taking the applicant considered and the reasons why such alternatives are not being utilized; and
(iv) such other measures that the Secretary may require as being necessary or appropriate for purposes of the plan.
(B) If the Secretary finds, after opportunity for public comment, with respect to a permit application and the related conservation plan that—
(i) the taking will be incidental;
(ii) the applicant will, to the maximum extent practicable, minimize and mitigate the impacts of such taking;
(iii) the applicant will ensure that adequate funding for the plan will be provided;

(iv) the taking will not appreciably reduce the likelihood of the survival and recovery of the species in the wild; and

(v) the measures, if any, required under subparagraph (A)(iv) will be met;

and he has received such other assurances as he may require that the plan will be implemented, the Secretary shall issue the permit. The permit shall contain such terms and conditions as the Secretary deems necessary or appropriate to carry out the purposes of this paragraph, including, but not limited to, such reporting requirements as the Secretary deems necessary for determining whether such terms and conditions are being complied with.

(C) The Secretary shall revoke a permit issued under this paragraph if he finds that the permittee is not complying with the terms and conditions of the permit.

(b) Hardship exemptions

(1) If any person enters into a contract with respect to a species of fish or wildlife or plant before the date of the publication in the Federal Register of notice of consideration of that species as an endangered species and the subsequent listing of that species as an endangered species pursuant to section 1533 of this title will cause undue economic hardship to such person under the contract, the Secretary, in order to minimize such hardship, may exempt such person from the application of section 1538(a) of this title to the extent the Secretary deems appropriate if such person applies to him for such exemption and includes with such application such information as the Secretary may require to prove such hardship; except that (A) no such exemption shall be for a duration of more than one year from the date of publication in the Federal Register of notice of consideration of the species concerned, or shall apply to a quantity of fish or wildlife or plants in excess of that specified by the Secretary; (B) the one-year period for those species of fish or wildlife listed by the Secretary as endangered prior to December 28, 1973, shall expire in accordance with the terms of section 668cc–3 [1] of this title; and (C) no such exemption may be granted for the importation or exportation of a specimen listed in Appendix I of the Convention which is to be used in a commercial activity.

(2) As used in this subsection, the term "undue economic hardship" shall include, but not be limited to:

(A) substantial economic loss resulting from inability caused by this chapter to perform contracts with respect to species of fish and wildlife entered into prior to the date of publication in the Federal Register of a notice of consideration of such species as an endangered species;

(B) substantial economic loss to persons who, for the year prior to the notice of consideration of such species as an endangered species, derived a substantial portion of their income from the lawful taking of any listed species, which taking would be made unlawful under this chapter; or

(C) curtailment of subsistence taking made unlawful under this chapter by persons (i) not reasonably able to secure other sources of subsistence; and (ii) dependent to a substantial extent upon hunting and fishing for subsistence; and (iii) who must engage in such curtailed taking for subsistence purposes.

(3) The Secretary may make further requirements for a showing of undue economic hardship as he deems fit. Exceptions granted under this section may be limited by the Secretary in his discretion as to time, area, or other factor of applicability.

(c) Notice and review

The Secretary shall publish notice in the Federal Register of each application for an exemption or permit which is made under this section. Each notice shall invite the submission from interested parties, within thirty days after the date of the notice, of written data, views, or arguments with respect to the application; except that such thirty-day period may be waived by the Secretary in an emergency situation where the health or life of an endangered animal is threatened and no reasonable alternative is available to the applicant, but notice of any such waiver shall be published by the Secretary in the Federal Register within ten days following the issuance of the exemption or permit. Information received by the Secretary as a part of any application shall be available to the public as a matter of public record at every stage of the proceeding.

(d) Permit and exemption policy

The Secretary may grant exceptions under subsections (a)(1)(A) and (b) of this section only if he finds and publishes his finding in the Federal Register that (1) such exceptions were applied for in good faith, (2) if granted and exercised will not operate to the disadvantage of such endangered species, and (3) will be consistent with the purposes and policy set forth in section 1531 of this title.

(e) Alaska natives

(1) Except as provided in paragraph (4) of this subsection the provisions of this chapter shall not apply with respect to the taking of any endangered species or threatened species, or the importation of any such species taken pursuant to this section, by—
(A) any Indian, Aleut, or Eskimo who is an Alaskan Native who resides in Alaska; or
(B) any non-native permanent resident of an Alaskan native village;
if such taking is primarily for subsistence purposes. Non-edible byproducts of species taken pursuant to this section may be sold in interstate commerce when made into authentic native articles of handicrafts and clothing; except that the provisions of this subsection shall not apply to any non-native resident of an Alaskan native village found by the Secretary to be not

primarily dependent upon the taking of fish and wildlife for consumption or for the creation and sale of authentic native articles of handicrafts and clothing.

(2) Any taking under this subsection may not be accomplished in a wasteful manner.

(3) As used in this subsection—

(i) The term "subsistence" includes selling any edible portion of fish or wildlife in native villages and towns in Alaska for native consumption within native villages or towns; and

(ii) The term "authentic native articles of handicrafts and clothing" means items composed wholly or in some significant respect of natural materials, and which are produced, decorated, or fashioned in the exercise of traditional native handicrafts without the use of pantographs, multiple carvers, or other mass copying devices. Traditional native handicrafts include, but are not limited to, weaving, carving, stitching, sewing, lacing, beading, drawing, and painting.

(4) Notwithstanding the provisions of paragraph (1) of this subsection, whenever the Secretary determines that any species of fish or wildlife which is subject to taking under the provisions of this subsection is an endangered species or threatened species, and that such taking materially and negatively affects the threatened or endangered species, he may prescribe regulations upon the taking of such species by any such Indian, Aleut, Eskimo, or non-Native Alaskan resident of an Alaskan native village. Such regulations may be established with reference to species, geographical description of the area included, the season for taking, or any other factors related to the reason for establishing such regulations and consistent with the policy of this chapter. Such regulations shall be prescribed after a notice and hearings in the affected judicial districts of Alaska and as otherwise required by section 1373 of this title, and shall be removed as soon as the Secretary determines that the need for their impositions has disappeared.

(f) Pre-Act endangered species parts exemption; application and certification; regulation; validity of sales contract; separability; renewal of exemption; expiration of renewal certification

(1) As used in this subsection—

(A) The term "pre-Act endangered species part" means—

(i) any sperm whale oil, including derivatives thereof, which was lawfully held within the United States on December 28, 1973, in the course of a commercial activity; or

(ii) any finished scrimshaw product, if such product or the raw material for such product was lawfully held within the United States on December 28, 1973, in the course of a commercial activity.

(B) The term "scrimshaw product" means any art form which involves the substantial etching or engraving of designs upon, or the substantial carving of figures, patterns, or designs from, any bone or tooth of any marine mammal of the order Cetacea. For purposes of this subsection, polishing or the adding of minor superficial markings does not constitute substantial etching, engraving, or carving.

(2) The Secretary, pursuant to the provisions of this subsection, may exempt, if such exemption is not in violation of the Convention, any pre-Act endangered species part from one or more of the following prohibitions:
(A) The prohibition on exportation from the United States set forth in section 1538(a)(1)(A) of this title.
(B) Any prohibition set forth in section 1538(a)(1)(E) or (F) of this title.

(3) Any person seeking an exemption described in paragraph (2) of this subsection shall make application therefor to the Secretary in such form and manner as he shall prescribe, but no such application may be considered by the Secretary unless the application—
(A) is received by the Secretary before the close of the one-year period beginning on the date on which regulations promulgated by the Secretary to carry out this subsection first take effect;
(B) contains a complete and detailed inventory of all pre-Act endangered species parts for which the applicant seeks exemption;
(C) is accompanied by such documentation as the Secretary may require to prove that any endangered species part or product claimed by the applicant to be a pre-Act endangered species part is in fact such a part; and
(D) contains such other information as the Secretary deems necessary and appropriate to carry out the purposes of this subsection.

(4) If the Secretary approves any application for exemption made under this subsection, he shall issue to the applicant a certificate of exemption which shall specify—
(A) any prohibition in section 1538(a) of this title which is exempted;
(B) the pre-Act endangered species parts to which the exemption applies;
(C) the period of time during which the exemption is in effect, but no exemption made under this subsection shall have force and effect after the close of the three-year period beginning on the date of issuance of the certificate unless such exemption is renewed under paragraph (8); and
(D) any term or condition prescribed pursuant to paragraph (5)(A) or (B), or both, which the Secretary deems necessary or appropriate.

(5) The Secretary shall prescribe such regulations as he deems necessary and appropriate to carry out the purposes of this subsection. Such regulations may set forth—
(A) terms and conditions which may be imposed on applicants for exemptions under this subsection (including, but not limited to, requirements that applicants register inventories, keep

complete sales records, permit duly authorized agents of the Secretary to inspect such inventories and records, and periodically file appropriate reports with the Secretary); and

(B) terms and conditions which may be imposed on any subsequent purchaser of any pre-Act endangered species part covered by an exemption granted under this subsection;

to insure that any such part so exempted is adequately accounted for and not disposed of contrary to the provisions of this chapter. No regulation prescribed by the Secretary to carry out the purposes of this subsection shall be subject to section 1533(f)(2)(A)(i) of this title.

(6)(A) Any contract for the sale of pre-Act endangered species parts which is entered into by the Administrator of General Services prior to the effective date of this subsection and pursuant to the notice published in the Federal Register on January 9, 1973, shall not be rendered invalid by virtue of the fact that fulfillment of such contract may be prohibited under section 1538(a)(1)(F) of this title.

(B) In the event that this paragraph is held invalid, the validity of the remainder of this chapter, including the remainder of this subsection, shall not be affected.

(7) Nothing in this subsection shall be construed to—

(A) exonerate any person from any act committed in violation of paragraphs (1)(A), (1)(E), or (1)(F) of section 1538(a) of this title prior to July 12, 1976; or

(B) immunize any person from prosecution for any such act.

(8)(A)(i)[2] Any valid certificate of exemption which was renewed after October 13, 1982, and was in effect on March 31, 1988, shall be deemed to be renewed for a six-month period beginning on October 7, 1988. Any person holding such a certificate may apply to the Secretary for one additional renewal of such certificate for a period not to exceed 5 years beginning on October 7, 1988.

(B) If the Secretary approves any application for renewal of an exemption under this paragraph, he shall issue to the applicant a certificate of renewal of such exemption which shall provide that all terms, conditions, prohibitions, and other regulations made applicable by the previous certificate shall remain in effect during the period of the renewal.

(C) No exemption or renewal of such exemption made under this subsection shall have force and effect after the expiration date of the certificate of renewal of such exemption issued under this paragraph.

(D) No person may, after January 31, 1984, sell or offer for sale in interstate or foreign commerce, any pre-Act finished scrimshaw product unless such person holds a valid certificate of exemption issued by the Secretary under this subsection, and unless such product or the raw material for such product was held by such person on October 13, 1982.

(g) Burden of proof

In connection with any action alleging a violation of section 1538 of this title, any person claiming the benefit of any exemption or permit under this chapter shall have the burden of proving that the exemption or permit is applicable, has been granted, and was valid and in force at the time of the alleged violation.

(h) Certain antique articles; importation; port designation; application for return of articles

(1) Sections 1533(d) and 1538(a) and (c) of this title do not apply to any article which—
(A) is not less than 100 years of age;
(B) is composed in whole or in part of any endangered species or threatened species listed under section 1533 of this title;
(C) has not been repaired or modified with any part of any such species on or after December 28, 1973; and
(D) is entered at a port designated under paragraph (3).

(2) Any person who wishes to import an article under the exception provided by this subsection shall submit to the customs officer concerned at the time of entry of the article such documentation as the Secretary of the Treasury, after consultation with the Secretary of the Interior, shall by regulation require as being necessary to establish that the article meets the requirements set forth in paragraph (1)(A), (B), and (C).
(3) The Secretary of the Treasury, after consultation with the Secretary of the Interior, shall designate one port within each customs region at which articles described in paragraph (1)(A), (B), and (C) must be entered into the customs territory of the United States.
(4) Any person who imported, after December 27, 1973, and on or before November 10, 1978, any article described in paragraph (1) which—
(A) was not repaired or modified after the date of importation with any part of any endangered species or threatened species listed under section 1533 of this title;
(B) was forfeited to the United States before November 10, 1978, or is subject to forfeiture to the United States on such date of enactment, pursuant to the assessment of a civil penalty under section 1540 of this title; and
(C) is in the custody of the United States on November 10, 1978;
may, before the close of the one-year period beginning on November 10, 1978, make application to the Secretary for return of the article. Application shall be made in such form and manner, and contain such documentation, as the Secretary prescribes. If on the basis of any such application which is timely filed, the Secretary is satisfied that the requirements of this paragraph are

met with respect to the article concerned, the Secretary shall return the article to the applicant and the importation of such article shall, on and after the date of return, be deemed to be a lawful importation under this chapter.

(i) Noncommercial transshipments

Any importation into the United States of fish or wildlife shall, if—

(1) such fish or wildlife was lawfully taken and exported from the country of origin and country of reexport, if any;

(2) such fish or wildlife is in transit or transshipment through any place subject to the jurisdiction of the United States en route to a country where such fish or wildlife may be lawfully imported and received;

(3) the exporter or owner of such fish or wildlife gave explicit instructions not to ship such fish or wildlife through any place subject to the jurisdiction of the United States, or did all that could have reasonably been done to prevent transshipment, and the circumstances leading to the transshipment were beyond the exporter's or owner's control;

(4) the applicable requirements of the Convention have been satisfied; and

(5) such importation is not made in the course of a commercial activity,

be an importation not in violation of any provision of this chapter or any regulation issued pursuant to this chapter while such fish or wildlife remains in the control of the United States Customs Service.

(j) Experimental populations

(1) For purposes of this subsection, the term "experimental population" means any population (including any offspring arising solely therefrom) authorized by the Secretary for release under paragraph (2), but only when, and at such times as, the population is wholly separate geographically from nonexperimental populations of the same species.

(2)(A) The Secretary may authorize the release (and the related transportation) of any population (including eggs, propagules, or individuals) of an endangered species or a threatened species outside the current range of such species if the Secretary determines that such release will further the conservation of such species.

(B) Before authorizing the release of any population under subparagraph (A), the Secretary shall by regulation identify the population and determine, on the basis of the best available information, whether or not such population is essential to the continued existence of an endangered species or a threatened species.

(C) For the purposes of this chapter, each member of an experimental population shall be treated as a threatened species; except that—

(i) solely for purposes of section 1536 of this title (other than subsection (a)(1) thereof), an experimental population determined under subparagraph (B) to be not essential to the continued existence of a species shall be treated, except when it occurs in an area within the National Wildlife Refuge System or the National Park System, as a species proposed to be listed under section 1533 of this title; and

(ii) critical habitat shall not be designated under this chapter for any experimental population determined under subparagraph (B) to be not essential to the continued existence of a species.

(3) The Secretary, with respect to populations of endangered species or threatened species that the Secretary authorized, before October 13, 1982, for release in geographical areas separate from the other populations of such species, shall determine by regulation which of such populations are an experimental population for the purposes of this subsection and whether or not each is essential to the continued existence of an endangered species or a threatened species.
(Pub. L. 93–205, §10, Dec. 28, 1973, 87 Stat. 896; Pub. L. 94–359, §§2, 3, July 12, 1976, 90 Stat. 911, 912; Pub. L. 95–632, §5, Nov. 10, 1978, 92 Stat. 3760; Pub. L. 96–159, §7, Dec. 28, 1979, 93 Stat. 1230; Pub. L. 97–304, §6(1)–(4)(A), (5), (6), Oct. 13, 1982, 96 Stat. 1422–1424; Pub. L. 100–478, title I, §§1011, 1013(b), (c), Oct. 7, 1988, 102 Stat. 2314, 2315.)

16 U.S.C.
United States Code, 2017 Edition
Title 16 - CONSERVATION
CHAPTER 35 - ENDANGERED SPECIES
Sec. 1540 - Penalties and enforcement
From the U.S. Government Publishing Office, www.gpo.gov

§1540. Penalties and enforcement

(a) Civil penalties

(1) Any person who knowingly violates, and any person engaged in business as an importer or exporter of fish, wildlife, or plants who violates, any provision of this chapter, or any provision of any permit or certificate issued hereunder, or of any regulation issued in order to implement subsection (a)(1)(A), (B), (C), (D), (E), or (F), (a)(2)(A), (B), (C), or (D), (c), (d) (other than regulation relating to recordkeeping or filing of reports), (f) or (g) of section 1538 of this title, may be assessed a civil penalty by the Secretary of not more than $25,000 for each violation. Any person who knowingly violates, and any person engaged in business as an importer or exporter of fish,

wildlife, or plants who violates, any provision of any other regulation issued under this chapter may be assessed a civil penalty by the Secretary of not more than $12,000 for each such violation. Any person who otherwise violates any provision of this chapter, or any regulation, permit, or certificate issued hereunder, may be assessed a civil penalty by the Secretary of not more than $500 for each such violation. No penalty may be assessed under this subsection unless such person is given notice and opportunity for a hearing with respect to such violation. Each violation shall be a separate offense. Any such civil penalty may be remitted or mitigated by the Secretary. Upon any failure to pay a penalty assessed under this subsection, the Secretary may request the Attorney General to institute a civil action in a district court of the United States for any district in which such person is found, resides, or transacts business to collect the penalty and such court shall have jurisdiction to hear and decide any such action. The court shall hear such action on the record made before the Secretary and shall sustain his action if it is supported by substantial evidence on the record considered as a whole.

(2) Hearings held during proceedings for the assessment of civil penalties authorized by paragraph (1) of this subsection shall be conducted in accordance with section 554 of title 5. The Secretary may issue subpenas for the attendance and testimony of witnesses and the production of relevant papers, books, and documents, and administer oaths. Witnesses summoned shall be paid the same fees and mileage that are paid to witnesses in the courts of the United States. In case of contumacy or refusal to obey a subpena served upon any person pursuant to this paragraph, the district court of the United States for any district in which such person is found or resides or transacts business, upon application by the United States and after notice to such person, shall have jurisdiction to issue an order requiring such person to appear and give testimony before the Secretary or to appear and produce documents before the Secretary, or both, and any failure to obey such order of the court may be punished by such court as a contempt thereof.

(3) Notwithstanding any other provision of this chapter, no civil penalty shall be imposed if it can be shown by a preponderance of the evidence that the defendant committed an act based on a good faith belief that he was acting to protect himself or herself, a member of his or her family, or any other individual from bodily harm, from any endangered or threatened species.

(b) Criminal violations

(1) Any person who knowingly violates any provision of this chapter, of any permit or certificate issued hereunder, or of any regulation issued in order to implement subsection (a)(1)(A), (B), (C), (D), (E), or (F), (a)(2)(A), (B), (C), or (D), (c), (d) (other than a regulation relating to recordkeeping, or filing of reports), (f), or (g) of section 1538 of this title shall, upon conviction, be fined not more than $50,000 or imprisoned for not more than one year, or both. Any person who knowingly

violates any provision of any other regulation issued under this chapter shall, upon conviction, be fined not more than $25,000 or imprisoned for not more than six months, or both.
(2) The head of any Federal agency which has issued a lease, license, permit, or other agreement authorizing a person to import or export fish, wildlife, or plants, or to operate a quarantine station for imported wildlife, or authorizing the use of Federal lands, including grazing of domestic livestock, to any person who is convicted of a criminal violation of this chapter or any regulation, permit, or certificate issued hereunder may immediately modify, suspend, or revoke each lease, license, permit, or other agreement. The Secretary shall also suspend for a period of up to one year, or cancel, any Federal hunting or fishing permits or stamps issued to any person who is convicted of a criminal violation of any provision of this chapter or any regulation, permit, or certificate issued hereunder. The United States shall not be liable for the payments of any compensation, reimbursement, or damages in connection with the modification, suspension, or revocation of any leases, licenses, permits, stamps, or other agreements pursuant to this section.
(3) Notwithstanding any other provision of this chapter, it shall be a defense to prosecution under this subsection if the defendant committed the offense based on a good faith belief that he was acting to protect himself or herself, a member of his or her family, or any other individual, from bodily harm from any endangered or threatened species.

(c) District court jurisdiction

The several district courts of the United States, including the courts enumerated in section 460 of title 28, shall have jurisdiction over any actions arising under this chapter. For the purpose of this chapter, American Samoa shall be included within the judicial district of the District Court of the United States for the District of Hawaii.

(d) Rewards and certain incidental expenses

The Secretary or the Secretary of the Treasury shall pay, from sums received as penalties, fines, or forfeitures of property for any violation of this chapter or any regulation issued hereunder (1) a reward to any person who furnishes information which leads to an arrest, a criminal conviction, civil penalty assessment, or forfeiture of property for any violation of this chapter or any regulation issued hereunder, and (2) the reasonable and necessary costs incurred by any person in providing temporary care for any fish, wildlife, or plant pending the disposition of any civil or criminal proceeding alleging a violation of this chapter with respect to that fish, wildlife, or plant. The amount of the reward, if any, is to be designated by the Secretary or the Secretary of the Treasury, as appropriate. Any officer or employee of the United States or any State or local government who furnishes information or renders service in the performance of his official duties is ineligible for payment under this subsection. Whenever the balance of sums received under this section and section 3375(d) of this title, as penalties or fines, or from forfeitures of property, exceed $500,000, the Secretary of the Treasury shall deposit an amount equal to such excess balance in the cooperative endangered species conservation fund established under section 1535(i) of this title.

(e) Enforcement

(1) The provisions of this chapter and any regulations or permits issued pursuant thereto shall be enforced by the Secretary, the Secretary of the Treasury, or the Secretary of the Department in which the Coast Guard is operating, or all such Secretaries. Each such Secretary may utilize by agreement, with or without reimbursement, the personnel, services, and facilities of any other Federal agency or any State agency for purposes of enforcing this chapter.
(2) The judges of the district courts of the United States and the United States magistrate judges may, within their respective jurisdictions, upon proper oath or affirmation showing probable cause, issue such warrants or other process as may be required for enforcement of this chapter and any regulation issued thereunder.
(3) Any person authorized by the Secretary, the Secretary of the Treasury, or the Secretary of the Department in which the Coast Guard is operating, to enforce this chapter may detain for inspection and inspect any package, crate, or other container, including its contents, and all accompanying documents, upon importation or exportation. Such person may make arrests without a warrant for any violation of this chapter if he has reasonable grounds to believe that the person to be arrested is committing the violation in his presence or view, and may execute and serve any arrest warrant, search warrant, or other warrant or civil or criminal process issued by any officer or court of competent jurisdiction for enforcement of this chapter. Such person so authorized may search and seize, with or without a warrant, as authorized by law. Any fish, wildlife, property, or item so seized shall be held by any person authorized by the Secretary, the Secretary of the Treasury, or the Secretary of the Department in which the Coast Guard is operating pending disposition of civil or criminal proceedings, or the institution of an action in rem for forfeiture of such fish, wildlife, property, or item pursuant to paragraph (4) of this subsection; except that the Secretary may, in lieu of holding such fish, wildlife, property, or item, permit the owner or consignee to post a bond or other surety satisfactory to the Secretary, but upon forfeiture of any such property to the United States, or the abandonment or waiver of any claim to any such property, it shall be disposed of (other than by sale to the general public) by the Secretary in such a manner, consistent with the purposes of this chapter, as the Secretary shall by regulation prescribe.
(4)(A) All fish or wildlife or plants taken, possessed, sold, purchased, offered for sale or purchase, transported, delivered, received, carried, shipped, exported, or imported contrary to the

provisions of this chapter, any regulation made pursuant thereto, or any permit or certificate issued hereunder shall be subject to forfeiture to the United States.
(B) All guns, traps, nets, and other equipment, vessels, vehicles, aircraft, and other means of transportation used to aid the taking, possessing, selling, purchasing, offering for sale or purchase, transporting, delivering, receiving, carrying, shipping, exporting, or importing of any fish or wildlife or plants in violation of this chapter, any regulation made pursuant thereto, or any permit or certificate issued thereunder shall be subject to forfeiture to the United States upon conviction of a criminal violation pursuant to subsection (b)(1) of this section.

(5) All provisions of law relating to the seizure, forfeiture, and condemnation of a vessel for violation of the customs laws, the disposition of such vessel or the proceeds from the sale thereof, and the remission or mitigation of such forfeiture, shall apply to the seizures and forfeitures incurred, or alleged to have been incurred, under the provisions of this chapter, insofar as such provisions of law are applicable and not inconsistent with the provisions of this chapter; except that all powers, rights, and duties conferred or imposed by the customs laws upon any officer or employee of the Treasury Department shall, for the purposes of this chapter, be exercised or performed by the Secretary or by such persons as he may designate.
(6) The Attorney General of the United States may seek to enjoin any person who is alleged to be in violation of any provision of this chapter or regulation issued under authority thereof.

(f) Regulations

The Secretary, the Secretary of the Treasury, and the Secretary of the Department in which the Coast Guard is operating, are authorized to promulgate such regulations as may be appropriate to enforce this chapter, and charge reasonable fees for expenses to the Government connected with permits or certificates authorized by this chapter including processing applications and reasonable inspections, and with the transfer, board, handling, or storage of fish or wildlife or plants and evidentiary items seized and forfeited under this chapter. All such fees collected pursuant to this subsection shall be deposited in the Treasury to the credit of the appropriation which is current and chargeable for the cost of furnishing the services. Appropriated funds may be expended pending reimbursement from parties in interest.

(g) Citizen suits

(1) Except as provided in paragraph (2) of this subsection any person may commence a civil suit on his own behalf—
(A) to enjoin any person, including the United States and any other governmental instrumentality or agency (to the extent permitted by the eleventh amendment to the Constitution), who is

alleged to be in violation of any provision of this chapter or regulation issued under the authority thereof; or

(B) to compel the Secretary to apply, pursuant to section 1535(g)(2)(B)(ii) of this title, the prohibitions set forth in or authorized pursuant to section 1533(d) or 1538(a)(1)(B) of this title with respect to the taking of any resident endangered species or threatened species within any State; or

(C) against the Secretary where there is alleged a failure of the Secretary to perform any act or duty under section 1533 of this title which is not discretionary with the Secretary.

The district courts shall have jurisdiction, without regard to the amount in controversy or the citizenship of the parties, to enforce any such provision or regulation, or to order the Secretary to perform such act or duty, as the case may be. In any civil suit commenced under subparagraph (B) the district court shall compel the Secretary to apply the prohibition sought if the court finds that the allegation that an emergency exists is supported by substantial evidence.

(2)(A) No action may be commenced under subparagraph (1)(A) of this section—

(i) prior to sixty days after written notice of the violation has been given to the Secretary, and to any alleged violator of any such provision or regulation;

(ii) if the Secretary has commenced action to impose a penalty pursuant to subsection (a) of this section; or

(iii) if the United States has commenced and is diligently prosecuting a criminal action in a court of the United States or a State to redress a violation of any such provision or regulation.

(B) No action may be commenced under subparagraph (1)(B) of this section—

(i) prior to sixty days after written notice has been given to the Secretary setting forth the reasons why an emergency is thought to exist with respect to an endangered species or a threatened species in the State concerned; or

(ii) if the Secretary has commenced and is diligently prosecuting action under section 1535(g)(2)(B)(ii) of this title to determine whether any such emergency exists.

(C) No action may be commenced under subparagraph (1)(C) of this section prior to sixty days after written notice has been given to the Secretary; except that such action may be brought immediately after such notification in the case of an action under this section respecting an emergency posing a significant risk to the well-being of any species of fish or wildlife or plants.

(3)(A) Any suit under this subsection may be brought in the judicial district in which the violation occurs.

(B) In any such suit under this subsection in which the United States is not a party, the Attorney General, at the request of the Secretary, may intervene on behalf of the United States as a matter of right.

(4) The court, in issuing any final order in any suit brought pursuant to paragraph (1) of this subsection, may award costs of litigation (including reasonable attorney and expert witness fees) to any party, whenever the court determines such award is appropriate.
(5) The injunctive relief provided by this subsection shall not restrict any right which any person (or class of persons) may have under any statute or common law to seek enforcement of any standard or limitation or to seek any other relief (including relief against the Secretary or a State agency).

(h) Coordination with other laws

The Secretary of Agriculture and the Secretary shall provide for appropriate coordination of the administration of this chapter with the administration of the animal quarantine laws (as defined in section 136a(f) of title 21) and section 306 [1] of the Tariff Act of 1930 (19 U.S.C. 1306). Nothing in this chapter or any amendment made by this chapter shall be construed as superseding or limiting in any manner the functions of the Secretary of Agriculture under any other law relating to prohibited or restricted importations or possession of animals and other articles and no proceeding or determination under this chapter shall preclude any proceeding or be considered determinative of any issue of fact or law in any proceeding under any Act administered by the Secretary of Agriculture. Nothing in this chapter shall be construed as superseding or limiting in any manner the functions and responsibilities of the Secretary of the Treasury under the Tariff Act of 1930 [19 U.S.C. 1202 et seq.], including, without limitation, section 527 of that Act (19 U.S.C. 1527), relating to the importation of wildlife taken, killed, possessed, or exported to the United States in violation of the laws or regulations of a foreign country.
(Pub. L. 93–205, §11, Dec. 28, 1973, 87 Stat. 897; Pub. L. 94–359, §4, July 12, 1976, 90 Stat. 913; Pub. L. 95–632, §§6–8, Nov. 10, 1978, 92 Stat. 3761, 3762; Pub. L. 97–79, §9(e), Nov. 16, 1981, 95 Stat. 1079; Pub. L. 97–304, §§7, 9(c), Oct. 13, 1982, 96 Stat. 1425, 1427; Pub. L. 98–327, §4, June 25, 1984, 98 Stat. 271; Pub. L. 100–478, title I, §1007, Oct. 7, 1988, 102 Stat. 2309; Pub. L. 101–650, title III, §321, Dec. 1, 1990, 104 Stat. 5117; Pub. L. 107–171, title X, §10418(b)(3), May 13, 2002, 116 Stat. 508.)

16 U.S.C.
United States Code, 2017 Edition
Title 16 - CONSERVATION
CHAPTER 35 - ENDANGERED SPECIES
Sec. 1541 - Endangered plants
From the U.S. Government Publishing Office, www.gpo.gov

§1541. Endangered plants

The Secretary of the Smithsonian Institution, in conjunction with other affected agencies, is authorized and directed to review (1) species of plants which are now or may become endangered or threatened and (2) methods of adequately conserving such species, and to report to Congress, within one year after December 28, 1973, the results of such review including recommendations for new legislation or the amendment of existing legislation.
(Pub. L. 93–205, §12, Dec. 28, 1973, 87 Stat. 901.)

16 U.S.C.
United States Code, 2017 Edition
Title 16 - CONSERVATION
CHAPTER 35 - ENDANGERED SPECIES
Sec. 1542 - Authorization of appropriations
From the U.S. Government Publishing Office, www.gpo.gov

§1542. Authorization of appropriations

(a) In general

Except as provided in subsections (b), (c), and (d), there are authorized to be appropriated—
(1) not to exceed $35,000,000 for fiscal year 1988, $36,500,000 for fiscal year 1989, $38,000,000 for fiscal year 1990, $39,500,000 for fiscal year 1991, and $41,500,000 for fiscal year 1992 to enable the Department of the Interior to carry out such functions and responsibilities as it may have been given under this chapter;
(2) not to exceed $5,750,000 for fiscal year 1988, $6,250,000 for each of fiscal years 1989 and 1990, and $6,750,000 for each of fiscal years 1991 and 1992 to enable the Department of Commerce to carry out such functions and responsibilities as it may have been given under this chapter; and
(3) not to exceed $2,200,000 for fiscal year 1988, $2,400,000 for each of fiscal years 1989 and 1990, and $2,600,000 for each of fiscal years 1991 and 1992, to enable the Department of

Agriculture to carry out its functions and responsibilities with respect to the enforcement of this chapter and the Convention which pertain to the importation or exportation of plants.

(b) Exemptions

There are authorized to be appropriated to the Secretary to assist him and the Endangered Species Committee in carrying out their functions under sections[1] 1536(e), (g), and (h) of this title not to exceed $600,000 for each of fiscal years 1988, 1989, 1990, 1991, and 1992.

(c) Convention implementation

There are authorized to be appropriated to the Department of the Interior for purposes of carrying out section 1537a(e) of this title not to exceed $400,000 for each of fiscal years 1988, 1989, and 1990, and $500,000 for each of fiscal years 1991 and 1992, and such sums shall remain available until expended.

(Pub. L. 93–205, §15, Dec. 28, 1973, 87 Stat. 903; Pub. L. 94–325, June 30, 1976, 90 Stat. 724; Pub. L. 95–632, §9, Nov. 10, 1978, 92 Stat. 3762; Pub. L. 96–159, §8, Dec. 28, 1979, 93 Stat. 1230; Pub. L. 97–304, §8[(a)], Oct. 13, 1982, 96 Stat. 1425; Pub. L. 100–478, title I, §1009, Oct. 7, 1988, 102 Stat. 2312.)

16 U.S.C.
United States Code, 2017 Edition
Title 16 - CONSERVATION
CHAPTER 35 - ENDANGERED SPECIES
Sec. 1543 - Construction with Marine Mammal Protection Act of 1972
From the U.S. Government Publishing Office, www.gpo.gov

§1543. Construction with Marine Mammal Protection Act of 1972

Except as otherwise provided in this chapter, no provision of this chapter shall take precedence over any more restrictive conflicting provision of the Marine Mammal Protection Act of 1972 [16 U.S.C. 1361 et seq.].

(Pub. L. 93–205, §17, Dec. 28, 1973, 87 Stat. 903.)

16 U.S.C.
United States Code, 2017 Edition
Title 16 - CONSERVATION
CHAPTER 35 - ENDANGERED SPECIES
Sec. 1544 - Annual cost analysis by Fish and Wildlife Service
From the U.S. Government Publishing Office, www.gpo.gov

§1544. Annual cost analysis by Fish and Wildlife Service

Notwithstanding section 3003 of Public Law 104–66 (31 U.S.C. 1113 note; 109 Stat. 734), on or before January 15, 1990, and each January 15 thereafter, the Secretary of the Interior, acting through the Fish and Wildlife Service, shall submit to the Congress an annual report covering the preceding fiscal year which shall contain—

(1) an accounting on a species by species basis of all reasonably identifiable Federal expenditures made primarily for the conservation of endangered or threatened species pursuant to this chapter; and

(2) an accounting on a species by species basis of all reasonably identifiable expenditures made primarily for the conservation of endangered or threatened species pursuant to this chapter by States receiving grants under section 1535 of this title.

(Pub. L. 93–205, §18, as added Pub. L. 100–478, title I, §1012, Oct. 7, 1988, 102 Stat. 2314; amended Pub. L. 106–201, §1(a), May 18, 2000, 114 Stat. 307.)

HOW CASE LAW DEFINES A STATUTE – LEGAL REASONING EXERCISE

1. a) Explain the meaning of "knowingly" in Section 1540(b)(1) of the Endangered Species Act (E.S.A.). Cite a case defining "knowingly."
   b) Who may commence a civil action for an alleged violation of the E.S.A.? Who may commence a criminal action? Explain and cite any relevant statutory reference.
   c) Can a person who knowingly violates the E.S.A. be imprisoned? Use a case where this issue was litigated.
   d) Define "standing" under the E.S.A. Who has standing to obtain judicial review under the E.S.A.? Cite the section of the E.S.A. that addresses this issue and explain the meaning of this section. How is standing construed in *Overton Park*? Explain the court's reasoning.

2. a) Cite and briefly explain the relevant section of the Administrative Procedures Act (A.P.A.) that formed the basis for the judicial review obtained by the plaintiffs in *Carlton v. Babbit.*

b) What was the "negative finding" with regard to the Cabinet/Yak grizzly bear population that prompted the plaintiffs' lawsuit in *Carlton v. Babbitt*? What remedy did the plaintiffs seek?

c) Explain the judge's finding in the Cabinet/Yak portion of *Carlton v. Babbitt.* What was the remedy? How did this finding utilize the *Overton Park* case?

3. Cite the specific section(s) of the E.S.A. that extends habitat protection to private property? Explain how this is accomplished. In what case(s) was the issue of extending habitat protection to private property discussed?

4. a) How does the E.S.A. define "take"? Quote and cite the relevant section(s).

   b) How is the meaning of "take" further expanded in 50 C.F.R.17.3? Why is 50 C.F.R.17.3 so important to the meaning of take?

   c) Briefly state the issue and finding in *Palila v. Hawaii* and then explain how this case defined the meaning of "take." Refer to the relevant statutory and administrative provisions.

   d) Would the *Palila* II court have reached a different decision regarding critical habitat had there been no specific E.S.A. provision? Explain.

Chapter 11 – Environmental Statutes and the Modern Environmental Movement

Earlier in this book you read about the law as a dynamic social system. Environmental law obeys that principle too, and engaged citizens like you will continue to promote its values through all the law-making branches of our government, at the local, state, and federal level.

For instance, in *TVA v. Hill,* 437 U.S. 153 (1978), the Supreme Court of the United States stated that the "Endangered Species Act of 1973 represented the most comprehensive legislation for the preservation of endangered species ever enacted by any nation." Remember that this law was passed in the midst of an explosion of nearly twenty years of new, forceful environmental legislation, regulations, agencies, and, like the case above, powerful case law precedents.

For a while, there has been amazing legislative activity in this area. Below are only some of these statutes passed by Congress during a two-decade period. They are listed chronologically, including the agencies they created. When it comes to the environment, only national governments and their international organization can act in a meaningful way:

Wilderness Act 1964, Public Law 88-577 (16 U.S.C. 1131-1136)
Solid Waste Disposal Act 1965, Public Law 89–272 (42 U.S.C. 6901–6992k)
National Historic Preservation Act 1966, Public Law 113–287 (54 U.S.C. 300101 – 320303)
National Wildlife Refuge System Administration Act of 1966, Public Law 89–669 (16 U.S.C. 668dd et seq.)
Wild and Scenic Rivers Act 1968, Public Law 90-542 (16 U.S.C. 1271 et seq.)
National Environmental Policy Act 1969 (established the Environmental Protection Agency on December 2, 1970), Public Law 91–190 (42 U.S.C. § 4321 et seq.)
Occupational Safety and Health Act and Occupational Health and Safety Administration 1970, Public Law 91-596 (29 USC 651 et seq.)
Clean Air Act 1970, Public Law 88-206 (42 U.S.C. §7401 et seq.)
Environmental Quality Improvement Act 1970 (established the Council on Environmental Quality), Public Law 91–224 (42 U.S.C. §§4371-4375)
Geothermal Steam Act 1970, Public Law 91-581 (30 U.S.C. §1001 et seq.)
Wild Free-Roaming Horses and Burros Act 1971, Public Law 92-195 (16 U.S.C. § 1331 et seq.)
Noise Pollution and Abatement Act 1972, Public Law 92-574 (42 U.S.C. §§ 4901 - 4918)
Clean Water Act 1972, Public Law 92-500 (33 U.S.C. §1251 et seq.)
Marine Mammal Protection Act 1972, Public Law 92-532 (16 U.S.C. §1361 et seq.)
Coastal Zone Management Act 1972, Public Law 92-583 (16 U.S.C. §1451 et seq.)

Marine Protection Research, and Sanctuaries Act 1972 (Ocean Dumping Act), Public Law 92-522 (33 U.S.C. 1401-1445, 16 U.S.C. 1431-1447f, 33 U.S.C. 2801-2805)

The 1972 Amendments to the Bald and Golden Eagle Protection Act of 1972 (responsible for the DDT ban in 1972), Public Law 92-535 (16 U.S.C. 668-668d)

Endangered Species Act 1973, Public Law 93-205 (16 U.S.C. §1531 et seq.)

Safe Drinking Water Act 1974, Public Law 93-523 (42 U.S.C. §300f et seq.)

Energy Reorganization Act 1974 (established Nuclear Regulatory Commission), Public Law 93-438 (42 U.S.C. § 5801 et seq.)

Energy Policy and Conservation Act 1975, Public Law 94-163 (42 U.S.C. §6201 et seq.)

Toxic Substances Control Act 1976, Public Law 94-469 (15 U.S.C. §2601 et seq.)

Resource Conservation and Recovery Act 1976, Public Law 94-580 (42 U.S.C. §6901 et seq.)

Federal Land Policy and Management Act 1976, Public Law 94-579 (43 U.S.C. §1701 et seq.)

National Forest Management Act 1976, Public Law 94-588 (16 U.S.C. §1600 et seq.)

Fisheries Conservation and Management Act 1976, Public Law 95-87 (16 U.S.C. §1801 et seq.)

Hazardous Materials Transportation Act 1976, Public Law 93-933 (49 U.S.C. §1201 et seq.)

The Department of Energy Organization Act of 1977 (established the Department of Energy), Public Law 95-91

Surface Mining Control and Reclamation Act 1977, Public Law 95-87 (30 U.S.C. §1201 et seq.)

Public Rangelands Improvement Act 1978, Public Law 95-514 (43 U.S.C. §1901 et seq.)

National Energy Act of 1978, included Public Utility Regulatory Policies Act (Public Law 95–617); Energy Tax Act (Public Law 95–618); National Energy Conservation Policy Act (Public Law 95–619); Power Plant and Industrial Fuel Use Act (Public Law 95–620); and Natural Gas Policy Act (Public Law 95–621).

Uranium Mill Tailings Radiation Control Act 1978, Public Law 95-604 (42 U.S.C. § 7901 et seq.)

Comprehensive Environmental Response, Compensation, and Liability Act 1980 (Superfund or C.E.R.C.L.A.), Public Law 96-510 (42 U.S.C. § 9601 et seq.)

Energy Security Act 1980, Public Law 96-294 (42 U.S.C. § 8701 et seq.)

Low Level Radioactive Waste Policy Act 1980, Public Law 96-573 (42 U.S.C. § 2021b)

Nuclear Waste Policy Act of 1982, Public Law 97-425 (42 U.S.C. § 10101 et seq.)

Federal Oil & Gas Royalty Management Act 1982, Public Law 97-451 (30 U.S.C. § 1701 et seq.)

What concatenation of historically evolved forces, events, and issues made all of this possible? The confluence and interaction of five major factors provided the impetus for this revolutionary whirlwind of legislation, growth of the federal environmental administrative state, exponential growth of the environmental legal profession, expansion of environmental consciousness, and maturation of environmental organizations.

1. Let us first begin with growth of environmental consciousness. The publication of Rachel Carson's Silent Spring in 1962 was a transformative event. Her book was revolutionary and warned of the dangers of pesticides (especially dichlorodiphenyltrichloroethane or DDT) as well as nuclear fallout. The broad theme was toxification of the environment by human activities. This book not only warned that humans now had the capability to massively poison the environment and its life; but, in the case of nuclear weapons, obliterate it. Carson also taught her many readers about basic ecology and the "balance of nature." The assault by chemical and agricultural big businesses on her book, and on Carson personally, was unprecedented, but ended up popularizing Silent Spring and its message even more. Her impact is reported in an excellent manner in the film "Rachel Carson's Silent Spring," a part of the American Experience series. There is a long history of environmental consciousness and the environmental movement. The purpose here is not to recount this history because the history of the environmental movement is well-explained in the following books:

A People's History of Environmentalism in the United States, by Chad Montrie;
First Along the River: A Brief History of the U.S. Environmental Movement, by Benjamin Kline;
A Fierce Green Fire: The American Environmental Movement, by Philip Shabecoff;
The Shaping of Environmentalism in America, by Victor Scheffer;
The American Environment: Readings in the History of Conservation, by Roderick Nash.

There was an important, nationally recognized conservation movement in the early 1900s focused largely on forests, wildlife, and the first parks and nature preserves. Gifford Pinchot brought conservationist and "right-use" policies for forests into the federal government. Teddy Roosevelt supported the creation of our national park system. John Muir organized the Sierra Club. The Audubon Society was founded. Aldo Leopold and his Sand County Almanac moved beyond preservation and into basic ecology, placing humans as part of the earth ecosystem and not over and above it, controlling nature. These books tend to emphasize prominent individuals, their accomplishments, and their philosophy in their history of the environmental movement. While these contributions are important, they miss the contributions and perceptions of the common working person.

A People's History of Environmentalism in the United States provides a useful antidote by discussing the perceptions of the working people, their unions, and their important role in protecting the workplace and the environment. Also significant was the contribution of the Hudson River School of painting. This movement popularized a transcendental and romantic reverence for wilderness, the sublime in nature, as well as providing an impetus for nature tourism that is well described by Kenneth Myers in "The Catskills: Painters, Writers, and Tourists in the Mountains 1820-1895."

The point is that there was a strong and developing thread of environmental consciousness that existed before the revolutionary whirlwind of the 60s and 70s. Rachel Carson's Silent Spring was published at a time when the environmental consciousness of the people was at a peak, had reached a crescendo. Why? The post-World War II excesses of unrestrained industrial development had led to environmental damage that no one could escape. Nuclear testing had dumped large amounts of radioactive fallout across the country. The nuclear weapons arms race had made it clear to everyone that humans now had the capability of destroying life on the planet as we know it. Once clear rivers, lakes, and streams now yielded up frothy foams and decaying green mats of algae along with millions of dead fish in massive fish kills. The Cuyahoga River infamously caught fire, and the Santa Barbara Channel was devastated by a massive oil spill. These were two of many events that captured national attention. How could this happen? The threatened existence of the whooping cranes also became a national issue along with the slaughter of the whales and seals. People died in major cities from breathing the smog, ozone, and soot dumped into the air. Toxic dump sites filled with thousands of rusting metal barrels oozed poisons. Raw sewage poured into our rivers, lakes, and streams from every town and city. There was no escape from the toxification, acidification, and eutrophication. THE CLOSING CIRCLE by Barry Commoner was a best seller. Perhaps the best indicator of popular environmental consciousness was the first Earth Day celebration in 1970. Over 20 million Americans were involved, but none of the older conservation organizations (National Wildlife Federation, Audubon Society, Sierra Club, etc.) were significantly involved in the organization of the first Earth Day. This was a totally grass-roots response by the American public in which members of civil rights and antiwar movements played an important role. There was now a wave of deepening anger. Something needed to be done. The environmental crisis required a response. Public opinion demanded it.

2. This environmental consciousness grew alongside and interacted with the social upheavals of the 60s: the civil rights movement; the Vietnam War; the draft and a growing antiwar movement; the movement for women's rights; the assassinations of John Kennedy, Malcolm X, Martin Luther King, and Robert Kennedy; and massive riots in most major cities. Do not forget *Hernandez v. Texas, Brown v. Board of Education,* the murders of so many activists, the dogs and fire hoses, resistance by white supremacists at the highest levels, federal troops, *Browder v. Gayle, the Civil Rights Act, the 24th Amendment, Loving v. Virginia, the Freedom Riders, Bloody Tuesday* and *Bloody Sunday, the Voting Rights Act,* and so much more. This struggle on the path of righteousness lifted the environmental movement and showed the path of non-violent protest and political activism with a purpose. The antiwar movement did the same. With over 55,000 killed in action and many more maimed and addicted to drugs in a war directed by lies at the highest levels of government, this movement became intense and national. It also

involved race (because many on the front lines were black) as well as the environment (e.g., Agent Orange).

3 & 4. So with a newly evolved and fervent environmental consciousness fortified and enriched by powerful movements for social justice, a new and structurally different kind of environmental organization developed and this new style organization initiating environmental litigation to achieve ecologic and political goals. This new style of organization went well-beyond the organizational structures of the traditional environmental groups. These new organizational principles grew out of struggle. The finest example, the bellwether, and the link that pulled the chain of the environmental movement was the movement to stop the pumped storage hydroelectric facility at Storm King Mountain on the Hudson River. This project was proposed by Con Edison in 1962, and initially approved by the old-boys network in the Federal Power Commission. The pumped storage facility would pump billions of gallons of water from the Hudson River up to the top of Storm King Mountain in order to let it fall and generate the electricity needed at peak periods of energy consumption. The problems were that the scenic beauty of Storm King Mountain, an icon of nature, would be destroyed, that the pumping would seriously impact the reproduction of striped bass, and that there were easier, more economical ways to generate peak electricity with jet turbine engines. STORM KING MOUNTAIN AND THE EMERGENCE OF MODERN AMERICAN ENVIRONMENTALISM by Robert Lifset documents the details of this eighteen-year-long, successful effort to save Storm King. The organization that developed around the movement to save Storm King was called the Scenic Hudson Preservation Conference. This group transformed the environmental movement by using the law as well as a new style of organization. It had a multitude of grassroots workers and organizers, as well as fundraisers, public relations and media specialists, scientists, economists, fishermen, and, of course, lawyers. The use of science to prove ecologic damage in court was entirely new and the interdisciplinary array of talents became the new foundation for environmental organizations. The famous landmark case of *Scenic Hudson Preservation Conference v. Federal Power Commission,* 354 F.2d 608 (2d Cir. 1965) was the first case in which the court granted standing based upon the plaintiffs' "special interest in aesthetic, conservational, and recreational aspects" of the mountain. In addition, the plaintiffs obtained judicial review and had the Storm King license revoked and remanded to the Federal Power Commission (where the struggle continued for more than a decade). This legal battle is described by Skip Card in THE 40TH ANNIVERSARY OF SCENIC HUDSON AND THE BIRTH OF ENVIRONMENTAL LITIGATION, and by Albert K. Butzel (one of the attorneys for Scenic Hudson) in STORM KING REVISITED: A VIEW FROM THE MOUNTAINTOP. As the titles of the books and articles indicate, Scenic Hudson was the birth of environmental litigation, and the Scenic Hudson Preservation Conference with its new style of environmental organization gave birth to the modern environmental movement.

Scenic Hudson was not alone. The new style of environmental organization is also exemplified by the *Environmental Defense Fund* (EDF). The EDF was founded in 1967 and grew out of a movement (inspired by Rachel Carson's Silent Spring) to ban the aerial spraying of DDT in Suffolk County, NY. In the mid-1960s, the founders of the EDF, Dennis Puleston, Victor Yannacone, and Robert Smolker, had discovered that the populations of osprey and other large predatory birds at the top of the food chain were dwindling. Their research showed a direct correlation between the spraying of DDT to kill mosquitoes and the thinning of eggshells of large birds, which resulted in premature death. Again, like Scenic Hudson, the focus of their efforts in court was to obtain injunctions against the spraying. They succeeded in the state of New York, and, after taking their efforts nationally, DDT was banned in the U.S. in 1972. The EDF still exists to this day as a leading organization within the environmental movement. Its activities marked a new beginning in the environmental movement. They involved a new style of organization: scientists and lawyers that worked together to achieve environmental goals in court.

DDT Wars: Rescuing Our National Bird, Preventing Cancer, and Creating the Environmental Defense Fund by Charles F. Wurster is an excellent book describing the early efforts and establishment of the EDF. What is true for Scenic Hudson and for the EDF is also true for the Natural Resources Defense Council, which was founded in 1970 by a group of law students and attorneys involved in the environmental movement. All major environmental groups, including the Sierra Club and Audubon Society, now have dockets, with resources and attorneys allocated for carefully selected environmental lawsuits and legal actions.

The four major factors discussed above that came together and interacted to help create the revolutionary whirlwind of environmental legislation are: 1) growth of environmental consciousness, 2) social upheavals of the '60s, 3) a structurally different kind of environmental organization, and 4) use of environmental litigation to achieve ecologic and political goals.

The fifth critical factor required in order to bear fruit was 5) the development and growth of the administrative state. It is generally agreed that the birth of the administrative state began with the New Deal, though legislation to create agencies within the executive branch occurred before this time. The next great spate of legislation to expand the administrative state occurred during President Kennedy's New Frontier and President Johnson's Great Society. The major policy areas of focus were civil rights and the "war on poverty" (health, education, and welfare). There were other areas, but the impetus for environmental legislation starts here. Given the sophistication and critical mass of the administrative state at this time, these programs made possible the means by which the government could provide environmental regulation and protection.

Nearly two decades of environmental legislation (1964-1982) have completely transformed the environmental movement. Protecting the environment is now big business. The National Environmental Policy Act (NEPA) requires the production of an Environmental Impact Statement (the EIS) for every project that involves some form of federal action. The same is true of most state projects so that almost every project/ development now requires an EIS. The agencies responsible for preparing an EIS often hire private sector consulting firms with expertise in the proposed project as well as in the project's probable environmental effects. As a result, EIS-consulting firms are a big business.

The *Environmental Protection Agency* (E.P.A.) defines a brownfield as "real property, the expansion, redevelopment, or reuse of which may be complicated by the presence or potential presence of a hazardous substance, pollutant, or contaminant." The actual presence of contaminants on this "real property" must be determined by a carefully planned investigation known as an environmental site assessment (E.S.A.). The Comprehensive Environmental Response, Compensation, and Liability Act (C.E.R.C.L.A.) of 1980 made the purchaser of any real property liable for any contaminants on this property. C.E.R.C.L.A.'s retroactive liability has made the completion of an E.S.A. a practical necessity for any potential buyer of property, who naturally does not want to assume liability for the cleanup of any contaminants found there. E.S.A.s have evolved into a multi-step process carried out by trained professionals employed by an environmental consulting firm. The E.P.A. has now strictly outlined the steps necessary for an E.S.A., which must be completed by a licensed environmental professional. E.S.A.s have become a routine part of real estate acquisitions and, thus, big business. Many such examples can be cited with regard to environmental legislation. Laws and regulations do indeed create jobs. In addition, many of the new environmental statutes like the Clean Air Act, Clean Water Act, and Endangered Species Act automatically provide for citizen standing and a direct means for citizens and environmental organizations to be directly involved in carrying out the goal of the legislation.

To the list of statutes at the beginning of this chapter, we should note the many more recent amendments to many of these statutes. More recent legislation includes:

Emergency Planning and Community Right-to-Know Act 1986, Public Law 100-235 (42 U.S.C. §11001 et seq.)
Lead Contamination Control Act 1988 (an amendment to the Safe Drinking Water Act), Public Law 100-572 (42 U.S.C. §300f et seq.)
North American Wetlands Conservation Act 1989, Public Law 101-233 (16 U.S.C. §4401 et seq.)
Oil Pollution Act of 1990, Public Law 101-380 (33 U.S.C. §2701 et seq.)
Pollution Prevention Act 1990, Public Law 101-508 (42 U.S.C. §13101 et seq.)
Food Quality Protection Act 1996, Public Law 104-170 (7 U.S.C. §136 et seq.)

Of course, there was limited but significant environmental legislation passed before the 1960s, such as:

Rivers and Harbors Appropriation Act 1899, Ch. 425 (33 U.S.C. §403 et seq.)

Lacey Act 1900, Ch. 553 (16 U.S.C. §§ 3371–3378)

National Park Service Organic Act 1916, Ch. 408 (16 U.S.C. §§ 1-4)

Migratory Bird Treaty Act of 1918, Ch. 128 (16 U.S.C. §§ 703–712)

Taylor Grazing Act of 1934, Ch. 865 (43 U.S.C. §§ 315-315o)

Federal Food, Drug, and Cosmetic Act of 1938, Ch. 675 (21 U.S.C §301 et seq.)

Atomic Energy Act of 1946, Public Law 79-585, superseded by **Atomic Energy Act of 1954,** Public Law 83-703 (42 U.S.C. §§ 2011-2017)

Outer Continental Shelf Lands Act 1953 (Bureau of Ocean Energy Management 2010), Ch. 345 (43 U.S.C §1331 et seq.)

Price-Anderson Nuclear Industries Indemnity Act 1957, Public Law 85-256 (42 U.S.C §2012 et seq.).

Food Additives Amendment 1958, Public Law 85-929 (21 U.S.C §321 et seq.).

What determines the meaning of these statutes and subsequent regulations promulgated by the agencies? The answer, of course, is case law as produced by lawsuits and adjudications in a courtroom. The final two chapters will explain this brief answer.

Chapter 12 – Environmental Law Research Combines Decisional, Statutory, and Administrative Law Research

We are approaching the end of our environmental law, policy, and research journey. You have been exposed to policy reasons behind the enactment of major environmental law statutes, as well as behind the adjudication of major environmental law issues. Environmental law, while promoting public values, cannot exist without citizens' determination to alert the government to the work it needs to do to protect everybody's life: by lobbying for legislative initiative or going to court to remediate some public harm. Environmental activism thus benefits from a solid understanding of how the law works and how legal research is performed.

Environmental law research requires familiarity with the relevant primary sources: case law (decisional) research, as well as statutory and administrative law research. Because environmental law has a strong administrative law component, environmental law research, as illustrated below, mandates a strong familiarity with administrative law, as well.

When we talked about the basic principles of legal research, the fourth principle stated the need to be flexible and remember that legal research is not a linear process. Your research has to make sense, and if necessary, you have to go back and forth between secondary and primary sources until you find the correct answer.

This fourth principle is useful to remember especially when your research covers all three branches of the government. For instance, if you were to research a complex question, you would benefit from a rigorous research plan (macro-managing your research), and a systematic research log (micro-managing your research). Let's assume your question is the following:

> *Find the circumstances when the notice and comments requirements applied to a specific agency rulemaking procedure.*

Your research would cover all three branches of the government, and multiple secondary sources discussing both the administrative rule-making procedures and how those rules applied to the circumstances of your research. Before you would start the macro and micromanagement of the question at hand, you would be hard pressed to have some understanding of federal administrative law.

Within this pre-research phase, you would learn about the federal administrative rulemaking that takes place within the general authority prescribed by the Administrative Procedure Act (A.P.A.), Pub. L. 79-404, codified at 5 U.S.C. § 551 et seq. Furthermore, each federal statute can delegate rulemaking powers to specific agencies, and circumscribe those powers within very strict limits.

The A.P.A., 5 U.S.C. §§ 551-59-701-06, is one of those quasi-constitutional statutes, which is heavily litigated. To summarize its significance, a quick search for law journal articles brings an impressive number of relevant articles. One of them is Christopher J. Walker, *Modernizing the Administrative Procedure Act*, 69 ADMIN. L. REV. 629 (2017), states:

> The Administrative Procedure Act (APA) has set the default rules that govern the federal regulatory state since its enactment in 1946. Over the decades, the APA has assumed quasi- constitutional status. In 1978, for instance, then-Professor Antonin Scalia remarked that "the Supreme Court regarded the APA as a sort of superstatute, or subconstitution, in the field of administrative process: a basic framework that was not lightly to be supplanted or embellished." (p. 630)

Because of its complexity, it makes sense to simplify your research query. For instance, let's try to reformulate your question:

> *What are the A.P.A. provisions on rulemaking requirements?*

As mentioned in Chapters 2-4, we encourage you to perform legal research in a particularly organized manner. We want you to strategize, map out your research, and afterward— execute it.

In this instance, the macro-management of your legal research starts from the moment you strategize how to find the relevant statutory section or sections on rulemaking requirements. If you think about performing a Google search with those keywords, or going directly to https://www.govinfo.gov/, and then browse title 5 of the U.S.C for the relevant content, instead of just accessing a fee-based database and performing the keyword search, any of these paths represent a strategy or a research plan. No matter what path you have chosen, you will discover that Section 553 of the A.P.A., 5 U.S.C. § 553, establishes the rulemaking procedure requirements for all agencies. It states:

> (a) This section applies, according to the provisions thereof, except to the extent that there is involved—
>
> (1) a military or foreign affairs function of the United States; or
>
> (2) a matter relating to agency management or personnel or to public property, loans, grants, benefits, or contracts.
>
> (b) General notice of proposed rule making shall be published in the Federal Register, unless persons subject thereto are named and either personally served or otherwise have actual notice thereof in accordance with law. The notice shall include—
>
> (1) a statement of the time, place, and nature of public rule making proceedings;
>
> (2) reference to the legal authority under which the rule is proposed; and

(3) either the terms or substance of the proposed rule or a description of the subjects and issues involved.

Except when notice or hearing is required by statute, this subsection does not apply—

(A) to interpretative rules, general statements of policy, or rules of agency organization, procedure, or practice; or

(B) when the agency for good cause finds (and incorporates the finding and a brief statement of reasons therefore in the rules issued) that notice and public procedure thereon are impracticable, unnecessary, or contrary to the public interest.

(c) After notice required by this section, the agency shall give interested persons an opportunity to participate in the rule making through submission of written data, views, or arguments with or without opportunity for oral presentation. After consideration of the relevant matter presented, the agency shall incorporate in the rules adopted a concise general statement of their basis and purpose. When rules are required by statute to be made on the record after opportunity for an agency hearing, sections 556 and 557 of this title apply instead of this subsection.

(d) The required publication or service of a substantive rule shall be made not less than 30 days before its effective date, except—

(1) a substantive rule which grants or recognizes an exemption or relieves a restriction;
(2) interpretative rules and statements of policy; or
(3) as otherwise provided by the agency for good cause found and published with the rule.

(e) Each agency shall give an interested person the right to petition for the issuance, amendment, or repeal of a rule.
(Pub. L. 89–554, Sept. 6, 1966, 80 Stat. 383.) (emphasis added)

Upon reading an explanatory secondary source summarizing the A.P.A, and reading one or more times the legislative text, you understand that Section 553 is designed to standardize administrative procedures and "to improve the administration of justice by prescribing fair . . . procedure," but you are far from understating the exact requirements. The text is unclear and filled with exceptions. By now, you understand that finding this relevant statutory provision does not end your research. Furthermore, even after accessing its legislative history—The Legislative History of the Administrative Procedure Act, S. DOC. NO. 248, 79th Cong., 2d. Sess. 187 (1946)—and reading committee reports or various congressional testimony, so that you understand the legislative intent behind it, your research task is far from complete.

A superficial reading of Section 553 states that an agency is required to publish a proposed rule in the *Federal Register.* A comment period follows publication during which interested parties may respond with criticisms and suggestions. Upon receiving and considering comments, the agency may promulgate a final rule, which may differ considerably from the original one, along with a statement of basis and purpose. The final rule becomes effective thirty days after its publication in the *Federal Register.* All interested parties have the right to petition for modification or repeal of the rule and may seek judicial review of the rule. The final rule is then published in the *Code of Federal Regulations.* Is this answer satisfactory?

In a civil law country, this sounds like a good beginning. An attorney could argue for the reading expounded above and suggest incorporating or excluding such requirements based on her understanding of the A.P.A. provisions. Anything would work as long as the rules of logical interpretation tolerate the argument.

But, in a common law country like ours, statutory interpretation has to incorporate case law jurisprudence as much as common-sense logic. Additionally, often the statutory language is complemented by agency rules detailing it. For instance, Section 553 is detailed by thousands of administrative rules. Among them is the following rule, entitled *Categories of documents,* which describes the categories of documents publishable in the Federal Register. This rule, *Categories of documents,* is codified at 1 C.F.R. § 5.9 (2019), and states that each document published in the *Federal Register* shall be placed under one of the following categories, as indicated below:

> (a) The President. This category contains each Executive order or Presidential proclamation and each other Presidential document that the President submits for publication or orders to be published.
>
> (b) Rules and regulations. This category contains each document having general applicability and legal effect, except those covered by paragraph (a) of this section. This category includes documents subject to codification, general policy statements concerning regulations, interpretations of agency regulations, statements of organization and function, and documents that affect other documents previously published in the rules and regulations section.
>
> (c) Proposed rules. This category contains each notice of proposed rulemaking submitted pursuant to Section 553 of title 5, United States Code, or any other law, which if promulgated as a rule, would have general applicability and legal effect. This category includes documents that suggest changes to regulations in the Code of Federal Regulations, begin a rulemaking proceeding, and affect or relate to other documents previously published in the proposed rules section.

(d) Notices. This category contains miscellaneous documents applicable to the public and not covered by paragraphs (a), (b), and (c) of this section. This category includes announcements of meetings and other information of public interest.

The rule about *Categories of documents* does add clarification to the reading of the A.P.A. statutory provision codified at 5 U.S.C. § 553. But, the final meaning of 5 U.S.C. § 553 is given by case law, and your research needs to incorporate it.

Case law interprets and gives authoritative meaning to all statutory language. For you as a researcher, the meaning of 5 U.S.C. § 553 depends on the relevant jurisdiction. It depends on the holding of a court decision coming from the court of last resort within the specific jurisdiction. For a federal statute, such as the A.P.A., that court is the United States Supreme Court.

The A.P.A. contains certain express exemptions from the notice and comment requirements. These exemptions are described in Section 553(b)(3)(A) and (B). The first exemption applies to interpretative rules, general statements of policy, and rules of administrative organization, procedure, or practice. Interpretative rules are an agency's interpretation of statutes or regulations that it administers. Such rules are supposed to clarify existing laws or regulations. It is possible that a rule can be both legislative and interpretive. Who would make the new rules to distinguish among the type of agency rulemaking?

Let's apply the third principle of legal research and reformulate our research question, so that we first identify the exceptions:

- Can an agency follow the *notice and comments* requirements even if the rules it wants to pass do not reach that level of importance?

Or, maybe it should be changed into:

- Should a court ask an agency to follow the *notice and comments* requirements procedure, on grounds of fairness on a case by case basis?

- Are the *notice and comments* requirements mandatory for an agency even when the A.P.A. is silent?

Let's assume you choose to reformulate your research question. It could be as it follows:

Are the notice and comments requirements mandatory for an agency even when the A.P.A. is silent?"

The answer becomes the following:

Under 5 U.S.C. § 553, there are instances when the notice and comments requirements are expressly mandated, but because Congress established these notice and comments procedures to give interested parties a reasonable opportunity to participate in the rulemaking process, they should apply to other situations too. To satisfy notions of elementary fairness, those requirements should apply when the rules passed would have a significant impact.

How does one find this answer?

After finding the statutory provision, then you need to find how the courts themselves have explained when notices and comments are required. You go back to macro-managing your research and strategizing your case law research and find that there is no comprehensive way of performing federal case law research using Google Scholar or any of the free-of-charge databases. You will have to access one of the fee-based mega databases, as case law research is a necessary research step. Without finding cases discussing the statutory provision of your choice, you cannot give a correct and comprehensive answer to any statutory research question. Thus, for instance, by doing a full-text search where the keyword is the statutory citation itself, or by using the citators embedded in any of the three mega databases, *LexisAdvance, Westlaw,* or *Bloomberg Law,* you could find more than a thousand cases discussing Section 553 of Title 5 of the *United States Code.*

Performing a keyword search on this issue brings up a multiplicity of cases, some of them so diverse, that their lack of uniformity caused a split within the circuit court decisions. In such situations, the United States Supreme Court intervenes to clarify the jurisprudential split. The case where the United States Supreme Court handed down a unanimous decision, in an attempt to unify the rulemaking issue discussed here was *Vermont Yankee Nuclear Power Corp. v. Natural Resources Defense Council, Inc.*, 435 U.S. 519 (1978).

Let's use *Vermont Yankee Nuclear Power Corp.* to continue our briefing exercises. In *Vermont Yankee,* the Supreme Court addressed the procedure surrounding a rule promulgated by the Nuclear Regulatory Commission (N.R.C.). That rule specified which spent fuel hazards it would consider in making adjudicatory decisions to license specific plants. *Vermont Yankee* faced the issue of whether courts could require more of an agency than the minimum procedures of notice and comments in accordance with Section 553. The Court in *Vermont Yankee* held that courts should not mandate rulemaking procedures that Congress had not required. But it did not stop there. For a unanimous Court, Justice Rehnquist expounded, that in extremely rare circumstances agencies should be free to fashion their own rules of procedure.

Thus, the holding in *Vermont Yankee* seems to nuance and add meaning to the answer to the research question posed earlier: where the enabling statute or the A.P.A. does not require preliminary notices and comments, whether courts may mandate those procedures.

Before we find the complete answer to your question, it is worth reading what the current Justice Stephen Breyer wrote in connection to this case when he was only a Harvard Law School faculty member. He addressed a version of the question posed earlier in this chapter. We still need to know when an agency needs to follow the "notice and comments" rulemaking procedure, and when it can rely on the A.P.A. exemption, if ever, on grounds of fairness. Justice Breyer had addressed a somewhat reformulated research question.

What is a reviewing court to do when it is uncertain whether an agency has dealt adequately with a complex and important scientific or technical issue?

If we were to look at Breyer's writing in Stephen Breyer, *Vermont Yankee and the Courts' Role in the Nuclear Energy Controversy*, 91 Harv. L. Rev. 1833 (1978), as a form of case briefing, then in addition to the legal issue he also identified the holding, the facts and the procedural history of *Vermont Yankee.* He wrote:

> In the Vermont Yankee case, the Court of Appeals for the District of Columbia Circuit sought to require additional agency procedures needed for a "thorough ventilation of the issues." The Supreme Court has correctly reversed that approach but the Court did not dictated the lower court the approach to follow, thus imposing a greater than ordinary burden of inquiry upon the agency. (at 1834).

We can continue quoting his language, as it is very instructive in terms of what we have come to call "dicta," or "reasoning":

> The judges are, I believe, intruding too deeply upon the administrative process, perhaps without full realization of their implicit premises or of the potential consequences. My argument will draw in part upon a discussion of the "substantive" issues in the case, since I believe that, in practice, the reviewing standards courts apply often reflect unarticulated assumptions about, or attitudes toward, the substantive aspects of the subject matter being reviewed (at 1834).

Because students rarely have the opportunity to read a case brief by a Supreme Court Justice, perhaps the following passage is also worth mentioning:

> My own recent review of the literature suggests that most experts would accept the following facts. Without an increased supply of oil, a radical breakthrough in solar technology, or the like, the major alternatives to nuclear power plants are inaction or increased reliance upon coal plants. Each approach (nuclear, coal, inaction) threatens the health and safety of many persons, bears the seeds (however improbable) of potential catastrophe, and risks major harm to the environment.
>
> The most recent comparison of the health and safety effects of coal and nuclear energy suggests that coal plants are likely to cause seven to twelve times as many deaths as nuclear plants, and four to six times as much sickness and injury. A study of nuclear power supervised by a group of prestigious experts and sponsored by the Ford Foundation in 1977 also suggested that coal is considerably more dangerous than nuclear power. The health and safety effects of not building any power plants depend upon the probability of blackouts or shortages. A

> Federal Power Commission study in 1976 indicated that a failure to license plants would create serious power loss risks by 1985. While these figures and other data available may not provide certainty as to precisely how much more dangerous coal is than nuclear energy, they do preclude any certainty that nuclear energy is more dangerous than coal. (at 1835–36)

Nevertheless, *Vermont Yankee* does not represent the end of the jurisprudential interpretation of Section 553 of the A.P.A. There are hundreds of cases using it as a point of reference; some incorporate its holding as *stare decisis.*

In fact, courts have explained the Section 553 notice and comments requirement by connecting it to the types of administrative rules agency issues. The type of rule determines when the requirement is applied. The distinction among administrative rules is differentiating whether rules are legislative, or substantive, and thus binding, or whether they are merely interpretative, and thus, only receiving deference from the court.

For instance, the Supreme Court in *Chrysler Corp. v. Brown,* 441 U.S. 281 (1979), created the legislative and substantive rule terminology, and distinguished between substantive rules having the binding effect of law and general statements of policy, which received only deferential treatment. The Court in *Chrysler Corp. v. Brown,* found that substantive rules affected individual rights and obligations. A general policy statement, on the other hand, prospectively advises how an agency will exercise a discretionary power.

> In order for a regulation to have the "force and effect of law," it must be a "substantive" or "legislative-type" rule affecting individual rights and obligations (as do the regulations in the case at bar), and it must be the product of a congressional grant of legislative authority, promulgated in conformity with any procedural requirements imposed by Congress. (*Chrysler Corp.,* 441 U.S. at 282).

In *Chrysler Corp.,* the United States Supreme Court decided that there were agency rules which had impact, although it was not necessarily "substantive." They could have been excluded from some procedural burdens but fundamental fairness required those agencies to adhere to the notice and comment procedures.

However, finding one or more relevant cases, even if one is a United States Supreme Case is not enough. As mentioned in the seventh principle of legal research, your research has to contain only "good law," which means it should cover only cases that are still binding, so they represent *stare decisis.* The citators, *Shepards* on *LexisAdvance, KeyCite* on *Westlaw,* and *BCite* on *Bloomberg law* will guide your search in this direction.

An additional layer of difficulty arises when you research a complex question, such as the one raised here. For instance, even if *Chrysler Corp.* is still good law, because the A.P.A. is such a significant statute, many of its provisions have been under tremendous judiciary scrutiny.

Section 553 is an example on point, and you need to make sure that there are no additional, further clarifying, answers to your question. In particular, what happens if you reformulate your research question? Think about how your answer changes if you research the following question instead:

> Can courts create an additional procedural requirement for agencies which have not implemented a notice and comments requirements procedure, on grounds of fairness?

In a recent case, *Perez v. Mortg. Bankers Ass'n*, 575 U.S. ______, 135 S. Ct. 1199, 1203 (2015), Justice Sotomayor writing for the United States Supreme Court, referenced both *Chrysler Corp.* and *Vermont Yankee,* built on their jurisprudential approach to the A.P.A., but reached a different conclusion (holding). Justice Sotomayor concluded the opposite of what the previous courts held in *Chrysler Corp.* and *Vermont Yankee.* In a magisterial way, in the name of *stare decisis,* Justice Sotomayor eviscerated the previous cases and held that 5 U.S.C. § 553 established the maximum procedural standard, which agencies alone could incorporate, but courts were not free to impose it, overcoming the agencies' decision. The Justice held that it was not the domain of the judiciary to create such judge-made procedures, but that of Congress:

> The APA establishes the procedures federal administrative agencies use for "rule making," defined as the process of "formulating, amending, or repealing a rule." § 551(5). "Rule," in turn, is defined broadly to include "statement [s] of general or particular applicability and future effect" that are designed to "implement, interpret, or prescribe law or policy." § 551(4).
>
> Section 4 of the APA, 5 U.S.C. § 553, prescribes a three-step procedure for so-called "notice-and-comment rulemaking." First, the agency must issue a "[g]eneral notice of proposed rulemaking," ordinarily by publication in the Federal Register. § 553(b). Second, if "notice [is] required," the agency must "give interested persons an opportunity to participate in the rule making through submission of written data, views, or arguments." § 553(c). An agency must consider and respond to significant comments received during the period for public comment. See *Citizens to Preserve Overton Park, Inc. v. Volpe,* 401 U.S. 402 (1971); *Thompson v. Clark,* 741 F.2d 401, 408 (C.A.D.C.1984). Third, when the agency promulgates the final rule, it must include in the rule's text "a concise general statement of [its] basis and purpose." § 553(c). Rules issued through the notice-and-comment process are often referred to as "legislative rules" because they have the "force and effect of law." *Chrysler Corp. v. Brown,* 441 U.S. 281, 302–303. [...]
>
> The straightforward reading of the APA we now adopt harmonizes with longstanding principles of our administrative law jurisprudence. Time and again, we have reiterated that the A.P.A. "sets forth the full extent of judicial authority to review executive agency action for procedural correctness." *Fox Television Stations, Inc.,* 556 U.S., at 513, 129 S. Ct. 1800. Beyond the APA's minimum requirements, courts lack authority "to impose upon [an] agency its own notion of which procedures

> are 'best' or most likely to further some vague, undefined public good." *Vermont Yankee*, 435 U.S., at 549. To do otherwise would violate "the very basic tenet of administrative law that agencies should be free to fashion their own rules of procedure." *Id.*, at 544 [...].
>
> These foundational principles apply with equal force to the APA's procedures for rulemaking. We explained in *Vermont Yankee* that § 4 of the Act "established the maximum procedural requirements which Congress was willing to have the courts impose upon agencies in conducting rulemaking procedures." *Id.*, at 524. "Agencies are free to grant additional procedural rights in the exercise of their discretion, but reviewing courts are generally not free to impose them if the agencies have not chosen to grant them." *Id.* (at 1207).

Concluding, all legal research has a mandatory case law research component, because since *Marbury v. Madison*, 5 U.S. 137 (1803), the courts have the last word explaining the law. Thus, comprehensive and correct answers need to contain statutory provisions as explained or interpreted by agencies, if relevant to the research question, and the jurisprudence litigating their application, brought up to date.

Using this standard of research, what is your answer to the question posed earlier:

> *Does the "notice and comments" rulemaking procedure apply when the A.P.A. does not expressly require it?*

We have reformulated it, so it became clearer and easier to answer. Reformulating the question as mentioned below helped you understand its difficulty.

- *Can an agency follow the notice and comments requirements even if the rules it wants to pass do not reach that level of importance?*
- *Should a court ask an agency to follow the notice and comments requirements procedure, on grounds of fairness on a case by case basis?*
- *Are the notice and comments requirements mandatory for an agency even when the A.P.A. is silent?*

Writing your final answer, remember to start with the statutory provision, 5 U.S.C. § 553, and apply the administrative rule explaining what documents represent administrative "rulemaking," and then find the jurisprudence within your specific jurisprudence, making sure you include the most relevant U.S. Supreme Court decision. The most recent U.S. Supreme Court decision indicates that while agencies are free to adopt more requirements than those provided by the A.P.A., if they do not, courts are not free to require them to on any grounds (related to the type of the rule issued, or on grounds of fairness). You would then cite Justice Sotomayor.

Chapter 13 – The Role of Administrative Law in Protecting the Environment

In this final chapter, we will carefully analyze *Citizens to Preserve Overton Park v. Volpe*, 401 U.S. 402 (1971). We focus on this case because it offers a rare chance to see the tension raised by the judicial review of agency law in the context of environmental law. It is also a case study of governmental checks and balances, of judicial control of the executive branch.

The core of this case is judicial review of agency adjudication. In the process of analyzing this case, you will also see how case law interprets and defines statutory law. In fact, most of the E.S.A. cases discussed in this book involve agency rulemaking and adjudication.

Before we get started, it would be useful to review Chapter 2 again, especially the section entitled "Article II – The Executive Branch, Executive Orders, Agencies and Administrative Law."

CITIZENS TO PRESERVE OVERTON PARK V. VOLPE, 401 U.S. 402 (1971)

Citizens to Preserve Overton Park v. Volpe is a U.S. Supreme Court case. While reading the case from Justia, https://supreme.justia.com/cases/federal/us/401/402/, review the questions in *Study Questions for Overton Park* in the Companion Website, and at the end of this chapter. Note the location of Overton Park, Memphis, Tennessee, Route 40, and the Mississippi River on the maps. Download the opinion and read it online or print it. As you read, number the paragraphs and focus on how the information in each paragraph fits into the rubrics for a brief, again mentioned below.

1. Heading
2. Facts
3. Procedural History
4. Legal Issues
5. Holding or Decision
6. Reasoning

Overton Park is not only a landmark case, it is also a powerful teaching tool for administrative law. In paragraph 1, Justice Thurgood Marshall begins by making the point that is the basis of Chapter 9 of this book: "The History of Environmental Statutes and Regulatory Law." The opinion was handed down in 1971 when the modern environmental movement led to a crescendo of statutes and regulations aimed at protecting the environment in the United States. Footnote #1 in *Overton Park* lists a few of these statutes that are more fully enumerated in Chapter 9.

Justice Marshall recognizes the growing public concern about the quality of the environment and the consequent Congressional legislation designed to curb the accelerating destruction of the environment. He references two statutes, the *Department of Transportation Act* of 1966, § 4(f), 49 U.S.C. § 1653(f), as well as the *Federal-Aid to Highways Act of 1968,* § 18 (a), 23 U.S.C. § 138: "[i]t is hereby declared to be the national policy that a special effort should be made to preserve the natural beauty of the countryside and public park and recreation lands, wildlife and waterfowl refuges, and historic sites." (401 U.S., at 405). Further, the Secretary of the Department of Transportation "shall not approve any program or project which requires the use of any publicly owned land from a public park, recreation area, or wildlife and waterfowl refuge....unless (1) there is no feasible and prudent alternative to the use of such land, and (2) such program includes all possible planning to minimize harm to such park, recreational area, wildlife and waterfowl refuge or historic site resulting from such use."

The procedural history is outlined in paragraph 2. The Citizens to Preserve Overton Park along with a number of environmental organizations sued the Secretary of Transportation, John Volpe, for violating the aforementioned statutes by allowing the "expenditure of federal funds for the construction of a six-lane interstate highway through a public park in Memphis, Tennessee." Footnote 7 indicates that the case originated in the District Court for the District of Columbia but was removed to the Western District of Tennessee in the Sixth Circuit. The significance of this Supreme Court case was emphasized by the presence of the Solicitor General (Erwin Griswold at this time during the Johnson administration) who defended the Secretary of Transportation. The District Court dismissed the case on the defendant's motion for summary judgment. The Court of Appeals affirmed the dismissal. The plaintiffs then petitioned the U.S. Supreme Court for an injunction to halt construction and the Court granted a "stay," placing a temporary hold on the decision of the lower court, as well as certiorari. We learn that the decisions of the lower courts were reversed and the case was remanded to the District Court for "further proceedings."

The facts of the case are presented in paragraphs 3 and 4. The Court describes 342-acre Overton Park and the history of the planning and approvals for the interstate highway through the park. Rights of way and federal funding were obtained for both the east and west connectors, and the six-lane east connector (now Sam Cooper Boulevard) was built right up to the edge of the park. Developers then waited for the Secretary of Transportation to fulfill § 4 (f) of the *Department of Transportation Act* and give approval for the expenditure of federal funds for the building of the highway through the park. This approval did not include any factual findings nor did it provide any explanation about any "prudent and feasible alternative" or any "planning to minimize harm to such park."

In paragraph 5 we learn that the Citizens to Preserve Overton Park did, in fact, have several well-considered, prudent and feasible alternatives and ideas to reduce harm to the park. Using Section 555(e) of the *Administrative Procedures Act* (APA), 5 U.S.C. § 555(e), the plaintiffs sued the Department of Transportation and became involved in this agency's adjudication process. The plaintiffs claimed that the Secretary's approval was not valid because the decision did not include formal findings. Section 555 (e) states: "[p]rompt notice shall be given of the denial in whole or in part of a written application, petition, or other request of an interested person made in connection with any agency proceed-ing. Except in affirming a prior denial or when the denial is self-explanatory, the notice shall be accompanied by a brief statement of the grounds for denial."

In paragraph 6 the defendants replied, "that it was unnecessary for the Secretary to make formal findings, and that he did, in fact, exercise his own independent judgment which was supported by the facts." Paragraph 7 informs readers that both the "District Court and Court of Appeals found that formal findings by the Secretary were not necessary;" and in paragraph 8, the Court states: "[w]e agree that formal findings were not required." The adjudication process can, in fact, be accomplished formally in a full trial process, as described in § 554 and §§ 556-557, with discovery, motions, witnesses, cross-examination, introduction of evidence, and, of course, a complete record of all the proceedings along with a well-reasoned decision. The Secretary of the Department of Transportation had no statutory obligation to produce formal findings of this type and the A.P.A. provides no specific process for informal findings in this type of adjudication.

Paragraphs 6, 7, and 8 also refer to two other issues. First, the plaintiffs "sought to take the deposition of a former Federal Highway Administrator who had participated in the decision to route I-40 through Overton Park" but the District Court "refused to order the deposition" because they "believed that probing of the mental processes of an administrative decision maker was prohibited," and "that the Secretary's authority was wide and reviewing court's authority narrow in the approval of highway routes." This deference accorded to agency decision-making and the Secretary's "wide" authority was typical in the judicial review of agency actions by courts at this time and, as we shall see, is at the heart of this landmark case. This is well before *Chevron U.S.A. Inc. v. NRDC*, 467 U.S. 837 (1984), which set forth the framework for deciding how much deference to give formal agency rulemaking and adjudication. The Court noted that the Secretary's decision was entered by the respondents as affidavits. Affidavits are notarized or authorized statements or statements made under oath on behalf of (*ex parte*) one party. The District Court and Court of Appeals used them as evidence that the Secretary had acted legally and had not "exceeded his authority." They were also *ex post facto* (created after the secretary's decision) for the purpose of supporting the defendant's position in the District Court. For all of these reasons, the Court did not "believe that in this case judicial review based solely on litigation affidavits was adequate."

The "threshold question" (that probably should have been addressed earlier) is whether the plaintiffs have the right to judicial review. This is a judicial review of agency actions, not to be confused with judicial review inaugurated by Chief Justice John Marshall in *Marbury v. Madison,* 5 U.S. 137 (1803). In *Marbury,* Chief Justice Marshall held that courts were the arbiter of statutory constitutionality rather the legislative or executive branches. The right to judicial review is clearly stated by the A.P.A., in 5 U.S.C. § 702:

> (a) person suffering legal wrong because of agency action, or adversely affected or aggrieved by agency action within the meaning of a relevant statute, is entitled to judicial review thereof. An action in a court of the United States seeking relief other than money damages and stating a claim that an agency or an officer or employee thereof acted or failed to act in an official capacity or under color of legal authority shall not be dismissed nor relief therein be denied on the ground that it is against the United States or that the United States is an indispensable party. The United States may be named as a defendant in any such action, and a judgment or decree may be entered against the United States:
> Provided, that any mandatory or injunctive decree shall specify the Federal officer or officers (by name or by title), and their successors in office, personally responsible for compliance. Nothing herein (1) affects other limitations on judicial review or the power or duty of the court to dismiss any action or deny relief on any other appropriate legal or equitable ground; or (2) confers authority to grant relief if any other statute that grants consent to suit expressly or impliedly forbids the relief which is sought.

The Court quotes from 5 U.S.C § §701 that states in full:

> (a)This chapter applies, according to the provisions thereof, except to the extent that—
>
> (1) statutes preclude judicial review; or (2) agency action is committed to agency discretion by law.
>
> (b) For the purpose of this chapter— (1) 'agency' means each authority of the Government of the United States, whether or not it is within or subject to review by another agency.

After this follows a list of entities not included in the definition of an agency such as the Congress, the courts of the Unites States, and so forth.

Using these defining sections of the A.P.A., paragraph 9 makes it clear that the Department of Transportation is an agency and that the only limitations on the right to judicial review of this agency's actions are when "statutes preclude judicial review" or when "agency action is committed to agency discretion by law." *The Department of Transportation Act* places no restrictions on judicial review and in paragraph 10, we learn that action "committed to agency discretion by law" is a very "narrow exception" applicable only when "'statutes are drawn in such broad terms that in a given case there is no law to apply.'" (Quoting 5 U.S.C. § 701).

Paragraphs 11-14 discuss Congressional intent. The Court quotes Section 4 (f) of the *Department of Transportation Act* and similar language in the *Federal-Aid to Highway Act*, concluding that "this language is a plain and explicit bar to the use of federal funds for construction of highways through parks – only the most unusual situations are exempted." The defense then argues that in spite of this language, the Secretary "has wide discretion" "to engage in a wide-ranging balancing of competing interests" in order to determine a "prudent and feasible" route. The Court responds by saying that "no such wide-ranging endeavor was intended" and that "in most cases consideration of cost, directness of route, and community disruption will indicate that parkland should be used for highway construction whenever possible." The cost will be low because the state or local government already owns the property. It should be noted that during the height of interstate highway building between 1957-1965, (after the *Federal Aid to Highway Act* was signed by President Eisenhower in 1956) parklands were considered to be desirable locations for highway construction because they didn't require the federal government to pay the legal costs of eminent domain proceedings and then compensate the private property owners. Paragraph 14 states that the "very existence" of the statutes" (quoted above) "indicates that protection of parkland was to be given paramount importance." Paragraph 15 begins with the concluding statement that "plainly, there is 'law to apply' and thus the exemption for action 'committed to agency discretion' is inapplicable."

The key significance of this most instructive landmark case is introduced in paragraph 15 with the statement that "the existence of judicial review is only the start: the standard for review must also be determined." Six separate standards delineated in §706 of the A.P.A. define the lawful scope of judicial review. Section 706 reads:

> "To the extent necessary to decision and when presented, the reviewing court shall decide all relevant questions of law, interpret constitutional and statutory provisions, and determine the meaning or applicability of the terms of an agency action. The reviewing court shall—
>
> (1) compel agency action unlawfully withheld or unreasonably delayed; and
>
> (2) hold unlawful and set aside agency action, findings, and conclusions found to be—
>
> (A) arbitrary, capricious, an abuse of discretion, or otherwise not in accordance with law;
>
> (B) contrary to constitutional right, power, privilege, or immunity;

(C) in excess of statutory jurisdiction, authority, or limitations, or short of statutory right;

(D) without observance of procedure required by law;

(E) unsupported by substantial evidence in a case subject to sections 556 and 557 of this title or otherwise reviewed on the record of an agency hearing provided by statute; or

unwarranted by the facts to the extent that the facts are subject to trial de novo by the reviewing court.

In making the foregoing determinations, the court shall review the whole record or those parts of it cited by a party, and due account shall be taken of the rule of prejudicial error."

Paragraphs 15-28 are devoted to a discussion of these standards to determine which, if any, can provide a basis for judicial review in this case.

In paragraph 16 the plaintiffs argue that either "E," the "substantial evidence" test, or in the alternative, "F," the "unwarranted by the facts" test is applicable and that the Secretary's action must be subject to a *de novo* review. *De novo* review means that the reviewing court reconsiders the entire case anew. The Court rules that "neither of these standards is, however, applicable in this case."

Paragraph 17 points out that the 'substantial evidence test' ("E" above) is only warranted "in a case subject to 5 U.S.C. §§ 556-557 of this title or otherwise reviewed on the record of an agency hearing provided by statute." Sections 556 and 557 involve trial–type procedures or a "public adjudicatory hearing." *Overton Park* was not subject to 5 U.S.C. §§ 556-557, and so the "substantial evidence test" could not be the basis for judicial review. The Court rejects *de novo* review in paragraph 18. Yes, the agency's decision may have been "unwarranted by the facts," but in standard "F" they must be unwarranted "to the extent that the facts are subject to trial de novo by the reviewing court." The *de novo* standard is applied only when issues of law are the major focus of a lower court's decision. In this case, since the main issues are those of fact, the *de novo* standard fails.

Though it seems that the plaintiffs' attempts to obtain judicial review under 5 U.S.C. §§ 706 (E) and (F) have failed from the technical requirements of the law, in paragraph 19 the Court warns that "706(2)(E) of the Administrative Procedure Act ... require[s] the reviewing court to engage in a substantial inquiry" and provide "a thorough, probing, in-depth review." In paragraph 20, it is stated that in this case, "the reviewing court must be able to find that the Secretary could have reasonably believed that in this case there are no feasible alternatives or that alternatives do involve unique problems.." The emphasis here should be on the word "find."

Paragraph 21 presumptively addresses standard "C" by stating: "[s]crutiny of the facts does not end with the determination that the Secretary has acted within the scope of his statutory authority." The main issue turns out to be standard "A," that agency action was not "arbitrary, capricious, an abuse of discretion, or otherwise not in accordance with law," and in order to make this determination the Court "must consider whether the decision was based on a consideration of the relevant factors and whether there has been a clear error of judgment." The Court tempers this statement with an important caveat that: "although this inquiry into the facts is to be searching and careful, the ultimate standard of review is a narrow one. The court is not empowered to substitute its judgment for that of the agency." This is the true and accurate statement of deference.

Paragraph 22 jumps to standard § 706 (2) (D), that is whether the agency followed the "procedure required by law." The plaintiffs, as already discussed, claimed that the lack of formal findings was a procedural error, and the Court reiterates its finding that formal findings were not required by law in paragraph 23.

Paragraphs 24-27 deal with DOT Order 5610.1 that "requires the Secretary to make formal findings when he approves the use of parkland for highway construction but which was issued after the route for I-40 was approved." Using the rule established in *Thorpe v. Housing Authority* that "an appellate court must apply the law in effect at the time it renders its decision," the plaintiffs argue that formal findings should now be required in a remand to the Secretary. The Court, however, distinguishes *Thorpe*, where the issues remained static, from the circumstances in *Overton Park* that have continued to develop and change. Most importantly, the Court states that "there is an administrative record that allows the full, prompt review of the Secretary's action that is sought without additional delay which would result from having a remand to the Secretary."

The Court in paragraph 29 finds it necessary to "remand this case to the District Court for plenary review of the Secretary's decision. That review is to be based on the full administrative record that was before the Secretary at the time he made his decision." The reasoning for this remand is found in paragraph 28. The administrative record referred to in paragraph 27 "is not, however, before us. The lower courts based their review on the litigation affidavits that were presented. These affidavits were merely 'post hoc' rationalizations'" and "they clearly do not constitute the 'whole record' compiled by the agency: the basis for the review required by §706 of the Administrative Procedures Act."

In addition to the case being reversed and remanded to the lower court for a full (plenary) review of the "whole record," we learn in paragraph 30 that the District Court "may require the administrative officials who participated in the decision to give testimony explaining their action," perhaps by using its subpoena power. Paragraph 31 allows the District Court to rely instead on formal findings required by DOT Order 5610.1 that may "provide an adequate explanation" for the Secretary's decision-making, though this too would need to be viewed critically through the glass of potential *post hoc* rationalizations.

Miscellaneous Issues

The significance of this case is that it raised the bar and set a new standard for judicial review of agency actions. Agencies were put on alert that they must be able to justify all decision-making with a complete and transparent record. *Overton Park* provided an important advance for what is known as the "hard look" doctrine. This doctrine requires courts to take a "hard look" at administrative agency decision-making to make sure that the agency has also taken a "hard look" at all the issues involved in particular rulemaking or adjudication actions and can support its decisions with a well-reasoned and transparent record. It is important to remember that the enormous and far-reaching administrative "branch" of government is not elected, yet it makes and enforces regulations that affect every facet of our lives. It cannot be emphasized enough that judicial review is the single most powerful and effective restriction on agency action. It is because agency decision-makers and enforcers are not elected that the courts over time have evolved this important "hard look" doctrine.

Interestingly, the plaintiffs in *Overton*, though they won the case, never did get judicial review. The only standard that was applicable was 5 U.S.C. § 706(2) (A), the "arbitrary, capricious, an abuse of discretion, or otherwise not in accordance with law" test. But the Court was unable to provide judicial review under this standard because there was no record based upon which to determine whether the Secretary's decision-making was or was not "arbitrary, capricious, an abuse of discretion, or otherwise not in accordance with law." Remember that courts will never reverse an agency decision, but if they find that the decision-making cannot be supported by the record, they will remand the issue to the agency to return with a record of solid reasoning. Often, the agency will return with a supportable record and the agency's decision will then stand. So, what happened to *Overton Park* and the Secretary's decision to build I-40 through the park?

The End Game

The plenary hearing ordered by the Supreme Court was held in the District Court for the Western Region of Tennessee in the Sixth Circuit. This court's memorandum decision was issued in January of 1972 and can be found in 335 F. Supp. 873 (W.D. Tennessee, 1972) or the second to last lawsuit, 357 F. Supp. 846 (W.D. Tennessee, 1973), available on Justia at https://law.justia.com/cases/federal/district-courts/FSupp/357/846/2154770/. This will be discussed at the end of the section. This second lawsuit has an excellent summary of what happened next:

> In the memorandum decision, this Court held: (1) that Secretary Volpe had never actually made a route or corridor determination as is required by § 4(f) of the Department of Transportation Act of 1966, as amended, (49 U.S. C.A. § 1653(f)); and (2) that even if Secretary Volpe had made

> such a determination, his determination was based on an incorrect view of the applicable law. Accordingly, we remanded to the Secretary to make a route determination in accordance with the applicable law. We also ruled that the Secretary's approval of the proposed design of the interstate through Overton Park should stand and that he need not reconsider such approval (357 F. Supp. 848-9).

There was no appeal of this Court's decision remanding to the Secretary. On January 21, 1972, Secretary Volpe stated in a news release, in part:

> I have asked for a complete analysis of the entire record that was before the court, with particular attention to alternative locations for this highway. That analysis will be done in the context of a thorough, detailed environmental impact statement, which is required by the National Environmental Policy Act. Once this analysis is complete, a new decision will be made (*Id.* at 849).

Thus, the Secretary decided that, in making the determination under § 4(f) of the Department of Transportation Act of 1966, he must also comply with the National Environmental Policy Act of 1969, 42 U.S.C.A. § 4321 et seq., (NEPA). Secretary Volpe also decided to require additional route and design public hearings and such were held, combined, on September 14 and 15, 1972, in Memphis.

On January 12, 1973, the Acting Federal Highway Administrator wrote a memorandum to his superior, Secretary Volpe, attaching a 457-page final environmental impact statement prepared pursuant to NEPA. The memorandum concluded that it was the determination of the Administration under § 4(f) that there was no feasible and prudent alternative to the route through Overton Park and that the proposed design included all possible planning to minimize harm to the park.

On January 18, 1973, Secretary Volpe rendered his decision, which states in part: "[on the basis of the record before me and in light of guidance provided by the Supreme Court, I find that an Interstate highway as proposed by the State through Overton Park cannot be approved. On that record I cannot find, as the Statute requires, and as interpreted by the courts, that there are no prudent and feasible alternatives to the use of parkland nor that the broader environmental protection objectives of the NEPA and the Federal-Aid Highway Act have been met, nor that the existing proposal would comply with FHWA standards on noise."

The State of Tennessee then filed a petition before the District Court to remand this decision back to the Secretary so that he would make his decision based on the appropriate statutory requirements and explain what the "feasible and prudent alternative" was. This opinion is found in *Citizens to Preserve Overton Park, Inc. v. Volpe*, 357 F. Supp. 846 (W.D. Tennessee, 1973). The decision was appealed, and the Appellate Court for the 6th Circuit reversed the lower court's decision. *Citizens to Preserve*

Overton Park, Inc. v. Brinegar, 494 F.2d 1212 (6th Cir. 1974) let the Secretary's decision stand. The Supreme Court denied certiorari, see, *Citizens to Preserve Overton Park, Inc. v. Smith*, 421 U.S. 991 (1975).

But that was not the end. During the next three years, the State of Tennessee submitted several new designs, most including tunnels of various kinds, for an interstate through Overton Park. The designs were rejected, and the cost estimates grew and grew. Eventually, after twenty-six years of planning and lawsuits, the I-40 Overton Park interstate highway was officially removed from the federal highway system. In 1987, the State of Tennessee returned the park to the city of Memphis where it is a vibrant part of the city's life (see www.overtonpark.org).

Study Questions for Citizens to Preserve Overton Park

http://www.overtonparkforever.org/
https://www.overtonpark.org/

1. a) What are the two main functions of agencies? Briefly define them.

   b) What function was under scrutiny in the *Overton Park* case? Explain.

https://www.overtonpark.org/2016/02/03/recap-of-february-2-parking-meeting

2. a) Why did the petitioners in the *Overton Park* case have standing to intervene?

b) Is this standing broadly or narrowly construed by the courts with regard to judicial review? Explain.

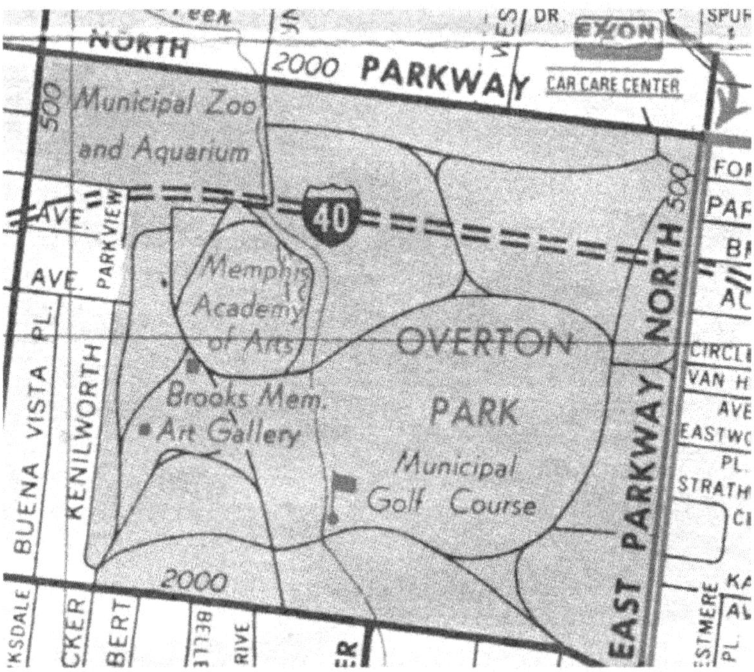

http://www.overtonparkforever.org/2011/03/forty-years-ago.html

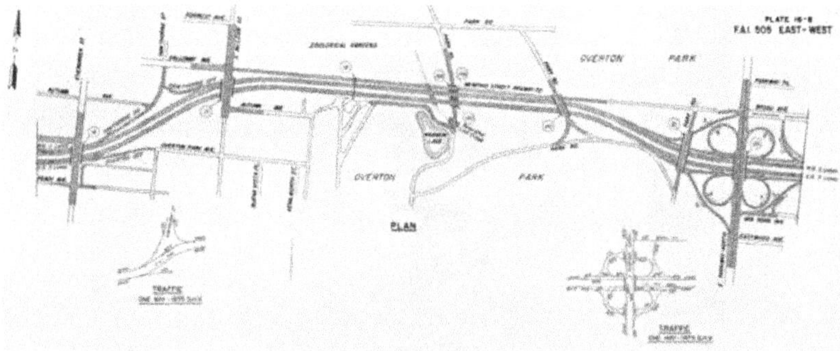

https://www.overtonpark.org/history

3. What were the main legal questions and holding in the *Overton Park* case? What was the rationale for this holding?

http://www.the19strongshow.org/council-corner.html

4. What was the remedy in the *Overton Park* case? What was the reason given by the court for choosing this remedy?

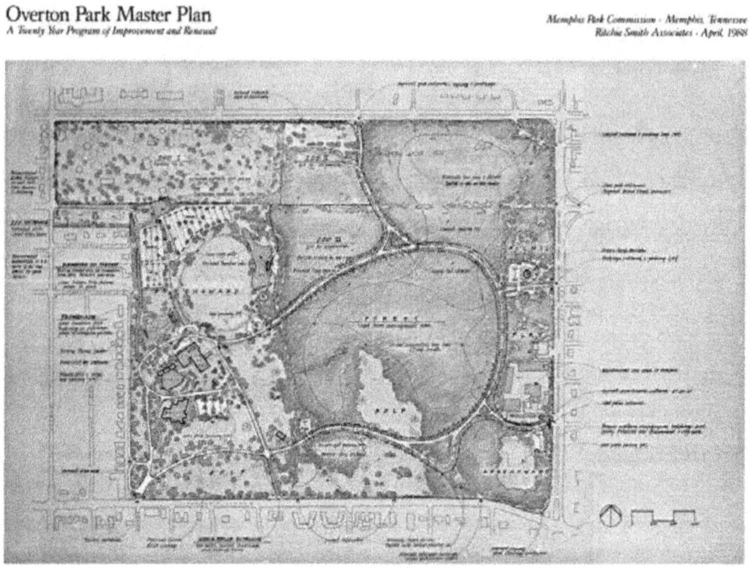

https://www.overtonpark.org/history

5. Did the petitioners win judicial review under the "substantial evidence," "de novo," or "arbitrary and capricious" tests? Explain.

https://www.overtonpark.org/2016/04/22/happy-earth-day-old-forest

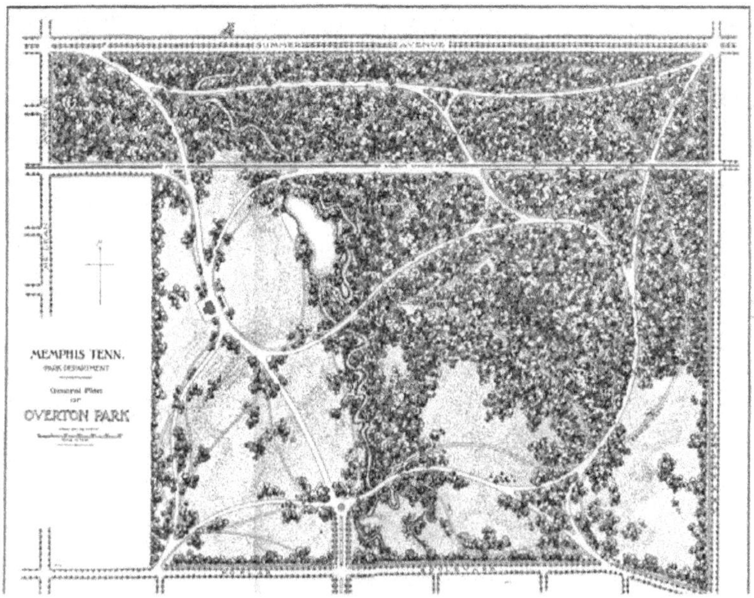

https://www.overtonpark.org/history

Overton Park Map c. 1901

Irma O. Sternberg (1915-2007), https://dlynx.rhodes.edu/jspui/handle/10267/11338 was a Memphis activist who worked to keep an expressway from being built through the center of Overton Park which is located in the Mid-town area of Memphis, Tennessee. Mrs. Sternberg's collection of over 1500 items relating to the Overton Park controversy includes published articles, correspondence, legal case descriptions, newspaper clippings, editorials and her personal notes all of which were used in building the case against the construction of the expressway. She also used these materials to write her booklet, "Overton Park is Your Park, Memphis" which she published in 1971. She gave these items to the Rhodes College History Department which then transferred them to the College Archives in 2005 where they are stored in the Archives' vault. Katie Lane, Class of 2007 who worked in the Archives from 2005 until 2007, processed the materials and created the finding aid to the collection which is published here. The Irma Sternberg Faculty Support Fund in American History was established in 2009 through the estate of Irma O. Sternberg to support research and teaching in American history. Researchers may consult the Sternberg collection during regular Archives hours.

Irma O. Sternberg Overton Park Expressway Collection

https://dlynx.rhodes.edu/jspui/handle/10267/11338

Instead of Conclusion:

The first part of the journey of this book has just ended. It will continue now with you, its users.

When its journey started, Peter was being elected a Council-member and then Mayor of a New Jersey municipality. There, he discovered environmental law, a hybrid of common law, as well as municipal, state, and federal law. More concretely, the journey started after Peter was sworn in as Mayor when he received a six-inch-thick ring-binder of the Municipal Code. Many issues he faced required reviewing the Code, using it, amending it, and when needed, creating new ordinances, which you know by now, are municipal statutes. Building a new police facility triggered state and federal law, including environmental impact statements produced by municipal agencies. Leaking underground storage tanks at private facilities, especially gas stations, as well as in the yards of the department of public works also triggered actions which would be regulated by state and federal law. Creating a park from publicly owned land or the town's first recycling program did the same. Negotiating police and fire contracts or strategies for lawsuits against the town required closed session meetings, attorneys, and then more public negotiations and litigation to issue regulations or pass ordinances.

You could say that Peter learned about the law while learning how to engage with it. His way is not too different than any attorney representing municipal interests in California, Virginia, Vermont, and Washington, where aspiring lawyers can take the bar exam and practice law without going to law school. Peter had no desire to make a living as an attorney. However, as an engaged citizen, he found it necessary to learn the law. He did it in a studious manner, as one might say, becoming a legal apprentice, so he could do his job as Mayor properly, and he hopes to inspire others doing similar work. As a geologist, environmental geochemist, and conservationist, Peter was instrumental in creating the Environmental Science Department at Barnard College. In that capacity as a scientist and, especially, because of his experiences as an elected municipal official, he created *Brownfield Action*, a web-based, interactive, three-dimensional digital space and learning simulation. Students form geotechnical consulting companies and work collaboratively to explore and solve problems in environmental forensics. They engage in an organic, evolving, laboratory exploration of a simulated brownfield and local community (see brownfieldaction.org).

But as an environmentalist, Peter needed to go further. In 1993, Peter created the course called *Environmental Law*, which incorporated all his formal and informal studies, as well as all his knowledge derived from teaching, and from life, including his work as an officer of a municipal government.

Environmental Law became a course rooted in basic civics (sorely lacking in our students, who rarely knew what a zoning code was and never knew what a ratable was). It was decided that the course would become a hands-on process-oriented class. With this experiential approach, Peter reached out to practicing attorneys and especially to law-trained librarians from the Columbia School of Law.

After having taught the class for a decade, this was how Peter met Dana *Neacşu*, a New York attorney and a Columbia Law School librarian. In 2003, she was working on publishing her first legal research book and creating a librarian-taught legal research program for LL.M. and 1L students. By then, the course incorporated a dialectical perspective and added a policy and research component to its already interdisciplinary bent.

Our students learned the ABCs of environmental law: the language, the meaning, the research; they used the Glossary and the Research Exercise you can find pages below, and the many other tools contained in the Companion Website, at http://www.environmentallaw-teach.org/. The course became *Environmental Law and Policy.*

For over ten years we have co-taught this class, co-teaching students the basics of legal research and writing: how to read and critically analyze cases, write briefs, and research precedent, as well as the role of common law environmental torts. We teach the way Dana hopes law students will eventually learn legal research and writing: as part of a doctrinal, interdisciplinary course. Students are taught of the various environmental statutes, but the course is not a description of each of these statutes. It is an analysis of one statute—the Endangered Species Act—its history, the politics behind its origin, its adoption and the administrative regulations enabling its application, as well as relevant case law that has defined the statute and guided its implementation.

Finally, this book is much indebted to Zygmunt Plater about whom we first learned when studying *TVA v. Hill.* Soon, his book, THE SNAIL DARTER AND THE DAM: HOW PORK-BARREL POLITICS ENDANGERED A LITTLE FISH AND KILLED A RIVER, became part of our stable of our course readings. Plater's other book, ENVIRONMENTAL LAW AND POLICY: NATURE LAW AND SOCIETY, continues to be a valuable resource for the *Environmental Law and Policy* course, having been read cover to cover several times, and of course, to Dana's 2005 introductory book to law and legal research.

We have written this book so many more generations of students will use our work, including the Companion Website, at http://www.environmentallaw-teach.org/. We hope they become a valuable tool for similar classes in universities all over. Based upon student reviews, especially those students who went on to law school, about one-third of each class, we believe this is a very successful approach to teaching law, policy and legal research.

Peter and Dana
New York City,
May 20, 2019

Glossary

APRIORI	From cause to effect, what goes before. The process of deducing facts that must follow from a general principle or admitted truth.
ACTION/ ACTIONABLE	Conduct, behavior, something done. Actions are divided into criminal and civil. A criminal action is a prosecution in a court of justice in the name of the government, against one or more individuals accused of a crime. A civil action is a legal demand of one's right, or it is the form given by law for the recovery of that which is due. Until judgment the writ is properly called an action, but not after. Civil actions are those brought for the specific recovery of goods and chattels; or for damages or other redress for breach of contract, or other injuries, of whatever description; the specific recovery of lands, tenements, and hereditaments only excepted. Personal actions arise either upon contracts, or for wrongs independently of contracts.
ACTUS REUS	Literally the criminal act, but more often the guilty act or deed of crime. The physicality of a crime as opposed to mens rea which is the mentality of the crime.
ADJECTIVE LAW	The rules of legal practice. The manner and means of enforcing legal rights.
ADMINISTRATIVE LAW	Synonymous with "natural justice." Administrative law is that body of law which applies for hearings before administrative tribunals. This includes the principles of natural justice. Many administrative tribunals supplement the rules of natural justice with their own detailed rules of procedure.
ADMINISTRATIVE HEARING	An oral proceeding before an administrative agency consisting of argument, trial, or both. Procedural rules are more relaxed at such hearings as contrasted with civil or criminal trials.

ADMINISTRATIVE LAW LITIGATION	Body of law created by administrative agencies in the form of rules, regulations, orders, and decisions to carry out regulatory powers and duties of such agencies. International law: Those laws governing the legal relations between nations. Rules and principles of general application dealing with the conduct of nations and of international organizations and with their relations inter se, as well as with some of their relations with persons, whether natural or juridical.
ADMIRALTY AND MARITIME JURISDICTION	Expansive jurisdiction over all actions related to events occurring at sea; "extends to all things done upon and relating to the sea, to transactions relating to commerce and navigation, to damages and injuries upon the sea, and all maritime contracts, torts, and injuries."
ADMIRALTY COURTS	Tribunals exercising jurisdiction over maritime matters, under the authority of the United States Constitution and the Judiciary Act.
ADMIRALTY LAW/ MARITIME LAW	The traditional body of rules and practices particularly relating to commerce and navigation, to business transacted at sea or relating to navigation, ships, seamen, harbors, and general maritime affairs.
AFFIDAVIT	A statement of facts which is sworn to (or affirmed) before an officer who has authority to administer an oath (e.g. a notary public). A statement which before being signed, the person signing takes an oath that the contents are, to the best of their knowledge, true. It is also signed by a notary or some other judicial officer that can administer oaths, to the effect that the person signing the affidavit was under oath when doing so.
AFFIRM	The act of an appellate court upholding a decision of a trial court or a lower appellate court is called affirming the decision. In the practice of the appellate courts, the decree or order is declared valid and will stand as rendered in the lower court.
AFFIRMATION	A solemn declaration and asseveration, which a witness makes before an officer, competent to administer an oath in a like case, to tell the truth, as if they had been sworn. Affirmation also means confirming; as, an affirmative statute.

AGAINST THE MANIFEST WEIGHT OF EVIDENCE	Evidentiary standard permitting a new trial after the verdict based on new evidence when it clearly appears to the judge that the jury's decision is unsupported by the credible evidence.
ALLEGATIONS	The assertion, declaration or statement of a party of what he can prove.
ALLEGE	An assertion of fact.
ALTERNATIVES	Solutions that everyone can live with.
AMICUS	Latin term meaning "friend of the court." Refers to a party that is allowed to provide information (usually in the form of a legal brief) to a court even though the party is not directly involved in the case at hand.
AMICUS BRIEF	Means, literally, friend of the court. A person with strong interest in AMICUS CURIAE or views on the subject matter of an action, but not a party to the action, may petition the court for permission to file a brief, ostensibly on behalf of a party but actually to suggest a rationale consistent with its own views.
ANSWER	In a civil case, the defendant's written response to the plaintiff's complaint. It must be filed within a specified period of time, and it either admits to or (more typically) denies the factual or legal basis for liability.
APPEAL	A request to a supervisory court, usually composed of a panel of judges, to review a lower court's decision.
APPELLANT	The party bringing the action to court (usually an appellate/appeal court).
APPELLATE COURT	A court of review to ensure that the findings of lower courts are correct.
APPELLATE JURISDICTION	The jurisdiction which a superior court has to bear appeals of causes which have been tried in inferior courts. It differs from original jurisdiction, which is the power to entertain suits instituted in the first instance.
APPRECIATION OF REALTY	The excess of the fair market value for the realty over the taxpayers cost or tax basis.

ARBITRATION	The process of resolving conflicts between parties or groups.
ARGUENDO	To put in clear light, for the sake of argument, hypothetically.
ARGUMENT	"A connected discourse based upon reason; a course of reasoning tending and intended to establish a position and to induce belief"
ARREST	To stop; to seize; to deprive one of his liberty by virtue of legal authority.
AT LAW	Pertains to or is governed by law as opposed to the rules of equity.
ATTORNEY-CLIENT PRIVILEGE	Privilege that confidential communications between an attorney and a client in the course of the professional relationship cannot be disclosed without the consent of the client.
BALANCING THE EQUITIES	The weight of conveniences, hardships, and policies as would be done in a Court of Equity.
BANKRUPTCY	The legal process to ensure fairness and equality amongst creditors and allow the debtor to start anew with property and free from old debts.
BAR	In procedure, barrier to the relitigating of an issue. Where causes of action are the same, final judgment on the merits in the first action is a complete bar to the second action. (2) A particular position in the courtroom is also termed a "bar," hence, the defendant standing before the judge is sometimes called the "prisoner AT BAR." The complete body of attorneys is called "the bar" because they are the persons privileged to enter beyond the bar that separates the general courtroom audience from the bench of the judge.
BARRISTER	In England one of two classes of legal practitioners, whose function is "the advocacy of causes in open court" and related duties. His function is somewhat similar to that of the American trial lawyer, but the barrister, unlike the American trial lawyer, does not prepare the case from the start. His solicitor assembles the materials necessary for presentation to the court and settles cases out of court.

BENCH TRIAL	Also called court trial. A bench trial is another term for a trial before a judge, only without a jury.
BENCH	The Court; the judges composing the court collectively. The place where the trial judge sits.
BENCH WARRANT	An order from the court empowering the proper legal authorities to seize a person; most commonly used to compel one's attendance before the court to answer a charge of contempt or for failure of a witness to attend in response to a subpoena which has been duly served.
BEYOND A REASONABLE DOUBT	The highest level of proof required to win a case. Necessary to get a guiltyverdict in criminal cases. See reasonable doubt.
BIPOLAR GOVERNMENTAL SYSTEM	A system in which there are two opposing great or super powers. These powers are highly competitive with no balancer.
BRIEF	A written argument concentrating upon legal points and authorities which is used by the lawyer to convey to the court the essential facts of his client's case, a statement of the questions of law involved, the law that he would have applied, and the application that he desires made of it by the court; it is submitted in connection with an application, motion, trial, or appeal.
CASE	An action, cause, suit or controversy.
CAUSATION	The fact of being the cause of something produced or of happening: the act by which an effect is produced: an important doctrine in fields of negligence and criminal law.
CAUSE OF ACTION	A set of facts or allegations that make up the grounds for filing a lawsuit.
CEASE & DESIST ORDER	An order from judicial authority prohibiting a person or entity from undertaking or continuing an activity or course of conduct.

CHARGE	In criminal law, the offense contained in an accusation or indictment.
CHATTELS	Any tangible, movable thing, personal, as opposed to real property.
CIRCUIT COURT	One of several courts in a given jurisdiction; a part of a system of courts extending over multiple counties.
CIRCUMSTANTIAL EVIDENCE	Indirect evidence that implies something occurred but doesn't directly prove it; proof of one or more facts from which one can find another fact; proof of a chainof facts and circumstances indicating that the person is either guilty or not guilty.
CITATION	An order of a court to either do a certain thing or to appear before it to answer charges. The citation is typically used for lesser offenses (such as traffic violations) because it relies on the good faith of the defendant to appear as requested, as opposed to an arrest or bail. The penalty for failing to obey a citation is often a warrant for the arrest of the defendant.
CIVIL	The branch of law that pertains to suits outside of criminal practice (contract, tort, etc.).
CLAIM	The assertion of a right to property or money.
CLASS ACTION	A lawsuit in which one or more parties file a complaint on behalf of themselves and all other people who are "similarly situated" (suffering from the same problem). Often used when a large number of people have comparable claims.
CLIENT	An individual, corporation, trust, or estate that employs a professional to advise or assist it in the professional's line of work. Professionals include but are not limited to: attorneys, accountants, architects, etc. A person who employs or retains an attorney or counselor, to appear for him in courts, advise, assist, and defend him in legal proceedings, and to act for him in any legal business
COMMON LAW	Judge-made law. Law which exists and applies to a group on the basis of historical legal precedents developed over hundreds of years. Because it is not written by elected politicians, but rather, by judges, it is also

referred to as "unwritten" law. Judges seek these principles out when trying a case and apply the precedents to the facts to come up with a judgment. Common law is often contrasted with civil law systems which require all laws to be written in a code or written collection.

COMPENSATORY	Also known as actual damages. Losses that are damages directly related to the breach of contract or tort and can be proven so. They should be compensated as a matter of right.
COMPLAINT	In a civil action, the document that initiates a lawsuit. The complaint outlines the alleged facts of the case and the basis for which a legal remedy is sought. In a criminal action, a complaint is the preliminary charge filed by the complaining party, usually with the police or a court. The complaint is the first court paper filed in a lawsuit. It briefly states the plaintiff's view of the crux of the legal dispute and asks the court to resolve the dispute.
CONCURRENT JURISDICTION	Equal jurisdiction; that jurisdiction exercised by different courts at the same time, over the same subject matter and within the same territory, and wherein litigants may, in the first instance, resort to either court indifferently.
CONDEMNATION	The legal process by which a governmental body exercises its right of "eminent domain" to acquire private property for public uses (highways, schools, redevelopment, etc.). Condemnation includes a resolution of public need, an offer to purchase, and, if a negotiated purchase is not possible, then a condemnation suit. The government may take the property at the time of suit if it deposits money with the court in the amount of the government's appraisal.
CONSENSUS	The making of decisions by general agreement and in the absence of any voiced objection.
CONSORTIUM	The conjugal fellowship between husband and wife and the right of each to enjoy the other's company, cooperation and aid.
CONSTITUENCY	The inhabitants of an electoral district.

CONSTITUTIONAL LAW	The original and fundamental principles of law that create a system of government and by which a country is governed.
CONSTITUTIONAL CLAIMS	Consistent with the constitution; authorized by the constitution; not conflicting with any provision of the constitution or fundamental law of the state.
CONTINUANCE	The adjournment or postponement of a session, hearing, trial, or other proceeding to a subsequent day or time; usually on the request or motion of one of the parties. Also, the entry of a continuance made upon the record of the court, for the purpose of formally evidencing the postponement, or of connecting the parts of the record so as to make one continuous whole.
CONTRACT	A promise or set of promises. In the event of a breach, the law can award remedies.
CONVICTION	The formal decision of a criminal trial which finds the accused guilty. It is the finding of a judge or jury, on behalf of the state, that a person has, beyond reasonable doubt, committed the crime for which he, or she, has been accused. It is the ultimate goal of the prosecution and the result resisted by the defense. Once convicted, an accused may then be sentenced.
CORPORATION	An association of shareholders recognized under the law as an artificial person. It is a legal entity that is completely separate from the individuals comprising the corporation.
COURT	Government entity authorized to resolve legal disputes. Judges sometimes use 'court' to refer to themselves in the third person, as in 'the court has read the briefs.
COURT OF EQUITY	The name of a court exercising jurisdiction at law, but mainly in equity. Example: bankruptcy court.
COURT OF LAW	A court that administers law based on common law (state or federal) as opposed to courts that follow the rules of equity. Courts of law are also referred to as chancery courts.

COURT OF LAST RESORT	This is the highest court in the system. It is the last place where litigants can appeal their cases. This court accepts appeals primarily from intermediate appellate courts, rarely from trial courts. The scope of review is limited to issues of law only. Often, the parties need permission to have their cases heard. Depending on the jurisdiction, this court may be called the Supreme Court (e.g. Federal), the Supreme Court of Appeals, the Supreme Judicial Court or the Court of Appeals (e.g. NY).
CREDIBILITY	Worthiness of belief. To entitle a witness to credibility, he must be competent. To gain credibility, we must be assured, first, that the witness has not been mistaken nor deceived. To be assured as far as possible on this subject, it is proper to consider the nature and quality of the facts proved; the quality and person of the witness; the testimony in itself; and to compare it with the depositions of other witnesses on the subject, and with known facts. Secondly, we must be satisfied that he does not wish to deceive: There are strong assurances of this when the witness under oath is a man of integrity and disinterested.
CRIMINAL	An act or omission which is prohibited by criminal law.
DAMAGES	A cash compensation ordered by a court to offset losses or suffering caused by another's fault or negligence. Damages are a typical request made of a court when persons sue for breach of contract or tort.
DE MINIMIS NON CURAT LEX	The law does not care for small things.
DECREE	The judgment or sentence of a court of equity which corresponds to the judgment of a court of law.
DEFENDANT	In criminal cases, the person accused of the crime. In civil matters, the person or organization that is being sued.
DEFERENCE/ DEFER	Putting off until later.
DICTUM	A statement or remark in a judicial decision that is not necessary for the decision.

DISCOVERY	Modern pre-trial procedure by which one party gains information held by another party; the disclosure by a party of facts, deeds, documents, and other such things.
DISTINGUISH	Determining that two cases are fundamentally different so that the case being cited as precedent has limited value.
DIVERSITY OF CITIZENSHIP	That basis of federal jurisdiction first promulgated in the First Judiciary Act which grants to federal courts original jurisdiction over cases and controversies between citizens of different states or between a citizen of a state and an alien, subject to a jurisdictional amount of $10,000.
DUE PROCESS OF THE LAW	The idea that laws and legal proceedings must be fair. The Constitution guarantees that the government cannot take away a person's basic rights to 'life, liberty or property, without due process of law.' Courts have issued numerous rulings about what this means in particular cases.
EASEMENT	Gives one party the right to go onto another party's property. Utilities often get easements that allow them to run pipes or phone lines beneath private property.
ELEMENTS	Fire, water, earth and air – the forces of nature. Caused by the elements is used interchangeably with caused by an act of God.
EMINENT DOMAIN	Government seizure of private property for public use. Just compensation is required by the Fifth Amendment.
ENJOIN	To command or instruct with authority. To abate, suspend or restrain.
EQUITY, EQUITABLE	A system of law designed to furnish remedies for wrongs which were not legally recognized under the common law or for which no adequate remedy was provided by the common law.
ESTOPPEL/LACHES	A bar or preclusion preventing a person from denying a truth that has already been established through legal proceedings.
ETIOLOGY	The causes of a disease or abnormal condition.

EVIDENCE	All the means by which a matter of fact under investigation in a judicial court is established or disproved. Evidence includes testimony of witnesses, records, documents, exhibits or any other probative matter.
EXHIBIT	A document or object shown to the court as evidence in a trial. They are each given a number or letter by the court clerk as they are introduced for future reference during the trial. Except with special permission of the court, exhibits are locked up in court custody until the trial is over.
EXPERT WITNESS	When knowledge of a technical subject matter might be helpful to a trier of fact, a person having special training or experience in that technical field, one who is called an expert witness, is permitted to state his or her opinion concerning those technical matters even though he or she was not present at the event. For example, an arson expert could testify about the probable cause of a suspicious fire.
FEDERAL QUESTION JURISDICTION	One kind of original jurisdiction given to federal courts by virtue of Article III of the Constitution and enabling legislation, it allows federal courts to hear cases wherein the meaning or application of something in the Constitution, laws, or treaties of the United States is being disputed.
FINDING, FOUND	That which has been ascertained, such as the ruling of the jury is conclusive as to matters of fact when confirmed by a judgment of the court. The basis of a decision, usually, but not always, in writing. For example, the reasons for a judge's rulings on matters like granting sanctions or summary judgment, holding a party in contempt, etc., should be explained, if for no other reason than to facilitate potential appellate review.
GOOD CAUSE	Substantial or legally sufficient reason for doing something.
GRAND JURY	A group of citizens convened in a criminal case to consider the prosecutor's evidence and determine whether probable cause exists to prosecute a suspect for a felony. At common law, a group of persons consisting of not less than twelve nor more than twenty-four who listen to evidence and determine whether or not they should charge the accused with the commission of a crime by returning an indictment. The number of members on a grand jury varies in different states.

GRAVAMEN	The material part of a grievance or complaint.
GUILT	Having been found by a jury to have committed a crime charged. Guilt may refer to the commission of a civil wrong or tort.
HEARING	A legal proceeding – other than a trial – held before a judge, magistrate, or court commissioner.
HOLDING	Property where one has the legal title and one has possession. Also, may refer to the findings in a court opinion.
HOMECENTRIC	Having the same center.
IMPANEL	To summon and select a jury. Into or against the person.
IN PERSONAM	Refers to an action in pleading founded on personal liability.
IN REM	Actions against an object rather than a person.
INDEMNIFY	To secure against a future loss or to make good on a loss that has already occurred. To insure.
INDEMNITY	The obligation of a person to make good on a loss or damage that has occurred or may occur.
INDICTMENT	A formal accusation of a felony, issued by a grand jury after considering evidence presented by a prosecutor. The formal charge issued by a grand jury stating that there is enough evidence that the defendant committed the crime to justify having a trial; it is used primarily for felonies.
INFORMATION	An alternative to an indictment for starting a criminal prosecution, it is a written accusation charging a person with a crime.
INFRA	Below, beneath. When used in text it refers to a citation below in the text. The opposite of supra.
INJUNCTION	A court order that prohibits a party from doing something (restrictive injunction) or compels them to do something (mandatory injunction).

INJURY	Any wrong or damage done to another. This covers person, property, reputation or rights.
INSTANT MATTER/ SUB JUDICE/CASE AT BAR	Under a court, before a court or judge before consideration.
INTENTIONAL TORT	A tort that was knowingly and purposefully caused.
INVERSE CONDEMNATION	An action brought by a property owner seeking just compensation for land taken for a public use, against a government or private entity having the power of eminent domain. It is a remedy peculiar to the property owner and is exercisable by him where it appears that the taker of the property does not intend to bring eminent domain proceedings. (Etc.)
JOINT LIABILITY	Shared liability among a group where one member being sued can insist the other members are sued as well.
JUDGE	A public officer, lawfully appointed to decide litigated questions according to law. This, in its most extensive sense, includes all officers who are appointed to decide such questions and not only judges properly so called, but also justices of the peace and jurors, who are judges of the facts in issue. In a more limited sense, the term judge signifies an officer who is so named in his commission and who presides in some court.
JUDGMENT	A court's official decision on the matters before it. The declaration, by a court, of the rights and duties of the parties to a lawsuit which has been submitted to it for decision. Can also include an "injunction," a specific order to do or not to do something.
JUDICIAL	Belonging to, or emanating from a judge, as such.
JUDICIAL ACTIVISM	Basing a decision on what the judge perceives to be best for public welfare rather than reaching a decision based on precedent.
JUDICIAL RESTRAINT	Reaching a decision based on precedent. The opposite of judicial activism.

JURISDICTION	The power to hear and determine a case. This power may be established and described with reference to particular subjects or to parties who fall into a particular category. In addition to the power to adjudicate, a valid exercise of jurisdiction requires fair notice and an opportunity for the affected parties to be heard. Without jurisdiction, a court's judgment is void.
JURISPRUDENCE	Technically, jurisprudence means the "science of law." Statutes articulate the bland rules of law, with only rare reference to factual situations. The actual application of these statutes to facts is left to judges who consider not only the statute, but also other legal rules which might be relevant to arrive at a judicial decision; hence, the "science." Thus, "jurisprudence" has come to refer to case law, or the legal decisions which have developed, and which accompany statutes in applying the law against situations of fact.
JURY	Persons selected according to law and sworn to inquire into and declare a verdict on matters of fact.
JURY TRIAL	A civil or criminal trial in which a jury decides any disputed issues of fact. The number of jurors is usually 12 in a criminal trial; the number varies from state to state in a civil trial.
LAWSUIT	A legal action started by a plaintiff against a defendant based on a complaint that the defendant failed to perform a legal duty, resulting in harm to the plaintiff.
LAWYER	A person that has been trained in the law and that has been certified to give legal advice or to represent others in litigation. Also known as a "barrister & solicitor" or an attorney.
LEGISLATION	The act of giving or enacting laws. The power to make laws.
LIABLE	Any legal obligation, either due now or at some time in the future. It could be a debt or a promise to do something. To say a person is "liable" for a debt or wrongful act is to indicate that they are the person responsible for paying the debt or compensating the wrongful act.

LITIGATION	A case, controversy, or lawsuit.
MEDIATION	Settling a dispute outside of a court.
MEMORANDUM OF LAW	Literally, to be remembered. It is an informal instrument recording some fact or agreement, so called from its beginning, when it was made in Latin. It is sometimes commenced with this word, though written in English; as "Memorandum, that it is agreed," or it is headed with the words, "Be it remembered that," etc. The term memorandum is also applied to the clause of an instrument.
MENS REA	The mental state of accompanying a crime. Guilty mind.
MUNICIPALITY	The body of officers, taken collectively, belonging to a city, who are appointed to manage its affairs and defend its interests.
N.O.V.	Non Obstante Verdicto: notwithstanding the verdict. A judgment N.O.V. is one that reverses the determination of the jury and is granted when a judge determines that the jury verdict had no reasonable support in fact or was contrary to law.
NEGLIGENCE TORT	Not only are people responsible for the intentional harm they cause, but also their failure to act as a reasonable person would be expected to act in similar circumstances (i.e. "negligence") will also give rise to compensation. Negligence, if it causes injury to another, can give rise to a liability suit under tort.
NGO	Non-governmental organization Public-interest citizen groups, with environmentalists at the forefront. They have reinvigorated a process of active pluralistic democracy.
NIMBY	"Not In My Backyard."
NO BILL	A determination by a grand jury that sufficient evidence does not exist for trial.
NOBLESSE OBLIGE	Because humans uniquely have been able to move beyond the basic existence demands of food, shelter, and survival to build an abstract

culture and to understand the effects of our actions upon the planet, our species has a high calling to protect the less powerful parts of the ecological community in which we live.

NOT GUILTY	A plea by the accused in a criminal court that denies every element of the offense charged.
NUISANCE	Nuisance is that activity which arises from unreasonable, unwarranted or unlawful use by a person of his own property, working obstruction, or injury to right of another, or to the public, and producing such material annoyance, inconvenience and discomfort that law will presume resulting damage.
OATH	A declaration made according to law, before a competent tribunal or officer, to tell the truth; or it is the act of one who, when lawfully required to tell the truth, takes God to witness that what he says is true. It is a religious act by which the party invokes God not only to witness the truth and sincerity of his promise, but also to avenge his imposture or violated faith, or in other words to punish his perjury if he shall be guilty of it.
OFFICE MEMORANDUM	An informal discussion of the merits of a matter pending in a lawyer's office; usually written by a law clerk or junior associate for the benefit of a senior associate or partner. It is protected from discovery by the work-product doctrine.
OPINION	The reason given for the court's judgment or conclusion. It defers from the decision because that is the judgment itself.
ORAL ARGUMENT	Legal arguments given in court by a lawyer.
ORDER	A direction of the court on some matter incidental to the main proceeding which adjudicates a preliminary point or directs some steps in the proceeding.
ORDINANCE	An executive decision of a government which has not been subjected to a legislative assembly (contrary to a statute). It is often detailed and not, as would be a statute, of general wording or application. This term is in

disuse in many jurisdictions and the words "regulations" or "bylaws" are preferred.

PANEL	The list of persons who have been summoned for jury duty and from whom a jury may be chosen.
PARETO EFFICIENT ALLOCATIONS	An allocation is Pareto efficient if there is no other allocation in which some other individual is better off and no individual is worse off.
PARTY	In a judicial proceeding, a litigant (plaintiff or defendant); a person directly interested in the subject matter of a case; one who could assert a claim, make a defense, control proceedings, examine witnesses, or appeal from the judgment.
PATRIMONY	An inheritance from a father or man, what one generation inherits from the previous.
PENALTY CLAUSE	A contract clause that provides for the payment of an amount as forfeiture in the event a party defaults.
PERJURY	Knowingly lying under oath. In order for a person to be found guilty of perjury the government must prove: the person testified under oath before [e.g., the grand jury]; at least one particular statement was false; and the person knew at the time the testimony was false.
PERMANENT DAMAGES	One-time compensation.
PERSON	"In law, an individual or incorporated group having certain legal rights and responsibilities." This has been held to include foreign and domestic corporations.
PERSONALTY	Tangible property (other than realty) and intangible property.
PETIT JURY	Ordinary trial jury. Its function is to determine issues of fact in civil and criminal cases and to reach a verdict in conjunction with those findings. Petit jurieshave Traditionally been composed of 12 members, whose verdict was required to be unanimous. This remains the case in most jurisdictions today, but six-person juries and less than unanimous

verdicts have been held constitutionally permissible in state criminal proceedings.

PETITION — A written application to the court asking for specific action to be taken.

PLAINTIFF — The person who initiates a lawsuit.

PLEADINGS — Written statements of the parties in a civil case of their positions. In the federal courts, the principal pleadings are the complaint and the answer. The claim, answer, counterclaim, and/or third-party claim filed in an action.

PRACTICE — Refers to the rules governing all aspects of a court proceeding.

PRAYER — That part of a bill (in modern practice, complaint) which asks for relief.

PRECEDENT — A case which establishes legal principles to a certain set of facts, coming to a certain conclusion, and which is to be followed from that point on, when similar or identical facts are before a court. Precedent forms the basis of the theory of stare decisis which prevents "reinventing the wheel" and allows citizens to have a reasonable expectation of the legal solutions which apply in a given situation.

PREPONDERANCE OF THE EVIDENCE — The level of proof required to prevail in most civil cases. The judge or jury must be persuaded that the facts are more probably one way (the plaintiff's way) than another (the defendant's).

PRESENTMENT — The result or finding of a grand jury on its own without the aid of a prosecutor.

PRIMA FACIE — On face value. Self-evident. Does not require additional support to establish validity.

PRIVATE/PUBLIC/PROSPECTIVE NUISANCE — Substantial interference with the right to use and enjoy land, which may be intentional, negligent, or ultra-hazardous in origin, and must be a result of the defendant's activity. Nuisances are either public or common, or private nuisances. A public or common nuisance is such an inconvenience or troublesome offense, that annoys the whole community in general, and not merely some particular person. To constitute a public nuisance, there must be such 'a number of persons annoyed, that the offense can no longer be considered a private nuisance': this is a fact to be judged of by the jury. A private nuisance is anything done to the hurt or annoyance of the lands, tenements, or hereditaments of another.

PRO TANTO	As far as it goes. Commonly refers to partial payments made by the government during eminent domain seizures.
PRO SE	On one's behalf, for himself.
PROBATE	The act of proving that an instrument purporting to be a will was signed and otherwise executed in accordance with legal requirements, and of determining its validity thereby; also, the combined result of all the procedural acts necessary to establish the validity of a will.
PROBATION	A procedure whereby a defendant found guilty of a crime is released by the court without imprisonment, subject to conditions imposed by the court, under the supervision of a probation officer.
PROBATIVE	Tending to prove a particular proposition or to persuade one as to the truth of an allegation.
PROCEDURE	Legal method; the mechanics of the legal process. The rules and practice by which justice is administered in the legal system rather than the laws themselves.
PROCEEDING	The succession of events constituting the process by which judicial action is invoked and utilized; the form in which actions are to be brought and defended, the manner of intervening in suits and of conducting them, the mode of deciding them, opposing them, and of executing judgments.
PROCESS	Any court document carrying the court seal or clerk's signature, that must be properly served on (that is, given to) the party or witness named in the document, is called a process document or process. A subpoena--a document requiring the appearance of a person or the

production of documents at a hearing--and a summons are examples of court process.

PROOF — The conviction or persuasion of the mind of a judge or jury, by the exhibition of evidence, of the reality of a fact alleged.

PROSECUTE — To bring judicial proceedings against a person and to administer them until the conclusion of the court proceedings.

PROSECUTOR — The government lawyer who investigates and tries criminal cases. Typically known as a district attorney, state's attorney, or United States attorney.

PROXIMATE CAUSATION — The natural and unbroken causation of an injury without the addition of any new, independent cause.

PUBLIC TRUST THEORIES — Provides that submerged and submersible lands are preserved for public use in navigation, fishing, and recreation and state, as trustee for the people, bears responsibility of preserving and protecting the right of the public to the use of the waters for those purposes.

PUNITIVE DAMAGES — Also known as exemplary damages. Damages awarded as a form of punishment that are in excess of actual damages.

RATABLE — Taxable.

REAL EVIDENCE — An object relevant to facts in a trial and produced at the trial as opposed to being described by a witness.

REALTY — An interest in land. Synonymous with real property or real estate.

RELIEF — The redress or assistance awarded to a complaint by a court. It includes such remedies as specific performance, injunction, rescission of a contract. It usually does not apply to money damages.

REMAND — When an appellate court sends an appealed case back to the trial court for further action, the case is said to be remanded. This usually happens if the trial judge has made an error which requires a new trial or hearing.

REMEDY — The means employed to redress or enforce an injury.

REMISSION — A release or extinguishment of a debt. It is conventional when it is expressly granted to the debtor by a creditor having a capacity to alienate; or tacit when the creditor voluntarily surrenders to his debtor the original title, under private signature constituting the obligation. At common law, the act by which a forfeiture or penalty is forgiven.

REMITTITUR — The process of the verdict being diminished by subtraction.

REMOVAL — A change in place or position; a petition made by a defendant to transfer a case from one court, where the plaintiff originally brought the action, to another. Generally used to refer to the transfer of a state action to a federal district court; the petition must be filed within 30 days of service on or receipt by defendant of plaintiff's pleadings and must allege jurisdiction in the federal court.

REPLY — A defensive pleading by the plaintiff, used to interpose a defense to a new matter pleaded in the answer.

RES — The thing; the subject matter of actions.

RES JUDICATA — The thing that has been decided. A matter has been adjudged.

RESPONDENT — The person being sued or responding to the suit. The party who makes an answer to a bill or other proceeding in chancery.

RETROACTIVE/ EX POST FACTO/ RETROSPECTIVE — After the fact.

REVERSE — When an appellate court sets aside the decision of a lower court because of an error. A reversal is often followed by a remand.

RULES OF CIVIL PROCEDURE	These rules govern procedure in the U.S. district courts in all suits of a civilnature whether cognizable as cases at law or in equity or in admiralty, with some exceptions.
SANCTION	This is a very unusual word with two contradictory meanings. To "sanction" can mean to ratify or to approve but it can also mean to punish. The "sanction" of a crime refers to the actual punishment, usually expressed as a fine or jail term.
SERVICE	The being employed to serve another.
SERVITUDE	Burden on the land (i.e. pollution); a charge or burden resting upon one estate for the benefit or advantage of another; a species of incorporeal right derived from the civil law and closely corresponding to the "easement" of the common-law except that "servitude," rather, has relation to the burden or the estate burdened, while "easement" refers to the benefit or advantage or the estate to which it accrues.
SEVERAL LIABILITY	Members of a party being separately responsible.
SHOW CAUSE ORDER	Requiring a party to appear and argue why something should not be done or permitted.
SLAPP	Strategic Lawsuit Against Public Partnerships
STANDING	The legal right to initiate a lawsuit. To do so, a person must be sufficiently affected by the matter at hand, and there must be a case or controversy that can be resolved by legal action. There are three requirements for Article III standing: (1) injury in fact, which means an invasion of a legally protected interest that is (a) concrete and particularized, and (b) actual or imminent, not conjectural or hypothetical; (2) a causal relationship between the injury and the challenged conduct, which means that the injury fairly can be traced to the challenged action of the defendant, and has not resulted from the independent action of some third party not before the court; and (3) a likelihood that the injury will be redressed by a favorable decision, which means that the prospect of obtaining relief from the injury as a result of a favorable ruling is not too speculative.

STARE DECISIS	A Latin term that means to stand by that which was decided. A basic principle of the law whereby once a decision (a precedent) on a certain set of facts has been made, the courts will apply that decision in cases which subsequently come before it embodying the same set of facts. A precedent which is binding must be followed.
STATUS QUO	The conditions or situations that exist. The current standing of a situation.
STATUTE/STATUTORY LAW	The written laws approved by Congress/legislatures/politicians. Also "legislation."
STAY	A judicial order forbidding an action until some event occurs or the court lifts its order.
STIPULATION	An agreement between parties to a dispute or court action that a certain fact is true or uncontested. Also, an agreement between parties to a specific procedure or action such as a stipulation to extend time to answer a complaint.
STRICT LIABILITY TORT	Liability, even when there is no proof of negligence. Often applicable in product liability cases against manufacturers, who are legally responsible for injuries caused by defects in their products, even if they were not negligent.
SUBJECT MATTER JURISDICTION	The authority of a court to decide a particular type/category of case is called subject-matter jurisdiction and is set by the federal or state Constitution, or by state statutes.
SUBPOENA	An order directed to an individual commanding him to appear in court on a certain day to testify or produce documents in a pending lawsuit. A process to cause a witness to appear and give testimony, commanding him to lay aside all pretenses and excuses, and appear before a court or magistrate therein named, at a time therein mentioned, to testify for the party named, under a penalty therein mentioned. This is usually called a subpoena ad testificandum.
SUBSTANTIVE LAW	The positive law which creates, defines, and regulates the rights and duties of the parties and which may give rise to cause of action.

SUE	To prosecute or commence legal proceedings for the purpose of recovering a right.
SUIT	Any proceeding in a court.
SUMMONS	A legal document that notifies a party that a lawsuit has been initiated, and states when and where the party must appear to answer the charges. A notice to the defendant requiring him to serve an answer to the complaint.
SUPRA	Above. When used in a written text it refers to text above the passage. The opposite of infra.
SURROGATE	A judicial officer of limited jurisdiction, who administers matters regarding decedents' and incompetents' estates and, in some cases, adoptions
TEMPORARY DAMAGES	Past injury/harm damages that allows for future action or lawsuits.
TEMPORARY/ MANDATORY PERMANENT INJUNCTION	A court order that orders a party to do or refrain from doing a certain act (or acts) as opposed to a money judgment. For example: An injunction might be obtained to prevent a copyright infringer from reprinting copyrighted materials; in divorces, there are frequently mutual restraining orders (a form of injunction) requiring both parties to leave another alone; a court order which restrains one of the parties to a suit in equity from doing or permitting others who are under his control to do an act which is unjust to the other party; if a party has threatened to remove marital property, or has threatened to kidnap, a court might prohibit the party from touching any marital property or removing the child from the county. Emergency injunctions that are in effect only a short time are called temporary restraining orders. Courts can also issue preliminary injunctions to take effect immediately and effective until a decision is made on a permanent injunction, which can stay in effect indefinitely or until certain conditions are met.
TEMPORARY RESTRAINING ORDER	Prohibits a person from an action that is likely to cause irreparable harm. This differs from an injunction in that it may be granted immediately, without notice to the opposing party, and without a hearing. It is intended to last only until a hearing can be held.

TESTIMONY	A statement made by a witness, under oath, usually related to a legal proceeding or legislative hearing.
TORTFEASOR	Name given to a person or persons who have committed a tort.
TORT, TORTIOUS	Derived from the Latin word tortus which means wrong. In French, "tort" means a wrong." Tort refers to the body of the law which will allow an injured person to obtain compensation from the person who caused the injury. Every person is expected to conduct themselves without injuring others. When they do so, either intentionally or by negligence, they can be required by a court to pay money to the injured party ("damages") so that ultimately, they will suffer the pain caused by their action. Tort also serves as a deterrent by sending a message to the community as to what is unacceptable conduct.
TRAGEDY OF THE COMMONS	This phrase refers to the over-exploitation of shared resources. Imagine a common pasture for livestock shared by a community of herdsman. Use of the pasture is free to all. Each individual herdsman gains the entire benefit of any of his livestock in the pasture. Since the costs imposed on the pasture are shared among all the herdsman, it is always to the immediate benefit of a herdsman to add an additional animal to the herd. This may continue for generations until the pasture collapses under the load.
TRESPASS	An action to recover damages for any unlawful injury of a person, property, or rights involving immediate force or violence.
TRIAL	A judicial examination of issues, of either law or fact, between parties before a court that has jurisdiction over the cause.
TRIAL COURT	The trial court is the court in which a lawsuit is filed, and where all litigation up to and including the trial is held.
TRUE BILL	When a grand jury, after having heard the witnesses for the government, are of opinion that there is sufficient cause to put the defendant on his trial.

VARIANCE	In procedure, a discrepancy between what is charged or alleged and what is proved or offered as proof.
VENUE	Venue is the legally proper place where a particular case should be filed or handled. Every state has rules determining the proper venue for different types of lawsuits.
VERDICT	The decision of a jury. In criminal cases, this is usually expressed as "guilty" or "not guilty." In a civil case, the verdict would be a finding for the plaintiff or for the defendant.
VICARIOUS LIABILITY	When the liability of one person is imposed on another (such as an employer being responsible for an employee's actions while on the job).
WITNESS	Person who comes to court and swears under oath to give truthful evidence. One who, being sworn or affirmed, according to law, is deposed as to his knowledge of facts in issue between the parties in a case.
WORK PRODUCT	That work done by an attorney in the process of representing a client which is ordinarily not subject to discovery.
WRIT	A judicial order. A formal written command, issued from the court, requiring the performance of a specific act. A mandatory precept issued by the authority, and in the name of the sovereign or the state, for the purpose of compelling the defendant to do something therein mentioned.
WRIT OF HABEAS CORPUS	The procedure for obtaining the judicial determination of an individual's custody. Also known as the Great Writ.
ZONING	The separation of municipalities into districts for the purpose of regulation, control and limiting the use of private property. Usually done on the municipal level.

Index of Cases

Borland v. Sanders Lead Co., Inc., 369 So. 2d 523 (Ala. 1979)

Boomer v. Atlantic Cement Co, 26 N.Y.2d 219 (N.Y. 1970)

Branch v. W. Petroleum, Inc., 657 P.2d 267 (Utah, 1982)

Carlton v. Babbitt, 900 F. Supp. 526 (D.D.C. 1995)

Citizens to Preserve Overton Park v. Volpe, 401 U.S. 402 (1971)

Palila v. Hawaii Dept. of Land and Nat. Resources, 649 F. Supp. 1070 (D. Haw. 1986)

Spur Industries, Inc. v. Del E. Webb Dev. Co., 494 P. 2d 700 (Ariz. 1972)

Tennessee Valley Authority v. Hiram Hill et al., 437 U.S. 153 (1978)

United States of America v. James E. Billie, 667 F. Supp.1485 (S.D. Florida, 1987)

Whalen v. Union Bag & Paper Co., 208 N.Y. 1. (N.Y, 1913)

Village of Wilsonville v. SCA Services, 86 Ill.2D 1 (Ill. 1981)

Selective Bibliography (Primary and Secondary Sources)

Boomer v. Atlantic Cement Co., 294 N.Y.S.2d 452 (1968)

Boomer v. Atlantic Cement Co., 257 N.E.2d 870 (1970)

Boomer v. Atlantic Cement Co., 340 N.Y.S.2d 97 (1972)

Borland v. Sanders Lead Co., 369 So. 2d 523 (1979)

Bush v. Palm Beach Canvassing Board, 531 U.S. 70, 121 S. Ct. 471, 148 L. Ed. 2d 366 (2000)

Bush v. Gore, (531 U.S. 98; 121 S. Ct. 525; 148 L. Ed. 2d 388(2000)

Plessy v. Ferguson, 163 U.S. 537 (1896)

Brown v. Board of Education of Topeka, 247 U.S. 483 (1954) *Brown v. Board of Education (II),* 349 U.S. 294 (1955) *Branch v. Western Petroleum, Inc.,* 657 P.2d 267 (1982)

Carlton v. Babbitt, 900 F.Supp 526 (1995)

Citizens to Preserve Overton Park v. Volpe, 432 F.2d 1307 (1970) *Citizens to Preserve Overton Park v. Volpe,* 400 U.S. 939 (1970) *Citizens to Preserve Overton Park v. Volpe,* 401 U.S. 402 (1971) *Citizens to Preserve Overton Park v. Volpe,* 335 F.Supp. 873 (1972) *Citizens to Preserve Overton Park v. Volpe,* 357 F.Supp. 846 (1973) *Citizens to Preserve Overton Park v. Volpe,* 494 F.2d 1212 (1974) *Loving v. Virginia,* 388 U.S. 1, 87 S.Ct. 1817, 18 L. Ed. 2d 1010 (1967)

Marbury v. Madison, 5 U.S. 137 (1803)

McCarty v. Natural Carbonic Gas Co., 189 N. Y. 40 (1907)

Palila v. Hawaii Dept. of Land & Natural Resources, 649 F. Supp. 107 (1986)

Palila v. Hawaii Dept. of Land & Natural Resources, 852 F.2d 1106 (1988)

U.S. v. Windsor, 570 U.S. (2013)

U.S. v. Virginia, 518 U.S. 515 (1996)

Roe v. Wade, 410 U.S. 113, 93 S. Ct 705, 35 L. Ed 2d 147 (1973)

Shelby County v. Holder (570 U.S. 2 (2013))

Spur Industries, Inc. v. Del Webb Development Co., 108 Ariz. 178,494 P. 2d 700 (1972)

Strobel v. Kerr Salt Co., 164 N.Y. 303 (1900)

Tennessee Valley Authority v. Hill, 437 U.S. 153 (1978)

Tennessee Valley Authority v. Hill, 549 F.2d 1064 (1977)

Tennessee Valley Authority v. Hill, 419 F.Supp 753 (1976)

State *v. Billie,* 497 So.2d 889 (1986)

U.S. v. Billie, 667 F.Supp 1485 (1987)

Vermont Yankee Nuclear Power Corp. v. Nat. Resources Def. Council, Inc., 435 U.S. 519 (1978)

Village of Wilsonville v. SCA Services, 426 N.E. 2d 824, 86 Ill.2d 1 (1981)

Village of Wilsonville v. SCA Services, 396 N.E. 2d 552, 77 Ill. App. 3d 618 (1979)

Whalen v. Union Bag & Paper Co., 208 N.Y. 1 (1913)

***

The Administrative Procedure Act of 1948, Constitution of the United States

E.P.A. Reorganization Plan No. 3 of 1970 Plum Book 2016

40 C.F.R. Part 230, Subpart A

1987-Army-Corps-Wetlands-Delineation-Manual Endangered Species Act

Convention on International Trade in Endangered Species of Wild Fauna and Flora - Text

Convention on International Trade in Endangered Species of Wild Fauna and Flora - Appendices 50 *C.F.R.* 17.1-17.8 - Harm and Harass

50 *C.F.R.* 17.95 - Palila Critical Habitat Map 50 *C.F.R.* 424.1-424.21 - Critical Habitat

50 *C.F.R.* 424.01-424.21

***

Agarkova E. et al., (2000) "Environmental Crimes," American Criminal Law Review, 37: 333.

Blackstone, William (1765). *Commentaries on the Laws of England.*

Davis, Michael & Dana *Neacşu* (2014). The Many Texts of Law, British Journal of American Legal Studies, 3: 481.

De Glanville, Ranulf (1187-89). The Treatise on the Laws and Customs of the Kingdom of England.

Dobris, J.C. (1990). "Boomer Twenty Years Later: An Introduction, with Some Footnotes About 'Theory'", Albany Law Review, 54:171.

Farber, Daniel, A. (2005). "The Story of Boomer: Pollution and the Common Law", Ecology Law Quarterly 32:113.

Garry, Patrick. M. (2006) "Judicial Review and the 'Hard Look'" Doctrine, Nevada Law Journal, 7:151.

Harr, Jonathan (1996). A Civil Action.

Holczer, E.M. (1997). "Boomer Revisited: Using Experimental and Partial Injunctions in Private Nuisance Actions." Defense Counsel Journal, 64:99.

Laycock, D. (2012). "The Neglected Defense of Undue Hardship (and the Doctrinal Train Wreck in Boomer v. Atlantic Cement)," Journal of Tort Law, 4:1.

Lewin, J.L. (1990). "Boomer and the American Law of Nuisance: Past, Present, and Future," Albany Law Review, 54:189.

Miller, Mary (2004). "Patching Up Paradise" - National History, http://www.environmentallaw-teach.org/uploads/1/1/2/6/112661613/palila-_nat_hist_article.pdf.

Morin, Tina (1992). "Indians, Non-Indians, and the Endangered Panther; Will the Indian/Non-Indian Conflict Be Resolved Before the Panther Disappears?", Public Land Law Review, 13:167.

Neacşu, Dana (2005). Introduction to U.S. Law and Legal Research.

Note, (1980). "The Distinction between Trespass and Nuisance in Alabama: Borland v. Sanders Lead Co.," Alabama Law Review, 31: 483.

Plater Zygmunt (2013). The Snail Darter and the Dam: How Pork-Barrel Politics Endangered a Little Fish and Killed a River.

Plater Zygmunt and William Goldfarb, (1998). Environmental Law and Policy: Nature Law and Society.

Washington, R.A.V. (1990). "The Misunderstood Law of Public Nuisance: A Comparison with Private Nuisance Twenty Years After Boomer," Albany Law Review, 54:359

List of Visuals

SPUR INDUSTRIES, 1962 (page 184): Court exhibit

SPUR INDUSTRIES, 1965 (page 185): Court exhibit

SUN CITY, AZ (page 187): http://www.city-data.com/city/Sun-City-Arizona.html

CATTLE FEEDLOT (page 188): https://www.farmsanctuary.org/learn/factory-farming/dairy/

A "BAG HOUSE" (page 203): permission from private collection

LITHIUM BATTERY RECYCLING (page 203): http://infohalifax.tk/hocis/lithium-batterien-recycling-qoc.php

LEAD STORAGE BATTERY CELL (page 203): https://chem.libretexts.org/Bookshelves/Introductory_Chemistry/Book%3A_Beginning_Chemistry_(Ball)/14%3A_Oxidation_and_Reduction/14.4%3A_Applications_of_Redox_Reactions_-_Voltaic_Cells

BATTERY RECYCLING DIAGRAM (page 203): https://www.mpoweruk.com/recycling.htm

ROTARY FURNACE FOR SMELTING LEAD (page 204): https://myportelizabeth.co.za/how-to-dispose-of-your-used-car-battery/21956

LEAD AND POLYPROPYLENE MATERIALS FROM CAR BATTERIES (page 205): https://www.eldan-recycling.com/en-us/lead-and-polypropylene-materials-car-batteries

MAPS, ROOSEVELT, UT (page 223): https://www.rooseveltcity.com/

MAIN STREET, ROOSEVELT, UT (page 223): https://www.rooseveltcity.com/

MOQUI INDIAN TRADING POST, ROOSEVELT, UTAH, 1976 (page 223): image from Flickr, https://thebookshelfofemilyj.com/2013/04/10/ethnocentrism-in-the-indian-in-the-cupboard/

OVERTON PARK (page 381): http://www.overtonparkforever.org/, https://www.overtonpark.org/

OVERTON PARK MAPS (page 382), https://www.overtonpark.org/2016/02/03/recap-of-february-2-parking-meeting & http://www.overtonparkforever.org/2011/03/forty-years-ago.html

OVERTON PARK MAP (page 383): https://www.overtonpark.org/history

Overton Park–Sign (page 383): http://www.the19strongshow.org/council-corner.html

Overton Park (page 384): https://www.overtonpark.org/2016/04/22/happy-earth-day-old-forest

Kessler Plan Overton Park (page 384 & 385): https://www.overtonpark.org/history

Irma O. Sternberg (1915-2007) (page 385): https://dlynx.rhodes.edu/jspui/handle/10267/11338

CPSIA information can be obtained
at www.ICGtesting.com
Printed in the USA
JSHW022250270120
3832JS00002B/3

9 781600 425028